Agricultural Standards

The International Library of Environmental, Agricultural and Food Ethics

VOLUME 6

# AGRICULTURAL STANDARDS
## THE SHAPE OF THE GLOBAL FOOD AND FIBER SYSTEM

*edited by*

Jim Bingen

*Institute for Food and Agricultural Standards,*
*Michigan State University, U.S.A.*

and

Lawrence Busch

*Institute for Food and Agricultural Standards,*
*Michigan State University, U.S.A.*

 Springer

A C.I.P. Catalogue record for this book is available from the Library of Congress.

ISBN-10  1-4020-3983-2 (HB)
ISBN-13  978-1-4020-3983-6 (HB)
ISBN-10  1-4020-3984-0 (e-book)
ISBN-13  978-1-4020-3984-3 (e-book)

Published by Springer,
P.O. Box 17, 3300 AA Dordrecht, The Netherlands.

*www.springeronline.com*

*Printed on acid-free paper*

# DEDICATION

To Linda and Karen,
who always set high standards

# CONTENTS

# CONTENTS

# CONTRIBUTORS

**Olivier Biencourt** is a Senior Lecturer in the Department of Law and Economics at the Université du Maine, Le Mans, France. His work deals with conventions theory and in 2003 he published *Conventions and Structures in Economic Organization, Markets, Networks and Organization*, with Olivier Favereau and Emmanuel Lazega.

**Jim Bingen** is a Professor of Community, Food and Agricultural Systems in the Department of Community, Agriculture, Recreation and Resource Studies at Michigan State University. He works on a range of food, farming and rural development issues from Michigan to sub-Saharan Africa. As one of the founding members of the Institute for Food and Agricultural Standards, he is currently studying the ways in which third party certification in organic agriculture embodies both science and values.

**Lawrence Busch** is a University Distinguished Professor in the Department of Sociology at Michigan State University and Director of the Institute for Food and Agricultural Standards. He has published numerous works on agrifood issues. He is currently working on the role of standards in structuring the new nanotechnologies, third party certification of food products, and problems associated with the global harmonization of food safety policies.

**John E. Chesebro**, a Certified Medical Technologist, MT (ASCP), Detroit Medical Center MT (ASCP), assisted during 1997-1998 with research contributing to Chapter 8 as part of the Undergraduate Research Opportunity Program (UROP) at Michigan State University.

**Jean-Marie Codron** is a Senior Researcher at the National Institute of Agronomic Research (INRA) in Montpellier, France where he heads MOISA, the Markets, Organizations, Institutions and Actors' Strategies program. His research focuses on the economics of contracts, the firm and market institutions in food sectors, such as the fresh produce industry, where product quality is difficult to measure and/or to signal to the consumer.

**H. Ade Freeman** is the Director of the Targeting Research and Development Opportunities program at the International Livestock Research Institute (ILRI). His research interests cover the areas of agricultural science and technology, poverty reduction, rural livelihoods, and natural resource management.

**Hervé Hannin** is a Senior Researcher with the Ecole Nationale Supérieure d'Agronomie (ENSAM) in Montpellier, France. He is currently the Secretary General of the French Institute for Higher Studies in Vine and Wine (IHEV), head of the International University Association of Vine and Wine (AUIV) and a delegate to the International Organization of Vine and Wine (OIV). His research focuses on the methods, marketing and economics of institutions in the international vine and wine sector.

**Suzan Ilcan** is Professor and Canada Research Chair in the Department of Sociology and Anthropology at the University of Windsor, Canada. Her recent work is in the field of globalization and international organizations, and focuses on questions of governance, social transformations, and social justice. She is the author of *Longing and Belonging: The Cultural Politics of Settlement* (2002) and co-editor of *Postmodernism and the Ethical Subject* (with Barbara Gabriel, 2004) and *Transgressing Borders* (with Lynne Phillips, 1998).

**Richard Jones** is Assistant Regional Director-Eastern and Southern Africa with the International Crops Research Institute for the Semi-Arid Tropics (ICRISAT). His research is oriented toward developing innovative institutional arrangements that will allow smallholder farmers to participate in high-value niche markets through the establishment of grades and standards, and to stimulate commercial investments in seed marketing for non-hybrid crops.

**Kevin Kennedy**, Professor of Law, Michigan State University College of Law, specializes in international trade regulation. He is the editor-in-chief of *The First Decade of NAFTA*, the author of *Competition Law and the World Trade Organization*, and the co-author (with Professor Raj Bhala) of *World Trade Law*. In addition to his teaching and scholarship, Professor Kennedy serves as a NAFTA Chapter 19 bi-national dispute settlement panelist.

**Steve Londner** is a Senior Advisor, Strategic Initiatives, TechnoServe Inc.

**Tonya Mckee** is studying for a Master of Arts degree in Geography and Environmental Planning.

**Michael Mascarenhas** is a PhD candidate in the Department of Sociology at Michigan State University. His interests include science, technology and society studies, and environmental and rural sociology, political economy, and globalization and development.

**Gerad Middendorf** is an Assistant Professor of Sociology at Kansas State University. He has published several articles and chapters on the social implications of agricultural technologies and on the formation of agricultural science and technology policy. He is currently studying transition in agricultural landscapes in eastern Kansas.

**Jacquelyn Miller** specialized in environmental sociology, science and technology studies, and feminist theory for her Master of Arts degree in Sociology from Michigan State University. She is currently a Lay Resident with the Bhavana Society.

**Gabriele Lo Monaco** was a Program Officer, MOVIMONDO, an Italian non-governmental organization supporting social, political and cultural development efforts in sub-Saharan Africa, Latin America, the Balkans, and the Middle and Far East. She is currently an independent consultant focusing on applied research for rural market development, including the role of farmer associations and relationships among the public, private and NGO sectors, in southern Africa.

**Lynne Phillips** is Head and Professor in the Department of Sociology and Anthropology at the University of Windsor, Canada. She edited *The Third Wave of Modernization in Latin America: Cultural Perspectives on Neoliberalism* and has published her current research on the United Nations (with Suzan Ilcan) in *Sociologia Ruralis, Canadian Journal of Development Studies*, and *Canadian Review of Sociology and Anthropology*.

**Elizabeth Ransom** is a Visiting Assistant Professor in the Department of Sociology and Anthropology at the University of Richmond. Her interests are in the areas of globalization and international development studies, the sociology of food and agriculture, and social studies of science and technology. Her recent work has focused on bovine spongiform encephalopathy and issues of meat safety in the United States.

**Maite P. Salazar** is a PhD Candidate in the Department of Community, Agriculture, Recreation and Resource Studies (CARRS) at Michigan State University. She is interested in sustainable development and community participation in conservation and environmental policy with a focus on the social justice implications of conservation agendas, particularly for low income communities.

**Ivan Sergio Freire de Sousa** is a Senior Researcher at EMBRAPA (Brazilian State Corporation for Agricultural Research). He has published several books and articles on scientists in agricultural research, standardization in food and agriculture, and food security and food safety. Currently, he is writing a book on the role of agricultural grades and standards in Brazil.

**Bertil Sylvander** is a Research Director at the National Institute for Agronomic Research (INRA) in Toulouse where he heads the research program on Organic Agriculture and Geographical Indications. He is a member of the Society-Action-Decision (SAD) research program and specializes on the management of quality supply chains in Europe dealing with protected denominations of origin, Red Label products, etc. He has coordinated several European Research Projects, especially the Dolphins project (www.origin-food.org) and will coordinate a new project (SINER-GI) that deals with transferring the concept of origin to developing countries.

**Paul Thiers** is an Assistant Professor of Political Science at Washington State University, Vancouver. His research focuses on the political, economic and environmental issues relating to agricultural production and international food trade, with a particular emphasis on the politics of globalization in rural China and elsewhere in the Pacific Rim. His recent and ongoing research projects include the global and local politics of pesticides, international trade in organic food, and the renegotiation of the WTO Agreement on Agriculture. His articles have appeared in *Agriculture and Human Values, The Journal of Contemporary China, Society and Natural Resources, Government and Policy,* and *Asian Perspectives.*

**Dr. Sophie Thoyer** is a Senior Lecturer at the Ecole Nationale Supérieure d'Agronomie (ENSAM) in Montpellier. As a member of the Applied and Theoretical Economics Research Unit (Lameta), Dr. Thoyer works on environmental and agricultural policies, with a focus on decision-making processes and negotiated outcomes. In addition to her current research on the international regulation of trade and sustainable development, she is interested the incentive mechanisms to preserve biodiversity and water resources locally and internationally.

**Steve Walls** is the Chief of Party, Regional Agricultural Trade Expansion Support (RATES) Program.

# PREFACE

The Institute for Food and Agricultural Standards (IFAS) (www.msu.edu/~ifas) is a multidisciplinary teaching, research and policy analysis institute at Michigan State University (MSU) that focuses on the social, economic, political and ethical dimensions of the creation, enforcement and review of food and agricultural standards. From four faculty members and a small handful of graduate students, IFAS is now a part of a growing international network of scholars and practitioners.

IFAS was launched in 1999 with grants from the National Science Foundation (NSF), the Michigan Agricultural Experiment Station (MAES), and the MSU Center for Advanced Studies in International Development (CASID). The NSF grant (No. 9810149), "Making the Grade: Science and Values in Agricultural Grades and Standards," established the foundation for an international set of studies focused on identifying and analyzing: 1) the roles of science, technology, ethics and values in, as well as the sociopolitical dynamics surrounding, the creation, maintenance and modification of food and agricultural standards; and 2) accountability, transparency and democracy in standards setting and enforcement. This grant funded studies in the United States as well as studies of cotton in Mali and soybeans in Brazil. Additional funding from the MAES supported studies of dry beans, potatoes and grapes in Michigan, while CASID supported a seminar series, "Standards in Everyday Life," during 1999 and 2000.

An NSF training grant, "Societal Dimensions of Food and Agricultural Standards," provided two graduate fellows and one post-doctoral fellow the opportunity to incorporate multidisciplinary perspectives and skills into their more discipline-based studies in order to grapple with normative issues raised by grades and standards in an increasingly global and differentiated food and agricultural system. In addition, NSF and Fulbright dissertation fellowships enabled graduate students to complete studies of the red meat industry in South Africa and the wholesale vegetable market in Sâo Paulo, respectively.

Finally, IFAS directly addresses the relationships between food and agricultural standards, international trade, and development through two projects funded by the

US Agency for International Development. The Partnerships for Food Industry Development - Fruits and Vegetables (PFID - F&V) (www.pfid.msu.edu) is a global project aimed at helping small farmers to compete in local, regional, and international markets by meeting the appropriate standards. The RAISE SPS project, a multi-institutional project for which MSU has the technical lead, consists of a series of studies addressing sanitary and phytosanitary standards in developing nations. Both of these projects are jointly administered with MSU's Institute of International Agriculture.

With funding from Michigan State University, the German Marshall Fund, and the Farm Foundation, IFAS hosted an international workshop, "Markets, Rights and Equity: Food and Agricultural Standards in a Shrinking World" in the Fall 1999. Seventy participants from twenty-two countries came together for three days to analyze standards setting, implementation and the effects of standards in the global context of increased agricultural trade and lower trade barriers. During the workshop, the participants developed policy recommendations oriented toward producing effective, equitable, and transparent standards for our food and agricultural system in the 21$^{st}$ century. The workshop made four recommendations: 1) the need for more democratic mechanisms in international standards setting; 2) more complementary standards setting between private and governmental standards agencies; 3) more research to promote equitable standards setting and to improve understanding of the diverse impacts of standards; and, 4) revisions to the Agreement on the Application of Sanitary and Phytosanitary Measures (SPS) and the Agreement on Technical Barriers to Trade (TBT).

The papers presented and the discussions at this workshop motivated the preparation of this volume of essays. In short: this volume has endured a very long birthing and we are deeply grateful for the patience and forbearance of all the authors, some of whom have waited over two years for this publication. Given this long delay, we are especially appreciative that all of the authors reviewed and brought their chapters up-to-date.

Over the long time from idea to realization we must acknowledge the invaluable intellectual contributions from our colleagues. As found in many shared endeavors that span several years of countless brainstorming sessions, the attribution of authorship for a particular concept or approach often becomes collective. While this has certainly been the case for IFAS, we must acknowledge the very special roles of our founding colleagues at IFAS, Tom Reardon and Craig Harris. Tom's quick and incisive insights were instrumental in helping us to frame our approach and to structure sets of ideas coming from divergent economic, sociological and policy analyses. Similarly, Craig has always been there with key questions forcing us to re-think cherished assumptions and with the keen editorial sense that consistently improved the presentation of our ideas. In addition, we were fortunate to benefit from, and be informed by Brady Deaton's research and writing on the institutional economics of food and agricultural standards during his post-doctoral affiliation with IFAS.

We continue to depend upon the enthusiasm and intellectual curiosity of the graduate students from several disciplines who have been integral to shaping the research program of IFAS. Some of them are contributors to this volume, and most have publications dealing with food and agricultural standards. For enduring our numerous meetings, but always challenging us with fresh questions, we want to acknowledge the contributions of Brikena Bali, Sherlyn Bienvenida, Holly Dygert, Ivan Ivanov, Chet Kendell, Jason Konefal, Michael Mascarenhas, Gerad Middendorf, David Randals, Elizabeth Ransom, Taylor Reid, Tonya McKee, Jacquelyn Miller, Maite Salazar, Andile Siyengo, Patricia Aust Sterns, and Michelle Worosz.

We have profited as well from our undergraduate research assistants including, Kris Durocher and John Chesebro.

The preparation of the final manuscript was made possible only through the indispensable assistance from Richard Campau, MSU Office Services, Deborah Doherty, Springer Author Support, and Natalie Rieborn, Springer Humanities Department.

We are especially pleased that Michiel Korthals and Paul B. Thompson accepted this volume as part of the International Library of Environmental, Agricultural and Food Ethics. We hope we have been faithful in responding to the valuable comments from two anonymous reviewers.

We also want to thank the various funding agencies and their program officers who have supported our work over the last several years. Without their generous support, much of the work reported here would not have been possible. Of course, we, the editors and authors, are responsible for any errors of commission or omission.

Finally, we want to thank all of those in national and international private and governmental "standards agencies" from whom we have learned so much over the years, and for whom we hope this volume serves to recognize and appreciate their service and contribution.

Jim Bingen
Lawrence Busch
East Lansing, Michigan

I

# THINKING ABOUT STANDARDS

LAWRENCE BUSCH* AND JIM BINGEN†

# 1. INTRODUCTION:

## *A New World Of Standards*

Standards are the measures by which products, processes and producers are judged. Grades are the categories used to implement the standards. In the not too distant past, all grades and standards (G&S) were determined locally and informally, often between the parties to an exchange. In the early twentieth century, it was claimed that good quality wheat could be determined by anyone with patience and a good set of teeth (Buller 1919)! Today formal G&S are ubiquitous in the world. They affect the production, processing and condition of things, and also the judging of human performance and worth. Thus, there are G&S for apples, ketchup, toxic chemicals, and endangered species as well as for new entrants to graduate school, pesticide applicators, food handlers and government food inspectors. G&S may be set by publicly accountable government bodies (e.g., United States Department of Agriculture), by industry groups (e.g., National Food Processors Association), nonprofit organizations (e.g., Social Accountability International) or market leaders (e.g., McDonald's). G&S are of particular importance in an era marked by restructuring economies and polities from planned to market driven, and by increasing global trade and competition (OTA 1992). In a market economy, G&S define what is to be traded on the market (e.g., soybean standards), establish agreed upon conventions to order production processes (soybean meal processing), fix levels of consistent product quality (though not always the highest quality), and make possible the location of production around the globe by ensuring compatible products and processes (pallets and shipping containers).

The study of standards would seem to be a dry and rather narrow topic. Indeed, were they to be discussed from a solely technical point of view that would surely be the case. Who, other than the most specialized of practitioners, would be concerned over the determination of the best test for the *Salmonella* count on chickens, or the specification of the maximum allowable pesticide residue on fresh vegetables, or the wavelength of the precise shade of red considered desirable for tomatoes? This is the stuff of specialists and is far removed from the concerns of ethics, politics, economics, or of the larger society. Or is it? In this volume, we argue and provide several case studies showing the significance of understanding food and agricultural standards within a far broader social and ethical context, one which touches on many

* Lawrence Busch, University Distinguished Professor, Department of Sociology, Michigan State University.
† Jim Bingen, Professor, Department of Community, Agriculture, Recreation and Resource Studies, Michigan State University.

J. Bingen and L. Busch, (eds.), Agricultural Standards: The Shape of the Global Food and Fiber System, 3-28. © 2006 Springer. Printed in the Netherlands.

of the questions that concern us individually and collectively in a most profound way.

## 1. STANDARDS: A BRIEF HISTORY

Standards have been around for a long time. When ancient Egyptian priests counted the *hekats* (~4.6 litres) of grain in the royal storehouses, they employed standards of volume. Such standards not only permitted a clear accounting; they ensured that tax collections were consistent over time and space. Two thousand years ago, Virgil (1982) railed against the lack of standards that led to watered down wine, adulterated olive oil, and sundry other products. During the Middle Ages, cities set the length of a yard of cloth or the size of a bushel of grain based on the amount of work that an average weaver or farmer could do in a day. In fourteenth-century Venice new accounting standards developed including double entry bookkeeping – standards that permitted new approaches to business, including new concepts of profits (Swetz 1987). In Bavaria, a 1516 law created standards for beer requiring that only three ingredients be present: water, hops, and barley. Its express purpose was maintaining the purity of the brew.

For years as well, many benefited from the myriad of conflicting standards. For example, in eighteenth century France there were some 700 to 800 weights and measures with more than 250,000 variants. Measures were usually inextricably linked to particular objects. Thus, measures of wheat differed from those of barley, based on how much labor was required to produce a given measure (usually some fraction of a day's work at harvest). Trade was facilitated by taking advantage of the differences among the measures in different regions. Thus, a merchant might purchase three measures of wheat at a given and usually fixed "just price," in one town and sell four (smaller) measures with the same name in another town for the same price. The metric system met with considerable resistance even in Paris, where it originated during the French Revolution. Only in the 1840s did the French succeed in eliminating that resistance, requiring the use of the metric system throughout the nation (Adler 1995). And, even today, French shoppers at open air markets will demand *une livre* (one pound) of fish or meat, although the *livre* has been conveniently redefined as 500 grams.

As world trade began to grow in the eighteenth century, nations rapidly developed standardized weights and measures. Such measures were often met with stiff resistance from those who benefited from the myriad conflicting standards of earlier years. This resistance to changes in standards was not merely a matter of traditionalism. Standards are all about power – most obviously the power to determine what shall be sold on the market, but also the power to count, to tax, to observe, to record, and to rule (Scott 1998).

In other words, standards are commonplace in all aspects of social life, and as Walzer (1983: 10) has argued every set of goods is a distinct distributive sphere:

> There is no single standard. But there are standards (roughly knowable even when they are also controversial) for every social good and every distributive sphere in every particular society; and these standards are often violated, the goods usurped, the spheres invaded, by powerful men and women.

Walzer goes on to note that there are three universally recognized but rather different distributive principles – principles that sometimes overlap, but more often stand on their own. They are:

## 1.1    Free Exchange

Which may be defined as the open exchange of goods in a market. Markets are quite obviously distributive in nature. Moreover, they distribute based on a combination of wants (but not necessarily needs) and ability to pay. As we shall see below, a good standard for free exchange is (at the very least) one that permits and even encourages free exchange. In most contemporary societies free exchange is seen as desirable principle of distribution. But as the great Chinese sociologist, Fei Shaotong (1992 [1948]) reminds us, in many traditional societies, including that of rural pre-revolutionary China, all exchange within villages was gift exchange. Markets were usually placed outside of village environs where one could trade with strangers "without human feelings" [*wuqing*]. Similarly, in medieval Europe the notion of a "just price" was designed to limit the scope of the market so as to achieve other desired social ends.

## 1.2    Dessert

May be defined as the distribution of goods according to how much one deserves a particular good. Standards for things such as awards, medals, public recognition of great skill or courage, or conversely, prison sentences for those guilty of crimes, involve providing persons with their just desserts. Quite clearly, it is widely agreed that free exchange should play virtually no role in the creation or enforcement of such standards; to the extent that it does, it violates the principle of just desserts. But determining who should receive what desserts is often subject to abuse. A most egregious example in modern times would be the apartheid system in South Africa. Proponents argued that people of different racial groups *deserved* different treatment under the law (see, for example, Bowker and Star 1999). The same misuse of dessert was evident in the American treatment of citizens of Japanese origin during the World War II (Hata, Hills and Hata 1995).

## 1.3    Need

Standards for need are also commonplace in modern society. For example, scholarships, food stamps, Medicaid, and public housing are normally assigned based on written standards focused on need. Clearly, one should not be able to buy these goods, nor are they normally distributed based on dessert.[1] International treaties as well, often talk of need. For example, the right to food, enshrined in

United Nations documents, is based on the principle that food should be distributed based on need.

In this volume we focus on food and agricultural standards – standards that involve the free exchange of goods. As the reader shall see, a wide range of issues of distributive justice, of rights, of equity, and of virtues, are endemic features of food and agricultural standards, even though they are not ostensibly what such standards are about. Questions of dessert and need enter into the discussion as well, especially when free exchange is used to justify practices that ignore these distributive principles.

## 2. STANDARDS AND STANDARDIZATION

Standards and standardization were inseparable in the development of many of the first standards. Weights, measures and coinage appeared thousands of years ago as means of standardizing, of creating order out of chaos, and of facilitating trade and taxation. The Swiss-born republican, Benjamin Constant, understood this clearly when he wrote:

> The conquerors of our day, peoples or princes, want their empire to possess a unified surface over which the superb eye of power can wander without encountering any inequality which hurts or limits its view. The same code of law, the same measures, the same rules, and if we could gradually get there, the same language; that is what is proclaimed as the perfection of the social organization...The great slogan of the day is uniformity (quoted in Scott 1998: 30).

Adam Smith (1994 [1776]) was one of the first persons to theorize about standards as they applied to production and trade, albeit in a rather oblique manner. Smith chose a pin factory as a means to illustrate several points in his theory. The standardized products of the pin factory (according to Smith made in 18 steps) employed the division of labor to achieve greater productivity. Smith claimed that the pin factory permitted (1) greater dexterity on the part of workers who now only had to learn a few skills, (2) the saving of time between tasks, and (3) the greater use of machines to substitute for labor. Of particular note is that he chose an industry that was somewhat of an exception in his time. Had he examined the furniture or carriage making industries, he would have found a far less developed division of labor, fewer standards, and little standardization. And, agriculture, Smith lamented, was not subject to the same division of labor as the emerging world of industry.

Napoleon provided a boost to standardization by virtue of his military ambitions. Developing a modern mass army of conscripted men required tens of thousands of uniforms, guns, and ammunition. It required standardized rations that would not spoil on long marches. Canning was developed by Nicolas Appert in 1806 in response to Napoleon's call for better means of standardized food preservation. Thus, by introducing standardized mass production, Napoleon was able to rapidly feed, clothe, and arm his armies.

Standardization rapidly caught on in manufacturing in the nineteenth century, especially in the United States (Habakkuk 1962). The use of standardized (and hence interchangeable) parts proved to be a boon unto itself, as it facilitated repair of all sorts of manufactured goods. The practice became so widespread that it became known worldwide as the American system.

But Smith's theoretical insights with respect to standardization lay largely unexamined until the early 20th century when engineers began to exploit the potential benefits of standardization. For example, Frederick Winslow Taylor developed his program of scientific management (Taylor 1911). For Taylor, there was a single best way to accomplish any task, and it was engineers who would determine what that best way was using the principles of science. No longer would it be necessary to rely on the rules of thumb developed by workers; engineers would use a variety of techniques, including time and motion studies, to determine the most efficient way to accomplish a given task.

Taylor's approach sparked a spate of books, pamphlets, and management advice. Taylor's system was to be applied to the farm and the home as well as the factory (Jones 1917 [1916]). Agricultural economist, Milburn Wilson, formed Fairway Farms in 1933 with the express idea of applying Taylor's ideas to agriculture.[2] "It was 'a scientific and carefully planned effort to transfer the industrial efficiency of modern factory methods to the farm...'" (Kirkendall 1966: 13). Similarly, home economists embraced the standardization of the kitchen as a means to reduce the labor required to prepare meals. In an age when working class women were entering the labor force in record numbers, such standardization was seen as freeing up female labor for paid work outside the home. Not surprisingly, standardized recipes tended to be simpler and required fewer ingredients, but at the same time, they allowed easy calculation of nutritional value, making them of particular interest to nutritionists (Levenstein 1988). And, as late as 1973, a manual on the fast food industry quoted Taylor with enthusiasm. Indeed, as the Operations Manager at Burger King noted, "...fast-food restaurants operate like manufacturing plants today – not restaurants..." (quoted in Reiter 1991: 112).

Marketing, too, could be standardized. The emergence of marketing as a separate field of study in the early twentieth century was heavily influenced by, and was a part of the trend toward standardization. Even the terms of marketing were subjected to standardization by 1930. As one observer has noted, "With marketing, the circle of scientific management was closed: the whole economic *circuit*, from each business to the big market, was amenable to a systematic control – marketing was smoothly but surely sliding from microeconomics to macroeconomics" (Cochoy 1998: 205, emphasis in original).

Herbert Hoover, also an engineer, became convinced that the road to prosperity was to be based on standardization. Hoover became perhaps the most ardent advocate of standardization the world had ever known. For Hoover, factories themselves needed to be standardized. Efficiencies would be achieved by factories built according to a scientifically determined design, using equipment that was equally standardized, with standard jobs and standard organizations. Yet, Hoover was unaware of how standardizing factories would stifle innovation and perpetuate whatever inadequacies those factories had (Krislov 1997).

Enthusiasm with standards and standardization was not limited to the capitalist world. Lenin saw Taylorism as a central part of his program of rapid modernization of the Soviet Union. As he put it, "We must organize in Russia the study and teaching of the Taylor system and systematically try it out and adapt it to our purposes" (Lenin 1937: 333). Gosplan, the great Soviet bureaucracy in charge of planning, was headed by technical specialists with strong Taylorist views. Alexei Gastev, head of the Central Labour Institute, saw Taylorism as crafting the new proletariat that would build a prosperous Soviet Union (Bailes 1977). Under Stalin, the situation hardly changed. Wages were set using Taylorist principles. Henry Ford, one of Taylor's greatest admirers, had technical aid contracts with the Soviets through the 1930s (Bailes 1978). Hoover's book so impressed the Soviet elite that it was translated into Russian (Bailes 1974).

Even radical critic Thorsten Veblen was a great admirer of standardization. Veblen (1921) argued that since engineers were in charge and could increase productivity several fold if given the opportunity, the solution to the problems of capitalism was for the engineers to take control away from the "absentee owners." For him, standardization merely exacerbated the problems of industry by showing in stark relief how useless the capitalist class really was and how it had to restrict production in order to maintain control. Freeing the engineers from capitalist limits, and promoting widespread standardization, would bring unlimited abundance and the end of capitalism.

## 3. STANDARDS WITHOUT STANDARDIZATION

But standards do not necessarily make for standardization. They have had other meanings for some time. For example, companies like Standard Oil and American Standard have names that reflect not the desire for standardization, but the wish to be "the" standard, to be the best in the field. They drew on an older meaning of the term standard, meaning the banner at the top of a pole, used as a rallying point in battle. They claimed to lead their respective industries, not to merely meet some existing standard.

More recently, standards have been linked to product differentiation. For example, Henry Ford insisted that one could buy his Model T in any color, as long as it was black. Meanwhile, another vision for standards was being developed in another Detroit neighborhood – that of General Motors. Alfred P. Sloan, Jr. became President and Chief Operating Officer of General Motors in 1923 and proposed to use differentiated standards to segment the automobile market. By the end of the decade, General Motors sales had eclipsed those of Ford, and the company soon became the single largest enterprise in the world. Standards played a key role in this endeavor.

Food processors had begun to differentiate their products even before Sloan began to reorganize General Motors. Indeed, the H. J. Heinz Company was among the first to differentiate its products (Levenstein 1988). In 1896, the company's slogan, "57 Varieties" was festooned on every jar of pickles they sold. But such remained the exception until the latter half of the twentieth century. Then, food processors moved from having a few products, to inundating shoppers with a seemingly endless variety of processed foods. Importantly, that diversity was achieved by the creation of myriad specialized standards, each differentiated from others. Doubtless, the widespread adoption of Sloanism in food processing had to await the invention of the supermarket. Supermarkets offered the newly mobile suburbanites of the 1950s larger stores with a far greater diversity of products than the local grocer. Today, food processors produce thousands of new products each year, each attempting to further segment the market, each conforming to another standard.

In their Sloanist reshaping of the food supply, food processors had relatively little effect on agricultural production. In part, this was because food processors – a highly concentrated industry – continued to demand undifferentiated bulk commodities from suppliers. Even when new technologies have permitted greater differentiation among commodity suppliers, processors have resisted the use of those technologies. For example, soybean standards have been in existence for nearly a century, but the key aspects of soybeans of interest to processors – oil and protein content – have until recently been impossible to measure cheaply and rapidly. Yet, Hill (1994) notes that many in the soybean industry have resisted the use of new technologies to differentiate soybean quality by oil and protein content, even though it is now widely available and is relatively inexpensive. There are several different reasons why this is the case. First, the new technology would increase the ability of those farmers with high protein/oil soybeans to bargain with processors. Put differently, processors prefer to buy an undifferentiated product at a low price and sell a highly differentiated product at a high price, thereby capturing the added value at the processing stage. Second, farmers who, for whatever reason, were unable to produce high protein/oil soy would be at a disadvantage in a differentiated market.

For somewhat different reasons, fast food operators have remained highly Fordist in their approach to food production. Most of the larger fast food chains have very limited menus, differentiating meals largely by size. At the same time, they have been more than happy to impose strict standards on their suppliers. For example, McDonald's only uses Russet Burbank potatoes for its french fries. These oblong potatoes minimize waste for McDonald's while they permit the production of long narrow fries. Moreover, McDonald's is apparently pleased by their uptake of cooking oil during the frying process. Similarly, when various animal rights organizations picketed McDonald's over the treatment of chickens bound for McDonald's sandwiches and "McNuggets," the company imposed strict new animal welfare standards on its suppliers, restricting significantly the degree to which chickens could be de-beaked by suppliers. Other fast food chains quickly followed suit (Barboza 2003). However, some of the medium priced chains have begun to borrow a page from Sloan. They offer a varied menu but use a rather short list of ingredients. Whether this signals a trend for future fast food is unclear.

A much more recent change in the food system is the development and enforcement of private standards by supermarket chains. Until recently, supermarkets tended to remain within their country of origin. Tariffs and quotas on food imports limited the profitability of cross-national chains. But the formation of the World Trade Organization transformed the rules by which supermarkets had to source their products. Today, supermarket chains traverse the globe. Three companies stand far above the others, in terms of both sales volume and number of nations in which they operate: Wal-Mart (US), Carrefour (France) and Royal Ahold

(Netherlands). Numerous other firms have stores and/or subsidiaries in several nations. All the larger chains source globally in ways they did not (and could not) in the past.

As these chains have grown in scale, they have changed the way in which they source their products. The very largest chains can and do dictate their terms not only to farmers but to food processors. For example, Danone yogurt disappeared for several months from Wal-Mart's shelves in Mexico as a result of a price dispute with that firm (Smith 2002). In contrast, independent supermarkets and small chains tend to buy on the spot market or through food brokers. Supermarkets have also banded together to introduce a variety of industry-wide standards for producers. These include:

EUREPGAP. The European Retail Produce Working Group (EUREP), an association of European retailers, has produced a common set of standards – in the form of Good Agricultural Practices (GAP) – for food safety, food quality, environment, and labor that will shortly be required of all producers (EUREP 2002). Thus, whereas nations and international organizations have been reluctant to go beyond food safety, EUREP has brought environmental and labor issues to the center of the global debate. Of course, it is unlikely that the Boards of Directors of these firms woke up one morning to great concern over either the environment or farm labor. Far more likely, they realized that (1) a significant portion of their customers cared about these issues, and (2) the cost of compliance would have a negligible effect on the cost to consumers of food. On the other hand, the consequences for producers have been substantial, a point to which we shall return later.

COLEACP. The *Comité de Liaison Europe, Afrique, Caraïbes, Pacifique* is partly funded by the European Union and has as its goal, the reduction of pesticide residues in food products (COLEACP 2002). It does not so much set standards as it helps suppliers in Africa, the Caribbean, and the Pacific to meet European standards for maximum pesticide residues.

CIES Food Safety Initiative. CIES, the Food Business Forum, is a global association of food retailers and processors (CIES 2002). Its membership encompasses all the major supermarket chains in the world. Through its food safety initiative it intends to develop a set of meta-standards that encompass all the standards of the major food importing nations of the world. In doing so, it intends that producers would have to be certified only once to ensure compliance with food safety standards in Europe, North America, and Japan.

Others have adopted broader private standards including:

## 3.1    ISO 9000 and ISO 14000

The International Organization for Standardization (2002), a non-profit organization, has issued a series of management standards known as the ISO 9000 series. These standards focus on good management practices – means by which an organization can be run to ensure that high quality products or services will be produced. The standards are generic and can be applied to any organization within or outside the agrifood sector. The ISO 14000 standards focus on good environmental practices. Many agrifood organizations have adopted ISO 14000 as a means of reducing environmental pollution as well as of demonstrating their concern for the environment.

## 3.2   SA 8000

The SA 8000 standards were developed by Social Accountability International (2002), an NGO concerned about human rights. SA 8000 standards cover a range of issues from minimum wages, to worker rights, health and safety. Many producers have adopted SA 8000 to demonstrate their fair treatment of workers.

## 3.3   Fair Trade

In recent years a number of organizations have sprung up in both the US and Europe that argue for what has come to be called fair trade (e.g., Fair Trade Federation 2004). The central concern of fair trade advocates is that producers in developing nations should receive a fair and just return on their products (i.e., what they deserve), rather than being forced to accept low prices by the vagaries of the market. Many of these organizations maintain their own shops where various food and non-food products are sold. In general, such shops tend to sell shelf-stable products (e.g., coffee, tea) that require minimal infrastructure at the downstream end of the supply chain. Fair trade advocates have also been successful in getting some fair trade products onto supermarket shelves, especially in Europe.

Compliance to these and other private standatrds is rarely required by law. More frequently, compliance is required in order to effectively participate in a given market, while in a few instances compliance is entirely voluntary and may be seen by participants as a means to build market share (Caswell, Bredahl and Hooker 1998). But in nearly all cases, compliance must be measured by some external group if it is to be credible.

## 4. THE STANDARDS COMPLEX

Virtually every aspect of food and agricultural production, processing, transport, and retailing is subject to one or another set of standards by a myriad of government agencies and/or non-governmental bodies. This poses problems of multiple agencies with overlapping jurisdictions. Standards may also differ in scope and specificity. There may be conflicts among standards and standards bodies. Furthermore, standards may place unexpected constraints on farmer decision making. Let us consider each of these in turn.

### 4.1 Multiple Agencies

Given the diversity of standards which pertain to US fruits and vegetables, it is not surprising that they are the responsibility of many agencies, e.g., the Food Safety and Inspection Service, Food and Drug Administration, EPA Office of Prevention, Pesticides and Toxic Substances, regional marketing commissions and commodity groups, major processors and distributors and several international agencies (Nichols 1996). Each of these agencies and organizations has different, although sometimes overlapping jurisdiction with respect to G&S.

### 4.1 Differences in Scope and Specificity

For example, organoleptic standards for fruits and vegetables may be explicit (e.g., sugar concentration) or embodied in varietal specifications (e.g., Fuji apples). In addition, (sometimes different) federal and state environmental standards limit what compounds may be used for pest control and rates and times at which they can be applied. Regulations also specify the protections, amenities and accommodations which must be provided to hired agricultural workers. Other G&S may cover production practices as a whole (e.g., organic produce), or the social relations of production or exchange (e.g., Community Supported Agriculture).

### 4.2 Conflicts Among Standards

Given the proliferation of standards, standards can and do conflict with each other. For example, fruits and vegetables constitute one of the most dynamic standards arenas in US agriculture (Bordelon et al. 1997). Advertising emphasizes the superiority of products that conform to certain standards of size, shape and color. These standards have been codified for purposes of international trade (Organisation for Economic Cooperation and Development 1983). Concern about the safety of fruits and vegetables from chemical and biological contaminants has existed since the late 1800s, but has recently increased with outbreaks of fruit- and vegetable-borne diseases (Tauxe et al. 1997). These two emphases create contradictory pressures within the fruit and vegetable industry: efforts to produce cosmetic perfection by applying high levels of pesticides result in concern about toxic effects of residues (Pimentel, Kirby and Shroff 1993), especially for groups with high sensitivity (e.g., children, National Research Council 1998). Furthermore, efforts by producers to meet cosmetic G&S for fruits and vegetables by using high levels of insecticides may have negative impacts on beneficial organisms as well as on groundwater supplies. Yet, in some areas, pests that cause major economic damage are controlled by pesticides for which there are currently no alternatives (Harris and Whalon 1995); if new standards make it impossible to use those pesticides, production will shift to other regions where those pests are not a threat.

*4.3    Standards' Effects on Decision Making*

In recent years it has been claimed that stringent standards for fruit and vegetable safety from microbial contamination, and especially the mandating of particular production processes for accomplishing those levels of safety, will make it impossible for small-scale operations to be profitable. Similarly, standards for farmworker protection and accommodation may influence farm operators' decisions to replace hand harvesting with mechanical harvesting (Friedland, Barton and Thomas 1981), thus both limiting employment for farm laborers and increasing machinery sales. Standards for environmental and farmworker protection may restrict a grower's options for pest management to a subset of more expensive alternatives; this may have the effect of shifting production to other locales where those standards are not in effect. As a result, there may be less farmworker employment in the US and higher levels of pesticide risk in the exporting countries (Thrupp 1995). On the other hand, the establishment of federal organic standards may result in the greater availability of organic fruits and vegetables, thus leading to a reduction in the consumption of pesticide residues by US consumers (Harris et al. 1998).

## 5.  THEORIZING ABOUT STANDARDS

So how do we organize the study of this incredibly diverse and complex world of standards? G&S are implicated in decisions about who shall participate in decision making and who shall get to produce what, as well as in issues of distributive justice, and what constitutes the good life. To illustrate:

(1) Not everyone is admitted to the *negotiations* leading to the creation, modification or maintenance of G&S. Most standards are produced by technical committees that pay scant attention to the needs or desires of other groups not represented at the negotiating table. Moreover, negotiations are not limited to the creation of the standard which is then applied rubber stamp-like everywhere. Standards are always applied locally, and in their application there is always and necessarily negotiation. For example, grain elevator operators are likely to be more willing to accept grain of marginal quality when supply is short than when it is abundant. Similarly, they are more likely to accept grain that barely meets the standard from a large producer than from a smaller one. After all, they need the grain from the large producer in order to maintain their business – and they want that grain year after year. Clearly, who participates and how much say and sway they have in negotiations is a central issue of fairness and self-governance.

(2) Although G&S make the rules for entry into a given market transparent, they may also (intentionally or not) allow or deny *access* to particular product or labor markets. Those with insufficient capital or lack of certain raw materials may be blocked from entry to certain product markets. Similarly, others may be blocked from entering certain labor markets based on failure to obtain the necessary educational certificates (another standard) or, more insidiously, by virtue of their identification with a certain race, ethnic group, or gender. Similarly, G&S may be

used by nation states to protect national industry; G&S can be relatively effective when used as non-tariff trade barriers.

(3) Finally, G&S may also have either positive or negative *outcomes*. These outcomes include a wide range of distributive as well as environmental effects. G&S may redistribute income, wealth, power, status and prestige. For example, standards for vegetables may shift income to processors and away from farmers. Similarly, pollution may be encouraged in order to meet the standard (requirements for blemish-free fruits necessitates the excessive use of pesticides) or processes that produce pollution may be prohibited (as is the case with certain agrochemicals).

Furthermore, in today's world, science and technology (S&T) are central to virtually all systems of formal G&S. S&T are essential for the design, measurement, execution and enforcement of standards. For example, standards often change as a result of the realization by one or more parties to a given standard that technologies might be developed to increase speed, efficiency and/or accuracy – or even testing of some attribute previously too costly to examine. For example, today it is possible to measure many things accurately and rapidly using Nuclear Magnetic Resonance (NMR) imaging. Therefore, the question "Whose Knowledge?" (Harding 1991) is a critical one in the study of standards.

Standards have become an object of theoretical interest within several fields of study recently. Let us briefly examine each of these.

## 5.1    Economics

Within the economic literature it is possible to distinguish two major views. From the somewhat older neoclassical economic perspective of Jones and Hill (1994: 119), "G&S comprise one...set of rules that provide the guidelines for information signals in the market." G&S "facilitate marketing" by (1) reducing transaction costs (allowing the avoidance of visual inspection) (Farris 1960; Zulauf and Sporleder 1994), and (2) modifying the average and variance of quality characteristics of the product at various points in food supply chains in order to increase acceptance of the product at the consumption stage. The work of Lowell Hill (1990) is paradigmatic of this type of research. In his history of the rise of public grain grades and standards, he argued that standards serve several very important functions:

## 5.2    Standards Reduce the Cost of Doing Business

In each economic exchange, there are two kinds of costs: those related to the cost of the good and those related to the cost of doing business including inspection and identification of the product for sale. In economic terms, standards reduce transaction costs, i.e., the cost of each transaction. For example, if I wish to purchase one sack of wheat, I can inspect it rapidly myself just before purchase. The transaction cost is minimal, perhaps unnoticed. On the other hand, if I wish to purchase 2000 tons of wheat, the cost of inspection of that wheat becomes significant both in terms of labor necessary and time spent. An alternative is to have a set of grades and standards by which to classify wheat. Under those circumstances,

I merely have to specify to the seller that I wish 2000 tons of number 2 wheat. Since number 2 wheat is agreed upon by official definition, we may conclude our sale quickly and efficiently, minimizing the transaction cost.

### 5.3    Standards Increase Competition

Hill also argued that standards for bulk commodities increase competition. If there are many suppliers of wheat and each has different standards, or no standards at all, then comparison between the various lots is extremely difficult. In some sense, they are incommensurable. Put differently, if two lots are for sale but they have differing and unspecified quality characteristics, then I cannot determine which of the two is a better value. By having a uniform set of standards governing the sale of all lots of the same product, I can quickly determine which lot gives the greater value. This means that each seller and each buyer is put in direct competition with every other participant in the market for that good. Competition increases and, according to the theory, consumers benefit through lower prices.

### 5.4    Standards Reduce or Eliminate Information Asymmetries

Related to the increase in competition is the reduction or elimination of information asymmetries. In short, if the product for sale is unstandardized, then the seller will likely know far more about it than will the buyer. Indeed, the seller may be intimately familiar with both its strong and weak points, while both will be opaque to the buyer. In contrast, if standards are applied to the product for sale, and those standards capture the relevant qualities or attributes in the product, then the information held by the seller and buyer is more nearly the same. Thus, the buyer and seller negotiate a price with equal information about the item to be sold.

But the work of Hill and others is restricted largely to grains and other bulk commodities where the number of attributes of interest to buyer and seller is relatively limited and easily defined. Perhaps of greater importance, for Hill standards are only of interest when they are accompanied by standardization and uniformity (Hill 1991).

In contrast, for Grindley (1995) standards must be seen as a central feature of business strategy, and not merely as "received features" of the business landscape as implied from the neoclassical perspective. He notes that standards may benefit the market as a whole, but may still generate benefits that are distributed unevenly. Furthermore, the widespread use of a product or process, not superior technology, tends *de facto* to create a standard. Since products are often networked, compatibility across the network sets the standard. Grindley gives the example of video cassettes which must be fitted into players, but the internal workings of a given player can vary as long as the cassette can be read. This leads to counterintuitive results: By establishing an architecture that everyone could copy, IBM *increased* its share of the personal computer market. Similarly, with respect to food, the example of the New Zealand pipfruit industry is of particular relevance (McKenna 2001).

The French *Convention* school, in challenging the distinction between the production of goods and their diffusion, also recognizes the importance of standards. Eymard-Duvernay (1994) notes that it is not uncommon for clients to enter into the production process, specifying standards for products that do not yet exist. Similarly, Salais (1994) goes so far as to argue that firms make no sense organizationally unless considered through the trials of the market. Common practices or conventions among actors (including agreement on standards), not perfect information or shared goals, are the key concepts from this perspective. Convention theorists argue that various groups of persons associated with a given firm (e.g., owners, managers, workers) need not share any image of what the firm should be. What they do need to do is to have agreed upon practices or conventions that everyone more or less follows. Moreover, Favereau (1994) argues that the use of standards to create consistent quality requires an articulation of the internal environment of the firm (worker relations) with the external environment (customer demands) that can only be produced by rethinking current notions of equity.

## 5.5   Science and Technology Studies

Much of the recent science studies literature consists of empirical studies in which standards are implicated. Some of that literature is theoretically informed by the work of Foucault (1977; 1973) who argues that the modern world is characterized by discipline and surveillance of people and things which is sometimes referred to as "minute power." While Foucault is clear in noting that minute power need not be negative – the production of replaceable parts, for example – he tends to obscure the processes by which such relations come into being, i.e., negotiations (Fuller 1988; Stemerding 1991). Indeed, he tends to define terms as parts of semiotic systems rather than as modes of ordering the world (Law 1994).

As Rouse (1987) observes, science is thoroughly implicated in that form of power. However, only a handful of studies have made standards a central theme. Echoing sentiments shared in the 18th century (Brown 1979), Keating, Cambrosio, and MacKenzie (1992: 314), note that "...by standardizing tools, or by standardizing the world outside the laboratory, one effectively reduces the contradictions between abstract representations and concrete work." Similarly, Rouse (1987) argues that it is by virtue of standardization that scientific works circulate outside their original context of development. This can be easily understood by examining the Green Revolution. The improved varieties produced by scientists had to circulate far beyond the laboratory in order for it to be considered a success.

O'Connell (1993) notes that standards create universality by the circulation of particulars. Thus, weights are the same everywhere only by virtue of circulating particular "standard" weights to various locations. Moreover, O'Connell notes the connection to ethical concerns: "Whoever owns the particular that circulates to form the collective can collect money, prestige, and other goods from those who wish for access to the collective" (p.132). In contrast, Jordan and Lynch (1992) argue that even that which is highly standardized is still subject to variation. In other words, standardization is accomplished only with the precision necessary for the situation at hand. For example, a standard might require that apples be precisely 60 millimeters in diameter; however, the tolerance would most likely allow as much as ± 2.0 millimeters. That would be sufficient for the purposes at hand. In contrast, a tolerance of ± 2.0 millimeters for the seal on the top of a canned product might be unacceptable.

Pinch (1993) attempts to develop a phenomenology of testing, noting that in testing something is always at stake. "Valid test results depend upon the acceptance of a similarity relationship, and such a relationship can only be constructed within a body of conventions or within a form of life" (p. 31). He also documents the symmetry in testing: both the thing and the human are tested simultaneously. Similarly, Valceschini and Nicolas (1995) argue that quality standards test both objects and organizations. Using military aircraft as a case in point, Bugos (1993) asserts that testing is also designed to manufacture certainty. Busch and Tanaka (1996) attempt to extend the concept of symmetry specifically to ethics. Using the case of canola production in Canada, they argue that G&S simultaneously subject humans and non-humans to rites of passage that test their "goodness." Thus the good farmer and the good crop are simultaneously identified. From their perspective, standards also allow something resembling the neoclassical market to be established, create the conditions for economic analysis, and allocate power among human actors.

The recent link between science studies and ethics is proving fruitful. Callon (1991) has observed that engineers who design standards must act like sociologists, political scientists and moralists in order to do so. In other words, they must ask precisely the kind of questions posed by applied ethicists – although usually with far less persistence – in order to carry out their assigned tasks. Latour (1993) goes further to argue that ethics is embedded in mundane technologies such as seatbelts. Busch (2000) makes a more complete case for the link between ethics and standards. While not denying the transactions costs argument, he asserts that standards serve other purposes as well. These include (1) disciplining suppliers who do not meet the standard – either by removing them from the market or by relegating them to a lower grade, (2) reconstructing nature so as to make it conform to the G&S in use at a particular point in space and time, (3) creating localized conditions of objectivity through negotiating what shall count, for example, for soybeans, (4) building complex networks through which people and things may move by virtue of agreement on "what is the same," (5) standardizing markets such that personal contact is unnecessary and pricing is uniform, and (6) making capitalist markets possible by turning singularities into commodities (see also Appadurai 1986). Moreover, it may be argued that G&S make possible the collection of economic and statistical data about production and trade by defining what may be added up.

## 6. ETHICS AND STANDARDS

Although we are only beginning to understand the ethical ramifications of G&S through examination of empirical cases such as those described in this volume, we believe the following represent most of the major ethical and value issues associated with standards.

## 6.1 Distributive Justice

G&S distribute wealth, income, prestige, power and status among actors implicated in the standards. Yet, as both Walzer (1983) and Boltanski and Thévenot (1991) have pointed out, no single criterion can be used to distribute all social goods. Walzer (1983: 18) emphasizes that equality is "...a complex relation of persons, mediated by the goods we make, share, divide among ourselves; it is not an identity of possessions. It requires then, a diversity of distributive criteria that mirrors the diversity of social goods." Based on their notion of "worlds," Boltanski and Thévenot argue that there are different standards of goodness [*grandeur*]. They also note that persons may find themselves having to grapple with standards that conflict among worlds (e.g., environmental concern v. profits). Similarly, Rawls (1985) argues for a democratic concept of justice that is defined politically rather than metaphysically.

In contrast, most economists take a position which is consequentialist with respect to distributive questions, asking whether it could be that all are better off than before by handing the reins to the more efficient. In that case, distribution of means of production away from an individual does not necessarily mean Pareto non-optimality, or absolute decline of wealth for that individual.

In addition, economists pose a series of issues that underscore distributive issues of G&S that arise in the market: First, G&S may be flawed as information-diffusion tools: as descriptions, they may not provide uniform, consistent information, thus distorting market signals and concentrating market power in the hands of a subset of market participants (Jones and Hill 1994). The devices quantitatively measuring whether products meet the grade may be inadequate (subjective, inaccurate, inconsistent). Even if the signals are good descriptions, all market participants may not have access to the devices (because of barriers such as time cost, purchase cost, skill of participant, and so on). For example, Klitgaard (1991) notes that some grading services are costly while others are cheap.

Second, as noted above, there has been a shift in the nature of the market from "fungible agricultural commodities" (mass markets with homogeneous goods) to "differentiated agricultural commodities" with personal market niche characteristics (especially for fruits/vegetables, but increasingly for meat and grains) over the past two decades (Jones and Hill 1994). There has been a significant lag in standards leading to fears that standards may be hindering markets from dynamically adjusting to the new trade environment (Hill 1990).

Third, there may be a lack of coordination between market segments in developing legislation (or the private sector equivalent) to produce efficient and equitable results; there is confusion as to whether the burden of response to a changing market should be from the farmer (push) or from the processor (pull). Hence, there are equity issues not only *among firms* within a given market segment (e.g., among producers of asparagus) but also *between market segments* (e.g., farm v. processor v. retail).

Fourth, traditional G&S implementation systems are covering a waning portion of the market. Markets in many nations are becoming more vertically coordinated (e.g., direct farm-to-processor contracting). For example, prices on the National Cheese Exchange in Green Bay Wisconsin are less and less an indicator of US national prices and more and more a residual spot market. It is what economists call a "thin" market, not necessarily correlated with actual prices received elsewhere through contractual arrangements. Moreover, Identity Preserved[3] markets "tend to bypass grading systems that are used as the basis for pricing" (Barkema, Drabenstott and Cook 1993; Jones and Hill 1994: 125). In this case, the provision of information is for the purpose of differentiation, not standardization.

Finally, traditional grades and standards focus on characteristics of the product, not the processes involved at each stage of the food system. Requirements for change have implications for these processes (and thus access and outcomes at each level) (Jones 1993). Moreover, novel G&S systems focus on processes (e.g., the HACCP approach now used for meat and fish safety, or the recently-enacted organic G&S) rather than end-characteristics. But there is little known about how to fashion these new G&S in equitable ways, or what their impact will be on outcomes and access.

Economists have drawn on some of the above evidence to justify government provision of public goods/services in the form of facilitating G&S negotiations (to seek consensus over firms within a market segment and over market segments), providing access to testing services and information to producers, processors, and merchants, and information to consumers. Hence, for them public intervention in the face of market failure is a response to issues arising from negotiation, access, and outcomes of G&S. In contrast, Sagoff (1988) argues that social regulation expresses what we believe as a nation, not what we wish to buy as individuals (See also Buchanan 1985). Nevertheless, the challenges of the changing market structure calling for new types of G&S, as well as their monitoring and negotiation, make it unclear what the role of government should be in intervention, or how it should intervene.

These debates suggest the difficulties in sorting out the empirical, political and ethical questions: Does the new standard increase overall wealth? Does the change rest on political assumptions about who gains, thus precluding compensating the losers? (The first gets short shrift by non-economists, while the second often gets short shrift from economists.) What would a fair and just distribution of values be for a given grade or standard? To what extent are questions of distributive justice considered in developing or modifying G&S? To what extent *should* they be considered? Are these criteria generalizable across things being graded?

## 6.2   *Rights/Justice/Democracy*

In democratic societies citizens have a right to participate in decisions that affect their own lives. One school of theorists/practitioners of democracy defines a political or governmental sphere (i.e., law making and enforcement) that encompasses most if not all such decisions (cf. Feenberg 1995; Sclove 1995). Other decisions occur in the private sphere or civil society (Putnam 1993). But the very complexity and far-reaching transformative effects of our technological societies, and the growing number of private or corporate decisions that affect how we shall live, encourage us to challenge the separation of economic from political power (cf. Berle 1954) and of both from science and technology (Harding 1991). Thus, how private decisions may be influenced by public action (regulation, incentives, etc.) with respect to issues of food safety (Halloran 1986), labeling, and environmental soundness, among others, has become the subject of much debate. These are usually defined in terms of rights: the right to know (labeling), the right to safe and healthy food, the right to a clean environment, the right a safe workplace, etc. This, in turn, raises fundamental empirical and normative issues. For example, Avery et al. (1993) note that large corporations are heavily represented in Codex negotiations while public interest groups are barely present.[4] Should all parties be present or is it enough to have the opportunity to be present? Who actually participates in standard setting? How is the process organized? Are standards set by the industry, by a leading firm, by a non-profit organization, by a government body? How open or closed is the process? Who should participate and why? Are more open standards-setting processes feasible in an age of increasing product differentiation? What are the implications for democratic societies?

Furthermore, to the extent that they link raw materials producers to final consumers, G&S may be seen as a series of social contracts between various actors designed to produce a common good. Much like the social contracts of Hobbes, Locke and Rousseau, they impose order on the (social and natural) world. They pattern the behavior of people so that results make the grade. As such they pose a range of questions commonly asked by contemporary social contract theorists: Are the contracts made in a free and uncoerced manner? Are they fair? What would constitute a fair and equitable contract for a given grade or standard? What role does science and technology play in demonstrating fairness and legitimacy?

*6.3    Risk*

Toxic substances may now be detected at parts per trillion; some level of toxic compounds may be found in virtually all food products and agroecosystems. But the salience or relevance of this information is the subject of heated debate. Moreover, today scientists often define risks, estimate how great they are, devise schemes for reducing or eliminating them, and monitor them. And, scientists from different disciplines may disagree on the acceptable level of risk (Beck 1994). Therefore, today risk is increasingly a public issue (Beck 1992). Shrader-Frechette (1991) asserts that the two major positions are positivist (quantitative) and relativist (arbitrary). In contrast, Thompson and Dean (1996) assert that many risk debates start from competing conceptions running along a continuum between the probabilistic and contextual. Probabilists insist that statistical probability of harm is the essential defining feature of risk, while contextualists argue that there are many dimensions (e.g., voluntariness, catastrophic nature, reversibility, etc.), while none are essential to the conception of risk. G&S are implicated in risk analysis in several ways including: (1) G&S may define what level of risk is acceptable (e.g., what level of a toxicant is permissible in food), thereby limiting access by defining an outcome. (2) G&S may distribute risks and protection from risks differently across populations (i.e., some subpopulations may be at greater risk based on age, gender, ethnicity, labor force status, etc.) (Caplan 1986; Johnson 1986). (3) G&S may involuntarily impose risks on certain persons or populations. Thus questions of import here include: Who or what is at risk in standards design, implementation, maintenance, modification? In what ways (e.g., monetary, health, environmental)? What level (if any) of risk should be imposed? How should risks be distributed?

One major political debate about risk is that between competing notions of risk. In recent years the European Union has tended to argue for what has come to be known as the precautionary principle. Essentially, this approach argues that when confronted with unknown potential risks one should proceed slowly. The EU has taken this position with respect to genetically modified foods. In contrast, the US has adhered to what might be called the familiarity principle with respect to new potential risks. US officials argue that one should engage in a conventional risk analyses when confronted with such products as genetically modified crops. In a recent paper Busch (2002) has noted that there is little consistency in these positions across issues. Thus, the US takes the precautionary principle with respect to a disease of sheep that is well-known in Europe but is non-existent in the US (scrapie). In contrast, the Europeans (especially France) take the familiarity principle with respect to unpasteurized cheeses. Busch notes that these positions are based on a combination of what is at stake in each instance as well as reliance on homilies (e.g., haste makes waste) that are called upon when deemed appropriate by government officials and others.

## 6.4    Virtues

G&S are also means for demonstrating virtues (MacIntyre 1984; Winner 1995). For example, Henderson et al. (1983) argue that G&S force public reporting of prices. Thus, trust and truth are aided by virtue of the clarity and objectivity enacted through the standard. Similarly, honesty is always crucial in the determination of standards as well as in their enforcement (Olesko 1995). Other virtues may be implicated as well. Indeed, some creators of standards have seen in them the means for the building of character (Sweetnam 1995). As Maxwell noted in 1871: "The man of business requires these standards for the sake of justice, the man of science requires them for the sake of truth,..." (quoted in Schaffer 1995: 136).

## 6.5    Duty to Future Generations

In recent years, numerous philosophers have raised difficult questions with respect to our duty to future generations (cf., Ferry 1995; e.g., Jonas 1984). Sagoff (1988) asserts that we have not so much a duty to future generations as to the future itself.

Economists have noted the path dependency of technical change, although they have not noted this particular problem associated with it (North 1990). At the very least, it would seem reasonable not to impose undue burdens on future generations to maintain practices that we create today. Since G&S modify human behavior, we may ask whether decisions we make about them today will affect negatively (i.e., unduly restrict) the welfare of our progeny. Are such issues currently considered in the development and implementation of G&S? If not, how might they be incorporated into standards debates? To what degree should such issues be debated?

### 6.6    Environmental Ethics

G&S may have important implications for the environment (e.g., Norton 1987).[5] Meeting a particular standard may put undue stresses on the environment (e.g., by forcing producers to engage in environmentally harmful practices). Thus, G&S raise important, but largely unexplored, issues with respect to our duties toward the environment. Since G&S are focused around production, they tend to squarely face off against the positions of preservationists. Thompson (1995) has recently attempted to address this conflict, although he has not applied his proposed solution to G&S issues. For example, raising a crop or animal that meets certain standards may require use of environmental contaminants, undue soil erosion, restricted crop rotation, etc. To what degree are such issues incorporated into G&S decision making? To what degree ought they to be included?

In addition, there are issues of environmental justice, often exemplified by the NIMBY (not in my backyard) or NIABY (not in anyone's backyard) phenomena. G&S may distribute environmental problems in such a way that only those without means to resist must face the deleterious environmental consequences. For example, processing waste may only cause pollution in low-income neighborhoods. How are such issues addressed in practice? How should they be addressed?

## 7. THE PLAN OF THIS BOOK

Clearly, no single volume can address all of these complex issues. However, in this volume we do attempt to address some of them. In doing so we hope this volume can begin to define the scope of inquiry into the economic, social, political and ethical dimensions of food and agricultural standards. This volume brings together eleven case studies that help to illustrate these multiple issues and to provide a basis for outlining a future research and policy agenda.

The first set of three case studies discusses the roles of three distinctly different public, international organizations in setting and negotiating standards. Kevin Kennedy, in "The World Trade Organization: Ultimate Arbiter of International Sanitary and Phytosanitary Standards?" examines three Sanitary and Phytosanitary (SPS) disputes that have been resolved by the World Trade Organization in order to identify the ways in which the WTO has become the ultimate arbiter of international SPS standards. In a similar, but more provocative line of reasoning, Suzan Ilcan and Lynne Phillips in "Circulations of Insecurity: Globalization Food Standards in

Historical Perspective" argue that the Food and Agriculture Organization (FAO) of the United Nations deliberately sought to standardize approaches to thinking about world food and agriculture as a means to build a global model of food consumption. In doing so, the FAO deliberately set aside consideration of food diversity around the world. From a significantly different perspective, the chapter by Hervé Hannin, Jean-Marie Codron and Sophie Thoyer, "The International Office of Vine and Wine (OIV) and the World Trade Organization (WTO): Standardization Issues in the Wine Sector," examines the relationship between two radically different international standard setting organizations, the WTO and the International Office of Vine and Wine (OIV). For the authors, the history and organizational principles of the OIV suggests ways in which the OIV could serve as a model for issues related to the standardization of food production. Nevertheless, the authors argue that current international market forces, and the strategies of various actors threaten the stability of the OIV.

The next four case studies offer an opportunity to examine a range of relationships among private and public sector actors and the role of standards in the regulatory process. Bertil Sylvander and Olivier Biencourt in "The Negotiation of Animal Product Standards: A Procedural Approach Applied to Raw Milk" propose a conceptual perspective, a "procedural approach" and use the controversial standard for the use of raw milk in cheese production in France to understand how standards are negotiated. In their chapter, "The Indivisibility of Science, Policy and Ethics: Starlink™ Corn and the Making of Standards," Maite Salazar et al. take an equally controversial issue, the regulation of Starlink™ in the United States, to argue that the degree of scientific uncertainty, the indeterminacy of risk, and the issue of equivalency help to illuminate the indivisibility of science, politics and ethics in technoscientific controversies. Ivan Sergio Freire de Souza and Lawrence Busch in "Standards and State-Building: The Construction of Soybean Standards in Brazil" offer a comparative historical perspective on the role of agricultural standards in the consolidation of the 19th century Brazilian state and how new, "modern" standards for soybeans have gradually replaced the standards of the past. In the final chapter in this section, "Paradoxes of Innovation: Standards and Technical Change in the Transformation of the US Soybean Industry," Lawrence Busch et al. also look at soybean standards, but focus on how standards mediate among various actors in a sub-sector and in doing so create paradoxes related both to restricting and enhancing the flow of commodities and to promoting competition while requiring cooperation.

The final four case studies in this volume focus on the issue of access and ethical trade in global markets. They explore various dimensions of the relationships between food and agricultural standards and development. Elizabeth Ransom, in "Defining a Good Steak: Global Constructions of What is Considered the Best Red Meat," explores several cultural, economic, political and ethical issues that arise as the South African red meat industry adopts quality standards for the purposes of world trade. In "Improving the Access of Small Farmers in Africa to Global Markets through the Development of Quality Standards for Pigeonpeas," Richard B. Jones et al. describe how collaborative research between an international research agency, ICRISAT, a non-profit organization, TechnoServe, Inc., and private sector traders and processors that focuses on grades and standards can help to improve the competitive position of smallholder African farmers. Paul Thiers's chapter, "China and Global Organic Food Standards: Sovereignty Bargains and Domestic Politics" considers the ways in which global organic standards have become embedded in domestic political struggles at the national, inter-ministerial and local level in China, and how the transformation of organic standards by domestic politics has affected the organization of organic agriculture in China. The final chapter in this section by Jim Bingen, "Cotton in West Africa: A Question of Quality," examines several political questions related to farmer control, power and democratic processes that are raised as the national cotton company of Mali seeks to implement three different sets of quality standards from production through processing and marketing to enhance a specific world market reputation for its cotton.

The volume concludes with a chapter by Jim Bingen and Lawrence Busch, "Shaping a Policy and Research Agenda," that revisits the key themes of the volume and identifies a policy and research agenda to address key issues such as, the relationships between private and public standards, third party certification, the plethora of product and process standards, and concerns with standards and power.

## 8. NOTES

[1] Some would claim that dessert should be linked to need. The concept of the "deserving poor" suggests this sort of linkage. Yet, as numerous scholars have noted, linking need to dessert in this manner is quite problematic. See, for example, Piven and Cloward 1971.

[2] Wilson also planned a 500,000 acre farm in the Soviet Union from the comfort of a Chicago hotel room (Scott 1998).

[3] "Identity Preserved" is the term used for specialty products, the identity of which must be preserved from the initial producer to the final consumer.

[4] Recently, the Codex (Codex Alimentarius 2003) has made significant advances in opening up to broader stakeholder groups.

[5] We distinguish here between environmental standards (e.g., the Clean Air Act) and implications of standards for environmental ethics.

## 9. REFERENCES

Adler, K. (1995) A Revolution to Measure: The Political Economy of the Metric System in France. Pp. 39-71 in *The Values of Precision*, edited by M. Norton Wise. Princeton: Princeton University Press.

Appadurai, A. (1986) "Introduction: Commodities and the Politics of Value". Pp. 3-63 in *The Social Life of Things: Commodities in Social Perspective*, edited by Arjun Appadurai. Cambridge: Cambridge University Press.

Avery, N., M. Drake, and T. Land (1993) *Cracking the Codex: An Analysis of Who Sets World Standards*. London: National Food Alliance.

Bailes, K. E. (1974). The Politics of Technology: Stalin and Technocratic Thinking among Soviet Engineers. *American Historical Review* 79:445-469.

_____ (1977) A. Gastev and the Soviet Controversy over Taylorism. *Soviet Studies* 29:373-394.

_____ (1978) *Technology and Society under Lenin and Stalin: Origins of the Soviet Technical Intelligentsia*. Princeton: Princeton University Press.

Barboza, D. (2003) Animal Welfare's Unexpected Allies. Pp. C1 in *The New York Times*. June 25.

Barkema, A., M. Drabenstott, and M. L. Cook (1993) The Industrialization of the US Food System. Pp. 3-20 in *Food and Ag Marketing Issues for the 21st Century*, edited by D.I Padberg. College Station: Texas: The Food and Ag Marketing Consortium.

Beck, U. (1992) *Risk Society: Towards a New Modernity*. London: Sage.

_____ (1994) The Reinventing of Politics: Toward a Theory of Reflexive Modernization. Pp. 1-55 in *Reflexive Modernization: Politics, Tradition and Aesthetics in the Modern Social Order*, edited by U. Beck, A. Giddens, and S. Lash. Cambridge: Polity Press.

Berle, A. A. (1954) *The Twentieth Century Capitalist Revolution*. New York: Harcourt, Brace & World.

Boltanski, L. and L. Thévenot (1991) *De La Justification: Les Economies de la Grandeur*. Paris: Gallimard.

Bordelon, B., A. Hammer, B. Moser, J. Simon, G. Sullivan, and J. Uhl (1997) Horticultural Sector. Pp. 353-390 in *Food System 21*. West Lafayette: Purdue University Cooperative Extension Service.

Bowker, G. C. and S. L. Star (1999) *Sorting Things Out: Classification and its Consequences*. Cambridge, MA: MIT Press.

Brown, J. (1979) *Mathematical Instrument-Makers in the Grocers' Company 1688-1800*. London: Science Museum.

Buchanan, A. (1985) *Ethics, Efficiency, and the Market*, Totawa, N. J: Rowman and Allanheld.

Bugos, G. E. (1993) Manufacturing Certainty: Testing and Program Management for the F-4 Phantom II. *Social Studies of Science* 23:265-300.

Buller, A. H. R. (1919) *Essays on Wheat*. New York: The Macmillan Company.

Busch, L. (2000) The Moral Economy of Grades and Standards. *Journal of Rural Studies* 16:273-283.

_____ (2002) The Homeletics of Risk. *Journal of Agricultural and Environmental Ethics* 15:17–29.

Busch, L. and K. Tanaka (1996) Rites of Passage: Constructing Quality in a Commodity Sub-sector. *Science, Technology and Human Values* 21:3-27.

Callon, M. (1991) Technoeconomic Networks and Irreversibility. Pp. 132-161 in *A Sociology of Monsters: Essays on Power, Technology, and Domination*, edited by J. Law. London: Routledge and Kegan P.

Caplan, A. L. (1986) The Ethics of Uncertainty: The Regulation of Food Safety in the United States. *Agriculture and Human Values* 3:180-190.

Caswell, J. A., M. E. Bredahl and N. H. Hooker (1998) How Quality Management Metasystems are Affecting the Food Industry. *Review of Agricultural Economics* 20:547-557.

CIES. 2002. CIES, The Food Business Forum. CIES. Retrieved on October 7, 2002; http://www.ciesnet.com/.

Cochoy, F. (1998) Another Discipline for the Market Economy: Marketing as a Performative Knowledge and Know-How for Capitalism. Pp. 194-221 in *The Laws of the Markets*, edited by M. Callon. Oxford: Basil Blackwell.

Codex Alimentarius (2003) Codex Alimentarius. Retrieved on June 6, 2003; http://www.codexalimentarius.net/.

COLEACP (2002) Liaison Committee Europe -Africa- Caribbean-Pacific. COLEACP. Retrieved on Oct. 6, 2002; http://www.coleacp.org/.

EUREP (2002) EUREPGAP: The Partnership for Safe and Sustainable Agriculture. EUREP. Retrieved on October 6, 2002; http://www.eurep.org/sites/index_n.html.

Eymard-Duvernay, F. (1994) Coordination des Echanges et Qualité des Biens. Pp. 307-334 in *Analyse Economique des Conventions*, edited by André Orléan. Paris: Presses Universitaires de France.

Fair Trade Federation (2004) Welcome to the Fair Trade Federation Web Site! Washington, DC: Fair Trade Federation. Retrieved on May 29, 2004. http://www.fairtradefederation.com/.

Farris, P. (1960) Uniform Grades and Standards, Product Differentiation and Product Development. *Journal of Farm Economics* 42:854-63.

Favereau, O. (1994) Régle, Organisation et Apprentissage Collectif: Un Paradigme Non Standard Pour Trois Théories Hétérodoxes. Pp. 113-137 in *Analyse Economique des Conventions*, edited by A. Orléan. Paris: Presses Universitaires de France.

Feenberg, A. (1995) Subversive Rationalization: Technology, Power, and Democracy. Pp. 3-22 in *Technology and the Politics of Knowledge*, edited by A. Feenberg and A. Hannay. Bloomington: Indiana University Press.

Fei, S (1992) [1948]. *From the Soil: Foundations of Chinese Society*. Berkeley, CA: University of California Press.

Ferry, L. (1995) *The New Ecological Order*. Chicago: University of Chicago Press.

Foucault, M. (1977) *Discipline and Punish: The Birth of the Prison*. New York: Vintage.

(1973) *The Birth of the Clinic; an Archaeology of Medical Perception*. New York: Pantheon Books.

Friedland, W. H., A. E. Barton and R. J. Thomas (1981) *Manufacturing Green Gold: Capital, Labor, and Technology in the Lettuce Industry*. Cambridge: Cambridge University Press.

Fuller, S. (1988) *Social Epistemology*. Bloomington: Indiana University Press.

Grindley, P. (1995) *Standards Strategy and Policy: Cases and Stories*. Oxford: Oxford University Press.

Habakkuk, H. J. (1962) *American and British Technology in the Nineteenth Century*. Cambridge: Cambridge University Press.

Halloran, J. (1986) To Ban or Not to Ban? What are the Ethics of the Question? *Agriculture and Human Values* 3:5-9.

Harding, S. (1991) *Whose Science? Whose Knowledge? Thinking from Women's Lives*. Ithaca, NY: Cornell University Press.

Harris, C. K. and M. Whalon (1995) Mapping the Middle Road for Michigan Pest Management Policy. Pp. 103-138 in *Policy Choices: Creating Michigan's Future*, edited by F. Bickart. East Lansing: Michigan State University Press.

Hata, D. T., D. Hills and N. I. Hata (1995). *Japanese Americans and World War II: Exclusion, Internment, and Redress*. Wheeling, Ill.: Harlan Davidson.

Henderson, D.R, L.F Schrader and V. J Rhodes (1983) Public Price Reporting. Pp. 21-57 in *Federal Marketing Programs in Agriculture: Issues and Options*, edited by W. J. Armbruster. Danville, IL: Interstate Printers and Publishers.

Hill, L. (1994) Component Pricing in the Soybean Industry. Urbana-Champaign. Retrieved on May 29, 2004; http://www.agribiz.com/IQS/epv/epvsumm.html.

Hill, L. D. (1990) *Grain Grades and Standards: Historical Issues Shaping the Future*. Urbana, IL: University of Illinois Press.

Hill, L. D. (Ed.) (1991) *Uniformity by 2000: An International Workshop on Maize and Soybean Quality*. Urbana, IL: Scherer Publications.

International Organization for Standardization (2002) Welcome to ISO Online. ISO. Retrieved on October 7, 2002; http://www.iso.ch/iso/en/ISOOnline.openerpage.

Johnson, D. (1986) The Ethical Dimensions of Acceptable Risk in Food Safety. *Agriculture and Human Values* 3:171-179.

Jonas, H. (1984) *The Imperative of Responsibility*. Chicago: University of Chicago Press.

Jones, C. R. (1917) [1916]. Scientific Management as Applied to the Farm, Home, and Manufacturing Plants. Pp. 108-115 in *Proceedings of the 30th Annual Convention of the Association of American Agricultural Colleges and Experiment Stations*.

Jones, E. (1993) Structural Changes in the Commodity Markets: Implications for the Soft Red Winter Wheat Market. Blacksburg: Virginia Polytechnic Institute and State University, Dept. of Agricultural and Applied Economics Staff Paper SP 93.

Jones, E, and L. D. Hill (1994) Re-engineering Market Policies in Food and Agriculture: Issues and Alternatives for Grain Grading Policies. Pp. 119-29 in *Re-engineering Marketing Policies for Food and Agriculture*, edited by D.I. Padberg. College Station: Texas: The Food and Ag Marketing Consortium.

Jordan, K. and M. Lynch (1992) The Sociology of a Genetic Engineering Technique: Ritual and Rationality in the Performance of a 'Plasmid Prep'. Pp. 77-114 in *The Right Tools for the Job: At Work in Twentieth-Century Life Sciences*, edited by A. E. Clarke and J. H. Fujimura. Princeton: Princeton University Press.

Keating, P., A. Cambrosio and M. MacKenzie (1992) The Tools of the Discipline: Standards, Models, and Measures in the Affinity/Avidity Controversy in Immunology. Pp. 312-354 in *The Right Tools for the Job: At Work in Twentieth-Century Life Sciences*, edited by A. E. Clarke and J. H. Fujimura. Princeton: Princeton University Press.

Kiltgaard, R. (1991) *Controlling Corruption*. Berkeley, CA: University of California Press.

Kirkendall, R. S. (1966) *Social Scientists and Farm Politics in the Age of Roosevelt*. Columbia: University of Missouri Press.

Krislov, S. (1997) *How Nations Chose Product Standards and Standards Change Nations*. Pittsburgh: University of Pittsburgh Press.

Latour, B. (1993) *La Clef de Berlin et Autre Leçons d'un Amateur des Sciences*. Paris: Editions la Découverte.

Law, J. (1994) *Organizing Modernity*. Oxford: Blackwell.

Lenin, V. I. (1937) *Selected Works*. London: Lawrence and Wishart, Volume VII.

Levenstein, H. (1988) *Revolution at the Table: The Transformation of the American Diet*. New York: Oxford University Press.

MacIntyre, A. (1984) *After Virtue*. Notre Dame, IN: University of Notre Dame Press. Second Edition.

McKenna, M., R. Le Heron and M. Roche. (2001) Living Local, Growing Global: Renegotiating the Export Production Regime in New Zealand's Pipfruit Sector. *Geoforum* 32:157-166.

National Research Council. (1998) *Ensuring Safe Food: From Production to Consumption*. Washington, DC: National Academy Press.

North, D. C. (1990) *Institutions, Institutional Change, and Economic Performance*. New York: Cambridge University Press.

Norton, B. G. (1987) *Why Preserve Natural Variety?* Princeton: Princeton University Press.

O'Connell, J. (1993) The Creation of Universality by the Circulation of Particulars. *Social Studies of Science* 23:129-173.

Olesko, K. M. (1995) The Meaning of Precision: The Exact Sensibility in Early Nineteenth Century Germany. Pp. 103-134 in *The Values of Precision*, edited by M. Norton Wise. Princeton: Princeton University Press.

Organisation for Economic Cooperation and Development (1983) *The OCDE [sic] Scheme for the Application of International Standards for Fruit and Vegetables*. Paris: OECD.

OTA (1992) *A New Technological Era for American Agriculture*. Washington, D.C.: Office of Technology Assessment.

Pimentel, D., C. Kirby, and A. Shroff (1993) The Relationship Between 'Cosmetic Standards' for Foods and Pesticide Use. Pp. 47-84 in *The Pesticide Question: Environment, Economics, and Ethics*, edited by D. P. and H. Lehman. New York: Chapman and Hall.

Pinch, T. (1993) Testing-One, Two, Three...Testing: Toward a Sociology of Testing. *Science, Technology, and Human Values* 18:25-41.

Piven, F. F. and R. A. Cloward (1971) *Regulating the Poor*. New York: Random House.

Putnam, R. D. (1993) The Prosperous Community: Social Capital and Public Life. *The American Prospect* 13:35-42.

Rawls, J. (1985) Justice as Fairness. *Philosophy and Public Affairs* 14:223-251.

Reiter, E. (1991) *Making Fast Food: From the Frying Pan into the Fryer*. Montreal: McGill-Queens University Press.

Rouse, J. (1987) *Knowledge and Power*. Ithaca, NY: Cornell University Press.

Sagoff, M. (1988) *The Economy of the Earth: Philosophy, Law and the Environment*. Cambridge: Cambridge University Press.

Salais, R. (1994) Incertitude et Interactions de Travail: Des Produits aux Conventions. Pp. 371-403 in *Analyse Economique des Conventions*, edited by André Orléan. Paris: Presses Universitaires de France.

Schaffer, S. (1995) Accurate Measurement is an English Science. Pp. 135-172 in *The Values of Precision*, edited by M. Norton Wise. Princeton: Princeton University Press.

Sclove, R. E. (1995) *Democracy and Technology*. New York: Guilford Press.

Scott, J. C. (1998) *Seeing Like a State: How Certain Schemes to Improve the Human Condition Have Failed*. New Haven, CT: Yale University Press.

Shrader-Frechette, K. (1991) *Risk and Rationality*. Berkeley: University of California Press.

Smith, A. (1994) [1776] *An Inquiry into the Nature and Causes of the Wealth of Nations*. New York: Modern Library.

Smith, G. (2002) Mexico's War of the Megastores. *Business Week* September 23:60.

Social Accountability International. 2002. SA 8000 Standard. Social Accountability International. Retrieved on October 7, 2002; http://www.cepaa.org/sa8000_review.htm.

Stemerding, D. (1991) *Plants, Animals, and Formulae: Natural History in the Light of Latour's Science in Action and Foucault's The Order of Things*. Enschede, The Netherlands: University of Twente, School of Philosophy and Social Science.

Sweetnam, G. (1995) Precision Implemented: H. Rowland, the Concave Diffraction Grating, and the Analysis of Light. Pp. 283-310 in *The Values of Precision*, edited by M. Norton Wise. Princeton: Princeton University Press.

Swetz, F. J. (1987) *Capitalism and Arithmetic: The New Math of the 15th Century*. LaSalle, Illinois: Open Court.

Tauxe, R., H. Kruese, C. Hedberg, M. Potter, J. Madden, and K. Wachsmuth (1997) Microbial Hazards and Emerging Issues Associated with Produce. *Journal of Food Protection* 60:1400-1408.

Taylor, F. W. (1911) *The Principles of Scientific Management.* New York: Harper.

Thompson, P. (1995) *The Spirit of the Soil: Agriculture and Environmental Ethics.* London: Routledge.

Thompson, P. B. and W. Dean (1996) Competing Conceptions of Risk. *Risk: Health, Safety and Environment* 7:361-384.

Thrupp, L. A. (1995) Bittersweet Harvests for Global Supermarkets: Challenges in Latin America's Agricultural Export Boom. Washington. DC: World Resources Institute.

Valceschini, E. and F. Nicolas. 1995. La Dynamique Economique de la Qualité Agro-Alimentaire. Pp. 15-37 in *Agro-Alimentaire: Une Economie de la Qualité*, edited by F. Nicolas and E. Valceschini. Paris: INRA and Economica.

Veblen, T. (1921) *The Engineers and the Price System.* New York: B. H. Huebsch, Inc.

Virgil (1982) *The Georgics.* London: Penguin Books.

Walzer, M. (1983) *Spheres of Justice: A Defense of Pluralism and Equality.* New York: Basic Books.

Winner, L. (1995) Citizen Virtues in a Technological Order. Pp. 65-84 in *Technology and the Politics of Knowledge*, edited by A. Feenberg and A. Hannay. Bloomington: Indiana University Press.

Zulauf, C. and T. L Sporleder (1994) Assessing Federal Grade Criteria for Fruits and Vegetables: Should Nutrient Attributes be Incorporated? Pp. 130-9 in *Re-engineering Marketing Policies for Food and Agriculture*, edited by D. I. Padberg. College Station: Texas: The Food and Ag Marketing Consortium.

II

# PUBLIC AND INTERNATIONAL STANDARDS

KEVIN C. KENNEDY*

# 2. THE WORLD TRADE ORGANIZATION:

*Ultimate Arbiter of International Sanitary and Phytosanitary Standards?*

## 1. INTRODUCTION AND BACKGROUND

World trade in goods and services has grown dramatically in the post-war era, as have the levels of environmental degradation and natural resource depletion. Some observers consider trade liberalization and environmental degradation to be locked in a direct cause-effect relationship.[1] The linkages and frictions, both legal and economic, between trade, on the one hand, and human health and safety issues, on the other, are undeniable.

Admittedly, the fit of international trade law and health and safety law, especially sanitary and phytosanitary standards and rules, has not been well-tailored. Trade and food safety policies have proceeded at times on diverging tracks, at times on parallel tracks, and at other times on the same track but headed on a collision course.[2] Many environmentalists have been unrelenting in their WTO-bashing, casting the World Trade Organization in the role of environmental villain. The General Agreement on Tariffs and Trade (GATT) – the core WTO agreement – has few friends among environmentalists, who vilify GATT and have made it their *bête noire*.

Why has the WTO become the environmentalists' whipping boy? The short answer is that the WTO is viewed as at best indifferent to legitimate environmental, health, and safety concerns and at worst hostile to them. What are some of the misgivings about the WTO and free trade? In a nutshell, some groups fear that countries with comparatively more stringent environmental, health, and safety standards will relax them under pressure from their domestic industries in order to discourage capital and job flight to countries where similar environmental regulatory standards are lax or non-existent. A closely related concern is that under pressure from economically powerful developed countries, rigorous health and safety standards will be compromised or "ratcheted down."[3]

The World Trade Organization today finds itself cast in the role of ultimate arbiter of international sanitary and phytosanitary (SPS) standards, at least in the international trade context. How is it that the WTO has been cast in this role? The short explanation for this development is straightforward. As part of the Uruguay Round multilateral trade negotiations that were concluded in 1994, the international

* Kevin C. Kennedy, Professor of Law, Michigan State University College of Law.

*J. Bingen and L. Busch, (eds.), Agricultural Standards: The Shape of the Global Food and Fiber System, 31-50. © 2006 Springer. Printed in the Netherlands.*

trade community entered into two agreements to supplement the extant international trade legal regime, namely, the WTO Agreement on the Application of Sanitary and Phytosanitary Measures (the SPS Agreement) and the WTO Agreement on Technical Barriers to Trade (the TBT Agreement). The rationale for these agreements is equally straightforward. Experience had shown that SPS measures were frequently employed as other, more traditional barriers to trade, such as tariffs (i.e., customs duties) and quotas on goods, were reduced or eliminated. Many countries, including the United States, often had the unhappy experience of negotiating tariff reductions and quota eliminations, only to be met with a suspect SPS measure that wiped out the benefit of the earlier bargain.[4] Before the SPS and TBT Agreements were added to the international trade legal regime in 1994, GATT Article XX(b) (discussed below) was the only GATT provision – and a skeletal one at best – dealing expressly with the subject of sanitary and phytosanitary measures. In short, before the SPS Agreement, no multilateral trade agreement existed that contained a set of rules regulating a country's use of SPS measures in connection with imported goods. The SPS Agreement filled this gap by circumscribing WTO members' use of such measures when used as an impermissible nontariff barrier to trade.

The next part of this chapter provides an overview of the core GATT articles that bear on the question of when SPS measures are permissible in the trade context. After briefly reviewing the SPS Agreement, the chapter considers three SPS disputes resolved in the WTO to date. By the end of 1999, the WTO had resolved three SPS/international trade disputes. The first dealt with human health and safety, the *EC – Hormone Beef* dispute. The second addressed animal health and life, the *Australia – Salmon* case. The third resolved a phytosanitary dispute, the *Japan – Food Quarantine* case.[5] The chapter concludes by identifying some of the lessons to be learned from the WTO's SPS Agreement jurisprudence.

## 2. THE GENERAL AGREEMENT ON TARIFFS AND TRADE

The General Agreement on Tariffs and Trade (GATT) strives for equal treatment of imported goods, regardless of their source of origin, through a nondiscrimination principle that operates at two levels: (1) nondiscrimination by an importing country among importers (the most-favored-nation principle, codified in GATT Article I), and (2) nondiscrimination between imported goods and the domestic like product (the national treatment principle, codified in GATT Article III). Despite its commitment to the goal of liberal trade, GATT does permit WTO members to restrict imports on a number of limited grounds. Of the ten enumerated general exceptions contained in GATT Article XX, the public health and safety exception touches directly on the promulgation and enforcement of food safety laws, standards, and regulations. The GATT Article XX(b) public health and safety exception provides:

> Subject to the requirement that such measures are not applied in a manner which would constitute a means of arbitrary or unjustifiable discrimination between countries where the same conditions prevail, or a disguised restriction on international trade, nothing in

this Agreement shall be construed to prevent the adoption or enforcement by any contracting party of measures:

\* \* \* \*

(b) necessary to protect human, animal or plant life or health;...

Thus, in order for an importing country to impose a GATT-permissible health or safety import measure, that measure (1) must be necessary (*i.e.*, no less trade restrictive alternative is available), (2) must not arbitrarily or unjustifiably discriminate between countries where the same conditions prevail (*i.e.*, it must be consistent with the most-favored-nation and national treatment obligations), and (3) must not be a disguised restriction on international trade.

However, considering the open-ended quality of broad terms, such as "necessary," "arbitrarily," and "unjustifiably," the public health and safety exception has the obvious potential for being a rich source of formidable nontariff barriers to trade. Given the vagaries of the public health and safety exception, the potential for abuse by economically powerful countries anxious to foist their own brand of food safety standards on weaker trading nations is ever present. GATT practice generally has been to construe Article XX narrowly in favor of trade and against nontariff barriers to trade. In a highly instructive GATT panel report, *Thai Cigarettes,*[6] the dispute settlement panel concluded that Thailand's ban on imported cigarettes was not "necessary" within the meaning of the chapeau to GATT Article XX:

[A] contracting party cannot justify a measure inconsistent with other GATT provisions as "necessary"...if an alternative measure which it could reasonably be expected to employ and which is not inconsistent with other GATT provisions is available to it. By the same token, in cases where a measure consistent with other GATT provisions is not reasonably available, a contracting party is bound to use, among the measures reasonably available to it, that which entails the least degree of inconsistency with other GATT provisions.[7]

This interpretation of "necessary" restates what is known as the minimum derogation principle, *i.e.,* any measure taken under one of the GATT Article XX exceptions must be the least trade restrictive measure available among the various alternatives.

Given the obviously skeletal nature of GATT Article XX(b), the negotiators at the Uruguay Round of multilateral trade negotiations agreed in 1994 to expand upon the public health and safety exception by agreeing to the SPS Agreement.

## 3. THE SPS AGREEMENT

The most important WTO agreement on human, animal, and plant health and safety issues is, of course, the SPS Agreement. Before the SPS Agreement was added to the GATT-WTO legal regime, GATT Article XX(b) was the only GATT provision– and at best a skeletal one – dealing expressly with the subject of sanitary and phytosanitary measures. Until the SPS Agreement, no multilateral trade agreement existed with a fully articulated set of procedural rules governing a country's use of SPS measures in connection with imported goods. The SPS Agreement fills this gap by circumscribing WTO members' use of such measures as a nontariff barrier to trade.

The SPS Agreement does not establish any substantive sanitary or phytosanitary measures *per se*. Instead, the Agreement sets forth a number of general procedural requirements to ensure that a sanitary or phytosanitary measure is in fact a scientifically-based protection against the risk asserted by the country imposing the measure, and not a disguised barrier to trade. The Agreement expressly recognizes that importing countries have a legitimate right to protect human, animal, and plant life and health, and to establish a level of protection for life and health that they deem appropriate. The provisions of the SPS Agreement are designed to preserve the ability of importing countries to act, while at the same time guarding against abuses in the application of SPS measures that are primarily designed to protect a domestic industry from import competition. The Agreement establishes criteria and procedures to distinguish the former from the latter, emphasizing the need for transparency in the SPS standards-setting and enforcement process.[8] As discussed in the following sections, the Agreement's most important provisions are (1) the definition of an SPS measure, (2) the requirement that all SPS measures be based on science, and not conjecture or superstition, (3) the exhortation that WTO members use internationally-approved SPS standards, (4) the requirement that if an international standard is not used, that a member conduct a proper risk assessment when adopting its own SPS measures, (5) the exhortation that members enter into agreements on the equivalency of facially different standards and the mutual recognition of other members' standards, and (6) that inspections of imported goods be conducted expeditiously.

## 3.1    The Definition of SPS Measures

The SPS Agreement provides a broad definition of sanitary and phytosanitary measures. This is important for the simple reason that unless a WTO member's laws or regulations fall within the scope of the definition of an SPS measure, then those laws or regulations cannot be the subject of a complaint in the WTO under the SPS Agreement. The SPS Agreement defines an SPS measure as any measure applied

> (a) to protect animal or plant life or health within the territory of the Member from risks arising from the entry, establishment or spread of pests, diseases, disease-carrying organisms or disease-causing organisms;

> (b) to protect human or animal life or health within the territory of the Member from risks arising from additives, contaminants, toxins or disease-causing organisms in foods, beverages or feedstuffs;

> (c) to protect human life or health within the territory of the Member from risks arising from diseases carried by animals, plants or products thereof, or from the entry, establishment or spread of pests; or

> (d) to prevent or limit other damage within the territory of the Member from the entry, establishment or spread of pests.[9]

Sanitary or phytosanitary measures include all relevant laws, decrees, regulations, requirements, and procedures governing *inter alia*, (1) end product criteria; (2) processes and production methods; (3) testing, inspection, certification and approval procedures; (4) quarantine requirements including relevant requirements associated with the transport of animals or plants, or with the materials necessary for their survival during transport; (5) provisions on relevant statistical methods, sampling procedures and methods of risk assessment; and (6) packaging and labeling requirements directly related to food safety.[10] If a measure is not intended to protect against one of these six risks, then the measure is not an SPS measure and cannot be the possible target of a complaint in the WTO, at least not under the SPS Agreement. If a measure is an SPS measure, however, then it may be the target of a WTO complaint if the measure is not based on science. We turn to that question in the next section.

### 3.2    The Use of Scientifically-Based Measures

The basic right of WTO members under the SPS Agreement is the ability to take SPS measures necessary for the protection of human, animal, or plant life or health. However, that right is tempered by the requirement that all SPS measures have a scientific basis. At the heart of the SPS Agreement, then, is the requirement that SPS measures find their basis in science and not in unfounded fears, superstition, or other irrational grounds. Thus, a WTO member's right to adopt and implement SPS measures is qualified by three provisos. Such measures (1) must be applied only to the extent necessary, (2) must be based on scientific principles, and (3) must not be maintained without sufficient scientific evidence, except that such measures may be imposed temporarily when evidence is insufficient, pending receipt of additional information necessary for a more objective assessment of risk.[11]

Article 2.3 reiterates the threshold inquiry of the GATT Article XX chapeau, namely, that SPS measures must not constitute a means of arbitrary or unjustifiable discrimination between countries where the same conditions prevail, and must not constitute a disguised restriction on international trade.[12] An importing country's failure to satisfy Articles 2.2 and 2.3 would in itself constitute a violation of the Agreement, regardless of the measure's consistency with the remainder of GATT.

A WTO member is free to establish its own level of sanitary and phytosanitary protection, including a "zero risk" level if it so chooses. Regardless of the level of risk a member chooses to adopt, however, a measure must be based on scientific principles and on sufficient scientific evidence. One of the many lacunae in the SPS Agreements is nowhere in the Agreement is the phrase "sufficient scientific evidence" defined or explained. This gap leaves WTO members to draw their own judgments from that evidence. Because scientific certainty is rare, many scientific determinations require judgments among competing scientific views. Thus, flexibility or "play in the joints" in the SPS Agreement leaves the door open for marginal WTO complaints.

## 3.3    The Use of International Standards

One way of cutting down on WTO complaints is for all WTO members to adopt the same SPS standards and measures. To that end, the SPS Agreement encourages, but does not require, WTO members to harmonize their SPS measures by adopting international standards where such standards exist.[13] Such international standards, guidelines, and recommendations are developed by several international bodies. The most important are the Codex Alimentarius Commission, established in 1963 and jointly administered by the World Health Organization and the U.N. Food and Agriculture Organization;[14] the International Office of Epizootics, founded in 1924 and charged with the tasks of developing a worldwide livestock reporting system and expediting trade in livestock without increasing livestock disease;[15] and the Secretariat of the International Plant Protection Convention, an agreement intended to prevent the spread of plant pests.[16]

Although the SPS Agreement urges but does not mandate WTO members to adopt international standards where they exist, Article 3.2 of the Agreement dangles a carrot to encourage the adoption of international standards. This article offers members the opportunity to establish a rebuttable presumption that a national SPS measure based on an international standard not only is necessary to protect human, animal, or plant life or health, but also is consistent with GATT.[17] At the same time, the SPS Agreement recognizes the politically sensitive nature of SPS measures for many WTO members who desire to give their consumers and environment the highest levels of protection. To that end, the Agreement further provides that WTO members may adopt more stringent standards if, in their judgment based on a scientific justification, the relevant international standard fails to provide an adequate level of protection.[18] Thus, despite the encouragement to adopt international standards, Article 3.3 permits WTO members to adopt measures that result in a higher level of protection if there is a scientific justification for doing so.[19] Consequently, a WTO member's ability to adopt standards higher than those promulgated by these organizations is assured.

## 3.4    Making Risk Assessments

Because the levels of protection established by international standards-setting bodies are regarded as the minimum level attainable, Article 5 permits members to maintain higher levels of protection than those based on international standards. What if a WTO member does adopt an SPS measure that is not based on an international standard? What procedures must the member follow in order for that non-conforming standard to pass muster under the SPS Agreement? The short answer to this question is that the member must undertake a risk assessment. Annex A, paragraph 4 defines "risk assessment" in two ways, depending upon whether human or animal life or health is at stake, on the one hand, or whether plant health or life is the focus, on the other. As the following definitions make clear, a risk assessment is an exercise in probabilities:

...The evaluation of the potential for adverse effects on human or animal health arising from the presence of additives, toxins or disease-causing organisms in food, beverages or feedstuffs.

...The evaluation of the likelihood of entry, establishment or spread of a pest or disease within the territory of an importing Member according to the sanitary or phytosanitary measures which might be applied, and of the associated potential biological and economic consequences.

Despite their sweeping definition – or maybe because of it – this definition does not explain with any specificity when a risk assessment has been conducted in an acceptable or unacceptable manner. The WTO members apparently have left this legislative lacuna to be filled by the WTO "judiciary" – the dispute settlement panels and the WTO Appellate Body – a potentially dangerous abdication of power that threatens the legitimacy of the very organization the members are trying to strengthen. Surprisingly, reform of the SPS Agreement to plug these legislative holes was not placed on the agenda of latest round of multilateral trade negotiations launched in November 2001 following the Doha Ministerial Conference.[20]

Article 5 of the SPS Agreement identifies specific criteria to be used in evaluating the assessment of risk to human, animal, or plant life or health: (1) available scientific evidence; (2) inspection, testing, and sampling techniques; (3) relevant ecological and environmental conditions; (4) the existence of pest- or disease-free areas; and (5) production processes and methods.[21] In the case of risks to animal and plant life and health, the economic impact and effectiveness of SPS measures for both the exporting and importing members also are to be considered. In all events, the objectives of minimizing negative trade effects, of avoiding discrimination or disguised restrictions on trade, and of adopting measures that are not more trade restrictive than required to achieve the appropriate level of protection are to guide members when imposing a level of protection higher than that provided under international standards. A WTO member must have scientific evidence to justify such higher levels of protection, or must show that it is "the appropriate level of protection" as determined under the criteria of Article 5. As long as there is a scientific justification for a particular SPS standard, a WTO member is free to choose its own level of protection after determining that the health or safety risk is genuine. If a WTO member believes that another member's SPS measure violates the Agreement, the burden rests on the complaining member initially to identify a specific alternative measure that is reasonably available. A responding member need not take steps that are deemed to be unreasonable. Next, the complaining member must demonstrate that the alternative measure would make a significant difference in terms of its effect on trade. Once again, the responding member is not expected to adopt an alternative measure if doing so would make only an insignificant difference to the impact on trade.

The SPS Agreement does not require "downward harmonization" through the adoption of less stringent SPS measures.[22] At the same time, the agreement does not prevent downward harmonization or a country's adoption of national standards that are less stringent than relevant international standards. A country in its role as importer may permit entry of products that fail to meet relevant international standards. No process exists in the SPS Agreement for challenging the adoption of SPS measures that are less protective of human, animal, or plant life and health than international standards. A fair argument can be made that an importing country's decision to adopt weak SPS measures is of no concern to the WTO, although the international human rights community would certainly take a dim view of this argument.

## 3.5   Equivalency and Mutual Recognition of Standards

In the event that WTO members elect not to adopt an international standard, does that mean that harmonization has failed and SPS-based complaints in the WTO are inevitable? Not necessarily. Because a range of SPS measures may be available to achieve the same level of protection, there may be differences among WTO members' SPS measures that achieve the same level of protection. Thus, the principle of equivalency is a key component of the SPS Agreement. Article 4 instructs members to accept the measures of other members as equivalent, even if they differ formally from those of the importing member, if the exporting member demonstrates that its measures achieve the importing member's appropriate level of protection.[23] WTO members are further obligated to enter into consultations with the aim of achieving bilateral and multilateral agreements on recognition of equivalence of specified SPS measures.[24]

In the opinion of some developing countries, a number of developed countries are requiring "sameness" rather than "equivalence" of measures.[25] In addition, experience suggests that recognition of equivalence is indeed very difficult to achieve even among countries that are economic equals, that share a common cultural heritage, and that are close trading partners. Take, for example, the experience of the EU which in 1996 imposed a ban on exports of UK beef and related products from cattle possibly infected with "mad cow" disease. The EU imposed the ban over the objections of the UK that its beef products posed no health risk and a threat to withdraw from the EU. Even after the EU declared UK beef to be safe in late 1999, France continued to block its importation.[26]

In a more progressive vein, 1996 amendments to US legislation on poultry and meat inspections authorized the Secretary of Agriculture to certify that poultry and meat inspection systems of other countries are equivalent to those of the United States.[27] In 1997, the EU and the United States reached a framework agreement on veterinary equivalency.[28] In the follow-on negotiations to this framework agreement, on July 20, 1999, the United States and the EU signed a mutual recognition agreement covering trade in live animals and animal products, including meat, fish, pork, dairy products, pet food, hides, and skins.[29]

## 3.6   Control, Inspection, and Approval Procedures

Once exported goods have entered the territory of an importing WTO member, the SPS Agreement lays down procedures that are designed to ensure that inspection and approval processes do not become a nontariff barrier to trade. Conformity assessment procedures (*i.e.*, control, inspection, and product approval procedures) are to be conducted under guidelines found in Annex C of the SPS Agreement.[30] Procedures are to be undertaken and completed without undue delay and are to be nondiscriminatory vis-à-vis the procedures for the like domestic product.

The concept of disease-free areas and zones within an exporting member is to be recognized by importing members. This concept ensures that exports of a particular product are not banned on a country-wide basis, if it can be shown that the exporting member has implemented effective quarantine or buffer zone measures.

### 3.7   Administration

A Committee on Sanitary and Phytosanitary Measures is established to provide a forum for regular consultations. The Committee is responsible for maintaining close contact with the relevant international bodies in the field of sanitary and phytosanitary protection.[31] It also monitors the process of international harmonization and the use of international standards.[32] Articles 3.5 and 12.4 of the SPS Agreement require the Committee to develop a procedure for monitoring the process of international harmonization and the use of international standards, guidelines, or recommendations. A provisional procedure was adopted in 1997.[33]

Members must notify the Committee on SPS Measures of new, or modifications to existing, SPS regulations that are not substantially the same as an international standard and that may have a significant effect on international trade.[34] Article 12.7 directs the Committee to review the operation and implementation of the Agreement three years after its entry into force.[35]

### 3.8   Implementation at Sub-Federal Level

Under Article 13 of the Agreement, WTO members are responsible for ensuring that their sub-national levels of government and non-governmental organizations responsible for setting standards comply with the provisions of the Agreement. Members are required to formulate and implement positive measures and mechanisms in support of observance of the Agreement by sub-national government bodies. State and local governments within the United States remain free to set their our SPS standards under the terms of the Agreement. They are under no obligation to adopt federal standards, unless Congress so mandates under its commerce clause power.[36]

### 3.9   Extraterritoriality

The definition of sanitary and phytosanitary measures in Annex A of the SPS Agreement - "measures to protect human or animal life or health *within the territory of the Member*" - revisits an issue that arose in the unadopted GATT panel report in *Restrictions on Imports of Tuna*.[37] The panel concluded that application of measures taken under Article XX(b) are limited to the territorial jurisdiction of the country imposing the measures. Conceding that the US ban on imports of tuna was not a disguised restriction on trade, but rather a bona fide measure designed to protect dolphins inadvertently caught with tuna in purse-seine nets, the panel nevertheless ruled that application of the US measure could not extend beyond its territorial jurisdiction. If the rule were otherwise, the panel observed, then each contracting party could unilaterally determine the life or health protection policies from which other contracting parties could not deviate without jeopardizing their rights under the General Agreement. The General Agreement would then no longer constitute a multilateral framework for trade among all contracting parties but would provide legal security only in respect of trade between a limited number of contracting parties with identical internal regulations.[38]

The GATT panel concluded that unilateral, extraterritorial application by the United States of health regulations under Article XX (b) is impermissible.

### 3.10   Relationship to the TBT Agreement

The WTO Agreement on Technical Barriers to Trade (the TBT Agreement) excludes from its scope of coverage sanitary and phytosanitary measures as defined in the SPS Agreement.[39] The SPS Agreement similarly provides that it does not affect members' rights under the TBT Agreement with respect to measures outside the scope of the SPS Agreement.[40] Despite their mutual exclusivity, the substantive provisions of the two agreements mirror each other in most respects. A significant difference between the SPS and TBT Agreements is the test used to determine whether a measure is impermissibly protectionist in nature. Whereas the TBT Agreement relies on a nondiscrimination test, the inquiry under the SPS Agreement is whether the measure has a scientific justification and is based on risk assessment. A strict requirement of nondiscrimination would be impracticable for SPS measures that discriminate against imported goods based on their origin. Goods may pose a risk of disease precisely because the goods come from a member where such disease is prevalent. The same situation might not be true for similar goods coming from another member. Discrimination is, therefore, tolerated under the SPS Agreement so long as it is not arbitrary or unjustifiable.

### 4. WTO RESOLUTION OF SANITARY AND PHYTOSANITARY DISPUTES

The WTO Appellate Body has issued three major decisions involving disputes under the SPS Agreement. In all three cases, the Appellate Body ruled in favor of the exporting member, invalidating the challenged SPS measure. In each case, the importing member failed to satisfy the risk assessment criteria of the SPS Agreement. The great value of these three cases is that they give us context in which to apply and interpret what are admittedly open-textured, broad-brush provisions, including the standards used for risk assessment, the precautionary principle, and acceptable science.

### 4.1   The EC Beef Hormone Dispute

The events leading up to the WTO dispute settlement proceeding spanned ten years. Following European consumer concerns over the safety of hormone-fed beef, in 1987 the EC imposed a ban on imports of animals and meat from animals fed six specific growth-promoting hormones.[41] The United States and Canada objected to this ban on the ground that the six hormones had been found safe for use in growth promotion by every country that had examined them. In addition, the Codex Alimentarius Commission had reviewed five of the six hormones and found them to be safe. What is more, the EC itself twice commissioned reviews of these same five hormones, and on both occasions found them to be safe.[42]

The United States raised the matter under the Tokyo Round Agreement on Technical Barriers to Trade (the Standards Code) in March 1987. Bilateral consultations between the United States and the EC failed to resolve the dispute. Contending that the EC ban was not supported by scientific evidence, the United States requested the establishment of a technical experts group under Article 14.5 of the Standards Code to examine the question. The EC rejected this request, arguing that the issue was outside the scope of the Code.

On January 1, 1989, the United States imposed retaliatory measures of 100-percent *ad valorem* duties on imports of certain EC-origin goods. A joint US-EC Task Force reached an interim agreement to permit imports of US beef that was certified hormone-free. The United States in return lifted some of its retaliatory tariffs. In June 1996, the EC requested the establishment of a WTO panel to examine the matter. A month later the United States removed the balance of its retaliatory tariffs pending the outcome of the panel proceeding.

In a 1998 decision, the WTO Appellate Body found that the EC measures on hormone-fed cattle violated Article 5.1 of the Agreement regarding risk assessments.[43] According to Annex A4 of the SPS Agreement (discussed above), the Appellate Body noted that a proper risk assessment is "the evaluation of the potential for adverse effects on human or animal health arising from the presence of ... contaminants...in food, beverages or feedstuffs." The EC thus had the burden of (1) identifying the adverse effects on human health caused by the presence of hormones in meat products, and (2) if any such adverse effects exist, evaluating the potential or probability of occurrence of these effects. To assist in determining the scientific basis for the EC ban, the WTO panel that initially considered this case appointed three scientific experts. After considering all of the sources cited by the EC in support of the first prong of the two-pronged risk assessment test, the experts concluded that none of the scientific evidence cited by the EC indicated an identifiable human health risk from the use of the growth hormones at issue. In fact, all of the studies cited by the EC indicated that such hormones are safe when used in accordance with good practice. Because there was no scientific evidence of an identifiable risk associated with the growth hormones, the panel found no basis under the SPS Agreement for the EC's adoption of any measure to achieve any level of protection. If it were otherwise, the panel concluded that the obligations of Article 5 would be eviscerated.

Taking the phrase from Article 5.1 of the SPS Agreement that an SPS measure must be *"based on* a risk assessment," the panel insisted that under Article 5.1 the competent EC authorities had to *take into account* risk assessment studies at the time they promulgated their SPS measures in order to satisfy the "minimum procedural requirement" of Articles 5.1 and 5.2. However, the Appellate Body rejected the panel's interpretation of Article 5.1. The Appellate Body concluded that a WTO member could rely on risk assessment studies performed by another member when making its Article 5 risk assessment, and that risk assessment studies did not have to precede the promulgation of the SPS measure under challenge.[44]

Despite this small victory for the EC, the EC measures on hormone-treated beef in the end failed to pass muster under the SPS Agreement on two counts. According to the Appellate Body: (1) all available scientific evidence, as well as the experts consulted by the panel, stated that the hormones in question were safe when used in accordance with good practice; and (2) the EC had failed to conduct a risk assessment that satisfied the provisions of the SPS Agreement.

Importantly, the Appellate Body rejected the argument that the importing member has the burden of proving that its SPS measures do not violate the SPS agreement where the challenged SPS measure is not based on an international standard. Instead, the Appellate Body ruled that the complaining member must present evidence and legal arguments sufficient to demonstrate that the challenged measures are inconsistent with the SPS Agreement.[45]

In addition, the Appellate Body responded to the EC's claim that the panel had failed to apply the appropriate standard of review in assessing certain facts and scientific material. The Appellate Body observed that the SPS Agreement was silent on the question of the appropriate standard of review. Turning to Article 11 of the WTO Dispute Settlement Understanding, the Appellate Body concluded that the proper standard of review was neither a de novo nor a deferential standard, but rather an "objective assessment" standard.[46] Based on its judgement of the panel's assessment of the facts, the Appellate Body was constrained to conclude that the panel had not failed to discharge its duty under DSU Article 11. While conceding that the panel's assessment was not error free, the Appellate Body stated that the panel had not deliberately disregarded evidence, wilfully distorted evidence, or wilfully misrepresented evidence.[47]

Finally, the EC defended its measures in part on the ground that they were based on the "precautionary principle," *i.e.,* in the face of scientific uncertainty, and so long as there is some scientific basis for adopting a particular SPS measure, such a measure should pass muster at least temporarily under the SPS Agreement. The Appellate Body agreed that Articles 5.7 and 3.3 of the SPS Agreement reflected the precautionary principle, but declined to state whether it was part of customary international law. However, it agreed with the panel that the precautionary principle does not override the provisions of Articles 5.1 and 5.2 of the SPS Agreement dealing with risk assessment.[48] In this case, the Appellate Body concluded, the EU had failed to carry out a proper risk assessment.

## 4.2    The Australia Salmon Dispute

In 1996, Australia imposed an import ban on uncooked salmon from the Pacific rim of North America ostensibly to prevent the introduction of certain exotic diseases. Fresh, chilled, or frozen salmon could be imported into Australia only if it was heat treated prior to importation. Canada complained that the import ban violated the SPS Agreement to the extent that the Australian import ban was not based on a risk assessment conducted in conformity with Article 5 of that Agreement.

The central question presented to the Appellate Body was the same as that presented in the *Hormone Beef* dispute: Did Australia carry out a proper risk assessment under Article 5.1 of the SPS Agreement?[49] Australia contended that a 1996 "Final Report" constituted a risk assessment for purposes of Article 5.1 of the SPS Agreement. (This 1996 Final Report concluded that imports of uncooked salmon should be prohibited in order to prevent the introduction and spread of exotic diseases within Australia.) Turning to the definition of "risk assessment" in Annex A of the SPS Agreement, the Appellate Body found that a proper risk assessment must (1) identify the diseases whose entry or spread the Member wants to prevent, (2) evaluate the *probability* of entry of a pest or disease, not just the *possibility* of such entry, and (3) evaluate the likelihood of entry, establishment or spread of these diseases according to the SPS measures which might be applied. Because the 1996 Final Report did not contain (1) an evaluation of the likelihood of entry, establishment or spread of the diseases of concern, or (2) an evaluation of the likelihood of entry, establishment or spread of these diseases according to the SPS measures which might be applied, the 1996 Final Report could not qualify as a risk assessment. Australia, therefore, acted inconsistently with Article 5.1 of the SPS Agreement.

The Appellate Body also concluded that Australia's import prohibition was arbitrary, unjustifiable, and a disguised restriction on international trade. While agreeing that herring and ornamental finfish presented an equal or greater risk of the introduction and spread of disease that could threaten domestic stocks, the Appellate Body noted that the Australian import ban was strictly limited to salmon. This strongly inferred that the import ban was intended and designed to protect the domestic salmon aquaculture industry from import competition.

The Appellate Body reconfirmed that WTO members have the right to determine their own appropriate level of SPS protection as long as the actual SPS measure adopted is rationally related to achieving this appropriate level of protection. Moreover, whatever appropriate level of protection a Member chooses, a Member may choose "zero risk" as an appropriate level of protection under the SPS Agreement. The Appellate Body clarified that:

> it is important to distinguish...between the evaluation of "risk" in a risk assessment and the determination of the appropriate level of protection. As stated in our Report in *European Communities – Hormones*, the "risk" evaluated in a risk assessment must be an ascertainable risk; theoretical uncertainty is "not the kind of risk which, under Article 5.1, is to be assessed." This does not mean, however, that a Member cannot determine its own appropriate level of protection to be "zero risk".[50]

What a proper risk assessment will be in the context of additives or contaminants to food remains to be seen.

### 4.3   The Japan Food Quarantine Dispute

In order to prevent the introduction of codling moth, since 1950 Japan has required that the efficacy of quarantine treatment for each variety of certain agricultural products be tested and confirmed before importing those products. The United States challenged the varietal testing requirement as applied to eight products (apples, cherries, nectarines, walnuts, apricots, pears, plums, and quince) as violative of the SPS Agreement. The United States claimed that the testing-by-variety versus a testing-by-product requirement lacked scientific justification. Japan countered that since the products in question were host plants of codling moth, Japan was justified in taking a precautionary approach and, therefore, that its varietal testing requirement was warranted under the precautionary principle.

While conceding that Japan could apply a standard that was stricter than an international standard, the Appellate Body noted that Japan was free to do so only if there was a scientific justification for such an SPS measure. According to the Appellate Body, "there is a 'scientific justification' for an SPS measure...if there is a rational relationship between the SPS measure at issue and the available scientific information."[51]

The Appellate Body concluded that the varietal testing requirement as applied to apples, cherries, nectarines, and walnuts lacked sufficient scientific evidence. In addition, and in response to Japan's claim to rely on the precautionary principle, the Appellate Body added that this principle, while reflected in the preamble, Article 3.3, and Article 5.7 of the SPS Agreement, had not been written into the SPS Agreement as grounds to justify SPS measures that were otherwise inconsistent with the specific obligations of WTO members under the Agreement.

With regard to the varietal testing requirement for apricots, pears, plums, and quince, the Appellate Body struck down Japan's SPS measure on the grounds that Japan had failed to conduct a risk assessment as required under Article 5.1 of the SPS Agreement. A risk assessment must (1) identify the diseases to be prevented, (2) evaluate the likelihood of entry of such diseases, and (3) evaluate the likelihood of entry according to the SPS measures that might be applied. Because Japan's 1996 risk assessment did not take into account the third factor, i.e., what alternative SPS measures might be applied, the Appellate Body invalidated the varietal testing requirement in connection with apricots, plums, pears, and quince.

## 5.   WHAT ARE THE BROAD LESSONS?

Why have importing countries been uniformly unsuccessful in WTO dispute settlement proceedings? While the pro-trade bias of the WTO might explain this result in part, the ultimate outcome of SPS disputes brought to the WTO are not a foregone conclusion. The Appellate Body jurisprudence teaches at least five valuable lessons for future respondents:

1. Reliance on the precautionary principle is misplaced. Although the precautionary principle is reflected in Articles 5.7 and 3.3 of the SPS Agreement, it can only be invoked when scientific evidence is "insufficient." For example, as was demonstrated in the *EC - Hormone Beef* decision, all the available scientific evidence pointed to the conclusion that the hormones in dispute are safe when used in conformity with good practice. The WTO's own "precautionary principle" seems to be, "If in doubt, trade wins out." The burden of proof certainly favors the exporting WTO member and, consequently, trade.

2. Be active in the international standards-setting process. To the extent that importing countries' sanitary and phytosanitary measures are a barrier to trade with an insufficient basis in science, then international standards can act as a sword to cut down such measures.

3. Use (or don't use) international standards, but be clear on the consequences.

4. In the absence of a genuine SPS emergency, *e.g.*, mad cow disease or the introduction of tainted food, if an importing country elects not to use a relevant international standard, it must be exhaustively thorough in the preparation of SPS measures that are not based on, and that do not conform to international standards. An importing country that adopts its own SPS standards must do so on the basis of "sufficient scientific evidence" (whatever the term "sufficient" means).

5. Conduct a proper risk assessment. A proper risk assessment must (1) identify the diseases whose entry or spread the member wants to prevent, (2) evaluate the *probability* of entry of a pest or disease in the case of plant diseases, and the potential for adverse effects on human or animal health arising from the presence of additives, toxins or disease-causing organisms in food, beverages or feedstuffs, not just the *possibility* of such entry or adverse effects, and (3) evaluate the likelihood of entry, establishment or spread of these diseases according to the SPS measures that might be applied. Do not merely make *some* evaluation of the likelihood of entry or spread of a disease or pest; rather, establish a likelihood that a pest or disease will enter or be spread in the absence of the SPS measure. In the *Australia – Salmon* decision, for example, Australia's ban on the importation of fresh salmon could not be justified on the basis of a risk assessment that considered only the *possibility* of entry of disease. Likewise, in the *Japan – Food Quarantine* decision, Japan's SPS measure violated the SPS Agreement because its risk assessment did not take into account what alternative SPS measures might be applied.

Although the burden of proof of a violation of the SPS Agreement rests with the complaining WTO member, the WTO jurisprudence to date shows that that burden is a relatively low hurdle to clear. This is not a surprising result: The WTO is first and foremost the premier international organization for the enforcement of rules designed to promote open trade, and only incidentally an institution that enforces SPS standards.

## 6. CONCLUDING OBSERVATIONS

The World Trade Organization has been buffeted by a storm of criticism from almost every conceivable front. The 1999 street demonstrations in Seattle during the

WTO's third ministerial conference showed the disdain of many groups and organizations of every stripe and persuasion, from environmental, human rights, labor, to consumer, for the WTO and their disaffection in general with globalization. The demonstrations also proved that the WTO and GATT 1994 are poorly understood, if they are understood at all. Broadly, non-governmental organizations have criticized the WTO for being undemocratic, closed, and secretive. Specifically, environmental and labor rights groups have condemned the WTO as being callous to environmental and labor rights issues, respectively. Consumer groups have blasted the WTO for being insensitive to food safety issues.

The debacle at the WTO's Seattle ministerial meeting in December 1999 was in part fueled by myths and misinformation about the WTO, free trade, and globalization. It is true that accelerated trade liberalization worldwide has led to the increased globalization of business and the interdependence of national economies. Environmental fear-mongers proclaim that we are on the brink of a global environmental collapse, thanks in large part to free trade. Labor unions condemn the labor rights record of developing countries. But many environmental and labor rights groups view the world as a zero-sum game: to the extent the WTO succeeds at promoting globalization, then in equal measure do the environment and labor rights suffer. One can only pause and wonder whether they silently fear global economic interdependence and wish *sub rosa* for autarchy. In the words of former presidential economic adviser Murray Weidenbaum:

> If the full policy agenda of the anti-global activists were adopted, the long-run effect would be for the United States and other industrialized nations to lose the benefits of the specialization of labor, and suffer severe declines in standards of living. Ironically, the economic costs would soon be translated into environmental costs. Wealthier countries can afford to devote more resources to achieving a cleaner environment, and they do so. Poorer countries do far less to clean up the environment.[52]

Unilateralists/isolationists within national legislatures (here, read "some members of the US Congress") view the WTO as a threat because to them it represents a loss of national sovereignty. "Dismantle the WTO" is the rallying cry for many of its critics. But most of the criticisms of the WTO appear to be the product of misinformation, distortion, and a lack of understanding of what the various WTO agreements actually provide. On the other side are the WTO's supporters who sometimes fall into the trap of viewing the WTO as a panacea that should have its portfolio enlarged to include multilateral agreements on everything tangentially related to trade, including labor, the environment, foreign direct investment, and competition policy.

What the critics fail to fully appreciate is that the WTO is not a top-down, supranational organization that directs nations what to do. Rather, it is a bottom-up forum where member governments meet and, occasionally, reach agreement on the conduct of world trade. The main attraction of the WTO for many non-trade groups is the WTO's binding dispute settlement mechanism. When environmentalists criticize the WTO, they speak with the voice of the green-eyed monster of envy. The WTO's dispute settlement mechanism is coveted by environmental and labor rights groups that have been unsuccessful in creating their own parallel international dispute settlement body. Because they have been unsuccessful in co-opting the WTO, they now want to trash it.

A December 1999 article in The Economist asked rhetorically, "Who needs the WTO?"[53] The article makes the following bold but highly defensible claim that "[f]or five decades the world's multilateral trade-liberalising machinery – known first as the General Agreement on Tariffs and Trade (GATT) and more recently as the World Trade Organisation (WTO) - has, in all likelihood, done more to attack global poverty and advance living standards right across the planet than has any other man-made device."[54] In answer to the question, "Who needs the WTO?" the answer is, of course, everyone. By increasing people's economic freedom, the WTO has enhanced people's political freedom and made most of them economically better off than they would have been in the absence of such an organization.

## 7. NOTES

[1] See, e.g., Steve Charnovitz, Exploring the Environmental Exceptions in GATT Article XX, 25 J. *World Trade* 37, 39-43 (1991)[hereinafter Charnovitz I]; Scott Vaughan, Trade and Environment: Some North-South Considerations, 27 *Cornell Int'l* L.J. 591 (1994); John Hunt, Free Traders Heading for Clash with Greens, *Fin. Times*, Sept. 5, 1991, § I, at 6.

[2] See, e.g., *World Bank, International Trade and the Environment* (Patrick Low ed. 1992); *World Bank, World Development Report* 1992: *Development and the Environment* (1992); Ernst-Ulrich Petersmann, International Trade Law and International Environmental Law: Prevention and Settlement of International Environmental Disputes in GATT, 27 J. *World Trade* No. 1, at 43 (1993); Christopher Thomas & Greg A. Tereposky, The Evolving Relationship Between Trade and Environmental Regulation, 27 J. *World Trade* No. 4, at 23 (1993); Jeffrey L. Dunoff, Institutional Misfits: The GATT, The ICJ & Trade-Environment Disputes, 15 *Mich. J. Int'l L.* 1043 (1994); Daniel C. Esty, GATTing the Greens, Not Just Greening the GATT, 72 *For. Affairs* No. 5, at 32 (1993); Charles R. Fletcher, Greening World Trade Law: Reconciling GATT and Multilateral Environmental Agreements Within the Existing World Trade Regime, 5 J. *Transnat'l L. & Pol'y* 341 (1996); Robert Housman & Durwood Zaelke, Trade, Environment and Sustainable Development: A Primer, 15 *Hastings Int'l & Comp. L. Rev.* 535 (1992).

[3] See Kym Anderson, The Entwining of Trade Policy with Environmental and Labour Standards, in *The Uruguay Round and the Developing Economies* 435 (Will Martin & L. Alan Winters eds. 1995); Hilary F. French, The GATT: Menace or Ally?, *WorldWatch* 12 (Sept.-Oct. 1993); US Int'l Trade Comm'n, Trade Issues of the 1990s - *Part I, Int'l Econ. Rev.* 17 (Nov. 1994); US Int'l Trade Comm'n, Trade Liberalization and Pollution, *Int'l Econ. Rev.* 17 (March 1995); The Race for the Bottom, *The Economist*, Oct. 7, 1995, at 90.

[4] See Jennifer Haverkamp, Provisions of the Uruguay Round with a Potential Effect on US Environmental Laws and Regulations, in *The GATT Uruguay Round* (Institute on Current Issues in Int'l Trade 1995).

[5] For additional analysis of these disputes, see Terence P. Stewart & David S. Johanson, The SPS Agreement of the World Trade Organization and the International Trade of Dairy Products, 54 *Food & Drug L.J.* 55 (1999).

[6] Report of the GATT Panel, Thailand – Restrictions on Importation of and Internal Taxes on Cigarettes, BISD, 37th Supp. 200 (1990).

[7] Id., quoting Report of the GATT Panel, United States – Section 337 of the Tariff Act of 1930, BISD, 36th Supp. 345, ¶ 5.26 (1989).

[8] Article 7 and Annex B of the SPS Agreement establish a number of transparency obligations. Among them is a requirement that SPS measures be published promptly and that a period for comment be made available before SPS measures take effect.

[9] SPS Agreement, Annex A, ¶ 1(a)-(d).

[10] Id.

[11] See id. arts. 2.3, 5.7. Article 2.2 provides: "Members shall ensure that any sanitary or phytosanitary measure is applied only to the extent necessary to protect human, animal or plant life or health, is based on scientific principles and is not maintained without sufficient scientific evidence, except as provided for in paragraph 7 of Article 5." Article 5.7 of the SPS Agreement in turn provides: "In cases where relevant scientific is insufficient, a Member may provisionally adopt sanitary or phytosanitary measures on the basis of available pertinent information, including that from the relevant international organizations as well as from sanitary and phytosanitary measures applied by other Members. In such circumstances, Members shall seek to obtain the additional information necessary for a more objective assessment of risk and review the sanitary and phytosanitary measure accordingly within a reasonable period of time." In tandem these two articles represent the SPS Agreement's version of the precautionary principle.

[12] Article 2.3 provides: "Members shall ensure that their sanitary and phytosanitary measures do not arbitrarily or unjustifiably discriminate between Members where identical or similar conditions prevail, including between their own territory and that of other Members. Sanitary and phytosanitary measures shall not be applied in a manner which would constitute a disguised restriction on international trade."

[13] SPS Agreement Art. 3.1 provides, "Members shall base their sanitary and phytosanitary measures on international standards..." (emphasis added). These international standards, guidelines, and recommendations are further defined in Annex A:3 of the SPS Agreement to include those of the Codex Alimentarius Commission, the International Office of Epizootics, and the Secretariat of the International Plant Protection Convention.

[14] The Codex Alimentarius Commission, with over 130 members, has issued more than 200 commodity standards and approximately 2,000 maximum limits for pesticide residues. General information about the Codex Alimentarius Commission, including the contents of the Codex Alimentarius; http://www.fao.org/waicent/faoinfo/economic/esn/codex/codex.htm.

[15] See International Agreement for the Creation at Paris of an International Office for Epizootics, entered into force Jan. 17, 1925, 57 L.N.T.S. 135. General information about the governing body, the International Committee, including its publications, is available from its website; http://www.oie.org.

[16] See International Plant Protection Convention, entered into force April 3, 1952, 150 U.N.T.S. 67. The IPPC was revised in 1997 to address the relationship of the IPPC to the SPS Agreement, in particular the role of the IPPC in promulgating internationally harmonized phytosanitary measures and standards. The revised text of the IPPC is reprinted in WTO, Committee on Sanitary and Phytosanitary Measures, Adoption of the New Revised Text of the International Plant Protection Convention (IPPC), Annex 1, G/SPS/GEN/51 (1998). General information about the Convention is available from the Food and Agriculture Organization: http://www.fao.org.

[17] Article 3.2 provides: Sanitary or phytosanitary measures which conform to international standards, guidelines or recommendations shall be deemed to be necessary to protect human, animal or plant life or health, and presumed to be consistent with the relevant provisions of this Agreement and of GATT 1994.

[18] The Committee on SPS Measures has established a system under which standards, guidelines, and recommendations developed by the Codex, OIE, and IPPC that have a major trade impact are to be monitored. It may invite the appropriate international standards-setting body to consider reviewing the existing standard, guidelines, or recommendation.

[19] Article 3.3 provides: "Members may introduce or maintain sanitary or phytosanitary measures which result in a higher level of sanitary or phytosanitary protection than would be achieved by measures based on the relevant international standards, guidelines or recommendations, if there is a scientific justification, or as a consequence of the level of sanitary or phytosanitary protection a Member determines to be appropriate in accordance with the relevant provisions of paragraphs 1 through 8 of Article 5. Notwithstanding the above, all measures which result in a level of sanitary or phytosanitary protection different from that which would be achieved by measures based on international standards, guidelines or recommendations shall not be inconsistent with any other provision of this Agreement." Footnote 2 of the SPS Agreement provides: "For purposes of paragraph 3 of Article 3, there is a scientific justification if, on the basis of an examination and evaluation of available scientific information with the relevant provisions of this Agreement, a Member determines that the relevant international standards, guidelines or recommendations are not sufficient to achieve its appropriate level of sanitary or phytosanitary protection." The drafters of the SPS Agreement bowed to pressure from environmental groups that feared that the SPS Agreement

would lead to a ratcheting down of national standards if international standards became the mandatory maximum levels of protection a WTO member could adopt. This fear was based in part on the status of the Codex, the OIE, and the IPPC Secretariat as arbiters of human, animal, and plant health issues. In the eyes of environmentalists, these organizations' deliberations are largely influenced by transnational corporations.

[20] See World Trade Organization, Ministerial Conference Declaration Adopted 14 November 2001, WT/MIN(01)/DEC/1 (Nov. 20, 2001).

[21] SPS Agreement art. 5.2.

[22] An example of more stringent domestic standards are the pre-1996 US Delaney Clauses that prohibited the introduction of food additives or color additives in processed foods if the substances posed any risk of cancer in humans or animals. The Delaney Clauses established a level of protection that reflected a congressional decision that there should be zero risk of cancer to humans from the substances those clauses covered. That congressional determination was based on scientific evidence available at the time of its enactment and a risk assessment (i.e., an evaluation of the potential for adverse effects on human life or health, even though the risk of cancer was slight). The evidence and assessment resulted in a level of zero risk of carcinogenesis. See Federal Food, Drug and Cosmetic Act, 21 US C. § 348(c)(3)(A)(1994). Under pressure from domestic farm groups, Congress amended the Delaney Clauses in the Food Quality Protection Act of 1996 to remove chemical pesticides in processed foods from the definition of "food additives." See Pub. L. No. 104-170, § 405, 110 Stat. 1489 (1996). Advances in detection techniques had developed to the point that pesticide residues could be detected that fell far below levels considered to pose a serious health threat. A new health-based standard that permits less than a one in one million lifetime risk of cancer was enacted to replace the zero-risk standard set by the Delaney Clauses in connection with pesticide residues. However, the Delaney Clauses continue to apply to food additives, color additives, and compounds administered to food-producing animals.

[23] Article 4.1 provides: "Members shall accept the sanitary and phytosanitary measures of other Members as equivalent, even if these measures differ from their own or from those used by other Members trading in the same product, if the exporting Member objectively demonstrates to the importing Member that its measures achieve the importing Member's appropriate level of sanitary or phytosanitary protection. For this purpose, reasonable access shall be given, upon request, to the importing Member for inspection, testing and other relevant procedures."

[24] Id. art. 4.2.

[25] See World Trade Organization, Committee on Sanitary and Phytosanitary Measures, Statement by Egypt at the meeting of 7-8 July 1999, SPS Agreement and Developing Countries, G/SPS/GEN/128 (1999).

[26] See More at stake than steak: Britain aims to avert trade war, *Christian Sci. Monitor*, Fri., Oct. 29, 1999, at 7.

[27] See Poultry Products Inspection Act, § 17(d), 21 US C. § 466; Federal Meat Inspection Act, § 20(e), 21 US C. § 620. The United States and the EU have been engaged in intense negotiations to conclude mutual recognition agreements on food and labeling requirements. See US , EU Fail to Meet MRA Deadline; New Talks Slated for Later This Month, 14 *Int'l Trade Rep.* (BNA) 225 (1997).

[28] See US and EU Agree on Framework On Veterinary Equivalency Except for Poultry, 14 *Int'l Trade Rep.* (BNA) 807 (1997); US-EU Animal Trade Pact Set to Take Effect with New USDA Rules, 16 *Int'l Trade Rep.* (BNA) 1091 (1999).

[29] See US -EU Animal Trade Pact Set to Take Effect With New USDA Rules, 16 Int'l Trade Rep. (BNA) 1091 (1999); European Union and the United States Sign Veterinary Agreement, Press Release, July 20, 1999; http://www.eurunion.org/news/press/1999/1999048.htm.

[30] SPS Agreement art. 8.

[31] See Report (1999) on the Activities of the Committee on Sanitary and Phytosanitary Measures, G/L/315 (1999). The Committee's 1999 Report notes that "[t]he SPS Committee continued to maintain close working relationships with the IPPC, the OIE and Codex." Id. 10.

[32] See SPS Agreement arts. 12.1, 12.4.

[33] See Procedure to Monitor the Process of International Harmonization, Committee on Sanitary and Phytosanitary Measures, G/SPS/13 (1999). In July 1999, the Committee agreed to extend its harmonization work program until July 2001. See Decision to Extend the Provisional Procedure to

Monitor the Process of International Harmonization, Committee on Sanitary and Phytosanitary Measures, G/SPS/14 (1999).

[34] See WTO, Report of the Committee on Sanitary and Phytosanitary Measures, G/L/118 (1996). The Report is available from the WTO: http://www.wto.org/wto/agric/spsrp.htm.

[35] See WTO, Committee on Sanitary and Phytosanitary Measures, Procedure to Review the Operation and Implementation of the Agreement, G/SPS/10 (1997).

[36] In 1997, tension built between twelve states and the EPA over allegedly lax enforcement of clean air and clean water regulations by the states. The EPA threatened to cut off federal funds and to limit the authority of those states to enforce those laws. See States Feud with EPA Over Regulations, *Christian Sci. Monitor*, Feb. 19, 1997, at 4.

[37] Report of the GATT Panel, United States - Restrictions on Imports of Tuna, BISD, 39th Supp. 155, 198-200, 5.24-5.29 (unadopted 1991).

[38] Id. 5.27.

[39] See TBT Agreement art. 1.5.

[40] See SPS Agreement art. 1.4.

[41] Three of the hormones are naturally occurring in animals and humans; the other three are artificially produced. For additional background on the dispute, see Kristin Mueller, Hormonal Imbalance: An Analysis of the Hormone Treated Beef Trade Dispute Between the United States and the European Union, *1 Drake J. Agric. L.* 97 (1996); Note, The EC Hormone Ban Dispute and the Application of the Dispute Settlement Provisions of the Standards Code, *10 Mich. J. Int'l L.* 872 (1989); Office of the USTR, WTO Hormones Report Confirms US Win, Press Release 97-76, Aug. 18, 1997.

[42] See Report of the WTO Panel, European Communities    EC Measures Concerning Meat and Meat Products (Hormones), WT/DS26/R/USA (1998), at 6-8, 11, 2.17-2.25, 2.33.

[43] See Report of the Appellate Body, European Communities—EC Measures Concerning Meat and Meat Products (Hormones), WT/DS26/AB/R, WT/DS48/AB/R (1998).

[44] Id. at 74, 190.

[45] Report of the Appellate Body, supra note 43, at 39, 109.

[46] Id. at 43, 117.

[47] Id. at 50-55, 135-145.

[48] Id. at 46-47, 123-125. The EC believes it now has sufficient scientific evidence to support its import ban and has requested the establishment of a WTO dispute settlement panel to revisit this question. See World Trade Organizations, United States * Continued Suspension of Obligations in the EC * Hormones Dispute, Request for the Establishment of a Panel by the European Communities, WT/DS320/6 (Jan. 14, 2005).

[49] Report of the Appellate Body, Australia – Measures Affecting Importation of Salmon, AB-1998-5, WT/DS18/AB/R, at 72, V.7 (1998).

[50] Id. at 75 (footnote omitted).

[51] Report of the Appellate Body, Japan – Measures Affecting Agricultural Products, AB-1998-8, WT/DS76/AB/R, at 21, 79 (1999). See also Report of the Appellate Body, Japan Measures Affecting the Importation of Apples, WT/DS245/AB/R (2003) (Japan's import ban on fruit from host plants of fire blight bacterium is maintained "without sufficient scientific evidence," contrary to Article 2.2 of the SPS Agreement).

[52] Murray Weidenbaum, Globalization myths, *Christian Sci. Monitor*, Dec. 16, 1999, at 9.

[53] See Who Needs the WTO? *The Economist*, Dec. 4, 1999, at 74.

[54] Id.

SUZAN ILCAN* AND LYNNE PHILLIPS†

# 3. CIRCULATIONS OF INSECURITY:

*Globalizing Food Standards In Historical Perspective¹*

Insecurity affects us all, immersed as we all are in a fluid and unpredictable world of
deregulation, flexibility, competitiveness and endemic uncertainty. Z. Bauman (2001:
144)

## 1. INTRODUCTION

The new millennium is a time to reflect on the standards that feed our perceptions of
change and uncertainty in our so-called modern world. In the context of this volume,
it is especially useful to explore how our contemporary views of food insecurity,
especially as defined in terms of disease, malnutrition and overpopulation, have their
links to earlier efforts to create order and reduce risks related to the production and
supply of food around the world. This chapter identifies and discusses various ways
in which the Food and Agriculture Organization (FAO)² of the United Nations relied
on modern scientific thinking and practice to standardize approaches to thinking
about world food and agriculture issues immediately following World War II. At the
time, this approach paralleled other interests and initiatives to continue control of
specific national and local territories and their production and trade efforts, as well
as to reduce the political risks posed by food insecurities in a Cold War world.

More specifically, this chapter emphasizes how building a global model of food
consumption was based on an effort to set aside the diversity of food and people in
the world and to make these categories comparable. This was accomplished through
a process that involved mapping food and human bodies, and rendering them
separable from their localities, and then stabilizing them as representations of
standardized units that could be compared. In addition, we consider the ways in
which the FAO has been involved in identifying, managing, and communicating
information on risks related to food production and consumption, as well as global
food stability and security. This attention to the relations of risk and food
standardization is critical to understanding current international thinking about
improving and stabilizing food production.

* Suzan Ilcan, Professor and Canada Research Chair, Department of Sociology and Anthropology,
University of Windsor, Canada.
† Lynne Phillips, Head and Professor, Department of Sociology and Anthropology, University of
Windsor, Canada.

*J. Bingen and L. Busch, (eds.), Agricultural Standards: The Shape of the Global Food and Fiber
System, 51-72. © 2006 Springer. Printed in the Netherlands.*

Our discussion of how particular concerns over food production and consumption become targets for standardization and risk management draws insights from Ulrich Beck (1999, 2000) and Nicholas Rose (1999, 2000) on issues of risk, and from Bruno Latour's (1987) work on inscription devices. Through the use of historical FAO documents that marked several geographical regions considered in need of transformation, and that highlighted Latin America as a key site of intervention, we argue that the inscription process fragmented food and agriculture into specific categories that were made presentable and representable, and that were reconstituted into standardized units. The final section of the chapter discusses the implications of this process for understanding the contemporary situation of global food security as it relates to the proliferation and dissemination of food information, or what we call the informatization of food. Specifically we examine the FAO-based Codex Alimentarius and the Global Information and Early Warning System on Food and Agriculture (GIEWS) as significant international information systems for elaborating, forecasting, and communicating the insecurities associated with food production, food trade, and food consumption.

## 2. TRANSFORMING FOOD IN A WORLD OF INSECURITY

Everyone is caught up in defensive battles of various types, anticipating the hostile substances in one's manner of living and eating (Beck, 1994:45).

Scientific thinking about the post-WWII agro-food system provided the basis for a new orientation toward food at a time when there was considerable interest in transforming national and local territories and their trading practices. In a Cold War context of concerns about future global stability, including political insecurities regarding de-colonization, this type of thinking about the world food situation focused FAO's efforts on malnutrition and disease as risks that appeared resolvable by advances in the agricultural, biological, and medical sciences. Consequently, many scientists, working directly or peripherally in the area of food, found support for work on particular topics such as: the emergence of agricultural and development planning, food and crop classification systems, diet and nutrition standards, plant breeding, and food genetic engineering.[3] In doing this work, the food knowledge generated by these scientists can be seen as a set of organized statements of facts or ideas that is transformed by the very medium through which it is communicated. In addition, the FAO approach, and the assumptions and methods of scientists, helped to appropriate and theoretically separate the local or indigenous knowledge of food sustained in oral traditions (rather than in texts) and embedded in the collective memory as living know-how, or what Bauman calls "internalized intuition" (2001: 11).

Latour (1987) refers to such a process as an inscription, wherein local information of the other is charted and mobilized to become the explicit, universal knowledge of the scientist. Inscriptions, in this sense, involve a three-part process executed by centers of calculation: (1) the mapping of other people, goods, and places to render them separable from their localities; (2) the stabilization of these representations in time and space to keep them "familiar, finite, nearby and handy" (1987: 230); and, (3) the translation of these facts into combinable products to permit further calculation. The scientist's knowledge consists of facts and ideas about food that is communicated or displayed through a variety of means or inscription devices, such as agricultural training centers, dietary surveys, food composition tables, and food balance sheets and bulletins. In this way, scientists were thought to play an effective role in managing risk, that is, in eliminating or reducing the possibility of incurring misfortune in relation to food (Rose 2000, 1999).

In transforming internalized intuition into immutable mobiles (Latour 1987), science becomes particularly effective in settling controversies – marshaling resources around its claims, establishing normative thinking about them, and holding these claims constant, as facts, in often jargon-laden texts. Far from a benign process, Latour's work compels us to consider how the process of inscription not only enters into a variety of networks but is used as a means to manage insecurities, such as those related to food, nutrition, disease, and populations.

For our purposes, an emerging scientific knowledge of food manifests both mobilized local knowledge, and the technical devices, styles of reasoning, theoretical languages, practical skills, and social strategies that make possible the modern world (see Hacking 2002). This emerging scientific knowledge is forged from tensions between local practices and the attempt to translate them into global and universal categories (see Appadurai 2001; Fischer 2000; Latour 1986, 1987; Bourdieu 1977). The resulting inscriptions – of standardized substances, places, bodies, and information – become the foundation for calculations of food supply and demand, agricultural and nutritional deficiencies, and production probabilities.

The inscriptions themselves also act as a means to manage risks, that is, the manner by which malnutrition or overpopulation are surveyed, compared against norms, trained to conform to these norms, and rendered productive. As Busch insightfully notes, science changes the context of debates by shifting the context from specific food products to the world of probabilities. Citing Beck, he argues that science "introduced notions of risk into food consumption as it did into all other areas of social life...as a systematic way of dealing with hazards and insecurities..." (Busch 1997: 8). He also suggests that "what should be apparent...is that all tests of food safety are simultaneously tests of people and things. These tests are designed to discipline human and nonhuman actors such that they perform in ways deemed acceptable (or correct or good) by whatever agency is in authority at a given point along a commodity sub-sector..." (Busch 1997: 9).[4] Thus, modern science not only introduces new orientations toward the management of food, but disperses knowledge on the insecurities of food itself. Such dispersions, and all the scientific knowledge, practices, and organizations that are linked to them, permit us to know risk as a social product and to understand the various ways in which risk can be managed. As Beck (1996: 4) argues, risks are "social constructs which are strategically defined, covered up or dramatized in the public sphere with the help of scientific material supplied for the purpose."

A wide variety of science professionals and international agencies rely upon modern scientific knowledge of food to remind us that peoples and places all over the globe are besieged with risks related to food and the efforts to measure and control them. International agencies such as the United Nations, and its specialized agency, the FAO, have identified the means of, and the plans for managing the dangers related to food. It is within this context that the concept of risk is most pertinent to our analysis of food insecurities. Risk is a term widely used to address issues connected to insecurity and to what counts as deviations from the norm, as adversities, and as alarming events. In modernist discourses, the term is often employed to designate a phenomenon that has the potential to furnish substantial harm, regardless of whether or not this harm is actualized (Lupton 1999). We may think here of the demands to cleanse the food we eat from harmful and potentially fatal environmental pollutants, demands that are directed to a great many social groups living in particular communities and regions. We may think of other risks, such as biotechnology, global warming, and nuclear radiation that may add to our general sense of insecurity and to our specific grasp of how such risks impact on the production and consumption of food. These risks spill over territorial and temporal boundaries, and are dramatized through international agencies and international practices.

A voluminous range of risks is linked to food and to particular food growing areas of the world which, in many ways, is an effect of international decisions geared to promote the establishment of economic opportunities (Fischer 2000) and international trade practices. The international trading regime established in 1944 at Bretton Woods supervened in its aim to increase global trade without producing more worldwide depressions like the one that had culminated in WWII (see Leys 2001). The FAO, since its inception in 1945, has operated within the unprecedented expansion of output and trade that the Bretton Woods system made possible. Yet, like other international organizations, it has always confronted concerns about the production of risks. As a reflection of a series of FAO reports on food insecurity, one early report highlighted the world food situation as an element of risk:

> [T]he recent improvement in the world food situation, particularly as it concerns cereals, may too easily engender a false sense of security. First, this year's harvest was far above what could be expected in an average year. Second, the increased dependence of the world on supplies from North America enlarges the element of risk, because of the extreme fluctuations of output in the United States of America and Canada. Third, world stocks of food have been cut to the barest minimum...so that the world will again depend on the hazard of next year's harvest (FAO 1948g: no pagination).

That the FAO has actively participated in numerous efforts to reduce and manage risks related to specific commodities, populations, and activities is a process that involves, what we term, the *circulations of insecurity*. Similar to what Rose (1999: 160) calls a "culture of risk," the circulations of insecurity refers to the manner in which uncertainties are made known and linked to the modern development of new problems, new scientific explorations, and new answers. Following Beck (1999), these uncertainties are considered to pose new misfortunes that remain largely different from the threats posed to human life by the natural disasters of plagues, floods, and earthquakes. In the context of the uncertainty of food stability, numerous developments emerged during (and after) the early post-WWII era. Some developments underlined food itself as a vulnerable substance and traded commodity that required international standards, such as the standards first discussed in 1963 by the Codex Alimentarius Commission, the body charged with developing a food code (FAO/WHO 1999) or what is now known as the Codex Alimentarius. Other similar developments identified new forms of food stability designed to minimize the riskiness of the greatest insecurities, such as those related to famine, malnourishment, and overpopulation. These insecurities are represented in global terms; they are shown to cut across the borders of nation-states, to signal the global problems that can be solved through technological and managerial practices, and to serve as the basis from which to predict future events and future risks. Ulrich Beck (1999: 146) might suggest that such processes contribute to the development of how, in risk society, modern society becomes reflexive, that is to say "the foundations of its activity and its objectives become the object of public scientific and political controversies" (1999: 146). In this regard, reflexive modernization points to the transformation and the ambivalence of modernity.

The idea of risk has become a major concept in many sociological and anthropological analyses in recent years and provides a new intellectual viewpoint for understanding the ambivalence of modernity and modern science. A variety of critical historical research has analyzed risk as part of a particularized orientation toward the modern world that arose during the nineteenth century and that still characterizes, albeit in different ways, many aspects of social life today. For some scholars such as Rose, this particularized orientation entailed new ways of conceiving and acting upon misfortune in terms of risk. In his words, "risk thinking brought the future into the present and made it calculable" (Rose 1999: 247). It was made calculable through, for example, the use of demographic characteristics, statistical correlations, and probabilities to predict individuals, populations, and events liable to produce risks, a style of thinking or reasoning that some more broadly refer to as statistical (e.g., Hacking 2002). A similar kind of risk thinking is underscored by Beck (1999: 3) in his emphasis on risk as an approach for anticipating and managing the future. As he claims, "risk is the modern approach to foresee and control the future consequences of human action, the various unintended consequences of radicalized modernization. It is an (institutional) attempt, a cognitive map, to colonize the future." Based on this kind of risk thinking, then, there can be no determining relationship between the past and the present. Instead, and in line with Beck's notion of risk society as the self-endangering, devastating industrial destruction of nature, "the future – something non-existent, constructed or fictitious – takes its place as the cause of present experience and action" (Beck 2000: 100). The insights of both Beck and Rose on issues of risk encourage us to review how concerns related to insecurities in the world served as a mediating context for understanding the processes by which food stability was reconceptualized and food became standardized immediately following WWII.

## 3. THE FAO IN HISTORICAL CONTEXT

> The subject of developing and standardizing methods of investigating food consumption
> so that accurate and comparable data may be obtained is one to which considerable
> attention has already been given by international organizations. Work in this field
> should be continued and expanded by FAO (FAO 1946a).

During WWII, agriculture underwent massive war devastation in Europe, the USSR, in areas of Asia and the Pacific, and in North Africa. Sharp falls in agricultural production in those regions, coupled with a prevailing inability to finance food imports, encouraged both the identification of a "food shortage" and the need to be aware of and reduce such risks in the future. The FAO, established to improve the world food situation, immediately sought out science professionals to identify, catalogue, categorize, and monitor information related to the global supply of and demand for food (see also Ilcan and Phillips, 2003; Phillips and Ilcan, 2003).

Within this context, the FAO acknowledged that resolving food shortages on a long-term basis was not feasible as long as there existed a "grievous unbalance between the economies of the different regions" which, for the FAO, constituted "the principal economic problem of our time" (FAO 1948g: np). The FAO's mission to attend to global food and agricultural concerns thus translated into "developing and organizing production, distribution, and utilization of the *basic* foods to provide diets on a *health standard* for the peoples of *all countries*; [and] stabilizing agricultural prices at *levels fair* to producers and consumers alike" (FAO 1946b: np, our emphasis). Successfully linking the management of global food shortages with scientific knowledge about such things as basic foods, health standards, and fair prices for all, the FAO was able to garner significant support for, and a prominent role in, the development of global food and agricultural standards.

This link was achieved in part through the identification, organization, and global dispersion of what Latour (1987) would call technoscientists. Professional agronomists, biologists, economists, statisticians, and nutritionists were drawn largely from North American and European universities during the early post-war years to identify and translate agricultural knowledge throughout the world. In this process, local knowledge was inscribed in terms of statistical methods, food crop production, diet, and food consumption, enabling these technoscientists to compare and evaluate food and agriculture within a global economy. Local knowledge became universal knowledge, and technoscientists became global citizens whose function it was to analyze and re-align rural spaces within a social field of universal expectations. Thus, a world of standards arose from efforts to manage risks associated with global food production and consumption which, in turn, controlled or colonized the future (Beck 1999).

FAO initiatives in the agricultural domain during the late 1940s and 1950s concentrated on technical assistance to increase yields since "a large increase in production is called for in the world as a whole and is obviously most urgent in the deficit regions and the low-income regions" (FAO 1948g: np). Technical assistance meant introducing modern science into these deficit regions, including ideas about new improved seeds, irrigation, farm mechanization, and new forms of land tenure.

The communication of such knowledge involved the introduction of technical training programs in Africa, Asia, the Far and Near East, and Latin America, as well as fellowships for people from these regions to study in Europe or the United States.[5]

Numerous agricultural training centers, designed to help extend the reach of new thinking about food into national and local territories,[6] were also established at this time (see FAO 1953a, 1974). These centers made arrangements with scientists from all over the world to teach local agricultural personnel about modern food science protocols and thereby disseminate scientific knowledge on food and agriculture. For example, a National Training Center for the Grading and Inspection of Rice and the Economics of Rice Storage Operations opened in Thailand in 1953 shortly following a resolution of the 1951 FAO Conference on the "urgent problem of rice supplies." Through lectures and experiments offered by technical experts, the center trained local agricultural personnel in the principles of plant breeding, genetics, soils, insect control, and statistics (FAO 1953a: 13-16). Over this same period, agricultural training centers that operated in Thailand and in other countries, such as Turkey, Egypt, and the Philippines (FAO 1949c; FAO 1953[1952]; UN 1980/1955), also helped to spread a globally inscribed knowledge of agriculture that both incorporated and transcended local knowledge and skills.

In an attempt to prevent what was forecast as an "aggravated disequilibrium" (FAO 4th Session 1948: np) in global standards of living, the FAO also focused on controlling disease. The control of diseases in plants, animals, and humans was seen as an absolute necessity for different regions of the world to meet minimum standards for exporting their products. A "successful result" in combating plant and animal diseases was defined as being able to export the product (UN 1980 [1955]: 388). Thus, in 1955 for example, the FAO had various projects around the world to combat foot and mouth disease, desert locusts, olive flies, Newcastle disease (poultry), rinderpest, and cereal pests (ibid: 388), and to train local personnel in the appropriate prevention methods to ensure that standards would be met in the future.

Efforts to combat malnutrition followed a similar pattern. The problem of malnutrition was related to the need to raise food consumption levels in order to enable 'vulnerable groups' (UN 1980 [1955]) to work efficiently and establish purchasing power to buy imported products in the future. Scientific definitions of what constituted malnourishment preoccupied the Nutrition Division for much of this period – a debate which, interestingly, continues today (Smith 1999; Svedberg 1999; FAO 1999; WHO 1998). Moreover, debates about human food requirements were integrally connected to establishing what is referred to as 'nutritional targets,' an inspiration – based on what Beck would call "fabricated uncertainty" (1999: 19) – that translated into food standards to which the world is to aspire.

International organizations, including the FAO, have been notoriously unsuccessful in reaching their forecast targets. The important point for us, however, is that rather than abandoning such efforts or imagining alternative approaches to resolve nutritional problems, modern science (or what is usually referred to as 'better' science) continues to be enlisted to settle the matter. Even when the character of the crisis changes (for example, when the population 'explosion' in the 1960s is thought to outweigh all other risks), appeals to scientific solutions dominate (in this case, new methods are proposed for programming and mathematically calculating food quantities [see Sukhatme 1960: 10]).

Both dietary standards and agricultural production standards were seen by the FAO as essential for risk prevention. In the following two subsections we examine in greater detail how food consumption standards and food production standards were inscribed within this context.

## *3.1    Inscribing Food*

> [H]uman beings must not only be kept alive and free from disease during the period of postwar convalescence (that is, at the 'minimum subsistence standard'), but they must have more food if they are to achieve a normal work output (FAO 1946b).

By 1960 the globe was easily severed into "well-fed" countries and "low calorie" countries, with "nutritional targets" clearly being necessary for the latter (Sukhatme 1960). These new spatial designations of food consumption signaled the need for new measures and models for thinking about food that supported dietary standards, recommended dietary allowances, and household surveys as ways to compare food consumption practices in various parts of the world (FAO 1949d, FAO 1983). Building a global model of food consumption obliged the FAO to make diverse categories somehow comparable. This task was accomplished through a process of inscription: first by mapping food and human bodies, rendering them separable from their localities, and then stabilizing them as representations of standardized units that could be compared. Food was thus fragmented into component parts of nutritive composition, i.e., calories, protein, minerals, vitamins, etc., and the human body was reduced to a construction of what was 'average': average size, average energy expended (or, 'normal work output'), and average consumption requirements.[7]

This inscription process was central to the FAO's development of scientific ways to understand and organize the world's food supply. For example, food supplies could now be computed as specific nutrients that were plotted, compared, and subject to judgment in internationally recognized Food Composition Tables (FAO 1948a: 1). The FAO scientific staff argued as early as 1946 that if foods were to be expressed as nutrients, appropriate tables on food composition were needed (FAO 1946b). Systems for computing calories were constantly improved in order to achieve "uniformity and comparability in estimating energy values in calories" (FAO 1948a: 2). The standardization of the nutritive value of food even required that all reports identify nutritive value at the same stage in a particular food's movement from the point of production to the point of consumption (FAO 1946b). Cloaked in the language of modern science, this apparently objective and value-neutral method of standardization came to inhabit a world in which the claims of positivist science dominated institutional discourses and practices as well as people's production and consumption patterns. Translating food needs into the category of 'nutritional requirements' was intimately connected to the transformation of humans from cultural beings with a wide array of food preferences into standardized units of labor with specific nutrient requirements.

Although improving nutrition in most regions around the world was high on the FAO agenda, raising nutrition levels was considered "an urgent necessity" in Latin America (FAO 1948b). This urgency could be identified in a series of tables on the supply of food per capita for specific Latin American countries, with specific translations of corn, potatoes, wheat, etc. into calories, proteins, minerals, fats, and vitamins, on the one hand, and prices, imports, and exports on the other (FAO 1948b). In addition, a number of revealing reports, based on a conference on nutrition held by FAO in Uruguay in 1948, map out the Latin American problem: the two primary causes of the region's nutritional deficiencies (FAO 1948c: 4) are identified as inadequate agricultural production and poor eating habits, the latter spawned by a general ignorance of people about nutrition (FAO 1948: 8).

The problem of race, a significant feature of many colonial and modern state imaginations, is especially highlighted in these regional reports on food deficiencies. One report concludes that, in Bolivia, the "indigenous race" was considered to be "at the margin of all progress," though it comprised 56% of the national population (FAO 1948b). Citing other studies, this report notes that: "the indigenous population 'only eats fresh meat once a week.' In general, the Indian eats 'charqui,' or salted llama meat that is dried in the sun. It is incredible...that these people are able to feed themselves on so little" (ibid: 2). Such observations not only reflected the assumed standard of a high animal protein diet but employed race as a category of risk, an axis upon which arguments about the necessity of 'modern' eating habits could hinge. It is worth noting that racial distinctions are referred to throughout these discussions about nutrition: we hear of indios vs. ladinos in Guatemala, indios vs. mestizos in Mexico and Ecuador, and the indigenous and Hispanic populations in the southwest United States (FAO 1948c; FAO 1948f).

It is also worth noting that the FAO seemed to recognize that the standardized approach to food calculation might not operate in the interests of everyone. For example, after noting the (deficient) average consumption of calories, protein, riboflavin, etc. of the average Bolivian, one FAO study states that the indigenous population consumes many foods that are not part of the FAO's caloric calculations of diet and that therefore such populations may well eat better than their figures indicate (FAO 1948c: 6). Another FAO study contains the statement that: "Animal protein levels are particularly low among the Indians [in Latin America], but the diet of those retaining their old food habits and consuming many wild plants has been found superior in vitamin A value and ascorbic acid to that of other groups who have lost such habits" (FAO 1949a: 32-33).

It is testimony to the strength of the FAO's agenda to standardize risky populations and food consumption that admissions of divergent dietary practices did not in any way erase the perceived necessity to purge local food habits. Targets were still set by calculating the standardized caloric requirements for adults and comparing the actual (inevitably deficient) consumption of food in Latin America. Science was still enlisted to confirm and settle the region's nutritional problems (FAO 1948d). Not only were devices of inscription employed to make explicit comparisons of diet in the US and other developed countries (e.g., Norway) with the Latin American region (FAO 1948e), but technoscientists, in the form of various kinds of consultants, evaluated and retrained Latin American social workers, nurses, and rural teachers about modern nutrition (FAO 1948f; UN 1980[1955]). These local professionals in turn judged and retrained people living in the countryside, working with themes such as *una comida completa en un solo plato* [a complete meal on a single plate] (FAO 1948f: 4). In this context, women were often mobilized as a safe population for introducing new standards to manage food and diet risks.[8] As noted in one report: "One can teach them to improve methods of cooking, to plan better homes, to obtain a higher quantity of food from their small gardens, etc. Women have the responsibility of managing the home and preparing the meals, making it essential to bring educational programs to them and to influence them" (FAO 1948f: 2).

The impressions of one FAO consultant (Bosley 1960) summarizes the scientific assessment of food consumption risks in Latin America: noted are the diminished stature of indigenous rural people, the ignorance of the local professionals about the "scientific facts," the lack of animal protein in the markets, and the unhygienic conditions under which food was most often prepared. Managing these risks, this consultant concludes, required the continuing presence of nutritional experts to ensure that people change to "intelligent food habits" (p. 20) based on the "science of nutrition." From this example we learn how proposed solutions to food consumption risks may be highly problematic. This is because, as Beck reminds us, in risk discourses "experts can only supply factual information and are never able to access which solutions are culturally acceptable" (1999: 42).

We now have perhaps a clearer idea of what it means to inscribe standards for food. It has certainly implied devising new measures of food and building new models for the consumption of food. Following Latour (1987), it also obliged scientists to explore all kinds of networks – of nutrition and of populations – and to make linkages between them. As will be illustrated below, such activities of inscription were also devised for standardizing how food was to be produced.

### 3.2 Inscribing Agriculture

> [I]n cooperation with the statistical services of the United Nations, FAO should work out agreements on nomenclature and exact definitions of the various items of national income, in order that fluctuations of agricultural income in relation to the incomes of other sections of the populations may be kept under constant review [and] the revision of the handbook of conversion factors, nomenclature, units of measurement, and definitions [should] be regarded as an urgent project for precise appraisal and comparison of statistical data from the various countries (FAO 1946b).

While inscriptions of food knowledge generated food-as-nutrition in the context of averting malnutrition and building able bodies, promoting the products of agriculture as an increasingly valuable and necessary global commodity greatly transformed how food should be produced. Such a commodification process called for the invention of new agricultural standards, the conversion of a whole class of goods or services into commodities, and the increased mobilization of international trade.

Though foods were thought of as commodities long before 1945, the FAO played a significant role in facilitating the global mobilization of the food trade through its inscription of food as standardized commodities that could be safely bought and sold across national borders. As in the case of nutrition, this process involved identifying the risks (i.e., low and unreliable agricultural production; overpopulation) and standardizing them through a process of inscription. One of the key assumptions operating in the presentation of agricultural production risks in the early post-war period, as it continues to be today, was that food production levels were insufficient to feed everyone. The emphasis placed on insufficient production levels was largely influenced by Malthusian-oriented views[9] on food production and by the introduction of geographic categories that highlighted particular 'populations' as posing risks to the world's food supply. It was recognized by the United Nations Population Commission, for example, that "the earth's population is growing more rapidly than ever in the past...[but] since something like two-thirds of the world's people live in the less developed countries, it is principally the growth in these areas that is pushing up the world rate" (UN 1959: 3). In forecasting the world's future needs in 1960, the FAO argued that "the world's total food supplies would have to be nearly doubled by 1980 and trebled by the turn of the century in order to provide a reasonably adequate level of nutrition to the peoples of the world" (Sukhatme 1960: 19-20). This kind of risk thinking focused great concern on the 'fact' that less developed countries were not planning the necessary and appropriate expansion in agriculture (FAO 1949a). It was especially in relation to these geographic areas targeted for risk management – what Rose might call "zones of exclusion" (2000: 197) – that a great optimism existed for agricultural expansion, primarily because of improvements in what had come to be known as agricultural science.

In order to reduce insecurities related to agricultural production, the science of modern agriculture demanded an inscription of the earth and its products: global comparisons and judgments about agricultural quantity and quality could only be made with a new, strategic orientation to land and its utility. For example, soil classification tables were developed in order to identify what kinds of "requisites" were needed. Standards of certification for improved seeds were developed, and new knowledge about crops in tropical countries was compiled (e.g., the World Catalogue of Tropical and Subtropical Forage Plants). The production of fertilizers and pesticides was monitored to ensure sufficient supply for use in developing countries, and a Convention on plant protection was established "to simplify and rationalize procedures intended to prevent the spread of plant diseases and pests" (UN 1953 [1952]: 832). Assessments of, and outlooks for, grains, sugar, fats and oils, livestock, and fruits were charted for every region of the world (FAO 1949a: 47-88), with the production levels of North America and Europe clearly contrasting with the high risk regions of Asia, Africa, and South America (FAO 1949a: 48). Once appraisals had been made, technical assistance was made available to the regions at risk in the form of advice, training, high-yielding seeds, fertilizers, and better tools, since the technical knowledge and material equipment of these regions were judged to be "pitifully inadequate" (FAO 1949a: 2).[10] With the resources of modern science sustaining the organization's efforts, the FAO was able to present limitless possibilities for reducing future risks in agricultural production: "to help [member nations] bring new lands under cultivation, improve the yields of lands already cultivated, reduce the costs of production, improve the efficiency of international distribution, raise levels of consumption, and better the living conditions in rural areas" (UN 1953 [1952]: 831). Appropriate levels of agricultural efficiency were notions grounded in scientific programs on distribution and consumption, notions which, in turn, derived their strength from the "forging of alignments" (Rose 1994: 364) between the capacities of modern scientific knowledge and FAO aims to reduce agricultural risks.

Latin America was predicted to have the fastest growing population in the world (Sukhatme 1960: 18), and the FAO identified the region as having a "great need for technical assistance in the solution of agricultural production, storage, transport, marketing, and consumption. The region needs closer and more continuous attention from FAO" (FAO 1948g: np). Specific recommendations were: the improvement of livestock strains; increasing pasture management; continuing resettlement programs; improving conservation knowledge; monitoring agricultural income; combating diseases that "sap the strength of agricultural producers and render inefficient or impossible agriculture production in large areas of Latin America"; and the centralization of "intelligence" on pests and communicable disease (FAO 1946b; FAO 1948g: np). Technical consultation was also required to develop a uniform system for standardizing food commodities, "especially for export products" (ibid).

In addition to the necessary technical advice for increasing the yields of specific crops, FAO professional consultants in various regions of Latin America explicitly identified land tenure patterns as a potential risk to agricultural productivity. Because "the level of production of a holding has increasingly become one of the criteria determining whether the holding should be redistributed" (UN 1955: 21), Latin American governments experienced extensive FAO involvement in agrarian reform and colonization efforts throughout the 1950s and 1960s. Similar to the approach of the FAO to agricultural production problems in the Far East, Africa, and Asia, entire countries in Latin America were mapped and mobilized as standardized units for systematic assessment and scientifically-based proposals for change.

One report on colonization in Ecuador, for example, describes the main role of the ILO and FAO experts as establishing "normative principles that serve to determine the size of each new property, the class of colonists who should be given it, the type of houses that they should construct, the system of agricultural credit that they should adopt, the cooperatives that they should construct, and the social assistance and labour facilitation that will be necessary to mount" (Luscombe & Pereira 1957: 1). In order to undertake this task, the specialists identified and assessed the country's physical, economic, and social characteristics, including its climate, soil, transportation systems, crop/animal production, distribution of tenancy arrangements, population density, etc. An appraisal of a country's population characteristics also permitted these consultants to suggest the "type of intensive training or preparation required" (ibid.: 175) for farmers of new lands to be successful.[11]

As in the case of nutrition, the risks associated in Latin America with poor productivity levels or with occupants having limited 'entrepreneurial spirit' were racially framed. One report notes, for example, that "the majority of coastal and Highland Indians live in a closed economic system, of self-sufficiency, without influence in the money market. Their standard of living is extremely low and the entrepreneurial spirit is very limited by the modesty of their ambitions" (Luscombe

& Pereira 1957: 21). In this statement indigenous people are viewed as occupants located in dangerous spaces and deprived of the standards of modern life. It is recognized that convincing the indigenous population to "abandon their illogical insistence on possessing a piece of land" (ibid.: 191) will require an enormous effort:

> If you want to use the indigenous population for colonization it will first be necessary to integrate them into the active life of the country and citizenship, through the means of a special programme, using all the resources available, particularly through the basic services of the State. This, naturally, requires changes in many people, but principally in Indians themselves. Every effort should be made to maintain and expand their trust [including] civic courses to familiarize the leaders of indigenous communities with the organized life of the people in nearby provinces; specialized courses and demonstrations, with the goal of giving them knowledge about better cultivation methods [and] about better childcare; [and] supplying them with the elementary but important notions of hygiene... (ibid.: 190).

These and other similar reports help to remind us that increasing agricultural production levels were part of a much larger effort to link 'risky' behavior, whether in the realm of agricultural production, food consumption, or biological reproduction, to particular populations. That these populations happened to occupy rather large areas of the world known to have 'deficient' economies must have made the FAO's efforts in circulating and managing insecurities seem all the more indispensable. As we illustrate below, the current emphasis on the production and dissemination of information on food reflects a style of risk thinking that not only brings potential future events into "calculations in the present" (Rose 2000: 198) but manages the uncertainty of food and food trade through global communication frameworks that detail a host of food associated-risks.

## 4. THE INFORMATIZATION OF FOOD

> [A]n essential part of each technical program of FAO is to gather, analyze, evaluate, and disseminate information. The dissemination of information is particularly important in the work of an organization having mainly informational and advisory powers, and dealing with subjects of such broad human concern as does FAO (FAO 1948g).

The FAO's communication of its global food and agricultural inscriptions as 'up-to-date and reliable' information formed part of what is now commonly referred to as the information or network society (May 2002; Castles 2000; Luke 1990; Forester 1985). We understand the concept of information here to mean a representation of data that involves organizing and communicating data in systematic ways (Shields, Ilcan, O'Connor, & Taborsky 2002: 149), a process that often demands the enhancement of the role of the scientific specialist or technocrat in data management and distribution. Adapting Webster (1995), we call the heightened flow of food information following World War II the 'informatization of food'[12] in recognition of how pivotal the global communication of information was, and is, to the management of food-associated risks.[13] Since its inception, the FAO has been identified as a key reference center for economic and statistical information about the world's food production, distribution, and consumption.[14] As indicated in the above section, the FAO's activities in this regard went well beyond simply compiling huge quantities of data. With the global reach of its standardizing activities, the FAO greatly facilitated the dispersion of what constituted food and agricultural risks and which prescriptions might best manage them. The free exchange of information was the rationale for conducting annual world commodity reviews and establishing training centers and regional conferences on agricultural production and rural welfare. It was the basis for "opening the door to the farmer's mind," an assumed necessity both for "increasing the power of assimilating new knowledge of improved agricultural practice" and for introducing "the realization of the importance of [the farmer's] part in the production program" (FAO 1948g: np).

Therefore, scientifically-based inscriptions of food and agriculture were not developed simply to enable scientists to make comparisons but were also undertaken "with a view to making this information readily available" (FAO 1946b: 5) throughout the world so that action could be undertaken. Action was never questioned as an essential ingredient in the FAO's global effort to create and raise standards, as indicated in its own documents:

> "[T]he task ahead for member governments and for FAO is one of recognizing needs, arousing interest, and taking vigorous action. The means to be employed include the promotion of research, the dissemination of knowledge, and the exchange of services and technicians. It will be for FAO to assist the member governments in all such measures and to act as the international center for the furtherance of national and international action" (FAO 1946b: 3).

It is worth noting that, within this context, the persistence of marginalized, risk-prone populations – peoples who were either unable or unwilling to abandon all their consumption or production 'habits' – never discouraged the FAO from having faith in its processes of inscription, or its 'faith in bread' (as FAO's motto translates). Consistently, the FAO's response to divergence from food and agricultural standards has been the production of yet more information on food for the purpose of not only managing and broadcasting the uncertainties of the times but, as Bauman might say, "feeding uncertainty" and "feeding on uncertainty" (2002: 197). It is in this sense that we understand the global communication of a safe, standardized food system as an integral component of the FAO's circulations of insecurities that form part of what we call the informatization of food.

This historical process of identifying, managing, and communicating information on food and agricultural risks forms an essential backdrop for understanding the FAO's approaches to food security today. A current way in which information on food and agricultural insecurities is communicated is through the FAO's Global Information and Early Warning System on Food and Agriculture (GIEWS). This system circulates information on food markets, supplies, demands, prices, trends, and fluctuations to a worldwide network of information users. Following the world food crisis of the early 1970s, GIEWS was first established in 1975. Making use of the revolution in information technology and the advent of computer communications, it invested in methods for collecting, analyzing, and disseminating information. The GIEWS is one of the most significant sources today for information on food production and consumption problems. Specifically, it reports on the world food situation by providing information on the supply and demand of food globally from country-level aggregated data. Not only does the GIEWS estimate global food supply and demand (warning when either one is at risk) but it collects world market export prices on a daily and weekly basis. It also reports on major market events and notes the risk of dramatic food price changes. Within this thematic field, it engages in "food security" monitoring activities, activities which are divided into four main areas: global, regional, national, and subnational. These reports are linked to a worldwide network that includes: 115 governments, 61 non-governmental organizations, and numerous trade, research, media, and government organizations.[15]

The GIEWS information network has most certainly generated an awareness of difference and diversity, but within a standardized orientation toward food, other food cultures, and other lives. In this sense it operates as a "reality-creating force" (Delanty 1999) that attempts to manage food insecurities by identifying, problematizing, and rendering them calculable within a global framework of standards. This reading of the GIEWS follows from our analysis of earlier forms of such information networks, networks that managed and communicated risk as part of the global informatization of food.

In this respect, the GIEWS resembles the Codex Alimentarius, another important avenue for communicating current information on food concerns. The Codex Alimentarius Commission was created in 1963 by FAO and WHO to ensure safe food for consumers and to facilitate the international food trade. Its main work is to compile and revise the Codex Alimentarius, a significant and internationally acknowledged food code that was first produced in 1981. According to the Codex text itself, it is "...a collection of international food standards adopted by the Commission and presented in a uniform manner. It includes standards for all the principal foods, whether processed or semi-processed or raw" (FAO/WHO 2000: Preface). In the context of establishing food standards, the Codex assesses, analyzes, and outlines hazardous foods and specifies what procedures to follow when assessing risks in relation to contaminants (see FAO/WHO 2000). It has regulations involving a wide variety of items, including food labeling to standardize: how nutrients should be calculated (carbohydrates, protein, fat, using a particular conversion formula); how nutrient content should be presented; and, how food additives should be named and numbered according to an international numbering system. The Codex Alimentarius is now customarily used by a wide range of scientists, government food control officials, health authorities, and consumer advocates (FAO/WHO 2000). Within the Codex, all aspects of food processing and marketing are subject to standards which form part of the circulations of insecurity that the FAO has long facilitated. For example, the Codex is concerned with how a scientific 'harmonization' of food standards lowers risks in the food trade. It includes definitions of risk and outlines the process of risk analysis as it relates to food safety, noting that definitions "are subject to modification in the light of developments in the science of risk analysis and as a result of efforts to harmonize similar definitions across various disciplines" (ibid: 13). According to the Commission, risk analysis itself is a science, and includes a scientific methodology for assessing, managing, and communicating risk. The Codex Alimentarius stands today as one of the most explicit devices for standardizing food through a science-based process linked to risk-aversion.

These and other forms of communication reflect the ways in which circulations of insecurity may enter into different networks of information that focus on issues of danger, safety, and stability. In this respect it is noteworthy that, although the support and implementation of the Codex Alimentarius was always meant to be voluntary "in the larger interest of the world community" (FAO/WHO 2000: 18), with the 1995 provisions of the World Trade Organization (WTO)[16] the Codex Alimentarius has now come to involve a kind of 'forced voluntarism' (Cosbey 2000). It is consequently under much greater scrutiny today and entering new fields of information flow and management. Coincidentally (or not), the Codex has just undergone a long overdue evaluation, the first since its creation. Given the FAO's historical propensity to avoid an examination of its core assumptions about food standards and food insecurities, perhaps one need not be surprised that the report's 42 recommendations point to an even greater reliance on standardized scientific expertise to evaluate food risks and a continuing pattern of disseminating information about hazards and risks.[17]

## 5. CONCLUSION

For the greater part of its history, modernity was an era of 'social engineering' in which the unforced emergence and reproduction of order was not, Bauman (2001) reminds us, to be trusted. The single probable order was designed using the resources of modern science, the necessity of which was upheld by day-to-day monitoring and management. It was assumed that modern science could be trusted for it had the power of reason both to bring about change in ways that would serve the interests of those involved and to support the justice-related goals of modern development, such as increased stability and security of lives and livelihoods, health and welfare. Many dimensions of change became connected to the goals of modern development of which universalization formed an integral part. Universalization was believed to have its strength in numbers, in linear theories of knowledge, and in its ability to rule out differences and divergences through programs, information systems, and international policies that would attempt to direct people and populations toward the modern goals of progress and advancement. Many 'unintended consequences' (Beck 1999) grew from modern scientific methods including those processes of standardization that contributed to the re-making of the world and to the production and consumption of food in ways that seem almost unimaginable.

Throughout this chapter, we have emphasized how post-WWII food production and consumption efforts were managed, transformed, and standardized by the FAO through practices designed ostensibly to create a stable world agriculture devoid of the risks associated with global food shortages, malnutrition, and disease. In the context of modern scientific practices, we illustrated how this international agency linked the management of food and agriculture with scientific knowledge and technoscientists. Following Latour, we argued that this linkage was achieved through a wide array of inscription devices designed to produce an international understanding of food in terms of dietary standards and food composition tables, of human bodies in terms of average sizes and consumption requirements, and of agriculture in terms of new production models and patterns. This international understanding stemmed from the manner by which the uncertainties of food and agriculture were revealed and linked to new scientific developments following World War II, a process that we have called the circulations of insecurity. These circulations ultimately resulted in the transformation of peoples and populations into standardized units to be judged, monitored, and assessed by modern scientific specialists. By doing so, they also created new forms of inequalities, as risky behavior became associated with marginalized populations in particular regions of the world through the lens of the inscription process. Furthermore, we have shown how the FAO's communication of its global food and agricultural inscriptions, such as that of the Codex Alimentarius in the current context, has formed an integral component of the ongoing management of food-associated risks which in turn contributed to what we have called the informatization of food today. While the circulations of insecurity and the informatization of food have a long and diverse history, the FAO has been centrally located in a wide range of activities geared to identify and manage risks in the modern food system, and to disseminate scientific standards to 'colonize the future' (Beck 1999). In light of such activities that demand a hunger for certainty, it now seems necessary to ask whether the pervasiveness of science-based orientations offers any escape from the straight-jacketed present.

The seemingly never-ending expansion of circulations of insecurities today indicates that Houdini-like efforts to imagine risk and safety in less destructive ways may be increasingly imperative. A potential beginning can be found in rethinking the notion of standards as a linear framework of scientific criteria based on international interests and on, what Beck (1999: 125) would call, "closed circles of formally responsible expert groups and people who act on knowledge." As is indicated in this study, such an approach not only homogenizes or ignores what it considers 'minor' or 'irrelevant' knowledge from a global perspective but promotes an indifference to difference by putting aside the possible significance of diverse practices, such as those related to production, crops, and nutritional preferences. While much diversity in the world has indeed been reduced by the very practices of standardization discussed in this chapter, a close reading of local practices continues to show that complex, eco-systemic, and culturally diverse knowledges still inform agricultural and consumption practices in vital ways (van der Ploeg 1993; Bianco and Sachs 1998). Would it not be possible to develop standards through a matrix that recognizes different domains of knowledge as potential sources of food security and livelihoods, rather than as a recipe for insecurities – to trade, global health, etc.? Such a shift would mean, among other things, that different questions would have to be addressed well before standards were imposed. For example, within the current movement toward a supply chain view of food standards (or the 'plow-to-plate' approach to food safety), we would need to ask: whose plow, whose plate, and whose security? If global food standards are to be applied, what larger implications might there be for particular farmers and their particular farming systems? We often hear about how standardizing food greatly benefits international trade, but what does it do to local farming knowledge and practices? How might it produce polarized networks of people, with only some capable of inscribing and acting on particular forms of knowledge? How might it transform community and employment relations in environments where people struggle amidst difficulties to make a life for themselves? And, further, how might the 'internalized intuitions' of a diverse range of farmers and consumers help us to think of standards in ways that do not discount local-level political and ethical responsibilities? While such questions feed into debates around 'reflexive modernization' and its unintended consequences, they also complicate the work of standardizing food and provide a major challenge to the work of an international organization such as the FAO. Nevertheless it may well be that the long-term sustainability of the world rests precisely on the ability and willingness of such organizations to test, rethink, and complicate the underlying assumptions that buttress future global security.

In light of our analysis of global food standardization, there is an urgency to be conscious of the implications that standardization practices impose upon the world which we inhabit. We cannot escape these practices by claiming that they belong to an isolated historical time frame or a set of social activities. They have been, and continue to be, created in spaces of production and consumption, in geographic places where we work and visit, and in disparate events and times. These practices not only transform our habitat and our habitual relations, but they work through a multitude of institutions and scientific knowledges which enter into contact with other practices that produce other effects, anticipated or not. However, if we are to understand the implications of standardization practices, we first need to focus on the agents and agencies that have the authority to invest in them, to constitute them, and to put them to work. It is at this level of analysis where greater attention is needed and where interrogations can be made about how objects, probabilities, classifications, and risks are generated and made knowable in universal terms.

## 6. NOTES

[1] As with this chapter and our other jointly published research, lead authorship alternates with every study produced through our collaboration. We acknowledge with appreciation the Social Sciences and Humanities Research Council of Canada for providing us with financial support to carry out this research. We thank our research assistants, Tarik Bereket, Christiana Gauger, and Marcia Oliver, for their excellent library acquisitions which have in turn contributed to our data archive on globalization, and on the United Nations and its specialized agencies. A version of this chapter was presented at the Rural Sociological Association meetings in Chicago in August 2002.

[2] Our focus on the FAO forms part of a larger project on the role of the United Nations in conceptually relocating people and place during its crucial years of development, 1946-1970. This was a time period characterized by the introduction of new orientations and programs to manage world-wide populations, regions, and resources in ways that greatly relied upon modern knowledges, techniques, and devices. This larger project explores how the concept of spatialization helps us to understand the new global policies, practices, and hierarchies that have emerged through the early UN efforts to map the world into diverse configurations and social categories. One dimension of this work focuses on how a particular understanding of 'rurality' has been created by mapping populations through what we have called cartographical and narrative techniques (Ilcan and Phillips 2000).

[3] See Isin (2002) on the emergence of other areas of professional expertise.

[4] Speaking of the present situation, Busch (1997: 13) maintains that "food safety is best understood as the result of the restructuring of the food system along industrial and scientific lines, and the consequent new problems that [it] has posed for processors and the general public alike."

[5] According to the FAO, by the end of 1952, there were 315 FAO experts in countries all over the world (UN 1953[1952]). The number of experts in the field at the end of 1955 was 438, and 274 fellowships were awarded (UN 1980[1955]).

[6] Sassen (1999, 1991) and Brenner (1998) have made similar arguments with respect to the processes of the global economy.

[7] See Ilcan and Phillips (2000) for a discussion of the United Nations' participation in the global mapping of the 'standard person.'

[8] See Phillips and Ilcan (2000) for an analysis of the 'place' of gender in the practices and politics of development.

[9] See Edkins (2000) for a critical assessment of the influence of the work of Thomas Malthus on the contemporary problem of overpopulation and famine in relation to food shortages, and on solving such problems by increasing food production.

[10] Much of this assistance was made possible by the developments of US agriculture in the 1920s and 1930s, when "the main building blocks...tractors and combine harvesters, synthetic nitrogen and hybrid seeds" were developed for what Goodman and Redclift (1991: 105) refer to as the 'modern agri-food system'.

[11] High illiteracy rates in a population did not apparently disrupt efforts to promote these standards: "[T]he [FAO] Conference recognizes that a very large proportion of the agricultural producers in Latin America cannot effectively be taught improved practices by means of the printed word. It therefore wishes to emphasize the importance of strengthening and greatly expanding existing agricultural extension services" (FAO 1948g: np).

[12] In his analysis of a range of theories of information, Webster (1995) coins the term the 'informatization of life' by which he means the central role that information has played and continues to play in supporting particular social forms over time. We find this approach, which departs from the view that information flow today signals the coming of a new age, useful for illustrating the ways in which the communication of information manages risk within circulations of insecurities.

[13] Winseck (2002: 34) notes how, in contrast, neoclassical economics "offers a soothing definition of information as the reduction of uncertainty," assuring us, for example, that we have all the information we need to make informed choices.

[14] Since the early post-WWII period, the categorization and use of information have been critical organizing principles for diverse social, political, and institutional sites. It is relevant that, during this time, information and communication technologies permitted a growing number of transnational corporations to begin treating the "whole world not just as a single market, but also as a single production site – or, rather, as a limited number of linked regional sites, co-producing broadly similar products" (Leys 2001: 9). This process also parallels the way that new information technology radically increased the mobility of various economic units for financial and commercial organizations (Held 1995).

[15] See the GIEWS world wide website; http://www.fao.org/giews for more on this topic.

[16] The WTO Agreement on Sanitary and Phytosanitary Measures states that a country may base its food safety measures on existing international standards, such as that provided by the Codex Alimentarius. For more see WTO website; http://www.wto.org/english/docs_e/legal_e/ursum_e.htm.

[17] By suggesting that FAO/WHO support the collection of data covering a wider range of diets and production processes, Recommendation 35 nods in the direction of developing countries' concerns that the findings of expert committees may be of limited value to them. However, this one indication that the universal application of science-based standards may have limitations is overwhelmed by a much stronger emphasis on helping developing countries meet such standards through 'capacity building' or another form of what we refer to as informatization. For a copy of the report see FAO website; http://www.fao.org/docrep/meeting/005/y7871e/y7871e00.htm.

## 7. REFERENCES

Appadurai, A. (2001) Grassroots Globalization and the Research Imagination. Pp. 1-21 in *Globalization*, edited by A. Appadurai Durham, N.C.: Duke University Press.

Bauman, Z. (2001) *Community: Seeking Safety in an Insecure World*. Cambridge: Polity Press.
_____ (2002) *Society Under Siege*. Cambridge: Polity Press.
Beck, U. (1994) The Reinvention of Politics: Towards a Theory of Reflexive Modernization. Pp 1-55 in *Reflective Modernization: Politics, Tradition and Aesthetics in the Modern Social Order*, edited by U. Beck, A. Giddens, and S. Lash, Cambridge: Polity Press.
_____ (1996) World Risk Society as Cosmopolitan Society? Ecological Questions in a Framework of Manufactured Uncertainties. *Theory, Culture & Society* 13(4): 1-32.
_____ (1998) Politics of Risk Society. Pp. 9-22 in *The Politics of Risk Society*, edited by J. Franklin. Cambridge: Polity Press. Pp. 9-22.
_____ (1999) *World Risk Society*. Cambridge: Polity Press.
_____ . (2000) *What is Globalization*? Cambridge: Polity Press.
Bianco, M. and C. Sachs (1998) Growing Oca, Ulluco, and Mashua in the Andes: Socioeconomic differences in cropping practices. *Agriculture and Human Values* 15: 267-280.
Bosley, B. (1960) Evaluacion Experimental de los Programa de Ensenanza de la Nutricion y Educacion Alimentaria en Ecuador, Costa Rica y Guatemala. FAO/61/G/11271.
Bourdieu, P. (1977) *Outline of a Theory of Practice*. London: Cambridge University Press.
Brenner, N. 1998. Global Cities, Local States: Global City Formation and State Territorial Restructuring in Contemporary Europe. *Review of International Political Economy* 5(1): 1-37.
Busch, L. (1997) Grades and Standards in the Social Construction of Safe Food. Paper presented at a conference on The Social Construction of Safe Food, Trondheim, Norway, April.
Castles, M. (2000) *The Rise of the Network Society*. Second Edition. Oxford: Blackwell.
Cosbey, A. (2000) A Forced Evolution? The Codex Alimentarius Commission, Scientific Uncertainty and the Precautionary Principle. Winnipeg, Manitoba: International Institute for Sustainable Development.
Delanty, G. (1999) *Social Theory in a Changing World: Conceptions of Modernity*. Cambridge: Polity Press.
Edkins, J. (2000) *Whose Hunger? Concepts of Famine, Practices of Aid*. Minneapolis: University of Minnesota Press.
Fischer, F. (2000) *Citizens, Experts, and the Environment: The Politics of Local Knowledge*. Durham and London: Duke University Press.
FAO (Food and Agriculture Organization) Global Information and Early Warning System on Food and Agriculture; http://www.fao.org/giews.
_____ (1946b) Report on the Second Session of the Conference of the FAO. Sept., Copenhagen.
_____ (1946a) Report on the First Session of the Conference of the FAO. Quebec, 1945. Washington, D.C.: FAO.
_____ (1948a) El Valor Nutritivo de los Alimentos. Tema 1(c) de la Agenda Provisional. N48/Co.2/3
_____ (1948b) Informes sobre el Estado de la Nutricion en Algunos Paises Latinamericanos. Uruguay, July.
_____ (1948c) Problemas de la Nutricion en la America Latina. Uruguay, July, N48/Co.2/2.
_____ (1948d) Nota sobre la Agricultura y la Alimentacion. Uruguay, July, N48/Co.2/4.
_____ (1948e) Nota sobre los Programas de Alimentacion Infantil. Agenda Provisional, Tema 2 (b), Uruguay, July, N48/Co.2/5
_____ (1948f) Educacion del Publico sobre Nutricion. Uruguay, July, N48/Co.2/6.
_____ (1948g) Report on the Fourth Session of the FAO. November, Washington, D.C.
_____ (1949a) The State of Food and Agriculture: A Survey of World Conditions and Prospects. Washington, DC (October)
_____ (1949b) Fifth Session of the Conference of the FAO. Parts I and II, Nov.-Dec., Washington, D.C.
_____ (1949c) Statistical Training Center for the Near East. Lecture 1, Purpose of Statistical Training Centres, delivered by Dr. M. Hassanein. Cairo, Egypt. October-December. Rome: FAO.
_____ (1949d) Dietary Surveys: Their Technique and Interpretation. *FAO Nutritional Studies*, No. 4. Washington: FAO.
_____ (1953a) Special Rice Meeting. *International Rice Commission Newsletter*. No. 5. March. Bangkok, Thailand: FAO Regional Office, Bangkok.
_____ (1953b) Statistical Organization in Turkey and its History. International Seminar on Statistical Organization. Sponsored by the Government of Canada and the United Nations. 13-31 October, 1952.

_____ (1974) Report to the Governments Participating in the FAO Interregionals Programme for the Improvement of Olive Production on Olive Cultivation in the Countries of the Mediterranean Basin and the Near East. United National Development Programme. Rome: FAO.

_____ (1983) A Comparative Study of Food Consumption Data from Food Balance Sheets and Household Survey. FAO Economic and Social Development Paper. Rome: FAO.

_____ (1999) A Report on Nutrition and Food Security Situation and Related Rural Development Issues in Turkey. Report Prepared by Dr. P. Arslan, Department of Nutrition and Dietetics. FAO Regional Office: Ankara, Turkey.

_____ (2000) *The State of Food and Agriculture: Lessons from the Past 50 Years*. Rome: FAO.

FAO/WHO (1999) Understanding the Codex Alimentarius; http://www.fao.org/docrep.

_____ (2000) Codex Alimentarius. Vol. 1A: General Requirements. Rome: FAO.

Forester, T. ed. (1985) *The Information Technology Revolution*. Cambridge: MIT Press.

Goodman, D. & M. Redclift (1991) *Refashioning Nature: Food, Ecology, and Culture*. London and New York: Routledge.

Hacking, I. (2002) Inaugural Lecture: Chair of Philosophy and History of Scientific Concepts at the Collège de France, 16 January 2001. *Economy and Society* 31(1):1-14.

Held, D. (1995) *Democracy and the Global Order*. Stanford, California: Stanford University Press.

Ilcan, S. & L. Phillips (2000) Mapping Populations: The United Nations, Globalization, and Engendered Spaces, 1948-1960. *Alternatives* 25: 467-489.

_____ (2003) Making Food Count: Expert Knowledge and Global Technologies of Government. *Canadian Review of Sociology and Anthropology*. 40(4): 441-462.

Isin, E. (2002) *Being Political*. Minneapolis: University of Minnesota Press.

Keenleyside, H. (1952) Developing the World's Resources: Technical Resources. *1951 Annual Review of United Nations Affairs*. New York: Dept. of Public Information of the UN in cooperation with New York University.

Latour, B. (1986) Visualization and Cognition: Thinking with Eyes and Hands. *Knowledge and Society* 6:1-40.

_____ (1987*) Science in Action*. Cambridge: Harvard University Press.

Leys, C. (2001) *Market-Driven Politics*. London: Verso.

Luke, T. W. (1990*) Screens of Power: Ideology, Domination, and Resistance in Information Society*. Urbana: University of Illinois Press.

Lupton, D. (1999*) Risk*. London: Routledge.

Luscombe, D.T. and M. Pereira (1957) *Informe al Gobierno de Ecuador sobre Colonizacion*. Rome: FAO.

May, C. (2002) *The Information Society: A Sceptical View*. Cambridge: Polity.

Phillips, L. & S. Ilcan (2000) Domesticating Spaces in Transition: Politics and Practices in the Gender and Development Literature, 1970-99. *Anthropologica* XLII (2): 205-216.

_____ (2003) A World Free From Hunger: Global Imagination and Governance in the Age of Scientific Management. *Sociologia Ruralis* 43(4): 434-453.

Rose, N. (1994) Expertise and the Government of Conduct. Studies in Law, *Politics and Society* 14: 359-397.

_____ (1999) *Powers of Freedom: Reframing Political Thought*. Cambridge: Cambridge University Press.

_____ (2000) Government and Control. Pp 183-208 in *Criminology and Social Theory*, edited by D. Garland and R. Sparks. Oxford: Oxford University Press.

Sassen, S. (1991) *The Global City: New York, London, Tokyo*. Princeton, N.J.: Princeton University Press.

_____ (1999) Cracked Casings: Notes Toward an Analytics for Studying Transnational Processes. Pp 134-145 in *Sociology for the Twenty-first Century: Continuities and Cutting Edges*, edited by J. Abu-Lughod. Chicago and London: University of Chicago Press.

Shields, R., S. Ilcan, D. O'Connor, & E. Taborsky (2002) The Impact of a Knowledge-based Economy on Work in the Public Service: The 'Virtual Organization of Expertise and Knowledge. Pp 143-180 in *Alliances, Cooperative Ventures and the Role of Government in the Knowledge Based Economy*, edited by M. Nakamura. Vancouver, Centre for Japanese Research: University of British Columbia.

Smith, L. (1999) Can FAO's Measure of Chronic Undernourishment be Strengthened? *Food Policy* 23 (5): 425-445.

Sukhatme, P. V. (1960) The World's Future Needs in Food Supplies. *FAO Pamphlet* 38:63 (100).

Svedberg, P. (1999) 841 Million Undernourished? *World Development* 27(12): 2081-2098.

UN (United Nations) (1953) Yearbook of the United Nations, 1952. New York: Columbia University Press.

\_\_\_\_\_ (1955) International Survey of Programmes of Social Development. Social Commission, Tenth Session, Item 3 of provisional agenda, E/CN.5/301.

\_\_\_\_\_ (1959) Population Commission. Report of the Tenth Session. February 9-20. *Economic and Social Council Official Record: Twenty-seventh Session*. Geneva.

\_\_\_\_\_ (1980) Yearbook of the United Nations, 1955. New York: Columbia University Press.

van der Ploeg, J. D. (1993) Potatoes and Knowledge. Pp. 209-227 in *An Anthropological Critique of Development*, edited by M. Hobart. New York & London: Routledge.

Webster, F. (1995) *Theories of the Information Society*. London and New York: Routledge.

Winseck, D. (2002) Illusions of Perfect Information and Fantasies of Control in the Information Society. Pp 33-55 in *Citizenship and Participation in the Information Age*, edited by M. Pendakur and R. Harris. Aurora: Garamond.

WHO (World Health Organization) (1998) Comparative Analysis of Nutrition Polices. *Second Analysis of Nutrition Policies*. WHO: Geneva.

HERVÉ HANNIN*, JEAN-MARIE CODRON†, SOPHIE THOYER‡

# 4. THE INTERNATIONAL OFFICE OF VINE AND WINE (OIV) AND THE WORLD TRADE ORGANIZATION (WTO):

*Standardization Issues In The Wine Sector*[§]

The end of the Uruguay Round and the creation of the World Trade Organization (WTO) marked a turning point in the development of world trade. The Marrakech Agreements, in particular the Sanitary and Phyto-sanitary (SPS) and the Technical Barriers to Trade (TBT) Agreements, established rules for controlling the proliferation of non-tariff barriers that were once thought to be used for protectionist reasons.

The creation of international standards[1] is a slow and controversial process, and one which most often ends with the multiplication and diversification of existing standards. Traditionally, standards in the food sector largely applied to the composition (shape, color, etc.) of the final product and/or to health features (pesticide residues, etc.). However, in the last few years, process (or production) standards have been increasingly used (especially when a final product analysis is too expensive or not very discriminating) in order to include environmental concerns or some unique aspect of particular products.

In this constantly evolving situation, the wine sector, organized 75 years ago under the auspices of the International Office of Vine and Wine (*Office International de la Vigne et du Vin,* OIV), is unique in the food sector and could logically serve as a model for considering issues in the standardization of food production, trade and distribution activities.

The objective of this chapter is to analyze the relationship between WTO and OIV as two completely different international standard setting organizations in terms of their history, areas of competence and political legitimacy. First, we discuss traditional standards setting in the wine sector with an emphasis on the uniqueness of this process in the food sector. Second, we examine the ways in which market

---

* Dr. Hervé Hannin, Senior Researcher , Ecole Nationale Supérieure d'Agronomie in Montpellier, France.
† Jean-Marie Codron, Senior Researcher at the National Institute of Agronomic Research (INRA) in Montpellier, France.
‡ Dr. Sophie Thoyer, Senior Lecturer, Ecole Nationale Supérieure d'Agronomie in Montpellier, France, UMR Lameta.
§ This chapter is translated and updated from the original publication in French as "L'Office international de la vigne et du vin et l'Organisation mondiale du commerce: Les enjeux de la normalisation dans le secteur viti-vinicole" *Cahiers d'économie et sociologie rurales,* No. 55-56, (Spring and Summer 2000): 111-138.

*J. Bingen and L. Busch, (eds.), Agricultural Standards: The Shape of the Global Food and Fiber System,* 73-92. © *2006 Springer. Printed in the Netherlands.*

forces and the strategies of various sectoral and political actors currently threaten the stability of the OIV. Finally, we consider the OIV in the broader context of international standardization.

## 1. THE PROCESS OF STANDARDIZATION IN THE WINE SECTOR

The OIV is an intergovernmental organization designed to create standards for the development of international trade in wine by focusing on the suppression of fraud, the protection of names (appellations) of origin, the guarantee of authenticity, and the harmonization of methods of analysis. OIV also seeks to promote and distribute scientific studies addressing the beneficial effects of wine consumption (notably to counter the prohibition policies like that practiced by the United States in the 1920s).

Historically, the first efforts at standardization in the food sector were principally guided by food safety preoccupations. That was the case, for example, with the French anti-fraud law of 1905. Since that time, steps toward standardization in the wine sub-sector have diversified rapidly and have been aimed at protecting the cultural heritage, local skill, and traditional regions of production.

The process of standardization by OIV has led to a substantial number of resolutions (recommendations to member governments) to protect the interests of both producers and consumers. There are three major types of standards worked out by the OIV: standards on product identity, standards of information for the consumer, and standards for denominations of origin. "Identity" standards concern the definition and the quality of the product "wine" (NPV), the process of production (NPP) and the methods of analysis (NMA).[2] Consumer information standards are detailed in the International Standard for Labeling Wines and Spirits. The standards that define and protect the denominations of origin are contained in the 1992 OIV resolution on "Recognized Appellations of Origin" and "Recognized Geographical Designations."

Standards can play a double edged economic role. If they permit a considerable reduction of transaction costs by homogenizing products and production practices and by providing greater transparency and reliability of information, they can also sometimes be used strategically as barriers to market entry that benefit existing producers and thereby deter innovation and differentiation, and hinder competition and trade (Reardon, Codron et al. 1999). Thus, standards can create potentially significant economic stakes. As a result, the process of developing standards whether voluntary or through government decree, often gives rise to complicated sets of negotiations (Sylvander 1996).

In order to better analyze the dynamics of standards development and institutionalization, we use a policy grid developed by political scientists (Finnemore and Sikkink 1998). We identify three key phases in the development of standards: an emerging phase, which is most often carried out by private initiatives; a phase of adoption and diffusion; and, an institutionalization phase in which private or governmental rules are established. A standard may also be challenged and as a result, enter a phase of decline as its legitimacy is questioned or it faces competition from new, emerging standards. For each of these phases[3] we study the strategies of the dominant actors by assessing their interests and their influence and by describing the manner in which they defend the legitimacy of their actions.

*1.1    An Early Standardization Effort: The Interests and Roles of the Actors in the Emergence of Standards for Wine.*

The Agreement of 1924, which officially created the OIV, was the result of a unique and exceptionally long process that was started thirty years earlier with the Madrid Convention of 1891. The economic interests at stake help explain this process: the eight countries to the Agreement,[4] each of which were leaders in the international wine trade, had endured an unprecedented phylloxera crisis at the beginning of the century. Following this crisis, which profoundly destabilized the sector, and in the face of stagnating demand for wine, wine production and marketing entered an anarchic period characterized by fraudulent production practices. Given the highly specialized nature of most production, exchange rate instability and the threat of overproduction were equally alarming and difficult to handle. Each provided little room for maneuver to wine growers.

In France, growers of "label of origin" wines were especially hard hit as they saw their reputations threatened and incomes eroded by competition from imported musts and fraudulent wines in a market dominated by the wine traders. The growers reacted by advocating the establishment of a specific organization to control and protect the high quality wine sector. They succeeded in defending their corporatist interests by obtaining the creation of a French guaranteed label of origin (*appellations d'origine contrôlée*, AOC) in 1935. This AOC regulation was instrumental in securing rents to existing producers by reinforcing supply control, by creating higher barriers to entry of new producers and by artificially maintaining product scarcity (Boulet and Bartoli 1995). On the other hand, the same producers also lobbied for a liberalized international wine market based on low taxes and tariffs.

By the same token, the French growers of AOC wine were also actively involved in creating the OIV. In this regard, it is not insignificant to observe that the OIV headquarters office is in Paris, that the French have always led it, and that Edouard Barthe, the first president of the OIV, was also one of the leading proponents of the French debate on the creation of labels of origin in 1919. France played an uncontested leadership role in the development of OIV's initial objectives, its orientation and its operations. Indeed, French growers were concerned that the restrictions they were imposing on themselves would also be binding on their foreign competitors. The position defended by the French related mainly to two main priority areas: the definition of wine and the label of origin. In fact, it is often said that "the international orientation of OIV's is essentially an extension of the French conception of viticulture and of wine" (Boulet and Bartoli 1995). However, France understood that the defense of its interests could only be achieved through a collective legitimization of the proposed OIV standards. Many of its concerns were shared by other countries, thereby enabling France to establish favorable and effective alliances. The persistence of the countries in these negotiations testifies to the common need for an international body to fight (real or potential) fraud and to offer a means for preventing bilateral disputes between countries. The legitimization of the objectives defended by leading countries at the OIV was also facilitated by their success in putting together a set of federating principles that recognized the interests of all producer countries and seeded the standardization process.

## 1.2    The Justification of this Early Effort

OIV standards are based on some fundamental principles that are still relevant today despite changing economic and institutional conditions.

First, there was a widely shared assumption that the wine sector embodied distinguishing characteristics. It justified the strengthening of the OIV even after the creation of the UN Food and Agriculture Organization (FAO) in 1948. The OIV obtained an agreement with the FAO stipulating that the "FAO would recognize and respect the role and responsibilities of the OIV as the intergovernmental organization specialized in the wine sector." Based on this agreement, a joint FAO-OIV secretariat is responsible for compiling statistics and information regarding the wine sector and for organizing scientific exchanges and meetings.

Second, there was an early interest in maintaining a strict definition of what was allowed to be labelled "wine" and including a cultural dimension. As defined by the OIV in 1928, wine is "the beverage that results directly from the complete or partial alcoholic fermentation of fresh pressed or unpressed grapes or grape must." This definition specifically excludes any alcoholic products from raisins or other fruits and the use of artificial flavours. The definition also excludes any type of wine reconstituted with water from distilled or frozen concentrated juices. These strict conditions ensured that a close relationship would be maintained between the location of grape-growing and the location of wine-making.

Third, it was important to consider and incorporate the cultural dimension of wine by protecting the label of origin which is based for the OIV on both the natural and human elements responsible for defining the specificity of a particular wine.

Fourth, there was a continuing concern with food safety. Historically, the large wine growing countries were confronted with the problem of fraudulent and unacceptable practices. As a result, the OIV adopted a set of strict food safety standards that have evolved as testing procedures have become more accurate. For example, over a period of 20 years, the OIV has progressively reduced the maximum allowed levels of lead from 600 to 200 micrograms per liter, even though consumers have not paid particular attention to this issue.

These principles help to define a relatively novel process of standardization that seeks harmonization without uniformity. Based on a concern with protecting diversity among products, the OIV standards focus on the importance of production location and the wine-making process. Consequently, the standards deal with "good practices," traceability and other features related to characteristics of the process of making wine, and not at standardizing or ranking wine as a product. Another consequence, and illustration of the novelty of these standards, is the confirmation of a tight link between grower and consumer interests. This historical bond helps to justify the strict organization of the sub-sector and the technical barriers to entry.

In summary, the OIV process of standardization, and the principles upon which it is based, have allowed it to be recognized as a legitimate representative for both grower and consumer interests. In addition, the operating rules of the OIV discourage free-riding and flavour the development of stable compromises even for potentially conflictual issues.

## 1.3    The Adoption and Institutionalization of Standardization Rules

OIV decision-making and operations are characterized by: (i) the preponderant role of expertise; (ii) collective decision making by voting procedures involving all members; (iii) minimal control and enforcement means; and (iv) a balance of power which was for a very long time flavourable to French interests.

### 1.3.1    Expertise

All international resolutions are prepared by groups of specialists, chosen by OIV members for their scientific competency, in meetings closed even to OIV members. By limiting these posts to scientists and experts, the member governments seek to protect themselves from lobbying by business groups. Nevertheless, while most countries usually appoint government experts, the most economically liberal countries have also selected experts from the private sector, thus raising doubts about the objectivity of the decisions taken.

### 1.3.2    Collective Decision-Making

All resolutions are voted upon during the annual General Assembly, by governmental representatives. This facilitates the transposition of the decisions into the national regulatory systems. Each member country has a different voting weight which is negotiated upon joining the OIV on the basis of the membership contribution paid by the country. During the first 75 years of OIV operations, one of the major concerns of the member governments was how to enlarge membership and how to persuade consumer nations to participate. In recent years, this decision-making system has been subject to two major criticisms. First, it is not consistent with the one country – one vote decision-making rule of the United Nations. Second, the process can be seen as unduly favouring the interests of producer countries, which are more numerous within the OIV and pay the highest membership fees, therefore accumulating majority voting power.

### 1.3.3  Essentially Non-Existent Means of Control or Enforcement

The OIV does not have any means of enforcement. By statute, the OIV can only submit proposals to the member countries, which are assumed to be capable of implementing approved decisions. In fact, the OIV promotes dialogue between specialists and member governments and lacks any kind of dispute resolution mechanism similar to the WTO dispute settlement body. In the absence of such a mechanism, member countries which did not flavour a particular OIV resolution could either engage in retaliatory practices or indefinitely delay integration of the resolution into national policy. In the majority of instances, however, the OIV process is effective as member governments either directly integrate resolutions into national policy or law, or indirectly implement the resolutions through bilateral and multilateral commercial agreements.[5]

Enforcement is often a delicate issue. OIV's only means for managing enforcement is to minimize the likelihood of conflict among member countries. Consequently, the OIV has always sought to negotiate compromises that are acceptable by all members, instead of imposing decisions upon a discontented minority that might seek not to comply.

### 1.3.4  An Equilibrium in Favour of French Interests

It might be thought that the role of European interests, and in particular, French interests, in the OIV might be a source of destabilization and power imbalance within the OIV. Europe produces two-thirds of the world's wine and the European members of OIV seek to assure that OIV standards are compatible with European processes and regulations. It is equally true that French government positions in the OIV, even in the absence of an explicit pro-active OIV policy, are viewed favorably among the international representatives to the OIV. Many have received advanced degrees in agronomy or wine making from French institutions of higher education, and speak French, the international language of wine (cf. Arrangement of 1924). In this leadership position, France has historically exhibited a certain generosity in hosting the site for the OIV headquarters in Paris, foregoing the voting privileges associated with its significant membership contribution, and inviting other governments to follow its example in the name of the broader interests of the sector. But the tacit consensus that has traditionally recognized both the legitimacy of France and other European countries in representing the best interests of the wine sector has diminished in recent years.

In conclusion, the OIV has adopted a relatively novel sectoral model of standardization, oriented initially toward defending the interests of producer countries, but which has widened its alliance to include primarily consumer countries by focusing on quality instead of quantity concerns. OIV standards, based principally on a product's origin, its typicity and its quality have inspired other sectors to adopt comparable rules even if they have not achieved similar level of organization and institutionalization. The OIV strategy has been to favour the process of building common standards rather than taking the route of mutual recognition of national practices. However, evolving world market conditions and international institutional constraints have changed the balance of power within the OIV and oblige this organization to adopt a different strategy.

## 2. CHANGES WITHIN THE WINE SECTOR

The increasing market power of new producing countries, the rapidly evolving consumer demand for higher quality, and the uptake of technological innovations have profoundly altered the global wine market and have created new challenges to which the OIV must respond.

### 2.1 Market Changes

For several decades, the unchanging characteristics of the wine market structure were: (i) Europe's considerable share of the market, representing more than two thirds of world production, despite a drastic policy to control supply in order to maintain market stability; (ii) traditionally, a very high (80%-90%) proportion of wine was consumed in the country of origin; and (iii) a decline in consumption in traditionally high demand countries.[6] Since 1995, these long term trends are changing. About 30% of wine is now consumed outside the country of production. "New producing countries," such as Australia and South Africa, strategically have chosen to increase production for their traditional markets (United Kingdom) and for new markets, such as Japan. For example, since 1995 Australian production has increased about 12% per year and in 1998 exceeded seven million tons.

Second, there is a marked change in the demand for certain types of wine. In the traditional consumer countries, the demand is for higher quality wines instead of table wines. For example, in France the most sought after wines now have either a label of origin (AOC) or an indication of regional origin (*indication géographique*; *vins de pays*). On the other hand, world demand is shifting towards more varietal wines,[7] with a limited number of varieties in very high demand: 12.7 million hectoliters in 1998 compared to 4.2 million hectoliters in 1990. The world market demand for quality wine is also changing: in 1998, the market was composed of 20% of varietal wines, 40% label of origin wines and only 40% undifferentiated wines.

Finally, wine production in many of the newer producer countries is often characterized by controversial technological innovations. Certain innovations are considered a potential source of distortion in competition, and the OIV is regularly called upon to regulate these new production processes. Even the use of oak chips or wood extracts, instead of the traditional maturing in barrel process, has given rise to considerable controversy and has not been fully addressed yet in the OIV regulation. It can be expected that the use of genetically modified grape varieties will create another set of challenges for the OIV. More generally, many changes arising from laboratory work, especially in the use of artificial flavour illustrates the fragility of the sector with respect to technological innovations. Only well-defined and widely accepted standards can guarantee a continued production based on traditional growing and wine making practices.

## 2.2    The Expansion of the OIV Membership and Rising Internal Conflicts:
### A Typology of Interests

Changes in the world market have redefined the competition patterns and called into question many of the previously accepted conditions, at a time when OIV has had to bring in new members and accommodate their interests while balancing the already agreed upon compromises.

As of today the OIV has 45 member countries representing 94% of world wine production and consumption. From a historical perspective, this expansion has occurred in three major stages: (1) a phase of progressive growth that included all countries traditionally represented in both the major areas of wine production and consumption; (2) a phase during which "New World" countries (USA, Australia, Chile, etc.), many of which had been producing wine for years, became members, representing new oenological practices and significant volumes of wine to trade on the world market; and (3) a more recent phase of membership by countries, such as those of Scandinavia, that exclusively represent consumer interests.

As expected, membership is limited to those recognizing OIV standards. For example, China does not recognize the definition of wine (as coming exclusively from grapes) and therefore cannot become a full member of OIV. It should be noted, however, that the US and Australia became members without recognizing the label of origin definition. The acceptance of new members, and especially the "New World" producer countries, has created internal changes in the OIV, including challenges to its basic principles. In addition, some long accepted OIV standards have recently become the focus of new negotiations that have revealed the very different concerns among members. These concerns range from issues regarding the structure of production and the national markets to those concerning the mobilization of the main stakeholders and the defense of their interests within the OIV.

The *professionals* – wine producers and traders – generally favour more open markets through lower tariff and non-tariff barriers. They are aware that the international wine trade is growing after many stagnant decades and that the demand for quality wine is increasing. Thus, producers are inclined to seek a softening of standards that would allow them to increase their production and sales. But they are also aware that the quality standards defended by the OIV help to preserve their profitable market by partially sheltering them from unfair competition.

In the *traditional producer countries* wine growers do not have a federated organization nor were they able to adopt a common lobbying strategy. This weakens them in defending their interests. In general, they have few representatives in the official delegations of experts and are poorly prepared for OIV meetings. Thus, the highly regionalized policies in Italy or the heterogeneous farm trade unions in France make the development of any sort of coordinated structure or negotiating position, especially in response to governmental positions, quite difficult. Portugal is a notable exception to this situation, with its national OIV Committee composed of experts, government representatives and producers.

Besides the historically significant collective efforts to recognize traditional European practices, intra-European divergent positions (over enrichment, for example) often win out over a truly common strategy. This weakness of the European Union is reinforced by the absence of single representative who would be authorized to speak in the name of the member states of the European Union.

From a strategic perspective, the *"New World" countries* favour the interests of companies and consumers as well as relying upon market forces. But this strategy has never excluded an interest in achieving a global consensus. For example, rather than refusing to participate in the OIV, they have chosen to negotiate exceptions when they join and thereby seek compromise within the OIV structure.[8]

Since the 1980s, the "New World" countries have sometimes been developing winemaking practices that are not traditional in Europe and demanding more flexibility in the level of the standards involved. Such demands often are not without their own contradictions, notably on the part of producers. In order to develop and make profitable recent investments,[9] the latter are often led to develop standards of quality that essentially follow the basic principles of the OIV. Thus, among these newer members, one sees efforts by some representatives to reject the historical culture of the OIV, while others seek to reinforce this culture.

From an organizational perspective, these countries are well prepared for their participation in international negotiations. They collaborate closely with key economic actors in the sector especially in nominating and supporting the participation of experts. However, certain companies are so large that they can afford to finance work that is in the general interest and send researchers to the OIV, even while promoting their own interests against those of national and international competitors. This is especially the case with Gallo (representing 30% of the US market) which has successfully launched a "Peach Chardonnay." This initiative "outside OIV standards" is not accepted even by many US professionals, and consequently the coherence of the delegation has been threatened and its legitimacy may be called into question.

*For the exclusively consumer countries* that have recently joined the OIV, their principal concern involves understanding the basis of wine standards and integrating them into their own national food quality standards. While they are less directly concerned with the debates on labels of origin or approved production techniques, their concerns have strengthened the credibility of OIV with respect to consumer protection. Nevertheless, these countries (Belgium, Denmark, Finland, The Netherlands, The United Kingdom, and Sweden) represent only 15% of the member governments in the OIV.

In conclusion, the rapid increase in OIV membership is an inevitable consequence of the growth of the international wine market. As a result, there is a growing internal movement that challenges many of the strategic choices made by the OIV. But the debates are far from clear and they place OIV in a delicate situation. On the one hand the new producer countries accuse it of defending overly strict regulations, while the traditional producers argue that it has become too lax, even as they feel free to follow practices that they would not allow for others. Thus, the European Union sometimes criticizes the foreign competition in varietal wines and calls for stricter regulations, but at the same time is heavily invested in marketing varietals.

The central question is whether the OIV is bound to disappear or, on the contrary, whether it is simply undergoing the kind of growing pains experienced by any expanding organization. In part, the answer is to be found in the development of international trade regulations which can be seen as an alternative to the model supported by the OIV.

## 3. THE EVOLUTION OF INTERNATIONAL REGULATIONS: THE OIV AT THE CENTER OF AN INTERNATIONAL SYSTEM OF STANDARDS

Since 1947, the General Agreement on Tariffs and Trade (GATT) has provided the organizational framework for the progressive liberalization of world trade. But the creation of the WTO in 1994 marked a significant turning point by providing a means for regulating international trade disputes. The WTO recognized also that trade must be based on recognized standards and on organizations capable of defining such standards.

### 3.1     The Marrakech Agreements

Four agreements signed in Marrakech are of direct relevance to the wine sector: The Trade-Related Aspects of International Property Rights (TRIPS) agreement, the Agreement on the Application of Sanitary and Phyto-sanitary Measures (SPS), the Agreement on Technical Barriers to Trade (TBT), and finally the Agreement on Rules of Origin. These agreements marked the beginning of a new and complex set of organizing principles among all the actors involved in the wine sector. In effect, many of the stipulations in the Marrakech agreements can be seen to conflict with the already established OIV standards. Consequently, it is important to identify a hierarchy between the OIV and WTO standards, or at least be able to establish a means of information exchange and decision-making between these two bodies.

The WTO recognizes the standards established by "qualified international organizations". The OIV's request for direct and total recognition by the WTO has not been approved yet. It places the OIV in the uncomfortable position of wondering how to make the best use of its 75 years of work related to scientifically based standards, even though recognition by the WTO would not guarantee or accommodate all OIV standards. Conversely, in a number of instances, recognition by specialized committees in the WTO could be sufficient.

With respect to TRIPS, the World Intellectual Property Organization (WIPO) signed a cooperation agreement with the WTO on global rules regarding labels of origin (AOC) and regional names (*indications géographiques*). Consequently, while the OIV has spent considerable time on seeking to harmonize the interpretation of these two norms across country members, it finds itself as a third tier actor below the

WTO and WIPO on these issues as a result of an old agreement stipulating OIV's observer status in the WIPO.

Concerning the SPS agreement, the FAO-WHO (Food and Agriculture Organization – World Health Organization) Codex Alimentarius is the recognized standard-setting body for food safety. With observer status at the Codex, the OIV holds another third tier position since the recognition of the Codex depends upon the WTO SPS Committee.

The TBT Agreement seeks to assure that technical regulations do not create unnecessary barriers to trade. National bodies are expected to use international standards, "except when such international standards or relevant parts would be an ineffective or inappropriate means for the fulfillment of the legitimate objectives pursued, for instance because of fundamental climatic or geographical factors or fundamental technical problems."[10]

OIV's extensive experience in setting technical standards (the definition of the wine, oenological practices, labeling) certainly could make it the international standards reference in the wine sector. But the relationship of the OIV to the WTO continues to be both indirect and very fragile.

### 3.2   The Harmonization of OIV and WTO Standards

The weak standing of the OIV within the framework of the WTO raises the possibility that trade decisions concerning the wine sector might be contrary to the principles upon which the OIV consensus has been built and sustained, thereby disrupting the coherence of OIV as well as generating significant sectoral change. In order to identify these potential threats and to clarify the prospects for harmonizing WTO and OIV standards, this section examines the process and progress of standardization in the WTO and the Codex, as well as the internal contradictions and gaps with regard to OIV concerns. It focuses on standards related to food safety, the definition of a product, and regional names (*indications géographiques*).

### 3.2.1   The Harmonization of Sanitary Rules

The prospects for harmonizing food safety standards relative to wine are unclear and ambiguous. It is debatable whether the Codex offers any hope of including OIV concerns. For example, some initiatives appear to have been made either in ignorance of, or contrary to, OIV principles. In July 1999 the Codex proposed to consider the use of sweeteners (i.e., Aspartame) in wine making, although it is banned by OIV rules, while simultaneously referring systematically to OIV norms for all discussions concerning wine. This willingness to collaborate has also been expressed by the WTO Committee on Sanitary and Phyto-sanitary Measures which envisages jointly established standards "with the qualified international organizations," thereby offering an opportunity for closer collaboration with the OIV.

However, given the current discussions within the Codex, reconciliation appears quite fragile. According to Jean-Luc Angot, former head of the French Codex office, there are two opposing groups (Bureau, Gozlan, and Doussin 1999). One group argues that Codex should provide scientific information related to health issues that can be used by WTO committees; another group, led by the European Union, argues that Codex should rely on scientific information, but also consider others factors such as consumer perception and acceptability of risks, environmental protection, and safeguarding economic and social well-being. In order to accommodate these latter concerns, the "scientific basis" for decisions has been broadened to include not only technological sciences but also economics (cost/benefit calculations) and the social sciences (opinion surveys, etc). However, judgments based on "pure and hard" science can also be questioned. For example, Salter (1998)), Powell (1997), and Hillman (1997), all provide evidence of the ways in which "mandated" or "negotiated" science operates within boundaries that are often defined by non-scientific criteria.

These debates over principles concern three significant areas of concern: the criteria used for Codex to identify the food products which should be under its regulation; the principles used for the evaluation of risk ("hard" science versus "soft" science) and methods of risk management (product or process standards; compulsory standards versus voluntary agreements). These debates relate also to the definition of traditional products and to the concepts of typicity (*typicité*) or *terroir*. Therefore, they are of concern to both the Codex, which rules on questions of product definition and of labeling, and to the OIV as the following examples illustrate.

Codex criteria for products. Acceptance criteria are limited only to health hazards, it is envisioned that practices such as the use of distilled water to dilute wine, or even the use of artificial flavors be permitted by Codex. While OIV standards prohibit the use of processes that would "denature the product," even though they do not pose a health risk, such practices could be approved if Codex stipulated that only human health criteria should be applied.

Risk evaluation. A scientific assessment of the harmfulness of wine, independent of its cultural and social dimension, could lead to a prohibition of wine in international trade. Indeed, despite medical studies showing the benefits of moderate wine consumption, popularized in the media as the "French paradox" and the "Mediterranean diet," wine unquestionably contains alcohol, which is defined by WHO as a "psycho-active drug" (Tinlot 1999).

Risk management. There are two preferred methods or approaches to risk management. One approach uses voluntary agreements and product standards while another favors regulatory methods and process standards. English-speaking countries tend to prefer the first approach, while the second is favored in "Latin" countries. The contrast between these two approaches is especially clear in dealing with pathogens.[11] With respect to residues or additives, where it is more appropriate to use a product instead of a process standard, differences arise between countries like the US which uses "negative lists" (stipulating what is forbidden) and those like France and the European Union that use "positive lists" (those indicating what is allowed). A negative list approach poses fewer constraints on producers, but thereby also uses criteria that require expensive and often contested research.

### 3.2.2 The Harmonization of Product Standards

Identity or product definition standards were developed within the framework of national regulations. While such standards usually are appropriate for basic, mass market products, market segmentation and product differentiation complicate the management of such national standards. Current trends in international marketing as well as the importance of respecting cultural diversity make it difficult to harmonize nationally based standards. The European Union, which considered the harmonization of national standards across country members in the seventies, only managed to standardize ten products and then decided to give up. Currently, standards of identity have fallen into disarray (Padberg and Kaufman 1994).[12]

Based on the work of the OIV, wine is one of the few products with an international standard of identity. However, although it has been defined for some time, the standard must now be reconciled with more specialized standards developed in the context of horizontal, multi-product global marketing. Some characteristics (sometimes referred to as "orphans") are not permitted on the grounds that they represent a barrier to international trade. This is based on the WTO position that with the exception of intellectual property, food safety, or environmental concerns, adequate labeling is sufficient to inform consumers and thereby ensure trade honesty.

In ascending order of importance, the "orphaned" regulatory features of wine are: (i) the prohibition of some oenological practices such as the use of oak chips; (ii) requirements concerning the geographic origin of grapes (e.g., the prohibition against importing concentrated must for table or local wine) (iii) the requirement to use only fresh grapes for making wine (other types of wine could include wine from raisins, cut peaches, or with artificial flavors).

There are real threats to maintaining these identity regulations. The first arises from efforts to change oenological practices by allowing the use of oak chips, a practice that is less expensive, than using oak barrels, but perhaps equally effective. Some countries in the European Union have already started to experiment with this practice. The OIV has not yet adopted definitive recommendations on this subject, and appears to prefer concentrating its efforts on more serious identity threats such as: the importation of must concentrate from countries that have a great potential for producing grapes but have limited capacity to produce good quality wine (Eastern Europe, the Cairns group; and, efforts by some large national brand name companies, in traditional wine producing countries as well as elsewhere, that seek to capitalize upon their name rather than operating according to collective rules. The WTO is using all of its weight to permit imported musts. The European Union put this problem on the agenda for the 1999 meeting in Berlin, and confirmed its adhesion to a ban on imported musts, subject to compatibility with WTO principles.

The threat of losing the agreed upon and standardized definition of wine to a multiplicity of definitions is real. It is being pushed along by both abuses and fraudulent behavior even in traditional wine producing countries. Without doubt this could have strong implications for the organization of the wine sector and for consumer behavior. The product features defended by the OIV maintain a strong cultural identity that can be regarded as a public good. But in the absence of a collective agreement to protect this identity, there is a fear that it will be lost as the sector becomes more industrialized.

In conclusion, any definition of wine that is more liberal than that of the OIV could appear to encourage the industrialization of the wine sector. It would risk distorting the nature of the product by authorizing industrial growing and oenological practices, as well as the use of synthetic chemical and biological products. This could penalize both producers and consumers. Producers could find that their traditional practices, their vines, and the significance of their geographic location would be devalued by the industrialized process encouraged by a more liberal definition. Only a standardized product, without personality, would be available to consumers. It is easy to imagine the negative ecological, economic and social impact of abandoning wine production, particularly in those areas where the poor soils do not support other crops.

Confronted by these various threats, and in the absence of an international authority charged with standardizing these identity characteristics, the member governments and the OIV continue to be the best defense against the commercial and individualized strategies of brand names that disregard the importance of preserving the public good represented by the cultural identity of wine.

### 3.2.3    The Difficult Harmonization of Standards for Labels of Origin

A critical issue raised by the use of geographic indications (*indications géographiques*) in the wine sub-sector arises in the context of the agreement on intellectual property rights (TRIPS). In fact, this agreement provides special protection for geographic labels, thereby constituting a kind of specific recognition by the WTO of the distinctness of the wine sector.

The agreement treats geographic indication labels separately from brand names. It broadens the scope of the agreement beyond the 1958 Lisbon agreement on multiple products, but without including the distinction between labels of origin and natural and human factors allowed by Brussels in 1992 for products other than wine, with the creation of the Protected Designations of Origin, PDO, *Appellations d'Origine Protégée, AOP*) and Protected Geographical Indications, PGI, *Indications Géographiques Protégées, IGP*) pursuant to Article 17 of Regulation (EEC) No 2081/92.

The TRIPS agreement is also weaker than the Lisbon agreement with respect to implementation and control, and there is significant opposition to this point. The more market oriented countries that seem to be favored by the WTO desire a simple list with clearly stated consumer information that poses no constraints on trade. On the other side, countries such as those of the European Union favour a more restrictive system with categories that are more detailed than providing indications of source, referring to both natural and human factors.

In the absence of a clear and agreed upon rule, current efforts to bypass agreements are usually the subject of bilateral discussions, such as those between the European Union and certain countries, Hungary or Australia for example. The use of a review panel is possible, but the procedure for showing proof of damage is expensive and complex, and until now the OIV has not taken any action within the framework of TRIPS to address such problems. But behind this question of "enforcement," lies the more fundamental issue of the difference between the reliance upon a brand name and a reliance upon the concept of *terroir* (Peri and Gaeta 1999; Valceschini 1999).

Those who rely upon brand names, such as the United States and the large multinational companies, are critical of any benefits claimed by the use of labels of origin and generally refuse *a priori* to accept any claims of superior quality of taste associated with a label of origin. Furthermore, attention is drawn to the costs of monitoring labels of origin and the importance of process standards. In response, they argue that brand names represent responsible production methods and responsiveness to consumer demand. While denying that it represents a trade barrier, those who represent this position also defend the use of generic or semi-generic products on the grounds that they are solidly anchored in local consumption habits.

Those who rely on the concept of *terroir,* in particular European Union members, emphasize the advantages of such a system for consumers (respect of local traditions and diversity of tastes, consumer education, etc.), and for wine production systems that provide support for effective small-scale farming and local communities and a means to maintain traditional knowledge in the face of progress. They fear that given the inability of companies to protect the cultural identity of wine as a public good, an absence of protection and reliance upon brand names will lead to a worldwide decline in the overall quality of wine.

Despite the significant differences between these two approaches, the prospects for harmonization are not completely precluded. It seems however that the debate might be resolved in favour of the concept of *terroir*. The use of brand names, although widely adopted, appears to be less effective in the wine sector due to its characteristics (e.g., the level of education and "attachment" of consumers, an atomized supply, highly segmented markets, the costs of institutional change, etc). The economic and historical significance of *terroir* has led most new producer countries, in accordance with the law of increasing returns for innovation adoption, to choose this "convention" as a means to differentiate their product. In part this response follows that seen with other food products that are also associated with strong cultural identities, such as cheese and olive oil (Ruffleux and Valceschini 1996). It is also supported by many developing countries, as a result of EU technical assistance programs, and as a means for valuing and developing their natural and cultural local resources.

Without a doubt, many of the advantages of labels of origin must still be defended and the OIV spends considerable effort developing such arguments. It is seeking to demonstrate that labels of origin[13]: (i) establish a formal link between natural factors and distinctness of the product; (ii) decrease the consumer risk by providing reliable information; and, (iii) prove that the positive "externalities" outweigh the negative.

An examination of the various fields of standardization shows considerable uncertainty with respect to the future of wine. Basic problems, such as accounting for natural and human factors in the statements of origin, the justification used, and the use of science to support policy decisions, currently debated by the WTO and Codex, are equally significant for the OIV and the future of the wine sector.

Curiously, the OIV is not directly associated with these debates, and its marginal role raises questions about the reasons for this situation. Does this represent a strategic maneuver by liberal market countries that do not agree with OIV standards, or is it the result of OIV's limited operating and collective capacity for action? If this is the case, it is appropriate to examine the impact of operating regulations that OIV adopted in 2000.

## 3.3    Gaining Recognition for Standards: The OIV Approach

Both the GATT and WTO negotiations have led to the emergence of a system of standards based on an industrial model and supported by many professionals in the wine sector and in the new producer countries. The implementation of the Marrakech agreements, and launching of the Doha Development Round in November 2001 further weakened OIV rules.[14]

To strengthen its legitimacy within the international system of standards, the OIV chose to reform many of its operating rules and regulations to conform more closely to those of other international bodies. For example, the role of "political" delegates, whose only role was to vote in the OIV General Assembly, was criticized as early as 1990 as inadequate and disconnected from the work of the scientific experts. Since 1993, these political representatives participate at several stages. Resolutions are drafted through a final vote which is consistent with other international organizations that use at least two rounds of discussions between government representatives and scientific experts before putting resolutions to a vote. Moreover, the OIV has revised its voting criteria to move away from tying the number of votes per country to the level of contribution to a system of consensus decision-making based on the recommendations of OIV's Statutory Review Committee. These recommendations were ratified by the June 2000 General Assembly in Paris and they have improved the confidence of the member governments in OIV operations.

Thus, the OIV appears as a more effective, representative, and modernized body like other international organizations. Its role as an organization of reference, especially for the WTO and its expert committees, should be strengthened. Its new operational features should also allow the OIV to play a more proactive international role.

The OIV has three approaches for assuring its continuing contribution to the process of standardization in the wine sector:

First, the most straightforward approach involves assuring that OIV's position is effectively presented and defended in those organizations where OIV is represented. While the OIV was able to make its position known in the past, the WTO effort to avoid a proliferation of competing systems of standards by imposing its own standards has allowed it to assume a lead role in this arena. Consequently, the OIV finds itself in a weakened position relative to its level of expertise.

Second, another approach involves relying on member governments to present and defend OIV resolutions as they participate in discussions concerning wine standards. However, these governments reflect a certain inertia in carrying forward this approach, due in part to the ambiguous support from growers as well as by the difficulty in coordinating the positions of different ministries participating in various international discussions. In fact, most of the professionals in the wine sector have a difficult time identifying a clear position vis-à-vis the debate between the WTO and OIV. They are generally favorable to using WTO standards that in the short run are favorable to more open markets, but at the same time defend OIV regulations that in the long run protect the special nature of the wine sector. In taking these positions, the professionals are not always aware of the paradoxical character or the conflicting implications of their support. This is partly explained by the fact that wine growers and wine traders, even the most well-known, are generally unfamiliar with the rules of the game in the operation of international organizations. Even the OIV, an organization that is 71 years older than the WTO, is not fully understood by most professionals. This is partly due to an early decision by the OIV to develop its standards on scientific evidence rather than specific corporate interests. Consequently, professionals in the sector, with the exception of those who participate as delegates, are generally poorly informed and little heard. The second difficulty that arises in defending the interests of the OIV by member governments involves the difficulties in coordinating their various representatives, preparing for negotiations, or applying resolutions, a problem made more complex in the case of federal forms of government like the United States and with supranational[15] unions like the European Union, NAFTA (North American Free Trade Area) , or Mercosur where coordination requires separate national or interministerial negotiations.

Paradoxically, countries with the most regulated economies tend to be the least well prepared for international negotiations (Bureau, Jayet and Marette, 1998). Their bureaucrats concentrate more on the implementation of national policies than on their involvement in international negotiations. Consequently, it is easy to understand their difficulty in international negotiations: Is there sufficient collaboration among different ministries so they could develop an agreed upon national strategy?

The third approach involves a more in-depth assessment of the evolution of the founding principles of the WTO. In this regard, it is a matter of defending a different conception of competition, not based on products themselves, but on processes. For example, just as there is a coordinated European effort to promote the use of the precautionary principle with respect to the use of bovine growth hormones, would it be possible for the representatives from the EU, the US or Mercosur to defend their design of standards for wine?

In fact, in preparing for the WTO Millennium Round negotiations (which was finally called Doha Development Round), it was noted that the member states were quite supportive of the OIV, but at the same time not mobilized in face of the risks and threats previously noted, which weigh heavily on this organization. It is clear that the majority are divided between the two logics of standardization: the industrial logic defended by the WTO and the territorial logic still defended by the OIV. The future of the OIV will depend above all on the capacity of each member State to synthesize the differences among the preferences identified by various interest groups and find a lasting compromise with the other partner countries.

## 4. CONCLUSION

There are several reasons why the OIV was among the first to establish a system of standards for wine. It was concerned with a strict definition of wine as a product. As such, it focused on the origin of the raw material and the wine making process rather than the intrinsic characteristics of the product. Thus, the OIV has preferred harmonization and information rather than the uniformization. This process of standardization was initially heavily influenced by the French government, which was concerned about the defense of the *terroir* notion and by issues of fraud and competition. The growth and institutionalization of the French model in the international wine trade occurred gradually and without major opposition as the number of OIV member governments increased and accepted the founding principles of the OIV.

However, over the last ten years a certain number of difficulties have arisen. Internally, as the number of conflicts of interest increases, it becomes more difficult to find and maintain compromises. In the context of intensification of competition to acquire new markets, and growth in demand for quality wine, divergences are amplified between the new producer countries that prefer to take advantage of new markets with more flexible rules and the traditional producer countries that prefer to maintain already accepted regulations. But the OIV standards are also threatened by the hegemony of the WTO which, with its dispute settlement body, has the means to defend more liberal trade policies which often contradict the OIV standards. This situation highlights a critical question regarding the hierarchy among international standards organizations: No international authority is capable of legitimately deciding the architecture of a system of global governance.

The world hierarchy, in terms of trade rules should thus be negotiated. Are the member governments of the OIV ready to mobilize to defend a system that they have patiently contributed to building or will they adopt an opportunistic strategy of defending their particular interests at the expense of collective action? Will the internal OIV reforms be sufficient to improve cohesion among the member governments?[16] Can the OIV defend an alternative position that focuses on the production process and the origins of products? By accepting the coexistence of several systems, the WTO could provide a new spirit that would not have to be based on an exaggerated uniformity of regulations.

## 5. NOTES

[1] A standard (or *norme*) can be defined as those technical specifications that stipulate features to be manifested by a product or involved in a manufacturing or production process. Producers may choose to

impose standards on themselves or standards can be imposed by national or supranational governmental regulation.

[2] It is important to distinguish among (i).The International Code of Winemaking Practices with definitions of grapes, musts and special wines (NPV) and the detailed description of possible practices and treatments (NPP) accompanied by the advisory opinion of the OIV (accepted or not), (ii) the Collection of International Methods of Analysis of Wines and Musts establishing not only recognized methods, models of certificate analysis (NMA) but also the maximum acceptable limits (NPV), by virtue of the International Convention on the Unification of Methods of Analysis of 1954, (iii) the International Winemaking Codex defining the products used in winemaking (NPP), the techniques of analysis and the reagents or labeled solutions involved (NMA).

[3] Note that the dynamic of standards development can also take place in one or two stages: Thus, in the case of the OIV, most of the standards were established by common decision. As such, there was no process of diffusion as the emerging and the institutionalization phases were merged. On the other hand, voluntary adherence standards are built through these three phases.

[4] Spain, France, Greece, Hungary, Italy, Luxemburg, Portugal, and Tunisia.

[5] In this regard, neither the European Union nor MERCOSUR directly address relevant regulations without OIV approval, and state that unless otherwise specified, OIV standards apply.

[6] As an example, the French yearly average consumption went from 120 liters of wine in 1960 to less than 60 liters today.

[7] These are wines made from a single or dominant type of grape depending upon a country's regulations.

[8] For example, when the US joined, it negotiated a reservation clause concerning the European definition of label of origin (AOC). Yet since that time, the US has participated in several discussions concerning the ways to achieve convergence between the concept of "name of origin" under discussion in the US with the OIV concept of "geographical (or regional) indication" (*indication géographique*).

[9] The investments in the US occurred after the phylloxera crisis, and those in Australia were part of more ambitious development plans.

[10] World Trade Organization. (2003). Agreement on Technical Barriers to Trade; http://www.wto.org/english/tratop_e/tbtagr_e.htm.

[11] Alcohol and natural antioxidants in wine prevent the development of pathogens.

[12] Ed note: Under the 2002 Farm Bill (The Farm Security and Rural Investment Act of 2002), country of origin labeling is required for beef, lamb, pork, fish, perishable agricultural commodities and peanuts. US Public Law 108-199 (January 2004) delays implementation of mandatory COOL, with some exceptions, until September 30, 2006.

[13] The techniques for analyzing organoleptic characteristics demonstrate the high variability among products with the same name, often higher than that seen between names. These results show the difficulty – even for experts –of identifying differences between products of two different origins, or between an original authentic product and an imitation based on artificial ingredients or fragrances.

[14] Since then, the principles described in this text have not been modified on the WTO side. The Cancún agenda has only confirmed that the objective is clearly to establish a multilateral system in order to establish a list of Geographical Indications for Wines and Brandies (and possibly to extend this list to other candidate products). However, the collapse of the Cancún negotiations in September 2003 has not allowed this objective to be officially recognized in the WTO texts.

[15] On this subject, the wine sector is rich in lessons: A majority of the wine producing countries – members of the OIV and the UN – shared votes for a resolution favoring moderate wine consumption in the OIV and at the same time for the "use = misuse" (the first glass is dangerous) resolution in the WHO.

[16] A response to this question would need to account for the withdrawal of the United States from the OIV in November 2000.

# 6. REFERENCES

Boulet, D. and P. Bartou (1995) Fondements de l'Economie des AOC et Construction Sociale de la Qualité. *Série Etudes et Recherches* (INRA) 103.

Bureau, J.-C., E. Gozlan, and Q.-P. Doussin (1999) Les Normes Sanitaires et Techniques, Nouvel Enjeu du Commerce International. *Club Demeter, Cahiers 9*: 1-57.

Finnemore, M. and K. Sikkink (1998) International Norm Dynamics and Political Change. *International Organization* 52,4: 887-917.

Hillman, J. (1997) Nontariff Agricultural Trade Barriers Revisited. Pp. 1-32 in *Understanding Technical Barriers to Agricultural Trade*. The International Agricultural Trade Research Consortium, edited by D. Orden and D. Roberts. St Paul, Minnesota: University of Minnesota.

Padberg, D. and P. Kaufman (1994) Are Standards of Identity Obsolete or Redundant? Pp. 158-168 in *Re-engineering Marketing Policies for Food and Agriculture*, edited by D. I. Padberg. Food and Agricultural Marketing Consortium,. College Station, TX: Texas A&M University.

Peri, C. and D.Gaeta (1999) Designations of Origin and Industry Certifications as Means of Valorizing Agricultural Food Products. Pp. 59-68 in *The European Agro-Food System and the Challenge of Global Competition*, edited by ISMEA. Rome, Italy: ISMEA.

Powell, M. (1997) Science in Sanitary and Phyto-sanitary Dispute Resolution. *Discussion Paper Resources for the Future*, Washington D.C.

Reardon, T., J.-M. Codron, L. Busch, J. Bingen, and C. Harris (1999) Global Change in Agrifood Grades and Standards: Agribusiness Strategic Responses in Developing Countries. *International Food and Agribusiness Management Review 2* (3-4): 421-435.

Ruffleux, B. and E. Valceschini (1996) Biens d'Origine et Compétence des Consommateurs: Les Enjeux de la Normalisation dans l'Agro-Alimentaire. *Revue d'Economie Industrielle* 75: 133-146.

Salter, L. (1988) *Mandated Science: Science and Scientists in the Making of Standards*. Dordecht, The Netherlands: Kluwer.

Sylvander, B. (1996) Normalization et Concurrence Internationale: La Politique de Qualité Alimentaire en Europe. *Economie Rurale* 231: 56-61.

Tinlot, R. (1999) Les Risques de la Mondialisation et la Nécessaire Harmonisation Internationale Réalisée par l'OIV. Pp. 140-147 in *Communication au Congrés Mondial de la Vigne et du Vin. Mainz*, Germany.

Valceschini, E. (1999) Les Signaux de Qualité Crédibles sur les Marchés Agro-Alimentaires: Certifications Officielles et Marques. Pp. 147-166 in *Signes Officiels de Qualité et Développement Agricole: Aspects Techniques et Economiques*, edited by L. LaGrange. Paris: Technique et documentation.Actes du Colloque SFER, Clermont-Ferrand, 14-15 Avril 1999.

III

# REGULATORY PROCESSES

BERTIL SYLVANDER* AND OLIVIER BIENCOURT†

# 5. NEGOTIATING STANDARDS FOR ANIMAL PRODUCTS:

## *A Procedural Approach Applied To Raw Milk‡*

## 1. INTRODUCTION

This chapter presents a theoretical framework for analyzing the negotiation of agreements concerning *specific quality products.*[1] In the contemporary context of economic globalization, market economies typically do not favor a multiplication of standards that could be interpreted as barriers to trade by the WTO. Under these conditions, it becomes increasingly important to understand the process by which standards (*normes*) are negotiated. This chapter uses one controversial standard – the use of "raw milk"[2] in cheese production – to illustrate what we call a "procedural approach" to understanding this negotiation process.

For some time, marketing activities have been implicitly organized around an informal understanding about two issues: the name of products (the *désignation* or the *dénomination*) and safety standards. This chapter examines the negotiations regarding the standards for raw milk cheese and thereby focuses on two of the issues at stake: the differentiation of cheeses by a specific quality, with a specific name (raw milk cheese); and, the legal definition of the safety standard. Before addressing issues related to the negotiation of standards, it is useful to identify the economic significance of the question.

Market liberalization, in the name of free trade, sometimes pits producers of the same products against each other, even though they may employ different production techniques with different associated costs. This often also commonly involves competition between industrial and artisanal products that may have the same name and that are subject to the same health regulations.

Without question, the competition between these two types of products is perfectly legitimate. According to standard economic theory, this competition is good for everyone's well-being, especially if the substantive quality of the products is similar (and therefore the consumer is not deceived in purchasing one or the other product). In this case, the price advantage of industrially produced products usually out-competes the more expensive artisanal products. In the absence of policy

---

* Bertil Sylvander, Research Director, Research Department SAD (Society-Action-Decision, French National Institute for Agronomic Research, Toulouse France.

† Olivier Biencourt, Senior Lecturer, Department of Law and Economics at the Université du Maine, Le Mans, France.

‡ This chapter is translated and updated from the original publication in French as, "La négociation des norms sur les produits animaux: Une approche procédurale sur le cas du lait cru," *Cahiers d'économie et sociologie rurales*, No. 55-56, (Spring and Summer 2000): 71-90.

*J. Bingen and L. Busch, (eds.), Agricultural Standards: The Shape of the Global Food and Fiber System, 95-109. © 2006 Springer. Printed in the Netherlands.*

recognition of the positive externalities of artisanal products (environmental, rural and regional development, etc.), the process unfortunately appears altogether normal.

When these products are not equivalent in substance, it is possible to argue that they should not be called the same thing thereby protecting the legitimacy of the transaction. But sometimes products that are considered physio-chemically the same (based on the current state of science) are perceived by consumers as different because they are produced differently. In this case it becomes necessary to establish a difference among products using criteria other than the physio-chemical, or intrinsic, features of the product. This is the case with raw milk cheese or cheeses that are under an AOC label of origin (*Appellation d'Origine Contrôlée*).[3]

Free trade economists dispute this position and different labeling for products if the products are substantially equivalent (Chen, 1997). On the other hand, consumers appear to look for indicators of differences among products (a brand name, a specific, or a quality label) that permits them to distinguish among products and thereby allow for acceptable competition.

This right is based on an expectation that is at the very least *cultural* or *ethical* (Thompson, 2000). In order to establish this right, one can look at the example of organic production or products produced according to religious prescriptions (e.g., Kosher or Hallal). These products are labeled differently and these labels are accepted, even in those countries where free trade economics dominates.

Thus, there is an obvious contradiction. The US, Canada and Australia all have legislation regarding organic production that allows these products to be specifically labeled as organic even though it is well known that the intrinsic qualities of these products (the substance) is not scientifically established (AFSSA, 2003). The same argument holds for Kosher products where the essential difference is in the religious procedure without any difference in the intrinsic quality of the product.

The relationship between the name of a product and its conditions of production is broader in the case of safety issues. In the case discussed in this chapter, several questions continue to be unanswered. For example, while the European definition of milk is a "whole product from the continuous milking of healthy lactating females," in other countries "milk" can be the same product from cows treated with anabolics or growth stimulators, or even substitute and much less expensive products made from vegetable proteins.

When there is a consensus, the existence and the level of hygienic standards is defined on scientific grounds. When there is no consensus, they are based on more historical and cultural factors. In this latter case, the level of food safety standards can be used to restrict trade. The search for a scientific consensus as well as for food safety or sanitary barriers is at the heart of some very difficult controversies within the WTO and the Codex Alimentarius. This is exactly where we find the controversy over the use of raw milk for cheese.

The use of raw milk in cheese production is still being negotiated at several levels: local, national, European and global. And at each level, the negotiations continue to stumble over the same point: Actors with diverse interests seek to reconcile their productivity concerns, costs and market access with the need to protect product name recognition and specific features associated with a product's traditional image, its culture of production and consumption, as well as sanitary or public health requirements.

A "procedural perspective" on this kind of issue poses two questions. Will the actors negotiate? Will they negotiate in order to reconcile apparently insurmountable differences?[4] In order to address these questions, a brief overview of the case is followed by a discussion of both Simonian and conventionalist concepts[5] that are the basis for an analysis of engagement and the negotiation process. In conclusion we offer some observations on the theoretical and practical implications of this theoretical perspective.

For illustrative purposes, this analysis requires the use of field level empirical observations from the "Tome d'Ost " (a fictitious name). In this case discussions of the conditions for renegotiation began in 1994. Among the issues to be discussed (cattle breeds, animal feed, the maturation time for cheese, the conditions of control, etc.), the use of raw milk was a major point of contention among the negotiating parties. Considered as proof of its typicality, the use of raw milk was supported by small cooperatives, artisan producers and processors (with an understanding by some that large commercial enterprises would not be able to conform to the conditions of its use), while these large companies opposed its use. Contrary to most expectations, negotiations got underway in May 1997 with the intention of addressing the issue of raw milk use. The analysis in this chapter helps to understand this seemingly paradoxical decision.

## 2. THE EMPIRICAL CONTEXT AND THE QUESTIONS ASKED

### 2.1    The Controversy Surrounding the Definition of Raw Milk:
### The Encounter of Diverse Interests

From the official definition of raw milk in 1909 to the Raw Milk Regulation of 1985 and its reformulation in 1988, several strategies have marked the standardization of milk in France. As a result, the controversy over the definition, or standardization, of raw milk is best illustrated in the context of harmonization within the European Community.

The first effort to harmonize European texts concerning hygienic standards for milk dates from 1990 when a single standard for both heated and raw milk was proposed. This proposal created significant and lasting protests in many countries. In response to this reaction, the European Commission issued Article 1992/46 defining raw milk as milk that is not heated to more than 40 degrees Centigrade during processing. In addition, the EU regulation stipulates hygienic standards from the animal and the farm to the market. It also imposes standards for microbial levels in the raw product that farmers have the responsibility to monitor subject to agreement by the buyers. Thus, this regulation covers raw milk cheese. In principle, artisanal producers can seek special dispensation for cheese aged more than two months. In reality, the Commission has only accepted exemptions related to the traditional materials in contact with cheese (copper, wood, cheese cloth) during processing and to the management of processing rooms and cellars. In the final analysis, upon sale all milk must meet the stipulated microbiological standards.

Internationally this controversy was repeated when the 1990 General Assembly of the International Milk Federation approved a common standard for milk, thereby opposing the use of raw milk. Nevertheless, in November 1990 the Codex Alimentarius[6] recognized the specificity of raw or un-pasteurized – milk, even if, within this forum the US Government sought to require pasteurization as the standard for world trade in milk products. Most countries currently allow cheeses from raw milk to be imported under certain conditions.

### 2.2 What is at Stake?

The controversial nature of these discussions becomes more apparent when the important economic stakes are recognized. In 1998, world cheese production of cheese was 12.4 million metric tons; imports amounted to 730,000 metric tons while exports were 972,000 tons. The European Community and North America accounted respectively for 47% and 39% of this trade.

The following table summarizes 1996 cheese production and marketing data for France.

Table 1. French Cheese Production and Value, 1996

|  | Aged Cheese | Designation-of-Origin Cheese (AOC) | Raw Milk Cheese | Designation-of-Origin Raw Milk Cheese |
|---|---|---|---|---|
| Production (1000 MT) | 1,084 | 1,7333 | 210 | 125 |
| Retail Turnover (FF millions) | 36.7 | 10 | 11 | 7 |
| Annual Growth Rate % | 1.5 | 2.7 | 2.1 | 2.5 |
| Consumer Price (FF/kg) | 44.01 | 57.7 | 52.38 | 56.00 |

Source: Milk Statistics, CNIEL

The use of raw milk for cheese is part of a deeply embedded tradition for small farmers, artisans and even some companies in many French regions.[7] Some of these cheeses have a guaranteed trade, or designation-of-origin (AOC) name.[8] French consumers value raw milk highly as seen in 1990 when consumer groups mobilized to protect the country's "cheese legacy."[9] The value of designation-of-origin cheese and/or those with un-pasteurized milk noted in the above table confirms this interest.

Public health concerns also play a role in milk regulations. These concerns were reflected in the regulations covering the presence of germs in raw milk. Countries importing raw milk can specify particular standards for these types of pathogens. Along with monitoring these pathogens in the end product, public agencies have also implemented monitoring controls for cheese making.[10] Processing problems also arise closer to production where the equipment of small farmers or artisanal producers may not meet standards. Risks are also higher with soft cheeses or with those whose acidity is not sufficiently high during curdling. However, it should be noted that the risks are extremely minimal.[11] Still, studies indicate that it is not acceptable to all citizens (CREDOC 1995).

## 3. PROCEDURAL NEGOTIATION AND EMERGENCE OF A CONVENTION

The convention school of economic analysis, or "convention theory", offers a framework for examining interactions between actors who manifest an interest in coordinating, if not cooperating, in order to achieve their objectives.[12] In this vast range of relationships, convention theory is well-suited to situations characterized by a high level of uncertainty. In other words, while convention theory accepts the issue of actor coordination as a fundamental question of economics, it approaches this issue by borrowing Herbert Simon's hypothesis of procedural rationality.

A convention is defined as a "particular type of rule that embodies some measure of arbitrariness and that most of the time is not accompanied by juridical sanctions; its origins are obscure and while its formulation may be either vague or precise, there is no official version" (Favereau, 1991). From this perspective, a "dispute" between two actors is settled by recourse to a shared, higher order principle or convention (Boltanski and Thévenot 1991; Thévenot 1995). That is, convention theory operates at two different levels of logic: that of the rule and that of the higher order principle. As Favereau clearly states: "a constitutive characteristic of this form of convention is a set of rules and not merely a category of rules among others. All rules, or more generally, institutions, have an underlying convention" (Favereau 1999).

This point helps to improve our understanding of the definition of a convention, especially with its emphasis on what is commonly understood as a rule. A student of this literature might well be surprised by dropping from the definition, the phrase, "but without any official version" since this apparently contradicts numerous conventionalist school writings, and especially those that are of interest with respect to product quality standards.

As argued by Eymard-Duvernay (1989), the classical economic question of coordination can be addressed not only in terms of prices but in terms of "conventions of product quality" that enable actors to coordinate their behavior. For example, in order to assess the quality of their products, they may draw upon various criteria related to interpersonal relationships (trust and brand – domestic convention), standards (scientific measures, third party certification – industrial convention), or the market (direct assessment of quality, price – market convention).

Now, if a product is "standardized" in the industrial sense of reflecting some economies of scale, then "somewhere"[13] an "official version" of this standard must exist so that the conformity of the product to this standard can be assessed. Consumers, of course, are not able to list the various criteria used to certify the conformity upon which the standard is based. The standard itself is accepted as a guarantee of product quality. But it is also obvious that this "official version" of the standard embodies a variety of professional practices that earlier had been implicit, informal and often unstated. These characterize the conventional dimension of standards.

Taking the case of raw milk, our objective is to account for the *emergence of an agreement* among different actors in a climate of conflict, or more precisely, among actors whose negotiating positions are based on different *points of departure*. This contributes to convention theory in that it allows us to examine the process of reaching agreement based on a standard that is created through this process and that is based on a convention. Moreover, by incorporating Simon's concept of rationality into convention theory, we are freed from standard economic considerations of choice within a defined range of possibilities, and allowed to consider the ways in which *mutually satisfactory solutions are created in the process*. In short, convention theory allows us to focus on *the very process of negotiation among actors itself.*

Taking into consideration the context and the process from the perspective of procedural rationality, convention theory also accepts that an agreement corresponds to what Schelling (1960), refers to as a *focal point*.[14] However, this notion of an agreement is insufficient to explain the emergence of a convention. Agreement at a point in time *t* assumes that actors have met before (Bouvier-Patron, 1998). Thus, is it possible to argue that a focal point arises from a process? Perhaps not. The word "process" suggests a more or less organized activity. Nevertheless, in order to talk about the focal point, it is necessary for actors to have shared some experiences. In other words, there is a temporal dimension to the process.

In the case of raw milk, the temporal dimension is real since the actors are engaged in negotiations, and this reinforces the importance of Simon's hypothesis. That is, the negotiating parties do not seek to maximize the outcome as a function of their objectives, but seek a "satisfactory" outcome through a process of "satisficing" in the negotiating process.[15]

In the process of negotiating, actors figure out what satisfactory solutions might be and thereby use the process or "search" as a means to arrive at these solutions.[16] However, since rationality resides in the method and not the result, the process unfolds according to rules and any *agreement reached is not known beforehand by the negotiators.* Therefore, in the case of raw milk neither the manufacturers nor the artisans could have predicted the final agreement. The manufacturers initiated the discussions with a view to convincing the artisans to accept industrial hygiene standards, which for them were equated with heating. The artisans on the other hand were committed "politically" to raw milk as a symbol of tradition and taste consistent with designation-of-origin (AOC) conditions. During the process of negotiation it became clear that these initially contradictory points of departure could be unpacked and then re-packed using elements from each position. The negotiators did not anticipate the conditions of the final agreement, and they could not have been derived by examining *ex ante* their initial negotiating positions and strategies. The agreement represents a "satisficing" solution.

## 4. NEGOTIATION: PROCESS AND ENGAGEMENT

Before examining the process of negotiation based on the agreement, it is important to explain why the actors decided to come to the table. This discussion is based on interviews with the negotiators between 1993 and 1997. The negotiations took place among representatives of the milk producers, cheese makers and processors of a designation-of-origin association, and under the auspices of the INAO,[17] whose direct involvement varies according to the contentiousness of the specific dispute. With respect to the highly contentious raw milk negotiations, INAO served to assure the integrity of the negotiating process.

*4.1     The Engagement of Actors in Negotiations*

There are two types of engagement in negotiations. The first type involves simply participating in the discussions in order to be informed of the progress of the discussions and decisions, without active engagement in the discussions. The second type involves a direct investment and an active engagement in the substantive nature of the discussions.

What is of interest is identifying the conditions that help make engagement possible. The questions identified in Table 2 summarize these conditions. In the current case, our observations indicate that engagement is both necessary and justified.

The first question involves knowing if it is in the individual or collective interest of the negotiators to arrive at an agreement.

In the case of "la Tome d'Ost," the lack of agreement is not in the best interest of any of the negotiators (Barjolle and Sylvander 2002). Thus, the response to the first question would be "yes." Or in the spirit of R. Salais it would not be reasonable to question everything in order to arrive at an agreement that represented a collective effort (Salais 1997).[18]

The second and the third questions are derived from Livet's (1995) concept of the *"indecisiveness condition."*[19] In the context of procedural rationality, Livet emphasizes the effects of anticipation in the process of seeking agreement. He argues that each actor must perceive indecisiveness in the process in order to continue cooperating. He argues that when an actor is certain of reaching an agreement (that is, according to Livet, "achieving a common good") there is no interest in entering the negotiation process. But if an actor is uncertain about the outcome, there is interest in cooperating in the process.

In the case of "la Tome d'Ost," the antagonisms among the actors are sufficiently strong so that no one knows whether an agreement will be reached. But since everyone in this case has an interest – the members of the inter-professional committee on cheese (the assembly of producers, artisans and industrial processors) – each must participate in the process (Barjolle and Sylvander 2002).

It is important to refine the question of indecisiveness with respect to the way in which actors believe the contents of the agreement will reflect their positions. Indeed, during the negotiations, the content of the final agreement is the main concern. In the "la Tome d'Ost" case we know there were various points of discussion and that all of them were crucial with respect to the interests of the negotiating parties. The question for each actor was whether their specific production techniques were compatible or not with the agreement that was in the process of being negotiated: Is the actor included or excluded from the agreement?[20] If an actor feels included, there will be less inclination to participate in the discussions. In the case of "la Tome d'Ost," the dominant position of the industrial processors encouraged the artisanal processors to mobilize in defense of their interests as a means of assuring that the agreement included their interest in raw milk.

This condition of indecisiveness can be made more specific by considering the concept of a *plurality of rationalities*. Following Simon, building upon Knight's concept of uncertainty, Salais and Storper (1994) argue that if actors are capable of formulating a diversity of objectives and ways to achieve them, [21] then they can be seen as operating in "different worlds" or with a plurality of rationalities and possible worlds. Marty (1998) uses this idea to highlight the importance of agreements based on different modes of production. Using the case of designation-of-origin or geographical indication cured ham, he distinguishes four types of rationality: (i) the rational model in which decisions are made based on known variability and a general, repeatable model; (ii) the open rationality model in which decisions are based on adapting a general model to the specific context; (iii) the innovative rationality model in which decisions reflect the variability of the situation and are taken on a case-by-case basis; or (iv) a model in which decisions reflect known uncertainties and personal knowledge adapted to the specific situation. These rationalities are expressed during the production process, for example, as decisions are made for managing the raw materials used in processing ham.

Anticipating the terms of an agreement, actors will want to know if it will be compatible with their mode of production. In the case of a procedural approach to negotiations Livet's notion of undecidability is seen as actors are more or less sure of the compatibility of the agreement in terms of their own rationality, or in other words, its applicability to their mode of production.

This issue raises the question of innovation. In the case of designations-of-origin (AOC) that pre-dated the reform of the INAO, the process at issue involves the replacement of one convention by another, or a *translation* in Boyer's and Orléan's (1994) terms, that seeks to make a technical or organizational innovation compatible with a traditional practice. Over time, this can be analyzed as a composite of imperatives linked to the modernization of a designation-of-origin (AOC) product and what Casabianca and De Sainte Marie (1997) call "the technological memory of a product" which embodies numerous changes and potential innovations. From the perspective of Marty's rationality models, the end of the negotiation process will reflect the different principles of innovation included in each model. For example, in the case of industrial processors the interpretation of an agreement on raw milk could be seen as representative of the "open rationality" model (Sylvander and Marty 2000). Based on the distinction between two levels of participation (simple participation and/or full involvement in the discussion), Table 2 below summarizes the conditions of engagement in negotiations in terms of three questions confronted by actors and five possible results related to this engagement.

Table 2. A Decision Tree of Engagement in Negotiations

| Question 1: Necessity | | Question 2: Probability | | Question 3: Compatibility | | Result |
|---|---|---|---|---|---|---|
| Does each one think that there is a collective interest in an agreement? | Yes | Is the actor certain that the agreement will be reached? | Yes | Is the actor sure to be included in the agreement? | Yes | 1) Does not engage or only a little |
| | | | | | No | 2) Fully engaged in the negotiation |
| | | | No | Is actor sure to be included in the agreement? | Yes | 3) Engages in the negotiation without being strongly concerned with the terms |
| | | | | | No | 4) Fully engaged negotiating the terms of the agreement |
| | No | | | | | 5) Does not engage at all |

## 4.2    Process and Agreement

Some concepts from the field of social psychology help us to elaborate upon our approach. Bellenger (1990) suggests that all negotiations involve *protagonists with divergent interests who decide to compromise based on an objective and the room to maneuver in a conflict situation.* For several years, scholars of negotiation theory have turned their attention from concerns with bargaining (conflictual or cooperative negotiation) to the idea of negotiating "without losing."[22] This approach is of particular relevance to our argument since it assumes an unpredictable result, that is, one that emerges more as a composite of positions taken than as a compromise or average of positions.

Without question, a large number of factors affect an on-going negotiating process: awareness of individual and collective stakes, information on the known situation of each party, the use of this information, etc. In addition, as our approach suggests, the changing positions of the negotiators should also be included as one of these factors. Within the specialized literature that provides recipes for successful negotiators, we would pull out an idea from Fisher (1982) who discusses the importance of identifying the point of departure in the interests of the protagonists.[23] These interests are not supposed to be announced at the beginning of a negotiation process and they are supposed to justify the point of departure. However, the more the discussions advance, and the more these initial interests are not specifically brought into the discussions, the more they become subjects of interpretation and discussions. That is, the causal link to the point of departure can be challenged either by arguing that one effect cannot be attributed to just one cause or that one cause can have diverse unexplained effects. In other words, the discussion process cannot be completely controlled by the partners. Only an exploration of the different positions allows for the emergence of a mutually advantageous solution. If we assume that the interests become known in the course of the negotiations and that they can be hierarchically arranged, we identify three model phases in negotiation (Miller 1978). These are: Phase 1: Confirmation of the position of departure. Phase 2: Disclosure of apparent interests. Phase 3: Discovery of related interests.

### 4.2.1 Phase 1: The Point of Departure.

We earlier emphasized the paradoxical character of agreements. We believe they are impossible to understand, if one assumes that negotiations are based on the notion of substantive rationality. In fact, the industrial processors who dominate the sector, strategically oppose any result favoring "raw milk." Nevertheless they have accepted its use, and an analysis based on the procedural rationality can help us understand this position.

In the case of the "la Tome d'Ost" the industrial and artisanal processors have radically different points of departure based on their interests (see Table 3).

Table 3. Negotiating Points of Departure and Apparent Interests

|  | Cheese from raw milk | Cheese from pasteurized milk |
|---|---|---|
| Industrial Processors | Negative<br>Heterogeneity of milk<br>Sanitary and technological risks<br>Public relations risk in case of<br>health problems<br>Cost of separating good and bad<br>milk | Positive<br>Homogeneity of milk<br>Organizational and technical control<br>Risk reduction<br>Less cost |
| Artisanal<br>Cheesemakers | Positive<br>Respect for skill<br>Taste<br>Image and tradition<br>Conformity to INAO Policy | Negative<br>Destruction of skill<br>Lower product quality<br>Weakening of the designation-of-<br>origin (AOC) |

Industrial processors oppose including raw milk in an agreement because they believe that it encourages a laxness in dairy farming that would maintain or increase bacteriological problems that raise both health and public relations problems. This is why they prefer to keep specific brand names instead of the riskier institutional brands. Furthermore, they emphasize that given the heterogeneous quality of milk, they must either make several trips or find a way to separate the milk in the trucks, both of which are costly solutions, especially in more mountainous regions. Finally, they believe that pasteurized milk is more uniform and therefore easier to process (it can be standardized and later enriched).

The artisans' position opposes the use of pasteurized milk. They consider that its use will undermine their traditional skills and capabilities of accounting for daily differences in milk quality. They believe that raw milk cheese has more taste and has particular qualities typical to a place. In fact, this position is consistent with the designation-of-origin (AOC) policy in France which consumers feel quite loyal.

Given the diametrical opposition of these positions it is difficult to conceive of an agreement. Nevertheless, it was reached, but on grounds different from those expected by the parties to the negotiations. An analysis of the positions taken over time shows the following hierarchy of interests by each partner.

In Phase One, the interests are in considerable conflict. The positions are taken and argued with a view to showing the other party how difficult it will be compromise on any change.

### 4.2.2 Negotiation phase 2: The Apparent Interests

The discussion process leads each partner to make their position explicit by providing the practical reasons for the position. In this process the related interests of each partner are progressively disclosed. Thus, for example, a strategy for industrial processors could be based on an effort to exclude artisanal cheese makers as a relatively easy way to open up a part of the market. Banning the use of raw milk for la Tome d'Ost would mean the disappearance of one-half of these artisanal co-operatives and refiners. For the artisanal cheese makers on the other hand, acceptance of raw milk would be a way to weaken industrial processors since they lack the expertise and skills to use it.

### 4.2.3 Negotiation phase 3: The Underlying Interests and the Agreement

Apart from these points, the analysis of the reasons used by each partner allow us to focus on the possible areas of justification to be discussed, that is those that are sufficiently open to interpretation so that the points of view might come together. Once the two first phases are complete, the following elements appear in the course of the third phase.

Artisanal cheese makers are aware of the problems related to the hygienic quality of the milk received from their suppliers. This is a well-known problem. Some of these cases have even exceeded CEE norms for raw milk sanitary standards (Meyniel, 1994). If the negotiators accept that a short supply chain (immediate on-farm sales) presents the least risk, it appears that longer supply chains can be socially justified. The information on the low bacteriological quality of milk was known, but it was used and accepted here by negotiators. The industrial processors as well are aware of quality issues in their process. The fact that among themselves they adhere to a type of civic argument with respect to sanitary risk (i.e., in taking the position that "we do not poison people") facilitates and appears as a common point for discussion.

For the artisanal cheese makers, this adhesion to a "hygiene agreement" cannot in any case involve abandoning their point of departure. It does not foreshadow the agreement and thereby must be "translated" in the composite agreement. This is why this result cannot be considered more than an intermediary position between the two points of departure. On the other hand, the industrial processors note that an ambitious program to improve on-farm hygiene would be beneficial for the whole industry and thereby acceptable to the artisanal partners in the discussion. The artisans, in turn, accept that an improvement in the bacteriological standards is compatible with the choice of raw milk, a position gradually accepted by the industrial processors. Moreover, in contrast to the artisanal cheese makers, the industrial processors have the technical, organizational and financial means to carryout such a program with their suppliers, in terms of providing guidance and assuring milk collection. Finally, they have the means to combine advanced technology with the advantages of raw milk in terms of its image and the hygienic imperatives. In the process of negotiation, one sees that the industrial processors try to interpret the agreement in terms of their logic of production. For them, accepting certain conditions for raw milk could be part of the agreement and could even be turned into a market barrier for the artisanal cheese makers with less capital.

## 5. DISCUSSION AND CONCLUSION

For heuristic purposes we have discussed only one hypothesis in this chapter. Whether negotiations are local or global, the nature of the phenomenon is the same. The limited rationality hypothesis (incomplete information and the limited capacity of actors to deal with information) goes along with the procedural rationality hypotheses; it takes us away from the idea of a "bargaining" type of negotiating process ("this for that") and assumes that part of the solution resides in the construction of a "satisficing" agreement as identified by Simon. In this process, incomplete information and the limited capacity of actors to handle information strengthens the idea that neither the process nor the results are predicable for the partners.

Nevertheless, there are limits to this approach. The principal one arises with respect to the interaction between the local and global levels of negotiation and the aggregation of local agreements to a global level. The relation between these levels is easy to establish. In the global raw milk negotiations, it is clear that local agreements will carry considerable weight as those representing local agreements will seek to protect their investments in these agreements. Understanding this becomes even more important in a global judicial setting. Thus, the European agreement on raw milk, or its recognition by the Codex Alimentarius are significant vis-à-vis the World Trade Organization.

On the other hand, one cannot always assume that global institutions will influence local agreements. In the case of "la Tome d'Ost", the INAO certainly played the role of negotiator, among other roles, in order to facilitate an agreement in a conflict situation (Scheffer and Sylvander 1997). And one can cite in France many cases where raw milk has not been chosen, despite INAO's advice, because of power struggles (Fourme d'Ambert, Bleu d'Auvergne), previous practices (Picodon of l'Ardèche) or the particular fragility of a product (Maroilles). By the same token, in the Netherlands where pasteurized milk is the standard, several processors – and not necessarily the small processors – are interested in raw milk because of its marketing image and its organoleptic characteristics. Finally, European integration requires the establishment of common norms and thus the kind of negotiations that raise, as seen in the first part of this chapter, divergent points of view and compromises among national systems (Allaire and Sylvander 1997).

While we have emphasized the importance of detailed analyses of the origins of agreements from the perspective of procedural negotiations, the issue of aggregating agreements not discussed here remains crucial and important to examine a different level of interaction.

That will come about, in the first instance, by reflecting on how the mandate of a negotiation and legitimacy of an agreement fundamentally restricts the capacity to uncover and progressively construct a solution. Second, this assumes an assessment of the standing of the negotiators. If we assume, as we have here in order to simplify the argument, that they have the same standing, one could examine, following Hatchuel, the mediator's role, who can be considered both as a stakeholder (with their own interests) and as an external actor who guarantees that the common good is constructed. Finally, to move from constructing a common good to a public good assumes an understanding of the feasibility conditions for collective action.

## 6. NOTES

[1] A quality is specific if the conditions of production are based upon specific resources, that is, non-reproducible for technical reasons, specifics of the transactions or for regulatory reasons (Allaire and Sylvander 1997).

[2] In this chapter we will use the term "raw milk" as a synonym for "unpasteurized milk."

[3] Allaire et Sylvander (1997) refer to these products as "products of a specific quality." Their specificity is related to the standardization of the conditions of production that are based on voluntary schedules of conditions that are approved by the government. The AOC labels of origin, created in France in 1919, and under the auspices of the Institut National de Appellations d'Origine (INAO) since 1935, are subject to international agreements (such as the Lisbon Agreement of 1958) and European Union regulations (reg. 2081/92). These products are defined in terms of conditions of production in a specifically defined geographical area that gives the product its specific quality (typicité), and reserves the use of this geographic name to those who agree to the specified conditions of production that are approved by the government. These Geographical Indications are referenced in the international agreements on Intellectual Property Rights (art. 22, 23 et 24). See Sylvander (2004) and Barham (2003).

[4] In the case discussed in this chapter, the protagonists are quite aware of the difficulties in withdrawing from negotiations, given the impact of the global economy on their future business. The question is less one of deciding whether to negotiate and more one of deciding on the logic for their negotiating position.

[5] Jurists are beginning to use this type of approach. See (Lenoble, 1996). We emphasize that with the exception of the rationality hypothesis, a discussion of the multiple components of the process of negotiation (awareness of outcomes and commitment to the collective good, variations in the number of parties involved, or the mandates of negotiators, aggregation of decisions, etc.) is beyond the scope of this chapter. Our primary objective is to indicate the heuristic value of our procedural hypothesis and how it helps use to consider both the process and unpredictable results of negotiations.

[6] The FAO-WHO body responsible for setting food quality standards.

[7] For example, Besnier owns the Les Caves de Rocquefort Company.

[8] The following cheeses are required to be processed from raw milk: Abondance, Beaufort, Bleu de Gex, Brie de meaux, et de Melun, Camembert de Normandie, Laguiole, Mont d'Or, Roblochon, Salers, Roquefort. Raw milk is used, but not required for the following: Bleu des Causses, Cantal, Epoisses,

Neufchatel, Saint Nectaire, Crottin de Chavignolles, Chabichou du Poitou, Selles sur Cher, Sainte Maure de Touraine.

[9] See (Letablier and Delfosse 1995).

[10] For example, the 1969-70 law on milk payments (linked to quality) has been the basis for policy that has resulted in considerable progress during the last 30 years. Thus when the law was passed, 11% of collected milk contained less than 100,000 bacteria /ml, while today 93% of the milk contains less than 70,000 bacteria/ml. The bottom line is that one effort to deal with all bacteria (both harmless and pathogenic) is sufficient to control the latter.

[11] The weekly epidemiological bulletin of Ministry of Health stated in 1995 that there were 6,800 hospitalizations due to infections from food toxins (regardless the type of food); this represents 0.00016% of meals, of which milk products were responsible for only 5% of the cases.

[12] This discussion draws largely from material presented in the special issue of the *Revue Economique* (Vol.40, no. 2, March 1989). The approach discussed here should not be confused with conventions or game theory as more commonly used by many American economists and which does not draw upon Simon's rationality hypothesis. (Young's work typifies this game theory approach.)

[13] Often held by a professional trade union or interprofessional association.

[14] According to Bouvier-Patron (1998) this concept of a focal point corresponds to Simon's concept of a level of satisfactory aspiration.

[15] This concept of rationality as used by Simon (1976) highlights how decision-making must be adapted to the situation, or how the agent must apply certain rules (consideration of alternatives, calculating costs and benefits, risk assessment, etc.).

[16] In this discussion, we consider only the case of two actors negotiating in the context of an institution. We do not consider power and legitimacy issues that arise when negotiators act as representatives for others and thereby can be considered as a part of the negotiating process.

[17] INAO: Institut National des Appellations d'Origine (National Institute for Designations of Origin). This is the French public agency charged with registering products under the designation of origin and for their juridical protection.

[18] For the purposes of this discussion, this first hypothesis concerning the engagement of negotiators to protect their collective interest is taken for granted; this means that we do not address the conditions that make collective action possible.

[19] "Indecisiveness is necessary for cooperation... It can be argued that the idea of accepting indecisiveness helps to define the threshold at which individuals will commit to working to achieve a collective good... One only accepts contributions to achieving a collective good when its achievement remains undecidable. Convinced that a collective good cannot be obtained or that the best efforts will not achieve it, one will not invest in the effort and the collective effort will collapse" (Livet 1995).

[20] The third question is not always relevant. In effect, it is important to account for the number of participants engaged in the process in order to model decision-making. In the case of only two negotiators, if the answer to the first and second questions (necessity and probability) is "yes," then the third question does not arise. This of course assumes that a decision will be taken and that the degree of engagement of each actor depends directly on the second question. In the case of three parties to the negotiations, e.g., INAO in the case of raw milk, or the WTO in the case of beef hormones, the third question becomes relevant.

[21] We have studied the diversity of objectives and collective strategies within designation-of-origin (AOC) actor systems in (Barjolle, Chappuis and Sylvander 1998).

[22] See the work of the Stanford Center on Conflict and Negotiation and, in particular, that of Ross and Stillinger Ross, L. and C. Stillinger. 1991. "Barriers to Conflict Resolution." Negotiation Journal 7.

[23] We use the term "protagonist" in a "bargaining" type of negotiation and "partners" for a process negotiation.

# 7. REFERENCES

Allaire, G. and B. Sylvander (1997) Qualité Spécifique et Systèmes d'Innovation Territoriale. *Cahiers d'Economie et Sociologie Rurales* 44: 29-59.

Barjolle, D., J.-M Chappuis, and B. Sylvander (1998) From Individual Competitiveness to Collective Effectiveness: A Study on Cheese with Protected Designation of Origin. in *59th EAAE Seminar:*

*Competitiveness: Does Economic Theory Contribute to a Better Understanding of Competitiveness?* The Hague, The Netherlands: EAAE Seminar.

Barjolle, D. and B. Sylvander (2002) Some Factors of Success for Origin Labelled Products in Agri-Food Supply Chains in Europe: Market, Internal Resources and Institutions. *Economies et Sociétés*, série systèmes agroalimentaires, A.G., n°25, 9-10/2002: 1441-1461.

Bellenger, L. (1990) *La Négociation*. Paris, France: PUF.

Boltanski, L. and L. Thévenot (1991) *De La Justication: Les Économies de la Grandeur*. Paris, France: Gallimard.

Bouvier-Patron, P. (2001) Quelle Relation Possible entre Niveau d'Aspiration Satisfaisant et Point Focal? *European Journal of Economic and Social Systems* 15, 1: 1-38.

Boyer, R. and A. Orléan (1994) Persistance et Changement des Conventions. Pp. 219-248 in *Analyse Economique des Conventions*, edited by A. Orléan. Paris: PUF.

Casabianca, F. and Ch. De Sainte Marie (1997) Concevior des Innovations pour des Produits Typiques, in *52ned Séminaire de l'AEEA*: EU Typical and Traditional Productions: Rural Effects and Agro-Industrial Problems. Parma, Italy.

CREDOC (1995) *Les Comportementes Alimentaries des Français en 1995*. Paris: CREDOC

Eymard-Duvernay, F. (1989) Conventions de Qualité et Formes de Coordination. *Revue Economique 2*: 329-359.

Favereau, O. (1999) Salaire, Emploi et Économie des Conventions. *Cahiers d'Économie Politique* 34 (Printemps): 163-194.

Fisher, L. (1982) *Comment Réussir une Négociation?* Paris, France: Editions du Seuil.

Lenoble, J. (1996) Idéal de la Rasion et Rationalité Procédurale, in *L'Amour des Lois: La Crise de la Loi Moderne dans les Sociétés Démocratiques*. Montréal, Canada: Presses de l'Université du Québec à Montréal, Diké, Philosophie et Droit.

Letablier M. T. and C. Delfosse (1995) Genèse d'une Convention de Qualité. Cas des Appellations d'Origine Fromagères. Pp. 97-118 in *La Grande Transformation de l'Agriculture*, edited by G. Allaire and R. Boyer. Paris, France: INRA, Economica.

Livet, P. (1995) Conventions et Rationalité Limitée. Pp 549-564 in *Le Modèle et l'Enquête. Les Usages du Principe de Rationalité dans les Sciences Sociales*, edited by L. Thévenot. Paris, France: Editions de l'Ecole des Hautes Etudes en Sciences Sociales.

Marty, F. (1998) Action Économique et Adaptations Rationnelles: Gestion par les Firmes Agro-Alimentaires d'un Produit Protégé soumis à Règlement Technique, *Thèse d'Économie*. Paris, France: Université de Paris X-Nanterre.

Miller, G. (1978) *Living Systems*. New York: McGraw-Hill.

Ross, L. and C. Stillinger (1991) Barriers to Conflict Resolution. *Negotiation Journal* 7: 389-404.

Salais, R. (1997) Action Publique, Gouvernance et Convention de l'État: Éléments d'un Problème. Pp 255-284 in *Le Gouvernement des Villes*, edited by D. Paquot. Paris, France: Descartes et Cie.

Salais, R. and M. Storper (1994) *Les Mondes de Production. Enquête sur l'Identité Économique de la France*. Paris, France: Editions de l'École des Hautes Études en Sciences Sociales.

Scheffer, S. and B. Sylvander (1997) The Effects of Institutionnal Changes on Qualification Processes: A Survey at the French Institute for Denomination of Origins (INAO), in *52 Séminaire de l'EAAE: EU Typical Products and Traditional Productions: Rural Effects and Agro-Industrial Problems*. Parma, Italy.

Schelling, T. (1960) *The Strategy of Conflict*. Cambridge, MA: Harvard University Press.

Simon, H. A. (1976) From Substantive to Procedural Rationality. Pp. 129-148 in *Method and Appraisal in Economics*, edited by S. Latsis. Cambridge: Cambridge University Press.

Sylvander, B. and F. Marty (2000) Logiques Sectorielles et Territoriales dans les AOC Fromagères: Vers un Compromis par le Modèle Industriel Flexible? *Revue d'Economie Régional et Urbaine* 3: 510-518.

Thevenot, L. (1995) Des Marché aux Normes. Pp. 33-51 in *La Grande Transformation de l'Agriculture*, edited by Allaire G. and Boyer R. Paris, France: INRA-Economica.

MAITE P. SALAZAR*, JACQUELYN B. MILLER†, LAWRENCE
BUSCH‡, AND MICHAEL MASCARENHAS§

# 6. THE INDIVISIBILITY OF SCIENCE, POLICY AND ETHICS:

*Starlink™ Corn and the Making of Standards*[1]

## 1. INTRODUCTION

There has been an ongoing debate in the science literature and in practice as to what constitutes "good science." Karl Popper (1959) first advanced the falsification hypothesis[2] as a means to distinguish science from nonscience. According to Popper, scientists did not proceed by verifying theories or laws. He asserted that only falsifiable statements could be called scientific and in failing to falsify such statements we became increasingly convinced of their correctness. Later, Robert Merton (1973) advocated a set of universalistic norms to resolve this demarcation problem. Later still, and perhaps building on Merton's work, Thomas Kuhn (1962) argued that science was organized into paradigms, thereby distinguishing between science and nonscience. While this debate may seem to be an obscure philosophical issue, how we define "science" has direct implications to the ethical claims and social policies we can legitimate.

As a result, and in spite of its ambiguous definition, science has continued to be the foundation for good policy making. For example, a public affairs staff member at the Food and Drug Administration (FDA) writes, "it is the science that provides the knowledge needed to develop and apply the regulations in the right way.... [S]cience is the cornerstone of good regulatory decisions," says FDA Commissioner Jane E. Henney, M.D. "A high-performing, science-based agency like FDA reaps public health benefits for individual citizens and the nation as a whole" (Thompson 2000: 2). Similarly, "[t]he Office of Science Policy (OSP) in the Environmental Protection Agency's (EPA's) Office of Research and Development (ORD) integrates and communicates scientific information generated by or for ORD's laboratories and centers, as well as ORD's expert advice on the use of scientific information. EPA

---

* Maite P. Salazar, PhD candidate, Department of Community, Agriculture, Recreation and Resource Studies (CARRS), Michigan State University.
† Jacquelyn Miller, Lay Resident, Bhavana Society.
‡ Lawrence Busch, University Distinguished Professor, Department of Sociology, Michigan State University.
§ Michael Mascarenhas, PhD candidate, Department of Sociology, Michigan State University.

*J. Bingen and L. Busch, (eds.), Agricultural Standards: The Shape of the Global Food and Fiber System, 111-124. © 2006 Springer. Printed in the Netherlands.*

and the scientific community at large use this information to ensure that EPA's decisions and environmental policies are informed by sound science" (US Environmental Protection Agency 2002).

In stark contrast, Busch (2000) argues that scientific standards are not merely benign, technical devices for reducing transaction costs or improving efficiency or "quality". Rather, they embody the outcome of social processes of negotiation, persuasion, and coercion and they serve to shape social structures, distribute resources, and define power relations. As such, they comprise ethical decisions and assumptions that are inseparable from their technical mechanisms. However, once firmly established, the ethical and political negotiations and decisions embodied in science-based standards tend to be forgotten or black-boxed (Latour 1987).

This *invisibility* further enhances the power of scientific standards to influence socioeconomic relations, because the ethical assumptions become more difficult to call into question. The phenomenon of invisibility becomes compounded in the case of scientific research standards, since quality and standardization in science and technology are widely presumed to be unaffected and "uncorrupted" by social, political, or ethical considerations. The opportunity to observe negotiations in the setting of scientific standards thus presents a striking illustration of the inseparability of the technoscientific and the social.

The case of Starlink™ corn provides a window on the complexities of standards in the making, particularly scientific and technical standards surrounding agriculture and food safety. The novelty of Starlink™ required the production of new standards, policies, regulatory processes, agricultural practices, markets, economics, science, and ethical decisions, all at once. As the challenges of biotechnology become increasingly complex, understanding the indivisibility of technoscientific and ethical/political problems in the Starlink™ case helps us to appreciate the larger context surrounding standards setting and food safety.

This study is based on observations of the Scientific Advisory Panel (SAP) meetings on Starlink™ in November 2000 and July 2001. Analysis of transcripts and reports from the two meetings, as well as secondary sources, comprised the data sources for this study. Since the Starlink™ crisis, a number of articles appearing in the academic, popular, and trade presses have addressed its causes and the lessons to be gained for agricultural biotechnology policy. The present study seeks to build on these insights, but also to investigate in greater depth the implications of the Starlink™ case for understanding the intersection of science, policy, and knowledge in the negotiation of standards. We begin with background on the case, followed by an overview of approaches to science and policy, a discussion of the role of uncertainty in regulatory science, and a definition of standards before turning to details of the Starlink™ case and illustrations of standards in the making.

## 2. THE STARLINK™ CORN CRISIS

Starlink™ is one of several corn varieties modified with genes from the soil bacterium *Bacillus thuringiensis* (Bt) to express an insecticidal protein (Cry9c, in the case of Starlink™) that confers resistance to the European corn borer. Starlink™

was developed by Plant Genetic Systems (PGS) and later registered to Aventis CropScience (Aventis). The split registration granted by the Environmental Protection Agency (EPA) in 1998 authorized the sale of Starlink™ for animal feed and industrial use only, but not for human food or international commerce. This ruling was due to concerns about the potential allergenicity of Cry9c proteins. The registration conditions included a maximum yearly acreage and a 660 ft. buffer zone of non-Starlink™ corn. Additionally, the corn planted in the buffer zone was also limited to animal feed or industrial use.[3] Legally, Aventis was liable for the actions of its customers, in terms of ensuring that they met the conditions of the registration.

In September 2000, tests ordered by Genetic Engineering Food Alert, an environmental coalition, found traces of Starlink™ genetic material in food products on grocery store shelves. Following confirmation of these findings, EPA, the United States Department of Agriculture (USDA), Aventis, grocers, grain processors, elevators, and farmers became involved in a massive and costly national product recall. In addition, comingled corn had to be rerouted to approved uses, such as feed and certain non-food industrial uses. In an effort to control further contamination, local elevators and food processors also conducted tests on all shipments of domestic food or export corn and corn products. However, according to Lin, Price and Allen (2002: 34), "segregation to meet zero tolerance is impossible, given limitations of production and handling processes and testing technology." Shortly thereafter, numerous consumer reports surfaced alleging allergic reactions after consumption of corn-based products. Aventis cancelled Starlink™'s registration in October 2000 and subsequently requested a temporary tolerance level for four years. Such a request, if granted, would have made legal the small amounts of Cry9c remaining in human food from the 1998, 1999, and 2000 harvests.

In response to the petition for a temporary tolerance, EPA convened two Scientific Advisory Panels (SAP), one in November 2000 and another in July 2001, to evaluate the scientific evidence concerning the protein's allergenic potential and whether it posed a risk to human health. Both panels concluded that there was a "medium likelihood" that the protein was an allergen but that there was a low probability that the protein was causing allergic reactions. Nevertheless, the July SAP asserted that, while reducing the probability, the evidence presented to the SAPs did not eliminate Starlink™ Cry9c protein as a potential cause of allergenic reactions (Environmental Protection Agency FIFRA Scientific Advisory Panel, 2001a). Both SAPs recommended further allergy testing and biochemical experiments to aid in determining the protein's allergenic potential. The EPA ultimately decided to reject the Aventis petition and not grant a tolerance exemption for Starlink™. The EPA added that it would not make sense to grant the request because it could take years to determine whether Cry9c is an allergen and that levels of Starlink™ were dropping so rapidly that it would be gone from the food supply by that time.

## 3. SCIENTIFIC ADVISORY PANELS

The introduction of scientific advisory panels, or committees, was a partial result of the rapid expansion of social regulation in the mid-1970s. In tandem with this expansion was the need to provide more predictive analyses of the associated risks and benefits of processes and products. Concomitant with issues of risk was an impetus for more "apolitical," "expert" input along with stronger peer review processes in the regulatory decisions of these new government agencies.

At the most basic level, regulatory science is a phenomenon distinguished from academic science in that it is conducted for the explicit purpose of aiding policy decisions. But framing regulatory science in this unsophisticated manner "black boxes" (Latour 1987) the hybrid character of the decision making process. For example, Margarita Alario (2001) argues that, given the uncertainty about facts (science) and the uncertainty of interpretation (ethics), more attention should be given to negotiation and deliberation strategies of the various actors involved in the political process. Furthermore, Rushefsky (1986) observed that the raising of scientific doubt and uncertainty could be used as a strategem for postponing such political-scientific decision making processes.

Sheila Jasanoff (1990) has proposed that, just as the agencies themselves have been dubbed the fourth branch of government because of their strong, perhaps undue, influence on politics, Scientific Advisory Committees (SACs) likewise form a "fifth branch" of government with unrecognized influence. She argues that the activities of scientific advisors are poorly documented and their impacts on policy decisions are typically difficult to understand or evaluate (Jasanoff 1990). As such, the heterogeneity and complexity of what has been termed regulatory or mandated science does not lend itself to easy definition (Irwin et al. 1997). In fact, more often than not, SACs fail to resolve policy questions, especially when the policy arena is highly politically charged. As Miller (2001: 495) remarks, "neither science nor politics has a monopoly on truth or power."

The notion that the scientific component of regulatory standard making can be separated from the political has effectively been dismantled by recent contributions to the political and social studies of science (Hunt and Shackley, 1999; Jasanoff 1990, 1992, 1995, 1996; McDonell 1997; Miller 2001; Rushefsky 1986). In fact, Latour (1987) asserts that science is simply politics by other means. In spite of this recognition, the policy theme that emerges most forcefully in regulatory standard making is that scientific uncertainty and the pressures of decisionmaking actually sanctify the marriage between science and politics. However, if, as Janasoff (1990: 9) posits, "the scientific claims that these bodies are asked to evaluate are uncertain, insufficient, and inherently mixed with policy, then how can advisers selected for their technical expertise and political neutrality possibly certify them as valid science?"

The Starlink™ case highlights the complexities at this intersection of science, policy, and multiple forms of knowledge and practice that occur in the contentious arena of regulation. Three aspects – the degree of scientific uncertainty, the indeterminacy of risk, and the issue of equivalency – are especially relevant in illuminating the heterogeneity of regulatory science. They can provide a critical perspective that challenges the conceptual and ethical underpinnings of the science-based approach and use of SACs in the production of food safety standards.

## 4. SCIENTIFIC UNCERTAINTY

Issues involving scientific uncertainty are pervasive in debates on genetically modified organisms. This uncertainty is also a focus of most regulatory science in general, since it is the predictive aspects of science that are typically required for regulation. "Analytically, therefore, this concept of regulatory science is concerned with how science can make predictions on the basis of uncertainties" (Irwin et al. 1997: 19). How much comingling of Starlink™ with other corn may have occurred in the marketplace is uncertain. The USDA's Economic Research Service (ERS) estimated the potential volume of commingled corn at 124 million bushels, while Aventis' estimates were in excess of 430 million (Lin, Price and Allen 2002).[4] Furthermore, according to the grain industry, contaminated shipments varied by mode of transportation. Moreover, Lin, Price and Allen (2002) suggest that zero tolerance, although required by law, would be impossible given the limitations of production and handling processes, and testing technology.

In such cases, statistical and modeling tools are used to make predictions based on uncertainty, by at least quantifying the level of uncertainty. However, with novel technologies, even ascertaining the certainty of predictions with some level of confidence may be unattainable (Hunt and Shackley 1999).With Starlink™ corn, the mechanisms underlying allergic reactions are so complex that allergenic potential is exceedingly difficult to quantify, particularly the amount of exposure required for the sensitization phase and the differential effects on individuals and sub-populations. Given this *analytical ambiguity,* it became increasingly difficult to model uncertainty in the Starlink™ case.

In addition to the problems associated with predictive uncertainty, normative uncertainties also became an issue given a technology (and its associated practices and institutions) as new as a transgenic crop (Levidow et al., 1997). If the norms and standards underlying a predictive model are not agreed upon, then no prediction can be made. For example, in the Starlink™ case no norms existed for how data on potential allergic reactions should be obtained. Furthermore, it was unclear which agency should be responsible for data collection. On the one hand, the Center for Disease Control's (CDC) passive reporting system was not designed for this purpose. On the other hand, soliciting reports of customer complaints from industry introduced a conflict of interest. Both alternatives were unsatisfactory in gathering information regarding potential allergic reactions.

To cope with uncertainty in decision-making, the regulatory process works to conceptually narrow the range of uncertainties that need to be debated (Levidow et al., 1997). It is essential to recognize that this framing of the problem and bracketing of external concerns is at once necessary and political. In the case of transgenic crops, when the safety of the product is considered in isolation from the agricultural, commodity, ecological, and socioeconomic systems in which it is embedded, then the social is framed as external to the technical (Levidow et al., 1997). An alternative view would see the transgenic crop as inseparable from these networks that bring together such disparate actors as allergists, granary operators, and environmentalists. For example, the claim that there is no problem with the Starlink™ product itself, only with the agricultural system that "allowed" grain to be contaminated, frames the social as external to the technical. Moreover, although all the parties associated with Starlink™ appear to acknowledge the centrality of the agricultural system, questions related to it were almost entirely bracketed from the 2001 SAP, which was charged only with determining allergenic potential.

## 5. THE INDETERMINACY OF RISK AND THE ISSUE OF EQUIVALENCY

During the 2000 and 2001 Starlink™ SAPs, discrepancies concerning standards of research and testing became the focus of contention, subsequently eclipsing the debate over interpretations of the actual results. Three types of negotiations required by the Starlink™ SAP can be categorized. First, standards of scientific research regarding food safety needed to be negotiated. Second, the Starlink™ crisis highlighted the need for negotiation of new standard institutional practices for agencies and industries to cope with novel agricultural biotechnologies. Third, in the process of contesting knowledge claims, the SAP also brought head-to-head different norms of behavior, discourse, and language held by medical scientists, agricultural scientists, bureaucrats, industry representatives, citizens, etc. This chapter addresses primarily the first type of negotiations. The second type, regarding new institutional practices, has been addressed elsewhere (see Lin et al., 2002). The third type of negotiations concerns cultural norms which are often informal, tacit, or unacknowledged (Jasanoff, 1996). Their analysis is beyond the scope of this chapter, but they certainly form part of the context for the negotiations described here. All these negotiations are inherently political, and imbued with ethical valuations.

This draws attention to the lack of widely accepted standards for GM testing (Dorey, 2000). During the SAP deliberations it became evident that the development of standards related to this new technology was imperative if policymaking were to move forward. In particular, a series of specific tests were required to detect the level of contamination in the human food chain and to determine allergenic responses of people reporting reactions to corn-based foods. Assays were needed to (1) determine the presence of the Starlink™ protein in both processed foods and raw grain, (2) determine the presence of Starlink™ DNA in raw corn, (3) determine allergic response in humans, and (4) determine dietary exposure. It is important to note that the potential for allergenicity was attributed to the Cry9c protein and not the DNA.[5] This means that while detecting the DNA was important since it provided some indication of contamination, it was deemed by the SAP, EPA and Aventis to be insufficient to determine risk to human health.

### 5.1 The Detection of Cry9c in Processed Foods

The test commonly used to detect proteins is called an Enzyme Linked Immunosorbent Assay, or ELISA. ELISA tests are based on the ability of antibodies to react to and bind specific proteins and molecules. ELISA kits are typically developed by injecting a model animal, such as a rabbit, with the protein or molecule one wishes to detect. The specific antibodies created as a reaction to the foreign molecule are then purified. These antibodies are then used to both capture and detect the desired protein in the manner of an "antibody sandwich" (Figure 1). ELISA tests are commonly developed as commercial kits for speedy and widespread use (for example, pregnancy tests). Both Aventis and the FDA relied on a test kit developed by the EnviroLogix Company.

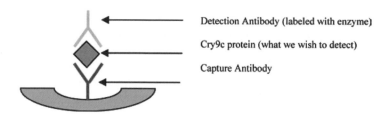

Detection Antibody (labeled with enzyme)

Cry9c protein (what we wish to detect)

Capture Antibody

The major controversy that arose surrounding the ELISA test for Cry9c protein in processed foods concerned the issue of equivalency. In generating the appropriate antibodies, the Cry9c protein injected into the model animal was produced from *E. coli* bacteria rather than from Starlink™ plants. This is a standard practice because it is easier, faster, and less expensive to produce proteins from bacteria than from plants. The concentration of Cry9c in the plant is lower than in bacteria and extraction is more difficult (Bucchini and Goldman, 2002). Nonetheless, the SAP panelists questioned whether the bacterial Cry9c was sufficiently similar to Starlink™ Cry9c and, therefore, whether the test's antibodies were able to adequately detect the plant protein.

Furthermore, questions were raised about the ability of the test to detect protein products produced during the cooking process, such as denatured or degraded products. Because the antibody in the test kit had been raised against the bacterial Cry9c instead of the corn Cry9c, some SAP panelists questioned whether it might fail to detect some or all of the denatured or degraded products that might be allergenic. The SAP final report stated:

> For the procedure to be accepted, it must be unequivocally shown that the two [bacterial and corn] proteins are the same. A recurring question, for which there are no definitive data, concerned whether all denatured and or degradation products of the Cry9c are being recognized. This is a critical concern for this analytical system (Environmental Protection Agency FIFRA Scientific Advisory Panel, 2001a).

The uncertainty about the equivalency of the plant and bacterial proteins was intensified by the transformative potential of the protein during cooking: The following dialogue illustrates the intensity of this issue:

> *SAP panelist:* Under the food conditions that these foods were produced, protein is not destroyed *[sic]*. That is illogical. The protein is still there. It may be insoluble; it may be

degraded. It may be bound to something, but it is still there. You do not destroy protein. Therefore, I have great problems with this data.

*Aventis representative*: I agree with you that there's a number of different ways that the antibodies will fail to pick up the Cry9c protein. It could be broken down in small pieces. It could be denatured. It could be degraded, and I'm using destruction as a general term to cover all those different cases.

*SAP panelist*: I don't think we can do that because the protein is still there in some form. Whether it's active or not, that's another question, but it's still there (Environmental Protection Agency FIFRA Scientific Advisory Panel, 2001b).

Even in the face of testimony from the National Food Processors Association[6] affirming the specificity, sensitivity, repeatability, and recognizability of this ELISA method for quantifying Cry9c protein in various processed foods (Environmental Protection Agency FIFRA Scientific Advisory Panel, 2001b), panelists remained intractable regarding the issue of equivalency in determining an acceptable level of risk. As the chair of the panel confirmed:

There has been a lot of good work that's gone into assessing the reliability and reproducibility of the assay. But if the antibody's not detecting everything that we want it to detect, then it's going to reliably and reproducibly give us the answer that's maybe not what we want (Environmental Protection Agency FIFRA Scientific Advisory Panel, 2001b).

The other concern regarding equivalency for the SAP panelists was glycosylation, a characteristic that could suggest allergenicity of the Starlink™ Cry9c protein. Regarding this concern, Aventis presented a 1997 report from Plant Genetic Systems providing evidence that Starlink™ Cry9c was not glycosylated. However, this report was also severely criticized for methodological problems and missing data. Thus, for the SAP panelists, it was unable to address the question of equivalence of the plant and bacterial proteins. Summarizing, a panelist declared:

... if this were presented for publication in the journals that I review for, it would be sent back to the authors with all of these questions. It would be rejected on the basis of the data here because lanes - and then lanes misnumbered and things like that are severe deficiencies. And, in fact, if one came back and said, I'm sorry, I mislabeled lanes and other things that were omitted, it might be rejected again because that's a very strange excuse for most investigators. In other words, the quality of this paper makes it difficult for us to judge whether the protein is glycosylated or not. Everyone around the table will make their own judgments. But it does make it difficult for us to make a decision because the quality of the data presented here and the discrepancies and mislabeled lines and lanes loaded with different quantities of protein all compound the difficulty in trying to draw a conclusion. And you've done an eloquent job, [name of Aventis representative], I think, of defending the data. But the data is not strong data and does have problems (Environmental Protection Agency FIFRA Scientific Advisory Panel, 2001b)

The issue of the equivalency between the bacterial protein and the plant-produced protein became such a central point of contention at the SAP meetings that disagreement over standards in testing methodology eclipsed discussion of the actual research results. The panel resisted moving beyond the question of the validity of the methodology to any debate on a specific tolerance level for Cry9c. Ultimately, the panel refused to recommend a tolerance level and EPA rejected Aventis's petition for a temporary tolerance level for four years.

## 5.2    *The Detection of Cry9c in Raw Corn*

Although the test for Cry9c in raw corn also relied on antibodies generated using the *E. coli* produced Cry9c, there is no denaturing of the protein, as in the case of cooked corn. As such, "The SAP accept[ed] the test in terms of its specificity" (Environmental Protection Agency FIFRA Scientific Advisory Panel, 2001b) and the test became the *modus operandi* for the detection of Cry9c in raw corn. Since this ruling, the Grain Inspection, Packers and Stockyards Administration (GIPSA) has validated particular proprietary tests and appears to be moving towards a laboratory certification process to minimize discrepancies among laboratories, such as different detection limits or varying sampling procedures, that had earlier resulted in disparate results among laboratories and test kits.

### 5.2.1 *Detecting Allergic Reactions in Human Serum*

The FDA relied on another ELISA test to detect allergic reactions to Cry9c in human serum. This type of test uses an IgE antibody specific to Cry9c[7] that would be present in the serum of a person who had an allergic reaction to the protein. This test also uses a Cry9c protein produced in *E. coli* bacteria, raising the same questions regarding equivalency of the plant and bacterial proteins. In this case, the *E. coli* protein is used to capture antibodies specific to the Starlink™ protein (Figure 2).

Figure 2. ELISA test to detect allergic reactions to Cry9c protein in human serum.

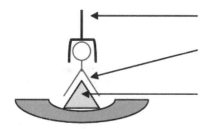

Anti-IgE antibody (coupled to a detection system) or "second antibody"

IgE antibody (what we wish to detect)

Capture antigen (recombinant Cry9c protein, in this case)

One major question concerned the sensitivity of the test. Because Starlink™ corn is a novel transgenic food, there is no positive control for the test, i.e., there is no patient with a known allergy to Cry9c from whom anti-Cry9c IgE antibodies can be obtained. Instead, the test is validated against other proteins known to be allergenic, specifically whole peanut, cat, and grass pollen. This validation process is intended to ensure that the second antibody is functioning properly. However, since this validation utilizes multiple proteins as opposed to a single protein (as would be the case for Cry9c), the SAP asked whether the test was sensitive enough to detect IgE antibodies developed against a single protein. The judgment of how sensitive is "sensitive enough" is a standard yet to be established to determine the allergenicity of transgenic foods.

In addition to sensitivity, the question of the equivalency of the plant and bacterial Cry9c proteins raised further concern about the possibility of false negatives. In this case, if the IgE reacts to additional or novel epitopes[8] existing in the corn protein but not in the *E. coli* protein, it might not be "captured" by the capture antigen and hence the test would not detect any IgE. The SAP also expressed concern that the IgE response might be masked by anti-Cry9c IgG.[9] In other words, IgG antibodies might be acting as inhibitors to the IgE-antigen reaction. This could compromise the reliability of the system to detect IgE and could also result in false negatives. The panel asserted that the results of the studies dependent on the ELISA test were inconclusive: "Taken together, the negative results are significant in that they reduce somewhat the likelihood that IgE-mediated allergic reactions are responsible for the symptoms observed, but the assay lacks sensitivity and specificity (to other delta endotoxins) to exclude the presence of Cry9C-specific IgE and the possibility of allergic reactions to the protein" (Environmental Protection Agency FIFRA Scientific Advisory Panel, 2001).

This test compounded the uncertainties related to transgenic foods with the uncertainty in the field of allergenics in general. Bucchini and Goldman explain:

> Assessment of exposure to food allergens is particularly challenging, in that adverse events are the result of a biphasic process. In the first phase, the immune system encounters the allergen and becomes capable of responding to it (sensitization). Later, the sensitized immune system encounters the allergen and allergic reaction is triggered. The doses and the frequency of exposure required for each process are not easily determined.... There are no standard methods for doing predictive modeling of dose response for potential food (Bucchini and Goldman, 2002:9).

Presumably to cope with this high degree of uncertainty, the EPA bracketed many potential issues related to assessment of allergenic potential. For example, they assumed that "exposure through inhalation and dermal contact would be negligible" thereby excluding workplace exposure to Cry9c and "did not address the potential for cumulative exposure to other *Bt* proteins along with Cry9c" (Bucchini and Goldman, 2002:9). This test illustrates the dangers of false negatives, particularly since the interpretation of negative results and uncertainty can be easy to manipulate.

## 5.3   Determining Dietary Exposure

Another area of controversy was the dietary exposure calculations, which estimated the exposure of the US population to Starlink Cry9c. Dietary exposure is calculated as the consumption of foods that would contain Cry9c protein multiplied by the level of Cry9c protein in the food and the fraction of Starlink corn in the grain stock. Although both panels characterized the high end level of dietary exposure as low, it was the assumptions that were necessary to make these calculations that became a point of contention for the SAPs. Furthermore, since these calculations were based on results from the ELISA to detect Cry9c in processed foods, the uncertainties described above regarding that test threw the dietary exposure calculations into question as well.

FDA and especially Aventis were criticized for not adequately calculating high end exposure and not representing it on a per user basis, as opposed to per capita or fixed percentiles.[10] The comments of one SAP participant suggest that the very exercise of pursuing a dietary exposure estimate itself embodies political and ethical decisions.

> If we really want to know, if it's important to get a number for the exposure estimates or whatever, that could be done. The various people could assemble and reconcile these sources of data and we could probably come [up] with a reasonable estimate of what's out there. Whether or not that exercise is worthwhile, I think I'll put that question to the Panel. Because in two or three months, we're going to have new stock, new supplies, and maybe at that point, such an exercise would be *more retroaction and accountability than it would be proaction and forecasting of dietary exposure.* So I'll leave that question to the Panel as to whether we want to reconcile all of these data sources (Environmental Protection Agency FIFRA Scientific Advisory Panel, 2001b) (emphasis added).

The goal of the SAPs was to address the standard of "reasonable certainty of no harm." However, as the above quote indicates, this standard was clearly open to interpretation. Moreover, the lack of transparency in proprietary research used to calculate the dietary exposure further aggravated the SAP panels. One panelist declared: "The exact reason for the apparent deficiency for defining high end exposure cannot be identified without further information from Novigen proprietary software used to perform the assessment ... the context of statistical expression is crucial to understanding the outcomes expressed" (Environmental Protection Agency FIFRA Scientific Advisory Panel, 2001a).

The problems with determining dietary exposure also demonstrate how, in the Starlink case, even questions as seemingly straightforward as "what is the reasonable certainty of no harm" became ambiguous and interpretive; assumptions had to be made about such factors in order to construct dietary exposure estimates.

## 6. CONCLUSION

The conception of science as a process separate from and unsullied by political or ethical considerations clearly contrasts with the actual SAP process, as exemplified by the Starlink™ case. We argue that the degree of scientific uncertainty, the indeterminacy of risk, and the issue of equivalency are especially important in shedding light on the indivisibility of science, politics and ethics. As Trevor Pinch has pointed out, all testing is based on the establishment of similarity relationships and evaluative judgments of sameness and difference.

> The way that scientists tell which differences are significant and which are irrelevant in part depends upon their theories and background assumptions or the *ceteris paribus* clauses assumed in the production of any experimental result. The background theories and assumptions, especially when a new phenomenon is claimed, are often themselves far from straightforward to elicit, as they are embedded within the very experimental claims at issue. In short, similarity and difference relationships that are constituted

within a wider framework of culture and action are at the very heart of how truth and falsehood are established in science (Pinch, 1993:31).

The Starlink™ case illustrates how the uncertainty and indeterminacy of the science and standards surrounding both novel transgenic foods and allergenics are hybrid processes situated within a context where different cultural assumptions about ethics, politics and science co-exist and collide.

It would be instructive to explore the meaning of the SAP process for its various participants through further qualitative research. At this point, we can reflect on the understanding articulated by the EPA representative at the close of the meeting.

> In any event, EPA must make its judgment on whether to grant the pending tolerance request guided by the statute under which we operate, which makes us conclude that the food will be safe if we authorize a level of this protein in the food. Congress through the statute has given us some guidance on what safe means; it's a reasonable certainty of no harm. Since the key word is reasonable certainty, what we need from you is an understanding of how far the science will take us and where we're left with unknown areas, what kind of uncertainty we're dealing with (Environmental Protection Agency FIFRA Scientific Advisory Panel, 2001b).

Clearly, the SAP is expected to play a key role in legitimating the decisions of the EPA in the eyes of the public. The panel is also expected to address questions apolitically, objectively, and within the bounds of sound science, while at the same time helping to frame which questions should and should not be asked. This conception of science as a process separate from and untarnished by political or ethical considerations clearly does not conform to the actual SAP process, as exemplified by the Starlink™ case. Understanding how standards, policies, and ethical decisions are generated simultaneously helps us to recognize the political and ethical assumptions embodied in scientific and technical standards. Perhaps explicitly addressing these political and ethical issues would serve to increase the transparency of this regulatory process.

## 7. NOTES

[1] This research was supported in part by National Science Foundation under Grant No. SBR 9810149. Any opinions, findings, and conclusions or recommendations expressed in this material are those of the authors and do not necessarily reflect the views of the National Science Foundation.
[2] Popper argued that science should be based on the falsifiability rather than the verifiability of hypotheses. In other words, for Popper, scientists did not proceed by verifying theories or laws, but by failing to falsify them and in so doing became increasingly convinced of their correctness.
[3] Since corn is open-pollinated, it was expected that a certain amount of pollen would drift into buffer zones.
[4] The ERS estimate was for the 2000 crop located near wet and dry millers prior to October 1, 2000. Aventis's estimate was for commingled corn stored at grain elevators as of March 2001 (Lin, Price, and Allen, 2002).
[5] Typically, it is proteins that produce allergic reactions. DNA is considered by the EPA to be a molecule generally recognized as safe (GRAS). Hence, the presence of Starlink DNA *per se* was not viewed as illegal. In this case, the presence of Starlink DNA was used as a means to determine contamination of food with Starlink *corn*, which constitutes an illegal pesticide if found in food. DNA tests are often used to determine the presence of GM crops, since these crops can be differentiated from their non-GM counterparts by the presence of specific DNA sequences inserted into their genomes.

[6] The National Food Processors Association had repeatedly used the EnviroLogix ELISA kits to detect Cry9c in processed foods.

[7] IgE is the only type of antibody that serves as a good marker for identification of immediate hypersensitivity in humans.

[8] Sites on the surface of an antigen molecule to which a single antibody molecule binds. An antigen has many different epitopes and reacts with antibodies of many different specificities.

[9] IgG antibodies are normally present at higher concentrations. Therefore, the presence of Cry9c-specific IgG may mask the IgE response, particularly at the high dilution rate used (1:2, necessary to ensure sensitivity).

[10] The subgroup with the highest potential estimated exposure was Hispanic children aged 7-12 (Bucchini, and Goldman, 2002). However, ethical questions concerning equity and justice in distribution of exposure were excluded from the SAP's deliberations.

# 8. REFERENCES

Alario, M., and M. Brun (2001) Uncertainty and Controversy in the Science and Ethics of Environmental Policy Making. *Theory and Science* 2(1): 1-7.

Bucchini, L. and L. R. Goldman (2002) Starlink Corn: a Risk Analysis. *Environmental Health Perspectives* 110(1): 5-13.

Busch, L. (2000) The Moral Economy of Grades and Standards. *Journal of Rural Studies* 16: 273-283.

Dorey, E. (2000) Taco Disputes Underscore Need for Standardized Tests. *Nature Biotechnology* 18 (November): 1136-1137.

Environmental Protection Agency FIFRA Scientific Advisory Panel (2001a) A Set of Scientific Issues Being Considered by The Environmental Protection Agency Regarding: Assessment of Additional Scientific Information Concerning StarLink Corn. Arlington, VA, US EPA.

_____ (2001b) Transcript of the FIFRA Scientific Advisory Panel Open Meeting of July 17-18, 2001. Arlington, VA., U.S Environmental Protection Agency. US EPA.

Hunt, J. and S. Shackley (1999) Reconceiving Science and Policy: Academic, Fiducial and Bureaucratic Knowledge. *Minerva* 37(2): 141-164.

Irwin, A., H. Rothstein, et al. (1997) Regulatory Science - Towards a Sociological Framework. *Futures* 29(1): 17-31.

Jasanoff, S. (1990) *The Fifth Branch: Science Advisers as Policymakers*. Cambridge, MA, Harvard University Press.

_____ (1992) Science, Politics, and the Renegotiation of Expertise at EPA. *Osiris* 7: 195-217.

_____(1995) Procedural Choices in Regulatory Science. *Technology in Society* 17(3): 279-293.

_____ (1996) Beyond Epistemology: Relativism and Engagement in the Politics of Science. *Social Studies of Science* 26(2): 393-418.

Kuhn, T. (1962) *The Structure of Scientific Revolutions*. Chicago, University of Chicago Press.

Latour, B. (1987) *Science in Action: How to Follow Scientists and Engineers Through Society*. Milton Keynes, England, Open University Press.

Levidow, L., S. Carr, D. Wield, and R. von Schomberg (1997) European Biotechnology Regulation: Framing the Risk Assessment of a Herbicide-tolerant Crop. *Science Technology & Human Values* 22(4): 472-505.

Lin, W., G. Price, et al. (2002) Starlink™: Where No Cry9c Corn Should Have Gone Before. *Choices* (Winter 2001-2002): 31-34.

McDonell, G. (1997) Scientific and Everyday Knowledge: Trust and the Politics of Environmental Initiatives. *Social Studies of Science* 27(6): 819-863.

Merton, R. (1973) *The Sociology of Science*. Chicago, University of Chicago Press.

Miller, C. (2001) Hybrid Management: Boundary Organizations, Science Policy, and Environmental Governance in The Climate Regime. *Science Technology & Human Values* 26(4): 478-500.

Pinch, T. (1993). Testing - One, Two Three...Testing!: Toward a Sociology of Testing. *Science, Technology, & Human Values* 18(1): 25-41.

Popper, K. (1959) *The Logic of Scientific Inquiry*. New York, Harper & Row, Publishers

Rushefsky, M. E. (1986) *Making Cancer Policy*. New York, SUNY Press.

Thompson, L. (2000) Science at FDA: The Key to Making the Right Decision. *FDA Consumer Magazine* 34(2): 1-5.

US Environmental Protection Agency (2002) The Office of Science Policy: the Link Between ORD's Labs and Centers and EPA's Regulatory and Program Offices; http://www.epa.gov/osp/. November 27, 2002.

IVAN SERGIO FREIRE DE SOUSA* AND LAWRENCE BUSCH†

# 7. STANDARDS AND STATE-BUILDING:

*The Construction of Soybean Standards in Brazil*

## 1. INTRODUCTION

This chapter discusses the long transformation of agricultural classification and standards in Brazil, from an individualized and intensively private practice to a general instrument for global competition. Public agricultural standards were introduced in Brazil as part of the nation's response to global markets and, to a large extent, to a shift of power to urban areas. During the gradual consolidation of the Brazilian State during the 19th century, the classification and standardization of agricultural products were part of broader strategies to establish new "rules" for Brazilian development. Universalizing values from an incipient capitalist market were imposed piecemeal upon traditional and familial values, founded in the agrarian patriarchy. Some label this whole set of social constructions as the "re-europeanization" of Brazil. The process was driven initially by anti-fraud laws that sought to overcome the effects of individualized, patriarchical standards for traditional products such as rice, corn, sugar, and cassava.

Following a brief historical overview that examines the emergence of concerns with classification and standardization of agricultural products in Brazil, this chapter examines the rise of standards first for fraud and then for various quality characteristics. Initially, the state was central to introducing food and agricultural standards. In contrast, we show that soybeans, a recent introduction to Brazil, are representative of the new, 'modern' standards that gradually replaced the older, private and often idiosyncratic standards of the past.

## 2. HISTORICAL BACKGROUND

In the 16th and 17th centuries, Brazil was merely an agglomeration of Portuguese "feitorias" and captaincies. What existed during this period was "an aterritorial space, a Portuguese archipelago composed of Portuguese-American outposts and the Angolan factorships" in Africa (Alencastro, 2000). Although ruled by the same crown and disputed by vessels of other European nations, the Portuguese lands on the American continent were not integrated socially, politically or economically. They were just a few dispersed outposts formed largely by people of European

---

* Ivan Sergio Freire de Sousa, Senior Researcher at EMBRAPA (Brazailian State Corporation for Agricultural Research).
† Lawrence Busch, University Distinguished Professor, Department of Sociology, Michigan State University.

*J. Bingen and L. Busch, (eds.), Agricultural Standards: The Shape of the Global Food and Fiber System, 125-135. © 2006 Springer. Printed in the Netherlands.*

origin. The Portuguese sail-powered vessels, the famous caravels, that depended on wind systems and the direction of the marine currents help account for the absence of integration. Simply, it was easier to connect parts of the Brazilian coast with Lisbon on the other side of the Atlantic, than to link the Brazilian outposts with each other. Clearly, dense tropical forests and natives not always cordial to the Portuguese reinforced the isolation of each capitaincy.[1]

In this "Portuguese archipelago," the products traded between the Brazilian and African Coasts were hardly inspected at all. Due to the long crossing, even the food imported from Portugal, usually butter and flour, almost always arrived rotten. Individual merchants and consumers established their own standards and classifications. There was no external intervention, nor were there laws that would standardize the goods. The standards were more private than public, characterized by a multiplicity of traditional, familial, individualized and patriarchical interests.[2] In this system, quality was a private rather than a public matter. Quality food production was tied to quantity, and a high quality product was simply one that did not have foreign matter in it.

The installation of the Portuguese Crown in Brazil in 1808 precipitated the creation of judicial, administrative and economic functions for the Brazilian State and the conditions for the development of standards to regulate trade. For example, one of the Regent Prince's first acts in Brazil was a Royal Letter regulating the Brazilian ports in foreign trade. Furthermore, the Crown "...decreed punishment for fraud in the export of sugar, to the detriment of the progress and the good name of this important national industry..." (Lima, 1996:148).

With the gradual consolidation of the Brazilian State during the 19th century, classification and standardization of agricultural products began. Universalizing values from an incipient capitalist market were imposed piecemeal upon traditional and familial values, founded in the agrarian patriarchy. To classify and to standardize were demands of the emergent system the "re-europeanization" of Brazil that Freyre (1968) argues would take years to impose.

Based on market demand and motivated primarily by combating fraud, new kinds of "rules of the game" began leaving the private sphere and slowly entering the public sphere.[3] For example, a 1918 law addressed the falsification of chemical fertilizers. For cotton, "typos officiaes" (official types) were defined in the 1920s with the express intent of avoiding fraud and thereby developing quality standards.

## 3. SOYBEANS IN BRAZIL

In contrast to rice, corn, and cassava, the traditional commodities of Brazilian food history, the soybean (*Glycine max* L. Merril) emerged on the agricultural and agro-industrial scene in Brazil in the second half of the 20th century as a product of science and modern technology. Consequently, Brazilian soybeans are intermeshed in a net of interlinked and interdependent social interests, where progressively, classification and standardization have assumed a central part in their role in the Brazilian economy.

Attempts to introduce soybeans began as early as 1822 (Miyasaka and Kiihl, 1979), but the first real soybean farm, with seed imported from the United States, was established in 1931 in the state of Rio Grande do Sul. Yet, until the 1950s soybean production had no significant economic importance and it was only between 1962 and 1968 that the wheat-soybean rotation became common in the southern part of the country.

Since soy is a photoperiod sensitive plant, one of the main challenges for soybean breeders in Brazil was to expand its planting to low latitudes, that is, closer to the equator. Until the 1970s, Brazilian farmers only possessed varieties with a very restricted planting period. In 1978, agricultural researchers in Brazil succeeded in developing cultivars with a long juvenile period, prolonging the pre-inductive period of blossoming from 14 to 30 days.[4] The first genuinely Brazilian cultivar with these characteristics, "Doko," entered the market in 1980 and offered Brazilian soybean producers the means to meet consistent quality and homogeneity standards in both domestic and international markets.

## 4. STATE OR MARKET?

Is it the "State" or the "market" that determines forms of classification and standardization? The most plausible tentative answer is that this became a joint responsibility. It has historically been this way.[5]

In the nineteenth century, there was no direct discussion of classification and standardization in any legal document. As noted above, what existed were a few measures to fight the generalized fraud in exports and also in local sales. Part of this fraud originated from the limited technology used in the production, transport and storage of the various products. In these cases, where there was no swindling, fraud would not exist technically. Nevertheless, technological limitations affected the integrity of the products leading importers to despise Brazilian merchandise, further lowering their prices.

However, the problem was not exclusively technological. Several contemporaries of that period perceived another force responsible for the adulteration. One of these contemporaries noted that it was tempting and profitable to deal with adulterated products so businessmen were unable to resist (Luccock, 1820). Adulteration was commonplace:

> ...we not only find ashes in the lime of this country, but lime-stone in its indigo, sand in its sugar, particles of feldspar in its rice, seeds in its cotton, and moisture in its coffee. As far as this is the effect of ignorance it punishes itself, perhaps sufficiently; but as before intimated, it is in part the contrivance of chicanery, and therefore ought to be severely chastised by the magistrate, as a crime against the state (Luccock, 1820: 364).

From its inception, the Brazilian State assumed the role as an instrument for socioeconomic development. While acting out this role, the classification and standardization of products - via anti-fraud legislation - was just one of the tools used.[6] It was part of the modernizing measures enacted by the Regent Prince's government.

Associated with the new legislation were measures that sought to limit the economy. Among those was the April 1, 1808 permit,[7] superceding that of January 5, 1785, which prohibited manufacturing plants and factories in Brazil. While the old ruling did not entirely prevent the beginning of some industries, it managed to inhibit the creative and manufacturing spirit in a social atmosphere that already devalued work and the use of innovations.

Whoever invested in a factory was always vulnerable, exposed to the extortion and prosecution of some colonial authority. In fact, one of the main objectives of the English merchant John Luccock's journey to Registro Velho was to examine the factory *Fábrica de Tecidos de Algodão e Lã* that operated there for 50 years. By the power of an old colonial law, the owner was required to go to Lisbon and,

> ... there, as in such cases was all too common, he was kept without a definite hearing for twenty years, while the fabric was every day going to ruin. When the Court, after its settlement in this country, had leisure to attend to such matters, attempts were made to revive the manufactory, but it was too late, a new direction had been given to the industry of the people more congenial with their general manners and habits... (Luccock, 1820: 535).

The objective of overcoming the Brazilian shortage of new technology in the early 19th century was central to the State that was emerging. However, slavery, as well as the patriarchal system that sustained it, conspired against progress. As a consequence, the use of machinery, whether in industry, agriculture, domestic work, or even mining, was always minimal or outdated.

Despite the fact that the modernizing State had brought along the incentive of internal capitalism, this initiative turned out to be timid, contained, and slow, especially when compared to Europe, of which Brazil was always a part, if only in a very peripheral and dependent way (Fernandes, 1975). One of the great obstacles to the dynamism of production and internal markets was the existence of very powerful institutions, formed and developed during the first three centuries of the Portuguese colonization of America.

When Brazil became the home of the Portuguese Monarchy and free commerce was declared, the merchants of Rio de Janeiro practiced a unique form of trade, especially when compared to European trade practices. They did not even know what credit was. The laws themselves reflected this atypical financial capitalism (see Luccock, 1820).

During the technical revolution that occurred in 19th century Brazil promoted classification and standardization as a necessary matter, although not as a high priority. In other words, it was the social transformations of the 19th century that made both classification and standardization, in terms of combating fraud, valid and important issues for society.

These new kinds of "rules" first permeated industry; only later did they affect transport and agriculture. The social agents that contributed to such were the same ones that facilitated the use of technologies in Brazil: the middle, lower middle, and lower classes of the population, that is, the free Blacks and mulattoes, the technicians, foreign artisans (English and French), and a few small entrepreneurs. They faced the problem of interchangeability of pieces and mechanisms, of making amendments and adaptations to the art they learned mostly from the English and French.

## 5. STATE REGULATIONS FOR STANDARDS

The legal documents with respect to classification and standardization can be grouped into three historical periods of the development of the Brazilian State. The first was marked by the presence of the Portuguese royal family in Brazil; the second by the constitution of the Brazilian Empire; and the third encompassed the whole republican period.

During the period when the Portuguese royal family was in Brazil (1808-1821) only three permits, all signed in 1810, were linked to the topic of standardization, and all attempted to combat fraud. One is the Permit of January 22 that assigned to the Major Purveyor of Health the taxing of any kind of corruption or fraud in wheat, flour, corn, dried and fresh meat, or any kind of edibles or drinkables, which could do harm to the population's health. Another permit, noted earlier, established punitive measures against those who falsified labels on boxes of sugar. Finally, the July 7 permit conceded favors to whoever introduced and cultivated Indian spices and set punishments for possible fraud or falsification.

It was during the period of the Brazilian Empire (1822-1889) that the nation state consolidated and enforced its anti-fraud laws in agricultural commerce. It should be noted that Brazil's first Constitution (1824) referred to standardized currency, weights and measurements. The *Constituição Política do Império*, in Article 15, section XVII, required the General Assembly to: "determine the weight, value, inscription, typography, and denomination of the coins, as well as the patterns regarding weights and measures."

During much of the imperial period, the units used remained Portuguese: the *vara* (32 to 43 inches), the *almude* (25 liters or 6.6 gallons), and the *canada* (1/12 of an *almude*), among others. However, measurements were not consistent across regions. Thus, it is not strange that on November 16, 1833, Decision no. 701 ruled that Rio de Janeiro's measurement standards were to be applied to the shipping of salt and other objects. The regional variations among weights and measures would only change later, during the reign of Dom Pedro II, with the passage of Law no. 1,157, on June 26, 1862. By this law, the whole system of weights and measures became metric. Nevertheless, the substitution process took place very slowly. Only in 1872, by Decree no. 5,089, of September 18, were the provisional instructions for the execution of that law defined. The final ruling of the Law no. 1,157, of 1862, was approved only a few months later, by Decree no. 5,162, of December 11, 1862 (cf. Adler, 1995).

Two laws, eleven decisions and three bills regarding the classification and standardization of agricultural products were enacted during the imperial period (Table 1). The November 5, 1827 law, for instance, abolished the inspection tables for sugar, tobacco and cotton. The content of these laws, decisions and bills focused mostly on inspection and taxation.

Table 1: Number of legal documents regarding classification and standardization of Brazilian food and agriculture. 1822-1889.

| Years | Laws | Decisions | Bills |
|-------|------|-----------|-------|
| 1822-1829 | 1 | 3 | - |
| 1830-1839 | 1 | - | - |
| 1840-1849 | - | 2 | - |
| 1850-1859 | - | 5 | - |
| 1860-1869 | - | 1 | 1 |

Source: Collecção das Leis do Brazil (1890), Collecção das Leis do Império do Brazil (1907-1910).

Beginning about 1850 several decrees and decisions were made guaranteeing to certain people the privilege of sole use, for a fixed number of years, of machines, mechanisms or agroindustrial processes they had invented. This corresponds exactly with the period of considerable growth of the economy and the long campaign against slavery. For example, the October 24, 1857 Decree (not included in Table 1) conceded to Frederico Sauerbrann the exclusive use, for five years, of a machine of his own invention, designed to pulverize and refine sugar. Similarly, the Decree of January 24, 1880 conceded to Álvaro Rodovalho Marcondes dos Reis the exclusive use of a coffee de-pulping machine based on improvements made to it. With respect to classification and standardization, the typical law attempted to fight fraud. An example of such a law was Decision no. 46, of May 15, 1850, referring to the confiscation of boxes of sugar "due to differences on the *varas*", i.e., in their sizes.

Concern for the quality of the agricultural products beyond fraud became more evident in the 20th century. Numerous factors contributed to the change in focus. Among them were the technological transformation of domestic agro-industrial processing, the struggle for the expansion of foreign agricultural commerce, the end of slave labor, the growth of the agricultural sciences, and urban expansion. The creation of the *Sociedade Nacional de Agricultura* (National Agricultural Society), founded on January 16, 1897, is an important sign of the concerns of the agricultural leaders not only with increases in production, but also with the quality of what was produced. However, this shift was a long and slow process.

The third period of the legal norms for classification and standardization begins in 1889 with proclamation of the republic and continues to the present. Nevertheless, until the 1920s, legislation regarding classification and standardization continued to emphasize fraud. This was the case for Decree no. 4,631, of January 1923, establishing penalties for fraud in pig fat and wine. The number of legal documents on the matter was, as in previous periods, very limited. This does not mean that some persons, such as exporters, were oblivious to what had to be done in terms of classification. In the magazine *A Lavoura* of the *Sociedade Nacional de Agricultura*, information about agricultural machines and implements as well as articles pointing to the need to increase the quality of what was produced, began to be published. In 1921, a foreigner, Arno Pearse, remarked with respect to cotton, "With the exception of coffee, it can be said that no Brazilian product receives the same remuneration as those from other nations, and this is due to the lack of classification."

And further, on the same page, he notes that: "Without exception, in Brazilian cotton, a complete absence of fiber uniformity can be observed" (Pearse, 1921: 214).

The absence of standards to guide the producer was also identified for other products. For example:

> The inferiority of our meat, classified as being of third and fourth quality among consumers, and, on the other hand, the low value of our beef cattle, require from breeders a patriotic sacrifice to improve breeding through the crossing with improved races for beef production (Riet, 1921: 269).

Table 2: Number of legal documents regarding classification and standardization of Brazilian food and agriculture. 1890-1999.

| Years | Law | Decree | Regulation | Resolution | Communication | Normative Instruction | Decision |
|-------|-----|--------|------------|------------|---------------|----------------------|----------|
| 1890-1899 | - | - | - | - | - | - | - |
| 1900-1909 | - | 1 | - | - | - | - | 1 |
| 1910-1919 | - | 5 | - | - | - | - | - |
| 1920-1929 | - | 8 | - | - | - | - | - |
| 1930-1939 | 7 | 1 | - | - | - | - | - |
| 1940-1949 | 10 | 11 | 2 | - | - | - | - |
| 1950-1959 | 2 | 15 | 7 | 1 | - | - | - |
| 1960-1969 | 4 | 22 | 7 | 2 | - | - | - |
| 1970-1979 | 3 | 5 | 83 | 148 | 7 | - | - |
| 1980-1989 | 5 | 5 | 45 | 21 | 2 | 3 | - |
| 1990-1999 | 6 | 7 | 140 | 19 | - | 8 | - |

Source: Collecção das Leis da República dos Estados Unidos do Brazil (1915-1937); LEX – Coletanea de Legislação (1937-1971) and LEX – Coletânea de Legislação e Jurisprudência (1972-2000).

The pressures to improve the quality of export products were finally successful in the following decade. Hence, in the 1930s, there was an evident change in focus of this specific legislation. Decree-Law no. 51, of December 8, 1937, already refers to different types of the same product with a focus on coffee. But the peak in the treatment of the matter was Decree-Law no. 334 of May 1938. This established classifications and taxation for the country's agricultural products and primary materials destined for exportation and targeted their standardization.

Beginning in the 1940s, the number of legal documents referring to classification and standardization grew rapidly. In the 1950s and the 1960s the focus was mainly on export products. This scenario, however, began to change in the 1960s, the same period in which soybean area began to expand in Brazil. On May 24, 1961, by means of Decree no. 50,647, the government began to require the payment of tariffs for classification. But the most important document appeared in 1975: It was Law no. 6,305 of December 15. It was strongly criticized by the private sector as a State-biased law. It made classification of plant products mandatory, along with their subproducts and their residues of economic value.[8] This law was later revoked by Law no. 9,972 of May 25, 2000, ending the State monopoly of classification and allowing a number of non-State agencies to perform classification activities via registration by the Ministry of Agriculture.

## 6. CLASSIFICATION AND STANDARDIZATION OF SOYBEANS

The production of soybeans in Brazil coincides with the internal strengthening of agribusiness. Soybeans were a symbol of a successful agribusiness, in part because of the number of byproducts of soybean processing ranging from meal to human food, e.g., oil, flour, bran, cookies, and margarine. Classification and standardization helped to assure compatibility from grain production in the field to factory processing.

If up to this point the central issue in standardization was the tension between the State and the market in the determination of classifications and standards, soybeans brought additional complexity, where the State-market dichotomy was gradually superceded by the entry of other agents. The expansion of soybean culture in Brazil coincided with the growing influence of several private organizations that were concerned with developing standards. Internationally as well, other standards organizations, such as the ISO (International Organization for Standardization), the WTO (World Trade Organization), Codex Alimentarius, and entities like Mercosur would begin to play a role. This is a new period in which the almost unilateral force of the State began to lose its strength. The initial matter of whether the State or the market should determine standards surrounding soybeans lost its meaning with the entry of these new agents including processors, export firms, the food industry and associations linked to them.

Since the 1960s there have been different decrees and regulations approving the specification and inspection of soybeans and their derivatives, but it was only in 1983 that the first legal instrument destined for the standardization, classification, and commercialization of soybean grain in Brazil appeared. This document was Regulation (*Portaria*) no. 262 of November 23, 1983, of the Ministry of Agriculture. Does this mean that Brazilian foreign trade in soybeans was paralyzed? Not at all. There were norms and international patterns that guided this trade and determined the shape of domestic production. State standardization was always a step behind what was common practice in the international domain.

Since the soybean grain is processed, it needs certain characteristics to be efficiently transformed into meal and oil. In the case of soybean grain, the law establishes an operational sequence to be followed in order to determine the classification of the sample of the analyzed soybean. This is what the official documents of classification and standardization try to guarantee. This official standard for soybeans offered a domestic legal base for inspections. It did not, however, impose anything that was not already practiced by those involved in this network. Domestically, soybeans were judged based on various quality factors: moisture content, broken grain, impurities and/or foreign materials, damaged grains, and green grains.

The official norms of identity, quality, packaging, labeling and presentation of oil and meal came into existence through Regulation no. 795, of December 15, 1993. Soybean oil is understood as the product obtained by mechanical pressing or extraction by solvent of soybean grain, free from mixture of other oils, fat or other materials foreign to the product. Soybean meal is the product resulting from the oil extraction of the soybean grain, whatever process was used: mechanical or chemical. Thus, the same processing unit that extracts the oil also produces the meal.

The Regulation also requires that legible characters be used in a noticeable place easily seen and hard to remove. The marking must include the following indications: 1) registration number at the Ministry of Agriculture, 2) product, 3) class, 4) type, 5) volume, 6) nutritional facts, 7) producer (name or company name), 8) address, 9) fabrication date and expiration date, and 10) lot number.

In the case of soybean meal, the classification involved classes, subclasses and types. This classification was performed, respectively, according to the treatment to which the meal was submitted, its presentation and its quality characteristics.

The classes originated from the treatments to which the soybean meal was submitted following the oil extraction. Since it is submitted to two treatments, two classes were created by the Regulation: crude and toasted meal.

## 7. SUMMARY AND CONCLUSIONS

One of the objectives of this analysis was to show the existence not only of a distance in time between soybeans and other traditional products of Brazilian food history, such as rice, corn, or cassava, but also to show that the current state of classification and standardization of agricultural and agro-industrial products was established in a different manner from those developed by traditional means. If State action was vital to the establishment of the quality of traditional products, it did not have the same significance for soybeans.

As discussed, Brazil had few food and agricultural standards when food was locally consumed. In fact, food and agricultural standards begin to appear with the creation of the Brazilian State, after the first decade of the 19th century. Historically, as exports began to grow, standards were introduced for that purpose, but the local market remained largely untouched. As Brazil became urbanized, new standards were developed to support the population shift to urban areas and to protect urban consumers.

This involved a full scale societal transformation, away from traditional values and towards the contemporary values of the global market. Universalizing values sprouted from an incipient capitalist market and were imposed piecemeal upon those familial values, founded in the agrarian patriarchy.

As was argued, to classify and to standardize were demands of the emergent system (of the "re-europeanization" of Brazil) that took years to impose themselves, but had their genesis at the time the Brazilian state was being created. From an initial focus on fraud, these new kinds of "rules" have expanded to include other concerns, such as technical instruments used by firms to reduce transaction costs and to assure higher product quality. Soybean production in Brazil emerged at this moment, becoming itself a social force in imposing these new universalizing values for agriculture and agribusiness. Today, with a focus directly linked to global competition, this applies to all seeds, crops, and food products (including nutrition and labeling).

# 8. NOTES

[1] Even as late as 1818, Luccock (1975: 376) referred to provinces that "were almost completely shut off one from another; they probably had no other resemblance besides the language."

[2] Nevertheless, it appears that the negative effect of fraud on trade was one of the incentives for the April 1, 1751 Resolution, establishing Inspection Offices, "that were created to allow the expansion and prosperity of agriculture and commerce."

[3] Busch (2000) notes that standards are first and foremost a means for establishing a moral economy. Hence, it is not surprising that fraud was of particular concern among early attempts to standardize.

[4] For further details about the introduction of soybeans in Brazil and the development of cultivars specific to tropical regions, see Miyasaka and Kiihl (1969), Miyasaka and Medina (1981), and Sousa and Busch (1998).

[5] See, for example, Krislov (1997), Brunsson (2000), and Vries (1999).

[6] An example would be the permit of February 27, 1810 that established punishments against those who falsified size on boxes of sugar.

[7] Nowadays, a permit (alvará in Portuguese) is understood as the instrument by which the Public Administration grants a license or authorization to several ends (Di Pietro, 1999:216). In that period, a permit was a much broader legal instrument. It could assume the characteristics of laws, decrees and decisions.

[8] Perhaps as a result, it took 3 years for the implementing regulation to be approved by Decree no. 82,110 of August 14, 1978.

# 9. REFERENCES

Adler, K. (1995) A Revolution to Measure: The Political Economy of the Metric System in France. Pp. 39-71 in *The Values of Precision*, edited by M. Norton Wise. Princeton: Princeton University Press.

Alencastro, L. F. de (2000) *O Trato dos Viventes – Formação do Brasil no Atlântico Sul*. São Paulo: Companhia das Letras.

Bowker, G. C., and S. L. Star (1999) *Sorting Things Out: Classification and its Consequences*. Cambridge, MA: MIT Press.

Brunsson, N. (2000) Organizations, Markets, and Standardization. Pp. 21-39 in *A World of Standards*, edited by N. Brunsson and B. Jacobsson. Oxford: Oxford University Press.

Busch, L. (2000) The Moral Economy of Grades and Standards. *Journal of Rural Studies* 16:273-283.

Collecção das Leis do Brazil (1810, 1815-1818, 1820). Rio de Janeiro, Imprensa Nacional, 1890.

Collecção das Leis do Império do Brazil (1823, 1825-1828, 1830, 1832, 1833-1834, 1836, 1840-1843, 1849-1852, 1856-1860, 1862-1865, 1878, 1880-1881, 1885). Rio de Janeiro: Thypographia Nacional, 1907, 1910.

Collecção das Leis da República dos Estados Unidos do Brazil (1890, 1903, 1909-1910, 1912-1913, 1915, 1918-1926, 1928). Rio de Janeiro: Imprensa Nacional, 1915, 1937.

Di Pietro, M. S. Z. Di (1999) *Direito Administrativo*. São Paulo: Editora Atlas. 11th edition.

Fernandes, F. (1975) *A Revolução Burguesa no Brasil*. Rio de Janeiro: Zahar Editores.

Freyre, G. (1968) *Sobrados e Mucambos – Decadência do patriarcado rural e desenvolvimento urbano*. Rio de Janeiro: L. J. Olympio Editora. 2 vols. 4th edition.

Holanda, S. B. de (1994) *Visão do Paraíso – Os Motivos Edênicos no Descobrimento e Colonização do Brasil*. São Paulo: Brasiliense.

Krislov, S. (1997) *How Nations Chose Product Standards and Standards Change Nations*. Pittsburgh: University of Pittsburgh Press.

Lima, O. (1996) *Dom João VI no Brasil*. 3rd Edition. Rio de Janeiro: Topbooks.

Luccock, J. (1820) Notes on Rio de Janeiro and the Southern Parts of Brazil; Taken During a Residence of Ten Years in that Country, from 1808 to 1818. London: Printed for Samuel Leigh, in the Strand.

Mattoso, K. M. de Q. (1986) *To Be a Slave in Brazil – 1550 – 1888*. New Brunswick, New Jersey: Rutgers University Press.

Miyasaka, S. and Kiihl, R. A. S. (1969) Genética e melhoramento da soja. Pp. 114-136 in *Melhoramento e Genética*. São Paulo, SP: Edições Melhoramento/Editora da Universidade de São Paulo.

Miyasaka, S. and Medina, J. C., eds. (1981) *A Soja no Brasil*. Campinas, SP: Instituto de Tecnologia de Alimentos – ITAL.

Nabuco, J. (1999). *A Escravidão*. Rio de Janeiro: Nova Fronteira.

Pearse, A. (1921) A lavoura do algodão no Brasil. Pp. 214-219 in: *A Lavoura – Boletim da Sociedade Nacional de Agricultura*. Rio de Janeiro: Year XXV, n. 8 e 9. August and September.

Riet, D. M. (1921) Pecuária Nacional: evoluir é progredir. In: *A Lavoura – Boletim da Sociedade Nacional de Agricultura*. Year XXV, n. 10 e 11, October/November: 269-270.

Salvador, F. V. do (1982) *História do Brasil: 1500-1627*. 7th Edition. Belo Horizonte: Itatiaia.

Sousa, I. S. F. de, and L. Busch (1998) Networks and Agricultural Development: The Case of Soybean Production and Consumption in Brazil. *Rural Sociology* 63(3): 349-371.

Souza, J. (2000) *A Modernização Seletiva – Uma reinterpretação do dilema brasileiro*. Brasília, DF: Editora UnB.

Vries, H. de (1999) *Standardization: A Business Approach to the Role of National Standardization Organizations*. Boston: Kluwer.

LAWRENCE BUSCH,* ELIZABETH RANSOM,† TONYA
MCKEE,‡ GERAD MIDDENDORF,§ AND JOHN CHESEBRO**

# 8. PARADOXES OF INNOVATION:

*Standards and Technical Change in the Transformation of the US Soybean
Industry*

> The very definition of the real becomes: that of which it is possible to give an
> equivalent reproduction. This is contemporaneous with a science that postulates that a
> process can be perfectly reproduced in a set of given conditions, and also with the
> industrial rationality that postulates a universal system of equivalency. Jean Baudrillard
> (1983: 146)

## 1. INTRODUCTION

In this chapter we examine the transformation of the soybean commodity sub-sector
in the United States. This discussion is based on the understanding that commodities
are not merely things given by nature, but that they are constructed via interaction
between humans, technologies and nature. We argue that, for certain purposes,
technologies may be considered to be of two sorts: (1) those that directly concern the
production and processing of a commodity and (2) those that are used to monitor
adherence to the definition of the commodity itself. The two sorts of technologies
are not independent, but rather open and foreclose paths of development. Put in the
words of economist Douglas North (1990), they create path dependence. Production
technologies have been widely studied (e.g., Barry et al. 2002, Bijker 1995, Molotch
2003), including studies of various aspects of agricultural production technologies
(e.g., Rogers 1995; Hayami 1997). However, the technologies of standards and
standardization have been virtually ignored (cf., Busch 2000; Grindley 1995).

Yet, standards are central to the entire process of industrial production and
exchange. The nineteenth century creation of the so-called American system of
interchangeable parts revolutionized production and led eventually to the widespread
use of assembly line production (Habakkuk 1962). Later in that same century, the

* Lawrence Busch, University Distinguished Professor, Department of Sociology, Michigan State
University.
† Elizabeth Ransom, Visiting Assistant Professor, Department of Sociology and Anthropology, University
of Richmond.
‡ Tonya Mckee, Master of Arts candidate, Geography and Environmental Planning.
§ Gerad Middendorf, Assistant Professor of Sociology, Kansas State University.
** John E. Chesebro, Certified Medical Technologist, MT (ASCP), Detroit Medical Center MT (ASCP)

J. Bingen and L. Busch, (eds.), Agricultural Standards: The Shape of the Global Food and Fiber
System, 137-155. © 2006 Springer. Printed in the Netherlands.

development of standard procedures for communication and control made possible large industrial establishments with operations in many places (Yates 1989). Indeed, today standards are ubiquitous. Not only are there standards for agricultural commodities, but for virtually all goods, services and people.

Below, we examine foreign material in soybeans as a case to illustrate how standards are implicated in commodity sub-sectors. Only through a review of the technical details can it be revealed exactly how standards participate in the construction of a sub-sector. Our intent here is not to provide a history as much as it is to examine the phenomenon of standards as illustrated by this case. First, we briefly present an overview of the literature on standards. Then, we examine the means by which foreign material is calculated. Next, we examine the roles played by farmers, elevator operators, transporters, European buyers, Japanese buyers, processors, grading equipment and climate. We conclude by noting that standards mediate between the various actors in the soybean sub-sector. But, like other technologies, the technologies of standards cannot be used to bend nature so as to fully meet the desires of any of the other human actors in the network. Thus, paradoxically, standards both restrict and enhance the flow of commodities. Equally paradoxically, standards may promote competition even while their use requires cooperation.

## 2. STANDARDS AND THE CREATION OF NEW COMMODITIES

Neoclassical and neoinstitutional economists are correct in arguing that the creation of formal grades and standards reduces transaction costs (e.g., Hill 1990; Williamson 1989). But standards also establish conventions that can be used to link (and more recently integrate) production and exchange (Eymard-Duvernay 1994; 1995). Thus, standards permit persons with little knowledge of each others' practices, and even less of each others' thoughts, to coordinate their action (Livet and Thévenot 1994; Orléan 1994). Moreover, since standards, like other conventions, are agreements to follow a course of action, they may be renegotiated in light of changes in technologies, organizations, and nature itself.

Classical economics felt little need to inquire into the origins of the market society. From that vantage point, it emerged from "...the propensity to truck, barter, and exchange one thing for another" (Smith 1994 [1776]: 14) and was common to all. Things to be traded were understood as commodities – that is to say, things that were "the same" for purposes of trade. Adam Smith chose a pin factory as his example of the division of labor, but it also was a clear example of a commodity, a fully identical product that could be produced for, and bought and sold "on the market." Neoclassical economists, while they have rejected parts of Smith's analysis, have largely accepted this account of the marketplace.

Yet, if Smith had chosen another commodity – grain, or furniture or fish – he would have found enormous variation in each lot. Only by a tedious, laborious and complex process could such singularities be transformed into commodities. For example, in their study of the development of canola in Canada, Busch et al. (1994) note, that when it was first introduced farmers initially complained of the 'weediness' of the crop. Plants grew to various heights, matured at different times, varied in color of the seed and oil, often had a mustard-like odor, and were otherwise unsuited to large scale cultivation as a commodity. Only by the labor of plant breeders, biochemists and others was canola normalized, standardized, socialized, and made to conform to the norms of the marketplace. In contrast, Smith's failure to notice the work involved in making singularities into commodities allowed him to immortalize the market society, for it is (at least) the process of creating and adhering to formal standards that distinguishes modern market economies from other epochs in history.

Standards and standardization contribute to the production of commodities, and because of this standards and standardization are often at the center of political and social struggles. Standards are not inevitable outcomes, but rather reflect choices made by actors or groups of actors. Thus, choices are made that construct what is positively and negatively valued. However, since standards and standardization are at first presented as purely technical details, the political and social are often hard to see (Bowker and Star 2000). Related to an understanding that standards reflect choices, an important aspect of standards is their symmetry. A grade for soybeans is simultaneously a grade for the beans and for the farmer that produced them.

There are complex symmetries among groups of actors and related types of technologies: farms, grading, export, meal and oil processing, and food processing. Soybeans flow from the farm to grading stations where they are weighed and graded to export ships and/or to crushing and processing firms. To aid in understanding these symmetries, our focus is entirely on post-harvest grading, although soybeans are graded again at ports of entry (for export soybeans) and at processing plants (for oil and meal) among other places. Of greater significance for our purposes are the symmetric constraints and opportunities that changes in farm, export and processing technologies pose with respect to grading systems.

A useful metaphor for considering the interrelationships among these various classes of technologies is that of plate tectonics. Geologists have shown that the earth's surface consists of tectonic plates of various shapes and sizes that rub against each other. Often that rubbing consists of only slight movements, but occasionally plates exert tremendous pressure on each other causing an earthquake that realigns the plates. Similarly, the six groups of actors and types of technologies described above form a system of interrelationships, what Callon (1991) has called a "technoeconomic network." Each actor pressures other actors to change their behavior. Most of the time, the actors cooperate as they compete. However, occasionally new technologies result in significant realignments – the earthquakes of technological change and industry coordination. Such changes in network organization are apparently irreversible; it is impossible to go backward although one may move laterally.

Consider the perspective of farmers: Farmers can only grow the seeds that are available to them in the soils and climates in which they find themselves. Thus, post-harvest standards and the grading technologies used to monitor and enforce those standards must be limited to the range of seeds, soils and climates available. For example, if the market only accepts yellow seeds but yellow seeded cultivars are unavailable, farmers will abandon that sub-sector and shift to another crop. In other words, failure to take the seed into account in imposing the standards might make it impossible for farmers to enter the market at all. But the reverse is true as well. If new yellow seeds become widely available grades may be modified to consider that characteristic or even to make its presence mandatory.

Thus, we can see that the farmers, their suppliers and those to whom they sell are all part of the *filière*, network, supply chain, or sub-sector. But, of equal importance the seeds, the climate, the soils, the farm equipment, the standards, the processing equipment, and the transportation available also form part of the network. Take away any element – human, technical, or natural – and the network will tend to break down.[1]

## 3. THE CALCULATION OF FOREIGN MATERIAL

The case of foreign material in soybeans reveals an interesting story of when, how, and why standards and standardization become important. Unlike a quality of interest that is directly sensed (e.g., color), foreign material requires much more elaborate testing. Merely looking at a truckload, a boxcar load, or a ship's hold filled with soybeans provides no means for estimating the proportion of dirt, brokens, weed seed and other foreign matter present in the grain.[2] In the US, the Department of Agriculture specifies that a sieve with round holes of 8/64 inch size must be used to measure foreign matter.[3] The procedure for sieving is quite elaborate. First, the grain must be sampled. Sampling is no small matter as the quantities from which the sample must be drawn are both very large and often very heterogeneous. Once the sample is drawn, it is necessary to divide it into subsamples for each of the various tests. For this, a special piece of equipment, known as a Boerner Divider, is used. This device consists of a large hopper into which the sample is dumped. The device then mixes the material in the hopper and divides it into smaller samples.

In testing for foreign material, first a sample of 1000 to 1050 grams is drawn. Foreign material is considered to be of two sorts: coarse and fine. The coarse pieces of foreign matter are removed by hand. Coarse foreign material includes whole kernels of corn, cockleburs, sticks one inch or more in length, pods, and other coarse material. The "cleaned" sample is then reduced in size to 125 grams. It contains both the soybeans and fine foreign matter, defined as broken corn kernels, popcorn, sunflower seed, edible beans smaller than soybeans, thistles, morning glory, small sticks, parts of pods, weed seed, and any other fine material. The reduced sample is then ready to be sieved. It is then poured into either a mechanical or hand sieve. The sieve is shaken five strokes (i.e., five complete cycles) such that much fine material drops through the holes. The sieve is then carefully removed from its bottom pan insuring that additional material does not drop through the holes. The material remaining in the sieve is sorted into soybeans and foreign material. This coarse foreign material is then added to the fine material that passed through the sieve. Both the coarse and fine foreign materials are weighed and the percent is calculated to the nearest one hundredth of one percent. Then the two percentages are summed and rounded to the nearest tenth of a percent. Rounding is always such that numbers greater than 0.05 are rounded up to next highest number (United States Department of Agriculture 1997).[4]

Of course, the purpose of all these elaborate procedures and strictly specified equipment is to ensure (i.e., create) objectivity in determining the percent foreign material. Despite that, for more than fifty years both the measurement procedures and the percent allowable have been the subject of considerable debate. Let us consider the perspectives of the parties to the ongoing negotiations.

The amount of foreign matter permitted is determined by (1) farmers' cultivation and (especially) harvesting practices which are themselves conditioned by the machinery available for harvesting, (2) the technologies used by rail transporters to ship the beans, (3) the technologies used by elevators to store, blend and transfer the beans, (4) the technologies and design of ships used to transport the beans overseas, (5) the demands of importers of soybeans (which are conditioned by alternative sources of supply, alternatives to soybeans in the marketplace, and the practices of shippers), (6) the kinds of crushing, oil refining and meal utilization technologies that are commonly used, (7) the food technologies used (especially in Japan) to make soybeans into food, and (8) the speed, cost and ease of use of grading technologies available at a given time and place. As each of these eight determinants change, so the grading technologies in use become subject to renegotiation and modification. It is for this reason that grading technologies and the standards they impose are in constant flux despite enormous efforts to pin them down. Below we examine the conditions, technologies and positions taken by each of the major actors in the longstanding debate over foreign material in soybeans.

## 4. FARMERS AND SOYBEAN PRODUCTION

Initially, US farmers grew soybeans for hay. Only in 1941 was more than half of the soybean acreage planted for beans (Goldberg 1952). They had no interest in harvesting the beans except for use as seed for the next year's crop. Thus, beans were commonly of a variety of colors, and bean quality was of virtually no concern. All that began to change in the early 1920s when oil was successfully produced from soybeans in Chicago Heights, Illinois.[5] But the key to the development of the US soybean industry was the so-called Peoria Plan. H.G. Atwood of Allied Mills agreed in 1928 to purchase on contract all the soybeans produced on 50,000 acres at a fixed price. This had the effect of convincing farmers that soybeans were a viable cash crop and convincing food and industrial processors that soybean oil would be available on a regular basis (Dies 1942). Even at the height of the depression, soybeans proved to be a profitable crop (Berlan, Bertrand and Lebas 1977).

When farmers switched from growing soybeans for hay to growing them for beans, a series of new problems emerged. First, the beans themselves needed to be more carefully selected. Oil producers – especially those producing cooking and salad oil – wanted clear, light colored oil. Yellow soybeans were preferred as black and brown beans gave a dark color to the oil. Second, farmers continued to harvest the beans as they had done the hay. Piper explained: "When cut with a mowing machine with an attachment or with a self-rake reaper, the plants may be raked in small piles or placed in small shocks. These piles or shocks should be left for four or five days in good drying weather, or until the grain is found to be fairly dry in the pods" (1923: 92-93). Then they would run the dried stalks through a stationary threshing machine. This led to considerable damage to the beans. A 1922 University of Missouri bulletin even gave advice on how one might separate broken and split beans from whole ones (Piper and Morse 1923). On the positive side, this harvesting procedure minimized foreign material.

Soybean harvesting equipment was developed by modifying equipment developed for other crops.[6] Although the combine was invented in 1836, it was too expensive for most Midwestern farmers until the late 1920s. Therefore, initially soybean harvesting was a laborious task involving the use of machinery that was not specifically designed for the task. Moreover, weeds abounded in soybean fields and only mechanical methods for their removal were available. As a result, weed seed and foreign matter were found in significant quantities in soybeans brought to the grading station. Finally, soybeans were prone to shattering and the considerable handling required to bring them to stationary threshers led to considerable losses in the field.[7]

In the 1930s the Garwood brothers of Stonington, Illinois convinced the Massey-Harris company to develop a suitable combine for soybean harvesting (Smith 1945). The development of new harvesting equipment (the soybean combine) reduced losses from 30% to only about 9%, a level at which they would remain until the latter part of the century (Kohn 1990). However, before 1930, combines had a fixed pickup bar which was unable to follow the contours of the ground. The development of the floating pickup bar undoubtedly both reduced foreign material and shattering (Hurt 1991) by cutting each vine at the proper location on the stalk. In addition, machines were developed that were lighter and therefore less likely to become bogged down in wet soil. And, self-propelled machines could travel over more uneven ground than those pulled by tractors. Improved combines, together with broad spectrum herbicides and new varieties of soybeans significantly reduced the foreign matter in soybeans – so much so that farmers and/or elevator operators began to add foreign matter so as to bring the amount up to just below the maximum permitted by law.

One final point worthy of note is that many farmers today store soybeans on their farms before sale. This creates yet another location where foreign material may enter the crop. Specifically, grain bins and augers must be cleaned before use with soybeans or corn grain will be mixed with the soybean crop. However, when comparing the grade that makes up the majority of US exports with the grade that makes up the majority of Brazilian and Argentinean soybean exports, the US grade remains relatively generous with respect to foreign matter. Brazil and Argentina, the major competitors, have a one percent limit on foreign matter compared to two in the US. However, US farmers remain largely unconcerned and equipment manufacturers have little or no incentive to develop better harvesting equipment. One author explains: "If soybean standards were more tightly drawn, combine engineers would quickly respond with even less crackage of beans, with even cleaner samples in the bin. When meaningful premiums are paid for whole beans and clean beans, combine engineers will be there to provide just that" (Buescher 1970: 86).

## 5. ELEVATOR OPERATORS AND ELEVATOR TECHNOLOGIES

Elevator operators engage in a practice known as blending. It takes advantage of the way in which US grain grades and standards are designed. Specifically, as is shown in Table 1, a variety of "factors" on which grain is to be graded are identified. For each of these, a maximum limit is imposed. Failure to meet any one of the grading criteria results in lowering the grade. Thus, for example, an elevator operator with 100 tons of No. 2 soybeans with low foreign matter (1.5%) might buy 10 tons of soybeans which meet all tests for No. 2 soybeans except that for foreign material, where the tests indicate a value of 2.5%. By blending the two lots, the elevator operator would have 110 tons with approximately 1.6% foreign matter, a value still considerably below the 2% limit for No. 2 beans.

Given the wide range of factors which are taken into consideration, the determination of potential advantages of blending is in practice a fairly complex procedure. Nevertheless, it is quite lucrative, making grain blending a very attractive business. As such, owners of elevators have been reluctant to change grading standards. For example, a Cargill spokesperson argued that "The proposed changes not only would restrict our ability to respond to the market. They also would impose substantial new costs for the industry and the producers" (Kohn 1992: 11).

Exporters tend to be more cynical about this, noting that No. 2 beans (the most common export grade) usually contain the maximum allowed on all factors. Indeed, when a shift from two to three percent foreign material occurred in 1949, one exporter noted: "it is only human for a country elevator or terminal elevator to add beans with excessive foreign material or even straight foreign material to the extent of bringing their deliveries to the 3 percent level" (Fox 1954: 60).

## 6. TRANSPORTERS AND TRANSPORTATION TECHNOLOGIES

One of the common complaints of foreign buyers of US soybeans is that the quality claimed on inspection certificates is not that provided when the boat reaches the foreign port. Of course, in some cases this is the result of fraudulent activities on the part of transporters. Indeed, in the early 1970s there was a major national scandal surrounding soybean grading, especially in exports. At one Congressional hearing a former grain company employee explained:

> I learned how to substitute a fake grain sample for the bona fide sample, and to manipulate or change valid samples when a substitute sample was not available. I did not feel that I was being taught how to break the law. At the time it simply seemed that I was being shown how the grain business was conducted.

> During my training in Chicago, I became adapt [sic] at switching and modifying samples to offset breakage, moisture and spoilage. I learned that we could cheat on soybeans even on appeal because we had access to and could modify samples.

Table 1. US Official Soybean Grades, 1935-1997.

| Year Grade | Minimum Test Weight Pounds per bushel | | | | Moisture Percent | | | | Splits Percent | | | | Total Damaged Kernels Percent | | | | Heat Damaged Kernels Percent | | | | Foreign Material Percent | | | | Other Classes[1] Percent | | | |
|---|---|---|---|---|---|---|---|---|---|---|---|---|---|---|---|---|---|---|---|---|---|---|---|---|---|---|---|---|
| | 1 | 2 | 3 | 4 | 1 | 2 | 3 | 4 | 1 | 2 | 3 | 4 | 1 | 2 | 3 | 4 | 1 | 2 | 3 | 4 | 1 | 2 | 3 | 4 | 1 | 2 | 3 | 4 |
| 1935 | 56 | 54 | 52 | 50 | 15 | 15 | 17 | 18 | 1 | 10 | 20 | 30 | 1.5 | 3.0 | 5.0 | 8.0 | | | | | 0.5 | 2.0 | 4.0 | 6.0 | 1 | 3 | 5 | 5 |
| 1941 | 56 | 54 | 52 | 50 | 13 | 14 | 16 | 18 | 10 | 15 | 20 | 30 | 2.0 | 3.0 | 5.0 | 8.0 | | | | | 1.0 | 2.0 | 3.0 | 5.0 | 1 | 3 | 5 | 5 |
| 1949 | 56 | 54 | 52 | 49 | 13 | 14 | 16 | 18 | 10 | 20 | 30 | 40 | 2.0 | 3.0 | 5.0 | 8.0 | | | | | 2.0 | 3.0 | 4.0 | 6.0 | 1 | 3 | 5 | 5 |
| 1955 | 55 | 54 | 52 | 49 | 13 | 14 | 16 | 18 | 10 | 20 | 30 | 40 | 2.0 | 3.0 | 5.0 | 8.0 | 0.2 | 0.5 | 1.0 | 3.0 | 1.0 | 2.0 | 3.0 | 5.0 | 1 | 2 | 5 | 10 |
| 1997 | 56 | 54 | 52 | 49 | | | | | 10 | 20 | 30 | 40 | 2.0 | 3.0 | 5.0 | 8.0 | 0.2 | 0.5 | 1.0 | 3.0 | 1.0 | 2.0 | 3.0 | 5.0 | 1 | 2 | 5 | 10 |

Notes:

[1] Includes off color soybeans in yellow green Soybeans.

Sources: USDA, 1935, 1956, 1980, 1997; Soybean Digest, 1955.

> Under the current system elevator employees can increase elevator profits by: Manipulating elevator equipment, falsifying or distorting grain quality, and influencing grain inspectors. Sampling devices can be circumvented by slowing the speed of the belt moving the grain, designing spouts to bypass the sampling device, and setting the sampling device to yield an unrepresentative sample. Scales can be circumvented by manually or electronically printing out any weights desired (U. S. Congress. Senate. Subcommittee on Foreign Agricultural Policy and the Subcommittee on Agricultural Production 1976: 4,6).

Such testimony eventually led to a major overhaul of the grain inspection system.

But equally problematic are the technological problems posed by the very process of long distance ocean shipping. First, given the measuring procedures described above, an increase in foreign material during shipping appears to be due in part to finely broken soybeans which can more easily pass through the sieve (Shaw 1956a). The finely broken soybeans are a consequence of the fact that as the marketing channels have been lengthened, grain is augured, dumped or otherwise handled at least 12 times between farm and final foreign customer (Brown 1977).

More was revealed when foreign complaints caused USDA inspectors to examine three ships loading at US ports and again when they arrived and unloaded in Europe. The team found that when beans are loaded on a ship, they build into a cone beneath the spout. Foreign matter and brokens remain there while round soybeans slide or roll to the side. Conversely, when suction is used to remove the beans from the ship at the receiving port, a reverse condition develops. Craters form around the suction tubes and foreign material builds up in ridges around edges. Thus, in discharging, part of the load may have much more foreign matter than other parts and sampling may not be accurate. Finally, the team concluded that there were enough differences in standards on the two sides of the ocean that they were not directly comparable (Shaw 1956b).

## 7. EUROPEAN BUYERS AND PROCESSING TECHNOLOGIES

As a result of farm practices, elevator blending, and transport problems described above, complaints from European buyers have been a consistent problem since the early days of world trade in soybeans. In the immediate postwar years, the US enjoyed a virtual monopoly on export soybeans. China, the only other serious contender at the time, was recovering from years of war and civil strife. The combination of price supports, export enhancement programs and programs limiting production of grains made soybeans the crop of choice for many US farmers (Berlan, Bertrand and Lebas 1977). However, by the 1970s Brazil and Argentina had entered the export market. Over time they have gained an increasing share of the overall market. Quoting C.J. M. Meershoek, executive director of the Dutch chapter of FEDIOL, the European oilseed processors association: "We try to stay away from US soybeans...Foreign matter is our main concern" (Kohn 1992: 10).

Yet, despite the complaints, repeated attempts to tighten the standards for foreign materials have failed. Moreover, USDA reports that most foreign material originates on the farm and that removing it at the elevator is quite costly – perhaps as high as $106 million per year, but at least $20 million (Lin 1996). Even though the US share of the world export market continues to decline, it is unlikely that change in foreign material will come easily.

## 8. JAPANESE BUYERS AND PROCESSING TECHNOLOGIES

Historically, while domestic processors and European buyers used soybeans for essentially the same final products, Japan uses soybeans for food. Smith (1958: 15) explained: "Exports to Japan are mostly a No. 2 grade, which permits 20% splits, 3% damaged beans, 2% foreign matter, and 2% brown, black or bicolored beans. These fractions add up to a total of 27% of material with varied characteristics that does not process properly in most Japanese foods." Farmers on 2.5 acres in Japan or China produce very clean beans because they harvest them by hand. Moreover, split beans absorb water and cook more rapidly than whole beans (although they are fully acceptable for oil and meal production), making them unsuitable for tofu. Furthermore, US standards do not consider green coated beans as green but as yellow. Japanese tofu processors found this unacceptable (Fox 1954).

In addition, by American and European standards, Japanese soybean *food* processors were quite small.[8] This posed yet another set of special problems. For example, given the small size of Japanese processors and uneven distribution of foreign material in ships, it is often the case that, even though foreign material is below the maximum allowable overall, some producer receives a great deal of foreign material. "In fact, it appeared that many of our past complaints on the foreign material factor have probably stemmed from this distribution problem" (Kurtz 1956: 41).

Today, most US food-grade soybeans destined for Japan are grown under contract. Farmers typically receive a premium for these beans, which are segregated from feed-grade beans throughout the supply chain (Leake 2001). This increases handling costs, but produces a bean satisfactory to Japanese processors and consumers.

## 9. DOMESTIC PROCESSORS AND PROCESSING TECHNOLOGIES

The processing industry has also had a significant effect on grades and standards. In the US, three types of oil processing equipment have been used: hydraulic presses, expellers, and solvent extraction. Hydraulic presses were used first in the United States, both with soybeans and with other oilseeds. The hydraulic press is quite simple: Cakes of cooked, crushed soybeans are enclosed in cloth and inserted into a press box. Each press holds 20-25 cakes 11 × 28 inches. The press itself consists of a base and head of cast iron. About 4000 pounds per square inch pressure is used such that the oil flows into a trough on the edges of the press and is drawn off. However, the hydraulic press required a great deal of hand labor. In addition, cloths used in the process were costly and lasted only a sort time, and the cake from the meal had an oil content of six percent. One positive feature was that the foreign matter was of little consequence.

Expellers started to come into general use about 1930 (Chicago Board of Trade 1956). They were designed to meet the need for continuous process oil-producing equipment. The expeller operates on a principle similar to that of a meat grinder. In short, an Archimedean screw rotates inside a cylinder made of steel rods. Pressure of 6 tons per square inch is exerted on the ground beans, dried to <3% moisture before entering the expeller, such that the oil is forced out of the small spaces between the steel rods. It is collected in a pan below for further refining. Unlike the hydraulic press, the expeller requires little or no attention; one person could monitor several machines. Like the press, the expeller produced a cake with 6% oil. However, a bonus was that the cake had higher digestibility for animal feed as it was cooked by the friction generated when the expeller turned (Horvath 1938).

The solvent method is most commonly used today. It is a continuous flow process that consists of three steps: (1) cleaning and rolling the beans, (2) treating them with a solvent, and (3) separation of the solvent from the oil by distillation. Unlike the expeller method, the solvent process requires that soybeans be rolled rather than crushed. Crushed beans would tend to clump during the solvent bath, thereby blocking the removal of oil. Instead the beans are rolled between two rollers which turn at slightly different speeds. The crushing process spreads the beans out and flakes them such that there is more surface area for oil extraction, and, therefore, more oil is removed. Then, the beans are bathed in hexane, a petroleum derivative, which dissolves the oil. Finally, the entire solution is heated. As hexane has a much lower boiling point than either soybean oil or water, it can be boiled off, distilled and reused at a later point in the cycle. Moreover, as with the expeller processing, the heating of the meal has desirable nutritional effects for animal feed.

Hydraulic and expeller methods were most commonly used until the 1950s when solvent processes began to replace them. Today, hydraulic presses are virtually unknown, while expellers are used only for specialized, small scale processing.[9]

The early solvent extractors were developed in Germany and used for oil extraction from a variety of oilseeds in larger mills in Europe, especially in England. In the mid-1930s Germany began to encourage soybean production in Romania and Bulgaria. In Romania production increased from 25,000 bu. in 1934 to 3 million bu. in 1939. Similarly, in Bulgaria production increased from 350,000 to 2.5 million bu. during the same time period. But World War II signaled the end of German-financed production and the communist regimes of the postwar era had little interest in rekindling the relationship (Burtis 1950).

In these European plants, benzine or gasoline was initially the preferred solvent. However,

> A large part of the early failure to develop the extraction process satisfactorily is traceable to the unsuitability of the solvent used. The solvent being incompletely removed from the oil and meal, imparted a very noticeable taste and odor to these products, which seriously affected their market value and built up prejudices against the solvent extraction system. At present, however, solvents which are easily and completely removable are used, and the oil and oilmeal is entirely free from solvent taste and odor (Horvath 1938: 44).

In interwar Europe, butter and olive oil were the most common edible fats; soybeans were only of use for industrial products such as soaps, paints and adhesives, so the odor was on no consequence. In contrast, although first used as a replacement for linseed oil in soft soaps and in hydrogenated form as hard soap (Piper and Morse 1923), in the US soybean oil soon entered into use as cooking and salad oil, margarine, and as an ingredient in prepared food products. Indeed, the first tank car of refined oil was sold to a margarine manufacturer in 1930 by Staley (Dies 1942).

Although the first solvent plant opened in the US in 1923 in Monticello, Illinois (Goldberg 1952), solvent extraction remained rare until hexane was discovered to be a satisfactory solvent. Then, it began to replace other forms of processing in the US. However, the high flammability of hexane proved to be a barrier to the establishment of small processing plants of the sort common for expellers and presses. Especially in its early years, hexane processing required extremely careful precautions for fire prevention, including situating the hexane bath some distance from electrical motors (Goss 1941). Indeed, today it is not uncommon for solvent plants to have the hexane bath in a "room" with just one wall (on the north side) so as to permit rapid dispersion of hexane fumes. Researchers at Iowa State University did attempt to develop small scale solvent processing arguing that "We believe that the concentration of industry in the form of large units in the cities is economically and socially undesirable" (Arnold 1941: 5). They believed that it would be possible to develop plants with a production capacity of 5-25 tons per day using non-explosive trichloroethylene as a solvent. However, most soybeans and some soy oil became important ingredients in cattle feed and trichloroethylene proved to be toxic to cattle (Goldberg 1952).

However, the flaking process posed new problems for processors. The rollers could be easily damaged by foreign materials. The manager of a processing plant explains: "We find that the cleaning operation is one that is a constant problem for us and the foreign material creates a lot of wear in all our machines and our highest maintenance cost in our mill is for maintaining the equipment which we use to handle the foreign material in the plant" (Pogeler 1954: 55). In addition, if moisture was too high, then the beans would gum up the flaking rollers; if moisture was too low, the beans would be pulverized causing loss of solvent and potential explosions (Goldberg 1952). The advantages and disadvantages of the three processing technologies are listed in Table 2.

## 10.    GRADERS, GRADING EQUIPMENT AND PROCEDURES

The grading equipment and procedures are themselves limits on grades and standards. As one observer noted:

> Grades or standards must necessarily be based on specific properties or characteristics of a commodity and these properties and characteristics must be susceptible of measurement. The measurement of these properties and characteristics depends, in turn, on the existence of applicable tests or methods of analysis which are sufficiently accurate for trading purposes. The existence of such methods, however, cannot be taken for granted. In fact, it may take a decade or more to develop a single method suitable for

evaluating some important characteristic even though a considerable number of scientists and technologists may apply themselves to the problem (Freyer 1950: 425).

Even relatively simple characteristics such as damage, splits and foreign material were often overestimated at country elevators, leading farmers to receive less than they might otherwise for their crop (Iftner 1942).

Table 2. Advantages and Disadvanteges of Several Types of Soybean Oil Extraction

| Type | Advantages | Disadvantages |
|---|---|---|
| Hydraulic Press | Low cost. Low water requirements. No solvent loss or parts that wear down. Capacity increased easily by adding another press. Insurance rates low. | High residual oil in meal. Protein in cake is coagulated. Press cloths expensive. High power requirements. |
| Expeller | Low labor cost. Low steam cost. Better oil. Little water needed. No cloths. Space requirements small. Small investment. Many oilseeds can be processed using same expeller. Heat of process removes antinutrional compounds. | Large amount of oil left in cake. High power requirements. |
| Solvent Extractor | Larger proportion of oil removed. Meal is lower in oil resulting in more satisfactory feed. Oil possesses superior bleaching properties. Protein in meal more concentrated. Beans not cooked making them more digestible. | Uses flammable solvents. Very high capital costs. Early solvents (benzene and gasoline) left odor and taste in oil and meal. Meal must be a toasted to eliminate antinutritionlcompounds. |

Source: Adopted from Horvath (1938).

From the very inception of the soybean industry in the US, there has been widespread agreement that oil and protein content are the characteristics most relevant to final users (e.g., Jordan 1944). At least one recent survey of farmers found that they were sympathetic to adding such measures to the grading process (Zhang 1991). However, while oil and meal tests have been available for many years, no test met the requirements noted above. That is to say, no test was sufficiently cheap, rapid and accurate, at least as measured by USDA scientists.[10] Thus, as early as 1950 it was possible to test for oil content, but the procedure was such that it was impractical to test less than five freight cars at a time (Freyer 1950). In 1978, one observer noted that the equipment necessary to measure oil and protein content would cost as much as $12-14,000 – far more than any country elevator could afford (Lee 1978). And, in 1986 a representative of the American Soybean Association lamented that "[w]hether current technology would allow such a system before the soybeans are exported and processed is, however, problematic at best" (U. S. Congress. Senate. Subcommittee on Rural Development 1986:129). As a result, moisture and foreign material were used as proxies for oil and protein content (Keirstead 1952). The development of Near-Infrared (NIR) analysis represents a major breakthrough in soybean grading. It is non-destructive, rapid, and highly accurate, although more costly than proxy measures. However, as yet it is still not in use at the first point of sale (Smith 1991).

## 11.   CLIMATE AND THOSE WHO LIVE WITH IT

Climate may also affect the quality of soybeans, often in ways not considered by the grades and standards. For example, in 1988 a drought led to high chlorophyll content and green oil, adding to processing costs considerably. In addition, the dry beans had wrinkled seedcoats, making dehulling more difficult. With 25% of the crop shriveled, the Federal Grain Inspection Service had to begin reporting shriveled beans, even though they were not part of the official standards (Mangold and Reeve 1988).

## 12.   CONCLUSIONS

Commodities are constructed objects brought into being in part by standards and the standardization of standards which are then applied to material objects (and, by implication, to those who produce them). Although they appear stable when viewed from a distance, in fact they are in constant flux as all parties to the negotiations over the standards jockey for position. By carefully inquiring into the technical conditions of soybean transformation throughout the supply chain we can make those negotiation processes visible. This adds a level of richness glossed over by conventional approaches to the study of standards.

Furthermore, commodities are constructed from the interrelationships among humans, technologies and nature in which the assignment of certain properties to each is subject to considerable dispute. Put another way, in the production of commodities, what aspects of the commodity are assigned to humans, technologies and nature is in some sense arbitrary – governed by conventions about such assignments. Thus, the good or poor qualities of soybeans may be assigned to the beans themselves, to the technologies that are used to transform them, or to the humans who are involved in using those technologies.

In addition, the relationship between nature and soybean technologies, on the one hand, and standards, on the other, may be stated as follows: Technological changes and changes in nature open new possibilities (and foreclose old ones) which are used by humans (individually or as part of organizations) to gain market share and to undercut competitors. However, technological changes in any given part of the soybean sub-sector exact changes among other parts of the sub-sector – changes that are not always accepted, and that are sometimes resisted. But even as standards can be used to enhance one's competitive position, cooperation in implementing standards is paradoxically needed if the sub-sector as a whole is, quite literally, to deliver the goods. (Here, we may argue, like Latour, that nature resists occasionally as well, by failing to rain or raining too much, failing to germinate, etc.). Grades and standards play an intermediary role in that they literally mediate among the various actors in the sub-sector. However, just as the technologies of production and processing are limited by the degree to which nature can be made to bend to human desires, so the technologies of grades and standards are so limited. If a particular character of a natural product such as soybeans is not susceptible to measurement that is rapid, accurate and inexpensive, then that character cannot be measured directly and those persons desiring to increase or decrease that character are at least partially blocked in their efforts.

Finally, grades and standards can have unexpected and unintended consequences for the sub-sector as a whole. For example, the separate evaluation of each grading factor tends to encourage practices such as blending and even illegal addition of foreign material. While certain individuals and firms may benefit from such practices, it is likely that the sub-sector as a whole does not.

## 13.   NOTES

[1] We agree here with Latour (1987) in arguing that the empirical study of actor networks must include humans and nonhumans, without giving priority to either.

[2] Brokens are parts of soybeans that pass through an 8/64 round-hole sieve. Splits are beans the seed leaves of which have separated.

[3] Until 1941 holes were 10/64" in diameter. The larger openings held back fewer soybeans as splits, thereby increasing the amount classified as foreign matter (Flumerfelt 1941).

[4] Until not too long ago, one rounded down. This led one senator to remark that "...our laws permit us to export grain knowing full well that it is not going to meet that standard once it arrives at the destination" (U. S. Congressional Senate. Subcommittee on Rural Development 1986: 9).

[5] The first soybeans processed in the US were brought to the country in 1911 from Manchuria. They were used to produce soybean oil meal for livestock and soybean oil for industrial use. The first crushing of domestic beans was accomplished in Elizabeth City, North Carolina in 1915 at a factory normally used to crush cottonseed (Dies 1942).

[6] So much was soybean cultivation in the US tied to corn, that even the space between rows (40") was initially the same. Only somewhat later was it discovered that narrower rows reduced weed infestation and increased yields (Merrill Lynch 1969).

[7] Soybeans themselves have been subject to considerable modification in order to meet grain standards. For example, varieties have been developed that have greater resistance to shattering and that have pods higher off the ground, thereby reducing foreign material in the harvest (Probst 1970).

[8] We distinguish between food processors and soybean crushers. Japanese crushers have factories about the same size as their American counterparts.

[9] Some expellers sold today heat the meal to about 300°F creating a feed particularly suitable for dairy cattle.

[10] One company did attempt to market a rapid tester for oil content in 1953 claiming that it was within ½ percent of official methods (Schmidling 1953), but for reasons unknown to us it was never widely used.

## 14.   REFERENCES

Arnold, L. K. (1941) A Call for Community Plants. *Soybean Digest* 1:4-5, 12.
Barry, A., D. Slater, and M. Callon (2002) Technology, politics and the market: An Interview with Michel Callon. *Economy and Society* 31:285-306.
Baudrillard, J. (1983) *Simulations*. New York: Semiotext(e).
Becker, H. S. (1974) Art as Collective Action. *American Sociological Review* 39:767-76.
Berlan, J.-P., J.-P. Bertrand, and L. Lebas (1977) The Growth of the American 'Soybean Complex'. *European Review of Agricultural Economics* 4:395-416.

Bijker, W. (1995) *Of Bicycles, Bakelite, and Bulbs: Toward a Theory of Sociotechnical Change.* Cambridge, MA: MIT Press.
Brown, E. (1977) Cleaning Up the Grain Inspection System. *Soybean Digest* 37:28-29.
Buescher, W. M. (1970) Farm Machinery and the Soybean. *Soybean Digest* 30:84-86.
Burtis, E. L. (1950) World Soybean Production and Trade. Pp. 61-108 in *Soybeans and Soybean Products*, edited by K. S. Markley. New York: Interscience Publishers.
Busch, L., V. Gunter, T. Mentele, M. Tachikawa, and K. Tanaka (1994) Socializing Nature: Technoscience and the Transformation of Rapeseed into Canola. *Crop Science* 34:607-614.
Callon, M. (1991) Technoeconomic Networks and Irreversibility. Pp. 132-161 in *A Sociology of Monsters: Essays on Power, Technology, and Domination*, edited by J. Law. London: Routledge and K. Paul.
Chicago Board of Trade (1956) *The Story of Soybeans.* . Chicago: Chicago Board of Trade.
Dies, E. J. (1942) *Soybeans: Gold from the Soil.* New York: Macmillan.
Eymard-Duvernay, F. (1994) Coordination des Echanges et Qualité des Biens. Pp. 307-334 in *Analyse Economique des Conventions*, edited by A. Orléan. Paris: Presses Universitaires de France.
_____. (1995) La Négociation de la Qualité. Pp. 39-48 in *Agro-Alimentaire: Une Economie de la Qualité*, edited by F. Nicolas and E. Valceschini. Paris: INRA and Economica.
Flumerfelt, W. (1941) The New Soybean Grades. *Soybean Digest* 1:9, 22.
Fox, W.B. (1954) Problems in Exporting Soybeans. *Soybean Digest* 14:60-63.
Freyer, E. (1950) Grading and Evaluation of Soybeans and Derived Products. Pp. 425-454 in *Soybeans and Soybean Products*, edited by K. S. Markley. New York: Interscience Publishers.
Goldberg, R. A. (1952) *The Soybean Industry With Special Reference to the Competitive Position of the Minnesota Producer and Processor.* Minneapolis: University of Minnesota Press.
Goss, W. H. (1941) Technological Problems in Soybean Processing. *Soybean Digest* 1:4-5.
Grindley, P. (1995) *Standards Strategy and Policy: Cases and Stories.* Oxford: Oxford University Press.
Habakkuk, H. J. (1962) *American and British Technology in the Nineteenth Century.* Cambridge: Cambridge University Press.
Hayami, Y. (1997) *Development Economics: From the Poverty to the Wealth of Nations.* Oxford: Oxford University Press.
Hill, L. D. (1990) *Grain Grades and Standards: Historical Issues Shaping the Future.* Urbana, IL: University of Illinois Press.
Horvath, A. A. (1938) *The Soybean Industry.* New York: The Chemical Publishing Company of New York.
Hurt, D. (1991) Combine Harvesters. *Journal of the West* 30:43-62.
Iftner, G. H. (1942) Recent Developments and Interpretations of Soybean Grade Standards. *Soybean Digest* 3:11, 38.
Jordan, G. L. (1944) Illinois Processors Meet. *Soybean Digest* 4:8, 18.
Keirstead, C. H. (1952) Marketing Study of Factors Affecting the Quantity and Value of Products Obtained from Soybeans, Washington, DC: United States Department of Agriculture, Production and Marketing Administration, Fats and Oils Branch.
Kohn, F. (1990) Reflections: A Tale of Battleships, Broilers and Billions of Bushels. *Soybean Digest* 51:7-10.
Kohn, F. (1992) Controversy Continues Over Cleaner Beans. *Soybean Digest* 52:10-12.
Kurtz, H. D. (1956) Marketing Problems of U. S. Soybeans in Japan. *Soybean Digest* 16:41.
Latour, B. (1987) *Science in Action: How to Follow Scientists and Engineers Through Society.* Milton Keynes, England: Open University Press.
Leake, L. L. (2001) Selling to Foreign Markets. *Successful Farming* 99:SB9.
Lee, K. W. (1978) Soybean Standards May Get Face-Lift. *Soybean Digest* 38:1SID-6SID.
Lin, W. (1996) *Costs and Benefits of Cleaning U. S. Soybeans.* Washington, DC: United States Department of Agriculture, Economic Research Service.
Livet, P., and L. Thévenot (1994) Les Categories de l'Action Collective. Pp. 139-167 in *Analyse Economique des Conventions*, edited by André Orléan. Paris: Presses Universitaires de France.
Mangold, G., and S Reeve (1988) Questions on Quality Surround Soybean Crop. *Soybean Digest* 49:8-9.
Merrill Lynch, Pierce, Fenner and Smith (1969) *The Soybean.* New York: Merrill Lynch, Pierce, Fenner and Smith.
Molotch, H. (2003) *Where Stuff Comes From: How Toasters, Toilets, Cars, Computers, and Many Other Things Come to Be as They Are.* New York: Routledge.

North, D. C. (1990) *Institutions, Institutional Change, and Economic Performance*. New York, Cambridge University Press.

Orléan, A. (1994) Vers un Modèle Général de la Coordination Economique par les Conventions. Pp. 9-40 in *Analyse Economique des Conventions*, edited by André Orléan. Paris: Presses Universitaires de France.

Piper, C. V. and W. J. Morse (1923) *The Soybean*. New York: McGraw-Hill.

Pogeler, G. (1954) The Processor Looks at Foreign Material. *Soybean Digest* 14:55-56.

Probst, A. H. (1970) Fifty Years of Soybean Variety Improvement. *Soybean Digest* 30:66-68, 70.

Rogers, E. M. (1995) *Diffusion of Innovations*. New York: Free Press.

Schmidling, J. (1953) Let's Put Oil in Its Rightful Place. *Soybean Digest* 13:14-15.

Shaw, E. A. (1956a) Marketing Problems of U. S. Soybeans in Europe. *Soybean Digest* 16:36.

Shaw, E. A. (1956b) Study of Sampling and Grading of US Soybeans for Export. Washington, DC: United States Department of Agriculture, Foreign Agricultural Service.

Smith, A. (1994) [1776]. *An Inquiry into the Nature and Causes of the Wealth of Nations*. New York: Modern Library.

Smith, A. K. (1958) Progress in Research on Soybeans. *Soybean Digest* 18:14-17.

Smith, H. C. (1945) 21 Years of Soybean Harvesting. *Soybean Digest* 5:11-12.

Smith, K. J. (1991) Constituent Pricing: How will it Impact Soybean Research Priorities? Pp. 17-21 in *Designing Value-Added Soybeans for Markets of the Future*, edited by R. F. Wilson. Champaign, IL: American Oil Chemists' Society.

U. S. Congress. Senate. Subcommittee on Foreign Agricultural Policy and the Subcommittee on Agricultural Production, Marketing, and Stabilization of Prices of the Committee on Agriculture and Forestry (1976) Grain Inspection : Hearings Before the Subcommittee on Foreign Agricultural Policy and the Subcommittee on Agricultural Production, Marketing, and Stabilization of Prices of the Committee on Agriculture and Forestry, United States Senate, Ninety-fourth Congress, Second Session, on Grain Inspection Irregularities and Problems. Washington, D.C.: US Congress. Senate.

U. S. Congress. Senate. Subcommittee on Rural Development, Oversight, and Investigations of the Committee on Agriculture, Nutrition, and Forestry (1986) To Amend the United States Grain Standards Act: Hearing Before the Subcommittee on Rural Development, Oversight, and Investigations of the Committee on Agriculture, Nutrition, and Forestry United States Senate Ninety-Ninth Congress Second Session on S. 1121. Washington, D.C.: U. S. Congress. Senate.

United States Department of Agriculture (1997) Grain Inspection Handbook. Washington, DC: Grain Inspection, Packers and Stockyards Administration, Federal Grain Inspection Service.

Williamson, O. E. (1989) Transaction Cost Economics. Pp. 135-182 in *Handbook of Industrial Organization*, edited by Richard Schmalensee and Robert E. Willig. Amsterdam: North Holland.

Yates, J. (1989) *Control Through Communication: The Rise of System in American Management*. Baltimore: Johns Hopkins University Press.

Zhang, S. (1991) Farmers' Attitudes Toward Grades and Standards for Corn and Soybeans. *Agricultural Economics*. Urbana: University of Illinois.

## 1. APPENDIX: HISTORICAL REVIEW OF US STANDARDS FOR SOYBEANS

| STANDARDS FOR SOYBEANS | YEAR |
|---|---|
| Standards for soybeans recommended by USDA | 1925 |
| Revised standards | 1935 |
| Soybeans brought under the Grain Standards Act | 1940 |
| **SPLITS** | |
| Increased the percentage of splits in grades No. 1 and No. 2 from 1.0 and 10.0% to 10 and 15%. | 1941 |
| The maximum limits of splits were increased from 15, 20, and 30% for grades Nos. 2, 3, and 4 to 20, 30, and 40 percent. | 1949 |
| Redefined splits as pieces of soybeans that are not damaged. | 1955 |

## MOISTURE CONTENT

| | |
|---|---|
| Reduced the maximum moisture limits from 15.0, 15.0, and 16.5% in grades Nos. 1, 2, and 3 to 13, 14, and 16%. | 1941 |
| Changed the method of determining moisture from the water oven to the air-oven. | 1942 |

## FOREIGN MATERIAL & DOCKAGE SYSTEM

| | |
|---|---|
| Established a dockage system based on an 8/64 round hole sieve and expressed on the certificate in terms of whole %. A fraction of a percent was disregarded. | 1941 |
| Classifying a part of the foreign material as dockage was eliminated. | 1949 |
| Increased the maximum percentage of foreign material from 0.5, 2.0, 4.0, and 6.0% in grades Nos. 1 through 4 to 1, 2, 3, and 5%. | 1941 |
| The maximum limits of foreign material were increased from 1, 2, 3, and 5% for grades Nos. 1 through 4 to 2.0, 3.0, 4.0, and 6.0%. This change was necessary due to elimination of the dockage factor. | 1949 |
| Reduced the foreign material in the numberical grades from 2.0, 3.0, 4.0, and 6.0% to 1.0, 2.0, 3.0, and 5.0%. | 1955 |

## DAMAGED KERNELS

| | |
|---|---|
| Increased the maximum percentage of damaged kernels permitted in grade No. 1 from 1.5 to 2%. | 1941 |
| Fixed the special limits on heat damage of 0.2, 0.5, 1.0, and 3.0 percent in the numerical grades. | 1955 |
| Stink-bug kernels considered damaged kernels at the rate of one-fourth of the actual percentage of the stung kernels. | 1969 |

## COLORS

A. YELLOW & GREEN

| | |
|---|---|
| Factor other colors was eliminated in the grade table. A footnote was added which applied to the No. 1 and 2 grade, providing the grade No. 1 of each of the classes Yellow Soybeans and Green Soybeans may contain not more than 2 percent and that grade No. 2 of each of these classes may contain not more than 3% of black, brown, or bicolored soybeans singly or combined. | 1941 |
| The definitions for the classes Yellow Soybeans and Green Soybeans were changed to provide that all soybeans with yellow or green seedcoats which were yellow in cross section be classified as yellow soybeans and only soybeans that wre green in cross section and had green seedcoats be classified as green soybeans. | 1949 |

B. BROWN & BLACK

| | |
|---|---|
| Limits for other classes were changed. Brown and black soybeans may contain not more than 10% of soybeans of other colors and yellow and green soybeans may contain not more than 10% of other colors, including not more than 5% of brown, black or bicolored soybeans. | 1941 |
| Provided that the term bicolored soybeans be construed to include soybeans with seedcoats of two colors, one of which is black or brown, when the black and/or brown color covers 50% or more of the seedcoat. The hilum of a soybean is not considered a part of the seedcoat. | 1966 |

## SPECIAL GRADES

| | |
|---|---|
| Established a special grade Weevily soybeans. | 1941 |
| Established a special grade Garlicky soybeans. | 1949 |

## PURPLE MOTTLED & STAINED

Required that purple mottled and stained soybeans be graded not higher    1955
than No. 3.

Provided that the term purple mottled or stained includes soybeans which    1963
are discoloured by a fungus. Purple mottled or stained soybeans would be
graded not higher than No. 3.

## DISTINCTLY LOW QUALITY

Provided that the term D.L.Q. (Distinctly Low Quality) be constructed to    1961
include soybeans which contain more than two crotalaria seeds in 1,000
grams.

## ADMINISTRATIVE CHANGES (Labels/Names)

Provided that the prefix US be shown on all official grain grades.    1970

The name of the soybean standards changed from "Official Grain    1974
Standards of the United States for Soybeans" to "United States Standards
for Soybeans."

Certification requirements changed so that a lot would be certified: 1) as    1977.
being of a specific US grade, or 2) as being equal to or better in quality, as
defined by the US Standards for Soybeans, than the grade specified by the
contract; i.e., US No. 2 or better, US No. 3 or better, etc.

---

Source: Historical Review of Changes in the Grain Standards of the United States. May, 1980. United States Department of Agriculture, Federal Grain Inspection Service. FGSI-5:25-27.

IV

# ACCESS AND ETHICAL TRADE

ELIZABETH RANSOM*

# 9. DEFINING A GOOD STEAK:

*Global Constructions of What is Considered the Best Red Meat*[†]

## 1. INTRODUCTION

Less than 50 years ago nearly all beef was grass fed and agricultural production was highly diverse around the world. By the late 1990s, approximately 37 percent of the world's meat supply emanated from industrialized livestock production (e.g., feedlot production) and this type of production was growing six times as fast as production in grazing systems (Delgado et al. 1999). Simultaneously, there is evidence of an increasing convergence of tastes that is often explained as "consumer preferences" among the top beef producing nations (Spriggs and Isaac 2001). Beyond the basic physiological need for food, taste and food preferences are largely learned. As such, we would expect these preferences to be diverse across time and space. This leads to the question: How do seemingly diverse consumer markets become aligned in similar ways? Through an analysis of standards in the South African red meat industry, this work contributes to an understanding of the impact of globalization on production and consumption.[1]

Globalization is a process that permeates major aspects of everyday life, including the food we eat (Bonanno et al. 1994). I argue that globalization processes within agriculture and food production contribute to the construction of what is considered the 'best' red meat. Globalization signifies the increasing movement of people and things (money, goods, services, etc.) around the globe (Held et al. 1999). Despite the shared consensus about the importance of globalization, scholars have vehemently disagreed over the nature and consequences of globalization. Globalization has been identified as the principal reason for increasing inequalities between and within nations (Barkin 2002; Held and McGrew 2002), while others see globalization as a means to promote free trade and investment flows thereby contributing to economic growth and the reduction of poverty on a global scale (Held and McGrew 2002 citing the World Bank 2001). At best, it can be said that

* Elizabeth Ransom, Visiting Assistant Professor, Department of Sociology and Anthropology, University of Richmond.
† Acknowledgments: I would like to thank Jim Bingen, Lawrence Busch, Matt Kleiman, and Toby Ten Eyck for their helpful comments on previous drafts of this chapter. Funding in support of this research was made possible by a Doctoral dissertation Research Improvement Grant from the National Science Foundation (#SES-0080335) and Michigan State University College of Social Science. The opinions expressed herein are those of the author.

*J. Bingen and L. Busch, (eds.), Agricultural Standards: The Shape of the Global Food and Fiber System, 159-175.* © 2006 *Springer. Printed in the Netherlands.*

globalization is a fragmented, incomplete, discontinuous, contingent, and contradictory process. Therefore, there is a need for additional research that evaluates the consequences of globalization, including its unexpected and unintended consequences (Guillen 2001). In order to shed some light on these debates this chapter focuses on the implementation of food quality standards in the context of a rapidly industrializing agri-food industry. Since food consumption is a basic necessity around the world, focusing on agri-food practices and the consequences of these practices is an excellent means to evaluate the impact of globalization on a diverse society.

Despite the long history of the food trade, changes occurring today are profoundly different from those of previous eras. Within agriculture and food (agri-food) studies, scholars note that the quantity of food traded and the speed and distance (time and space) at which food now travels has increased dramatically (Bonanno et al. 1994, McMichael 1991, Magdoff et al. 2000). Due to the increased globalization of capital in agriculture, rates of concentration and centralization have increased in agri-food sectors (Magdoff et al. 2000). In addition, the emergence of new trade rules over the past 25 years (disseminated through the General Agreement on Tariffs and Trade/World Trade Organization and the North American Free Trade Agreement[2]) has furthered the expansion of global sourcing of agri-food products and the growth of export-oriented production in developing countries (McMichael 2000).

As agri-food systems have become more global, there has been an increase in the use of standards[3] and a tendency for standardization of standards to take place. In modern capitalist societies, more things tend to become commodities at some point in their "lives," and standards for a given thing tend to become more uniform across nations and cultures (Tanaka and Busch 2003 citing Appadurai 1986). The global agri-food system reflects these same tendencies towards standardization and homogenization.[4]

Standards are more than simply technical details or tactical tools used as part of market strategy. In the past ten years scholars have focused on the ways in which standards and standardization have ethical and moral implications. In particular, standards and standardization construct the world in certain ways and not others (Busch 2000; Grindley 1995; Bowker and Star 1999; Brunsson and Jacobsson 2000). Linked with an understanding of the ethical and moral implications of standards, is the idea that standards are one means by which products, processes, and people are judged. A standard for a "good" steak also implies a standard for a "good" farmer and a "good" slaughter process.

This chapter explores the role of science, ethics, culture, economics, and politics in standards through an analysis of the "tools of the trade" that are used to achieve product quality (specifically tender meat) within the beef industry. Defined broadly, "tools" encompass any industrial technology that incorporates a standard or a set of standards to achieve consistent food safety or quality attributes. In particular, this chapter explores the consequences of focusing on quality standards that emphasize tender meat production, which in the case of South Africa may have deleterious effects on a large segment of the population. This discussion sheds light on the complexity and contradictory tendencies of globalization by focusing on the intricacies of standards and their impacts on actors within a commodity network.

The following section elaborates on South African history and the current state of its red meat industry. This is followed by a discussion of the use of standards in industrial meat production and the quest for tender meat on a global scale. Next is a presentation of the purpose of the quest for tender meat and the consequences of the pursuit of tender meat production in South Africa. Finally, the analysis concludes with an evaluation of the implications of adopting tender meat standards for different groups in South African society.

## 2. THE SOUTH AFRICAN CONTEXT

During the apartheid era[5] all of South African agriculture was government-directed and marketing boards controlled up to 80 percent of all commercial agriculture.[6] The Meat Board had statutory authority to oversee the registration of key participants in the industry, keep industry records, and collect a levy from farmers for each animal slaughtered. For example, in 1996 the Board collected more than R57 million in the form of statutory levies (NAMC 2001). In fact, until 1992, the Meat Board acted as the sole importer of red meat. However, in order to comply with the requirements of the General Agreement on Tariffs and Trade (GATT), import control as executed by the Meat Board was abolished (NAMC 2001).

As a result of apartheid policies, by 1983 at least 2.5 million rural people had been forcibly removed from their land and driven into the "homelands." From 1955 to 1969 population densities in traditionally black rural areas rose from 60 persons to 110 persons per square mile (Winberg 1996). Besides promoting overcrowding, and therefore, degradation of the available natural resources in the homelands, the government also intervened in ways that undermined black smallholder agricultural production. These interventions included taxes that forced blacks to earn wages in "white areas" (Lipton 1993). The government, in conjunction with the commercial agricultural sector, effectively created a two-tier agricultural system, establishing white farmers as commercial producers and restricting most blacks and coloreds to subsistence farming.[7] Today, South Africa is attempting to integrate its dual agricultural system into one and at the same time, to improve land distribution, agricultural productivity, and agricultural exports.

Reform of the agricultural sector began in 1996, when the government passed the Marketing of Agricultural Products Act to disband all marketing boards (Act No. 47 of 1996). After the passage of the act the Meat Board officially ended its operational activities in December 1997. Along with agricultural sector reform, the democratically elected government in South Africa adopted neo-liberal economic policies, which opened the doors to international trade in a way that South Africans had not experienced in the previous 40 years (see Hart 2003) for a more extensive discussion). Within agriculture the neo-liberal economic policies created a dramatic decline in government subsidies and a significant decline in protection from foreign imports through tariffs. Thus, South Africans involved in the agri-food sector started to grapple with the new constraints and opportunities of global capitalist markets.

Presently, the majority of black South Africans are confined to 13 percent of the land.[8] One quarter of the commercial farmers (97 percent of whom are white) produce 80 percent of food output, while approximately one million black families in the former homelands generate five percent of marketed production (Winberg 1996; de Wit 1997; Lipton 1993). Export marketing for livestock products could prove to be a growth promoter for the red meat industry and for rural areas of South Africa (mentioned as a general strategy for developing countries by Haen (1998). However, to compete internationally puts increased demand on maintaining animal health and food safety standards (Haan et al. 2001). According to the latest projections, by 2020 63 percent of meat will be produced in developing countries, up from 56 percent in 2002 (Haan et al. 2001). Higher-income developing countries with a fairly developed agricultural sector, such as South Africa, are likely candidates as future leaders in developing countries' industrial livestock production.

## 3. INDUSTRIAL MEAT PRODUCTION AND SCIENTIFIC PRACTICES

Industrial meat production can be thought of as a scientific practice. As Clark and Fujimura (1992, 5) note, agriculture, along with medicine and biology, has focused on "what is life" and more importantly, "how to control life." For the scientific practice of industrial meat production to occur there must be continuity and stabilization of production practices across time and space. This does not mean that industrial livestock practices are identical, but similarities and continuities can be found at all locations (Clark and Fujimura 1992). Standards or sets of standards contribute to the creation of continuity and stabilization in the red meat industry.

Contributing to continuity and stabilization across time and space, tools of the trade can be viewed as immutable mobiles (Latour 1987), "things that can travel without withering away ... do not fundamentally alter on the trip ... can be provided to and interpreted by others...and linked to other things" (Clark and Fujimura 1992: 12-13). Therefore, standards that are created in one space (e.g., a business, a country, or a region) become mobile by way of their incorporation into the "tools" of the industry. An important point made by scholars of science studies is the recognition that continuity and stabilization are the result of successful efforts to dominate (Clark and Fujimura 1992: 13).

At the very least, a standard that becomes "the" standard in an industry calls attention to some point of view and silences another. Bowker and Star (2000: 5-6) note that this is not inherently a bad thing, but "it is an ethical choice, and as such it is dangerous – not bad, but dangerous." Deciding on a specific standard is an ethical choice because it is one more technical detail that contributes to the construction of the world in some ways and not others. Standards are dangerous because the choices that are made to determine a standard are rarely made by democratic decision-making or with consideration of their societal impacts. Despite their ability to alter power relations, technologies of standards and standardization have generally been ignored by social scientists as an arena of investigation (Busch et al. 2005).

Before we move on to discuss standards that are used in the quest for tender meat, let us review four points to keep in mind when focusing on standards: First, creators of standards propose them as objective, but standards are always enacted in specific locations that have their own set of cultural and historical circumstances. Second, standards do not work equally well across time and place. For example, standards that suit the purposes of intensive industrial farming do not automatically suit the needs of agriculture organized in other ways, such as communal farming. Third, the question of who (which individuals or groups) gets to determine what is considered a "good" standard is an important point to consider. Currently standards are constructed within private industry and specific government bodies and thus will likely reflect dominant (or at least the most vocal) social actors' definitions of what a good standard is within these groups. Finally, some standards are unable to directly measure the desired characteristic, and in their place proxy standards are used. These standards will change as other standards are found that more closely measure the desired item or characteristic. Having highlighted these four points, let us move to a discussion of the quest for tender meat.

## 4. THE QUEST FOR TENDER MEAT

> SA Grainfed Beef is lean, tender young beef (0-2 teeth) selected according to the strictest A Class age specifications with a specified fat coverage (2, 3, or 4) over the whole carcase [sic] to ensure the ultimate eating experience. Technically speaking this means that animals are selected for their lean meat attributes from beef breeds known to produce tender beef. (From a brochure advertising South African red meat for export.)

The quest for tender meat is a curious example of the meshing of ethics, culture, politics, science, and economics. To look at the history and the resources that have gone into finding an economical way to produce consistently tender meat at the point of consumption is to see a set of principles and practices that can often be viewed as innovative and at times counter-intuitive. To comprehend the great lengths that the industry has gone to find consistently tender meat, let us review some of the better known cases of tender meat production.

One of the more common techniques for producing tender meat is to slaughter the animal while it is very young. (As animals age, the muscle gets tougher due to the presence of more connective tissue and the connective tissue becomes less soluble.) Veal is young meat produced by preventing the animals from exercising, and, therefore, developing stronger muscles. Similar to the concept of veal, are Kobe and Matsuzaka cows from Japan. (The Japanese locations are the names given to the meat.) The tender meat produced is a combination of a certain breed and production standards. For example, Wagyu is the breed for Kobe beef and production standards. Production standards include feeding beer to the cows to help them relax, massaging the animals, and a regimen of minimal exercise for the cow (which some have argued makes the massage a necessity rather than the luxury that humans associate with the concept). The terms Kobe and Matsuzaka are appellations and cannot be used unless the cows were raised in these regions. Wagyu, because it is a breed, can be marketed and sold in other regions of the world. Effectively veal, Kobe and Matsuka remain meats sold within a niche market of consumers who are willing to pay significantly higher prices.

A more common technique used throughout the industrialized red meat industry for tenderizing meat is "aging." Generally, immediately after an animal dies rigor mortis sets in and the meat actually becomes tougher within the next 6 to 12 hours. After this period the meat begins to become more tender. Depending on the breed, conditions at the point of slaughter and post-mortem, an animal can be "aged" from anywhere from 1 to 21 days, with the average length of time in the United States being seven days and in South Africa up to five days. The older the animal the more aging improves the tenderness of the meat, up to a certain point. In an effort to speed up the aging process scientists at a United States university in collaboration with a private agricultural biotechnology company successfully cloned a cow from a two-day old side of beef in 2002. According to the newspaper report this means "cattle producers could choose beef cells from a slaughtered cow after its meat has been graded, then create a herd of grade A clones" (Bacon, 2002). Of course, genetic appeals obfuscate the many intervening variables that produce tender meat for the consumer. These variables include: age and sex of the animal, breeds suitable to the production location, feeding regime, transportation to the slaughterhouse, conditions at the point of slaughter, post-mortem handling, and cooking methods.

Finally, the technology most commonly used in slaughterhouses[9] for promoting tender meat is electrical stimulation (ES). Recognized by many as first used by Benjamin Franklin in 1749 on a turkey, ES has been increasingly used in industrial slaughterhouses since 1976. During the slaughter process a cable is attached to the animal carcass and an electrical current is sent through the carcass, causing the muscles to contract involuntarily. Not only are there competing theories as to why ES works, but there are also different types of ES available (e.g., high voltage versus low voltage) and different points in the slaughter process where it is used (e.g., pre-hide removal in the bleeding area versus after dehiding, but before evisceration). ES combined with aging is considered the most efficient means of achieving tender meat in an industrial setting (Stiffler et al. 1982). Generally, these two practices combined produce tender meat more quickly which reduces inventory costs of keeping carcasses for extended periods of time, prevents shrinkage, and reduces energy use.[10] Although ES was first used to improve tenderness, its adoption by the meat industry in the United States likely resulted from findings that demonstrated that ES improves lean quality characteristics (Stiffler et al. 1982). In South Africa, they slaughter livestock at a younger age and lighter weight compared to the US One South African processor states that ES is widely used because the smaller, leaner carcasses are more prone to cold shortening during chilling than larger carcasses with more fat.[11] Therefore, in order to counter toughening of the product, ES is used.

Prior to the widespread implementation of electrical stimulation, a processor that was explicitly concerned with producing tender meat would utilize slow chilling techniques. However, slow chilling requires a large number of chillers (i.e., large refrigerators), resulting in more capital costs and increased working capital (costs associated with storing more meat prior to sale). In addition, slow chilling allows more bacteria to grow on the surface of the carcass in comparison to fast chilling. For consumption purposes, increased levels of surface bacteria are not a major concern because cooking the meat will kill the bacteria. However, as meat is shipped longer distances surface bacteria shortens the shelf life of meat and thus, increases the risk of meat spoiling while in transport to the final destination. Hence as red meat commodity chains grow longer, the slow chilling technique is ill suited to the changing circumstances.

## 5. WHAT IS THE PURPOSE OF THE QUEST FOR TENDER MEAT?

Similar to participants in the United States and other red meat producing countries, South Africans involved in the commercial red meat industry are very interested in producing tender meat for consumption. What is the purpose of the quest for tender meat? In order to capture the complexity of the answer to this question it is necessary to study the actors involved with and shaped by the quest for tender meat.

For producers, the South African grading system rewards those who bring relatively young cows to slaughter. This grading system is an example of a proxy standard, in that the age of the cow is only used as an imprecise measure of the tenderness of the meat.[12] Studies have shown that the younger the cow the more tender the meat (Crosley, et al 1994). As noted earlier, there are many variables that contribute to tender meat. Age as a proxy does not guarantee the consumer will get a tender piece of meat, but younger animals do increase the odds of tender meat at the point of consumption. Thus, South Africa's grading system favors producers who raise animals in feedlots as opposed to grazing systems. This is because livestock raised on grazing systems are generally older at the time of slaughter and have developed tougher muscle tissue.

The quest for tender meat also impacts cattle. Breeds of livestock are often selected, at least in part, based on the environment in which the animals are reared and the end purpose of the meat. Thus, native breeds in South Africa, such as the Nguni, are excellent for less organized grazing systems where "nature" is less controlled by humans.[13] Nguni adapt well to harsh conditions and have a high tolerance for parasitic and infectious diseases. However, the Nguni breed is not considered highly productive within intensive livestock conditions, where reproduction, feed, and the environment are regulated in order to promote rapid weight gain. Thus, most commercial producers (intensive or extensive) raise breeds of cattle that are better suited for industrial production that aims to have the animal gain weight quickly and in a consistent manner. In South Africa they use major continental livestock breeds, such as Angus and Simmentaler. Also utilized are Bonsmaras, a beef breed developed after WWII by cross breeding an indigenous breed with British breeds so that livestock farmers would have a breed that could produce beef economically in the subtropical savannah regions of South Africa (Campher 1998).

For slaughterhouses the technology used tends to be dependent on the size of the abattoir. High levels of technology are not cost effective in a smaller abattoir that slaughters fewer animals per week. For example, an abattoir that slaughters only 25 cattle a week is less likely to have the types of slaughter equipment found in abattoirs that slaughter 200 cattle or more a week. Thus, small abattoirs tend to be more labor intensive and they are not likely to use ES as part of the slaughter process. Thus, whatever benefits ES bestows on the meat, all cattle slaughtered in smaller facilities will not have these characteristics.

As a side note, it is important to note that ES is not automated, even in abattoirs where it is available. Rather the ES process requires workers to physically attach the wire to each cow that passes through the slaughter line and for the wire to then be physically removed, usually by another worker, after a certain period of time (approximately 10 to 14 seconds). Hence, ES entails properly trained workers who attach the wire at the proper time and who leave the wire attached for a discrete period of time.[14] The reason for raising this point is because unlike other industrial processes such as the automotive industry which have tried to minimize the human factor (e.g., human error) through increased automation of the production process, the abattoir is still highly labor dependent, regardless of its size. The labor-intensive aspect of the industry is due to the variability in size of the animals, which thus far has not allowed for fully automated lines. One interviewee in this study told a story of visiting one of the largest abattoirs in a particular region in South Africa where he witnessed every third or fourth carcass going through the line without an ES wire attached. This person found a worker on the floor and asked why some carcasses were without the wire, to which the worker replied that they were running short on wires that day. Obviously the worker failed to understand or to care about the purpose of attaching the ES wire. In general, slaughterhouses are increasingly under pressure from larger retailers to introduce new technological devices that promote tenderness. One research report from Ireland states, "[l]eading supermarkets already issue detailed specifications to abattoirs and some specify tenderising processes such as electrical stimulation, pelvic suspension and ageing times up to 4 weeks in chill" (Troy and Joseph 2001: np).

Retailers make up a diverse group in South Africa and include butchers, small independent retail stores, fast food and restaurant establishments, and large retail supermarkets. Retailers may have a variety of goals when selling meat to customers, including low price, large quantity, fresh product, or tender meat. However, regardless of the goals, it should be recognized that meat classification, with A as the highest-grade meat and C as the lowest, is directly coupled to the price that the consumer is going to pay. Therefore, any retailer who is selling a higher grade, and therefore higher priced meat, wants the consumer to feel they have gotten the appropriate value for their money. This is especially true among the large retail chains that are selling their store name along with the meat. Thus, retailers are concerned with how to ensure the consistent meat quality that its customers expect. A few strategies that the largest retail chains are pursuing include labeling or branding and offering in-store cooking instructions. For the largest retail chains in South Africa that are attempting to brand their product, the process involves consolidation and centralization of operations, thereby ensuring more control over the entire process. As mentioned in the previous discussion about abattoirs, increased control for a large retail chain involves hand-picking select abattoirs that they can trust to provide them with the types of carcasses they request. The retail chains also conduct more of the meat preparation in-house (e.g., deboning of the meat, packing specific cuts into family size prepackaged containers, and producing sausages). Of course, the centralization and increasing control also costs more, so stores that take branding to this extreme often charge higher prices for their meats than other retail stores.

Finally, there are consumers who are supposedly the persons driving the demand for tender meat. Curiously, tastes vary and change and are generally inconsistent across ethnic groups and regions of the world. In addition, taste is ambiguous and flavor is largely a learned reaction (Fiddes 1991). In South Africa, meat preferences fall along racial and class lines due to the socio-political and economic history. As such, there is a noticeable split in the population over what is considered a "good" piece of meat. Generally, urban populations prefer tender meat. Historically, the majority of the white population of South Africa lived in urban centers. The rural populations, primarily black South Africans, tend to prefer meat that is tougher and on the bone. The grading scheme within South Africa privileges tender meat (A grade) over tougher meat (C grade). One interviewee, concerned that the structure of the grading system disadvantaged non-feedlot producers, said, "rural people like B and C graded meat, yet producers get penalized for producing what rural consumers want. Why should a British, urban elite determine the grading system for everyone?"

If it is understood that continuity and stabilization are the result of successful efforts to dominate, then seemingly mundane ideas about what is considered "the best" meat can elicit much larger processes of domination and subordination. The grading system rewards industrial livestock producers and the production of cattle that is favored by a select group of upper- and middle-class consumers.

The grading system also reveals the international process of dominance and subordination. Historically, the need for methods of carcass description arose primarily from the lengthening of the distribution chains and the decline in face-to-face interaction. Carcass descriptions were introduced to facilitate trade at a distance, but these descriptions quickly took on promotional significance (Kempster et al. 1982). The promotional significance of tender meat as equivalent to good meat on a global scale is illustrated by the use of ES during processing in several exporting countries in the South. For example, in Brazil – one of the largest exporters of red meat globally - thirty percent of medium-size and forty percent of large-size plants use ES Significantly smaller participants in international beef trade include Costa Rica and Venezuela. Nonetheless, all three of the export slaughterhouses in Costa Rica utilize ES, while six out of eighteen export slaughterhouses in Venezuela utilize ES (personal communication). The use of ES in slaughterhouses in countries in the South partially supports Goodman and Redclift's (1991: 157) point of recognizing trends that move beyond the nation-state policies and brings attention to the "catalytic role of the transnational corporation in disseminating standardized technologies and labor processes and integrating commodity markets on a global basis." However, in contradiction to Goodman and Redclift's point, there is not one corporation that controls the red meat industry. Rather, red meat production continues to be organized within nation-states. However, a lack of unified corporate control globally, does not mean that the global influence of a few powerful actors within nation-states (primarily Western, industrialized countries, especially the United States) can be dismissed.

In order to explain the means by which a few actors can structure an industry, it is important to understand the process of livestock production. The scientific practice of livestock production requires standards and standardization throughout the process, not just at the end point. The extent that beef production is a process, in which scientific practices are always emphasized, is revealed when speaking with the largest feedlot operators in South Africa. These operators utilize a tracking system that allows them to collect data about the animal at the point of slaughter, but also data all the way back almost to the point of conception. After slaughter, the feedlot collects information on the grade and weight of the carcass, if the carcass was diseased, and how much the carcass sold for. This information is then combined with information regarding which group of livestock that cow arrived with at the feedlot and which cow calf producer sold the animal to the feedlot. The feedlot owner also has records documenting the type of feed and medication (antibiotics, hormones, etc.) the animal received each day since its arrival at the feedlot. Through this traceability system the feedlot develops a profile of humans and animals. Thus, the feedlot is concerned with identifying the most productive breeds *and* the most productive cow calf producers within the current grading scheme. If the grading system in South Africa were changed, the entire process of livestock production would require reorganization so that feedlots could maximize their profit. To reorganize the system would effectively alienate South Africa from international trade. Recall that scientific practices, such as national grading schemes, differ across locations. South Africa bases their quality grading system primarily on age by dentition (i.e., the number of permanent incisors – A grade is 0 permanent incisors) and carcass fat cover. In contrast, the United States bases its system primarily on maturity established through visual inspection of the carcass (such as the amount of hardening of cartilage into bone) and visual analyses of marbling in the rib eye muscle between the 12th and 13th rib. However, both systems operate because there is some semblance of continuity and stability in determining palatability.

Like most agricultural industries, South Africa has a strong interest in maintaining export options. As one South African industry leader states, "The future growth opportunity for the local beef industry lies in entering the international market, and in doing so, we will have to comply with the standards as set by the particular importing country" (personal communication). Aside from obtaining much stronger currencies, South African producers/processors are able to sell higher-end cuts elsewhere and import lower-end cuts for the majority of the population that does not have enough income to pay for higher priced pieces of meat.[15] This is one way to maximize the earning potential of producers and processors, whether or not it is the best way to organize the industry for the purposes of the majority of South Africans.

## 6. CONSEQUENCES OF THE QUEST FOR TENDER MEAT

While specific standards have very real material consequences, the issue of specific standards designed to produce tender meat might not appear as something that maintains or enforces power differentials. However, as Bowker and Star (2000: 6) note "for any group or situation, classifications and standards give advantage or they give suffering. Some regions benefit at the expense of others." Quality standards that emphasize tender meat have negative consequences for at least some of the South African actors discussed previously.

First, for extensive livestock producers, the grading system favors young animals that are finished (i.e., prepared for slaughter) much more quickly than animals in grazing production systems. Therefore, most extensive producers receive a lower price for their animals at the point of slaughter or they opt to provide the input (weaner calves) to intensive livestock producers, losing their ability to capture more profit by raising the animal until the point of slaughter.[16] Accompanying the disadvantaged position of extensive producers is the reality that the majority of emergent farmers in South Africa are extensive producers. Emergent farmers generally denote previously disenfranchised groups, who in agriculture for the most part consist of black South Africans. Therefore, an emphasis on quality standards that promote intensive livestock production in South Africa is counter to the government's initiatives to promote the advancement of emergent farmers. Of course, there are some initiatives underway (private, public, and not for profit) to cultivate and promote extensive production, for a niche market. While providing an opportunity for extensive production these niche markets generally promote the product based on claims associated with the environment, health or the ethical treatment of animals. The success of these initiatives remains uncertain, especially in terms of giving emergent farmers access to markets for selling the meat they produce.

Second, the emphasis on tender meat leads to a loss of genetic diversity among livestock. Industrial livestock production relies on a limited number of highly productive breeds (LEAD 1999). Currently, the FAO estimates that out of approximately 4,500 known breeds globally approximately 30 percent of breeds are in danger of extinction (FAO 1993). This means valuable genetic diversity is increasingly lost, including animals that are better equipped to resist certain types of parasites or diseases.

Abattoir owners who do not have the available ES technology in their plants are the next group of actors that indirectly and directly experience negative consequences from the quest for tender meat. Indirectly, the majority of abattoirs that do not use ES are small in size, and as the industry continues to move towards vertical integration and concentration, smaller abattoirs will be forced out of business. Directly, larger retail chains will increasingly expect abattoirs to utilize technology, like ES, that enhances the consistency of the final product. Furthermore, the majority of smaller abattoirs service rural areas that are not regularly serviced by larger abattoirs. If supermarkets continue the trend of increasing the number of stores in rural areas of Southern Africa (Weatherspoon and Reardon 2003), it is likely that meat coming from larger abattoirs will flow into the area via trucks delivering to rural supermarkets. The decline of smaller abattoirs in rural areas is important in the context of South Africa because of the high poverty and unemployment rates in these areas. The poverty rate in rural areas is about 70 percent (May et al. 2000) with approximately 58 percent of rural inhabitants currently unemployed (Tørres et al. 2000). Smaller rural abattoirs provide a form of employment for rural inhabitants. In addition, smaller rural abattoirs provide a source of income because the animals slaughtered are purchased from local producers, thus reducing the costs of transportation should these producers have to send their livestock to an abattoir located further away.

Linked to the decline of smaller abattoirs are retailers, especially smaller retailers, which will most likely also decline in the future. Because small abattoirs tend to source to smaller retailers, not large retail chains, small retailers including independent butchers will likely see increased costs associated with obtaining carcasses from non-local abattoirs. However, there are many more options for retailers. Thus the decline of this sector will not be as dramatic as in the abattoir sector. First, despite the increased costs of transport, it is possible that the carcasses coming from large abattoirs will decline in price due to economies of scale (i.e., more carcasses moving through one abattoir leads to a decline in the price per carcass). Second, creative retailers may work out alternative arrangements for acquiring meat, such as partnering with other independent butchers or selling more specialty items, such as cheaper imported meats or specialty sausages. Third, it seems likely that retailers will increasingly serve specific clientele. Thus, certain retailers will increasingly only serve upper-middle class consumers, while others will serve the working class. By serving specific clientele, retailers will be better able to control overhead costs based on how much their customers are willing to pay for their product. In other words, retailers serving upper-middle class customers will be able to charge a higher price for their meats thereby recouping costs associated with maintaining more rigorous standards and providing higher end meats. Having mentioned consumers it is important to discuss the consequences of the quest for tender meat for some South African consumers. Poorer consumers find that their choices in the market for affordable and healthy meat are reduced. At face value this conclusion may seem contradictory. By adopting a system that favors urban-middle class consumers, it appears that meat that is not desired by this group (i.e., lower grade meat) will be cheaper (remember that the grade and the price are linked). However, there are costs associated with implementing and maintaining standards. At the international level it is recognized that implementing and maintaining standards increases costs, and actions have been taken in an effort to offset these costs.[17] Nevertheless, at the local level increased costs are generally passed on to consumers through higher prices for a particular product. In the case of red meat, higher costs mean that some of South Africa's poorer consumers cannot afford to purchase any meat, regardless of the grade.

In addition, the adoption of standards shaped by international markets impacts the food preferences of consumers. Despite a large portion of the South African population preferring tougher meat they will increasingly get more tender meat. This is because, as the number of smaller abattoirs declines, and as more of the rural poor migrate to urban centers,[18] much of the meat obtained by these consumers will be from animals slaughtered in large abattoirs that use ES. Poorer consumers will still buy the cheapest meat, which is B or C grade, but all of the grades will have gone through ES, thereby increasing meat tenderness. Over time, this will likely change meat tenderness preferences. This point lends more evidence to support Goodman and Redclift's (1994) point that urban food systems in developing countries are becoming increasingly Westernized.

As stated previously, the entire industrial meat production process favors Western, industrialized consumers. While we should avoid romanticizing the more traditional approaches to meat production in third world countries, there is a paradox to the current situation. There is an increasing number of consumers in the EU and the US that seek 'all natural beef' that does not originate from modern industrial livestock production.[19] 'All natural' beef is the type of product that is in abundance in Third World countries. However, this type of beef is largely found in the informal sector and is increasingly being pushed out as a viable means of production by intensive livestock production that is striving to export to Western, industrialized markets.

## 7. CONCLUSIONS

A discussion of tender meat standards is not simply about the West's tender meat preferences extending out to "other" regions. Industrial meat production is clearly grounded in distinct material conditions, and likewise, food habits and preferences are locally situated and interact with a variety of historical, economic, and cultural factors that create diverse outcomes. Recall that despite claims of objectivity standards are always enacted in specific locations and standards do not work equally well across time and place. Focusing on a specific region and the actors within that region offers a more complex understanding of globalization, including an improved understanding of the contradictory processes at work.

Some actors in South Africa are actively supporting the trends in concentration and centralization, at least in the short term. These actors tend to be large feedlot producers, large retailers, and wealthy consumers. However, as should be obvious from the discussion in this chapter, as we evaluate standards it is also important to be aware of which groups or individual determine what is considered a "good" standard. Many other actors in South Africa do not benefit from the production of tender meat. For those actors interested in constructing a more democratic food system there are alternatives. Baker (1999: 254) proposes that "democratic food production is rooted in local economies and reconstructs the diversity (biological and cultural) that has been destroyed by the global food system." Baker's suggestion provides support for the continued development of some of the local initiatives currently underway in areas of South Africa.[20]

At the provincial government level, several provinces have implemented policies or laws that are more accommodating to smaller participants. In one region the policies led to the establishment of over 150 abattoirs that are only large enough to slaughter one animal per day. The establishment of these abattoirs encourages the production and distribution of meat that is more suited to local preferences, while also helping to ensure the meat has been handled in a manner that ensures food safety. In Durban (one of South Africa's largest cities) local health inspectors have modified the standards to facilitate the establishment of informal meat traders. These policy changes will ensure the continued existence of retailers that are not a part of the broader process of concentration and centralization. In addition, Durban's city inspectors also changed laws so as to accommodate the slaughter of animals for ceremonial purposes at individuals' homes. This will also help to ensure the continued existence of diversity in meat preferences among some consumers in urban areas. While none of the local initiatives just mentioned will bring a halt to the pursuit of tender meat, these local initiatives do create spaces of resistance and alternative practices. National and international bodies regulating global trade would do well in following the lead of local South African officials. That is, local officials have developed practices and standards that incorporate the values, politics, and history of a region, which required acknowledging who benefits and who loses economically and socially from the adoption of specific standards.

## 8. NOTES

[1] For an overview of the data and methods used in this paper see Ransom 2003.

[2] First signed in 1947, the General Agreement on Tariffs and Trade (GATT) was designed to encourage freer trade between signatory countries by reducing tariffs on traded goods and providing an arena in which to solve trade disputes. The 1994 GATT Uruguay Round formally established the World Trade Organization, which furthered the goals outlined by GATT.

[3] This is because standards help reduce transaction costs, increase the predictability of a product, and in general, simplify what could be a very tedious and complicated process. However, standards are also used as strategic tools for accessing markets, coordinating systems, assuring quality and safety, product branding, and creating niche markets (Giovannucci and Reardon 2000; Reardon et al. 2001). As a part of market strategy standards may benefit the industry as a whole and/or may be used as a means to distribute benefits unevenly in the industry.

[4] A good example of standardization and homogenization of food products on a global scale is the McDonald's Corporation, which is discussed in Schlosser's (2001) *Fast Food Nation*. Boston: Houghton Mifflin.

[5] While separation and inequality existed in South Africa from the very early days of Dutch settlement, apartheid officially began in 1948 when the Nationalist party was elected. Apartheid consisted of a series of laws that required people to be strictly categorized by racial group. These classifications were used to determine every aspect of a person's life, including where a person could live and work (Bowker and Star 2000; Wylie 2001).

[6] Commercial is used here to distinguish from the informal sector of South Africa, which for historical reasons, is very large. Approximately 25 percent of all livestock in South Africa are found in the informal sector.

[7] The racial classification system under apartheid had four basic groups: Europeans, Asiatics, coloureds or persons of mixed race, and Bantus, also called natives (Bowker and Star 2000).

[8] Black South Africans make up approximately 75 percent of the population, followed by 13.6 percent Whites, 8.6 percent Coloureds, and 2.6 percent Indian. Of all black South Africans, 60.7 percent are categorized as poor, while 38.2 percent of Coloreds, 5.4 percent of Indians, and 1.0 percent of all white South Africans are poor (May et al. 2000).

[9] The term abattoir is also used to refer to slaughterhouses. Generally, abattoir is used in South Africa and the EU, while the term slaughterhouse is used in North and South America.

[10] As meat ages it loses weight, which means if you are selling a product based on weight, you are effectively losing money.

[11] Cold shortening occurs when muscle fibers shorten during rigor mortis due to cold temperature producing tough muscle fiber. This tough muscle fiber is very difficult to break down, even through cooking.

[12] The US grading system also relies on proxy standards. One USDA web site explains "The quality grade factors, marbling and maturity, used to determine USDA beef quality grades (Prime, Choice, Select, etc.) do not explain all of the variation in beef palatability. However, they are capable of segregating a large dissimilar population of beef into more similar grade classes" (Morris 1999).

[13] Nguni actually originated from Northern Africa more than 8000 years ago. Nguni most likely arrived in Southern Africa around 800 A.D. Compared to breeds introduced to South Africa in the Twentieth century, Nguni is considered an indigenous breed.

[14] Most abattoirs control the amount of time the wire is attached by the actual structure of the slaughter line. In other words, the slaughterhouses where I witnessed ES being used prior to hide removal have a bleeding area that is inaccessible to workers without a significant amount of effort on their part. Once the animal has exited the bleeding area, the worker can easily remove the wire and the hide removal process begins.

[15] Many countries pursue the practice of exporting higher quality meat and importing lower quality meat, including the United States.

[16] Most extensive producers actually engage in a combination of practices, which includes selling calves to intensive producers and sending some animals to slaughter.

[17] A $40 million Trust Fund was recently established by the UN Food and Agriculture Organization (FAO) and the World Health Organization (WHO) to assist less developed countries in participating in Codex Alimentarius. The Codex Alimentarius Commission establishes international food safety and trade standards (FAO 2003).

[18] Due to high unemployment and poverty in rural areas many people migrate to urban centers in search of work (see Posel [2003] for a discussion of migration).

[19] Many US and EU consumers actually want "all natural" beef characteristics (e.g., meat with flavor not found from grain-feed beef) combined with characteristics achieved through industrial production (e.g., meat tenderness and consistent quality).

[20] This supports Bonanno et al.'s (1994) point that regulation of the global agri-food system is most likely to occur at the transnational or regional/local level, and not at the national level.

## 9. REFERENCES

Appadurai, A., ed. (1986) *The Social Life of Things: Commodities In Cultural Perspective.* New York: Cambridge University Press.

Bacon, J. (2002) What's for dinner? Cloned Cow. Pp. 3A *USA Today.* April 26, 2002.

Baker, L. (1999) A Different Tomato: Creating Vernacular Foodscapes. Pp. 249-260 in *Women Working the NAFTA Food Chain: Women, Food, and Globalization* edited by Deborah Brandt. Toronto: Second Story Press.

Barkin, D. (2002) Sustainable Regional Resource Management: A Strategy to Create New Beneficiaries from World Trade. Department of Economics, Universidad Autónoma Metropolitana-Xochimilco, Mexico. Unpublished Manuscript.

Bonanno, A., L. Busch, W. Friedland, L. Gouveia, and E. Mingione, eds. (1994) *From Columbus to ConAgra: The Globalization of Agriculture and Food. Lawrence,* Kansas: University Press of Kansas.

Bowater, F. J. (1996) The Preparation and Transportation of Meat Products with Particular Emphasis on Chilled Meat Shipments. Presented at Intermodal, 1996; http://www.fjb.co.uk/contentpreparationofmeatproducts.htm

Bowker, G. and L. Star. (1999) *Sorting Things Out: Classifications and Its Consequences.* Cambridge, Massachusetts: MIT Press.

Brunsson, N. and B. Jacobsson, eds. (2000) *A World of Standards.* Oxford: Oxford University Press.

Busch, L. (2000) The Moral Economy of Grades and Standards. *Journal of Rural Studies* 16: 273-283.

Busch, L., E. Ransom and G. Middendorf (2005) Paradoxes of Innovation: Standards and Technical Change in the Transformation of the US Soybean Industry. In this volume.

Campher, J. (1998) Bonsmara Synthetic Breed. DNAfrica (Pty) Ltd. Retrieved July 21, 2003; http://www.dnafrica.co.za/bonsmara.htm.

Clark, A. and J. Fujimura (1992) *The Right Tools for the Job: At Work in the Twentieth Century Life Sciences.* Princeton: Princeton University Press.

Cheit, R. E. (1990) *Setting Safety Standards: Regulation in the Public and Private Sectors.* Berkeley: University of California Press.

Crosley, R. I., P. H. Heinze and R.T. Naudé (1994) The Relationship Between Beef Tenderness and Age Classification in the South African Beef Carcass Classification System. The Meat Industry Centre, Irene Animal Production Institute, Irene, South Africa. Unpublished Report.

de Wet, C. (1997) Land Reform in South Africa: A vehicle for justice and reconciliation, or a source of further inequality and conflict? *Development Southern Africa.* 14(3): 355-362.

Delgado, C. and M. Rosegrant (1999) Livestock to 2020: The Next Food Revolution. Washington, DC, IFPRI.

Dunn, E. (2003) Trojan Pig: Paradoxes of Food Safety Regulation. *Environment and Planning A*. 35: 1493-1511.

FAO (2003) Codex Alimentarius – new $40 million fund for poor countries; http://www.fao.org/english/newsroom/news/2003/13489-en.html. (April 15, 2003).

Fiddes, N. (1991) *Meat: A Natural Symbol*. New York: Routledge.

Giovannucci, D. and T. Reardon (2000) Understanding Grades and Standards – and How to Apply Them, in D. Giovannucci (ed.) A Guide to Developing Agricultural Markets and Agro-Enterprises, Washington: *The World Bank*; http://wbln0018.worldbank.org/essd.nsf/Agroenterprise/.

Goodman, D. and Redclift, M. (1991) *Refashioning Nature: Food, Ecology*, and Culture. London: Routledge.

Grindley, P. (1995) *Standards Strategy and Policy: Cases and Stories*. Oxford: Oxford University Press.

Guillen, M. F. (2001) Is Globalization Civilizing, Destructive or Feeble? A Critique of Five Key Debates in the Social Science Literature. *Annual Review of Sociology*: 235-257.

Haan, C. de, T. S. van Veen, B. Brandenburg, J. Gauthier, F. Le Gall, R. Mearns, M. Siméon (2001) Livestock Development: Implications for Rural Poverty, the Environment, and Global Food Security. Washington, D.C.: *The World Bank*.

Haen, H. de, N. Alexandratos and J. Bruinsma (1998) Prospects for the World Food Situation on the Threshold of the 21st Century. Pp. 21-52 in *The Future of Food: Long-term Prospects for the Agro-food Sector*. Paris: OECD Publications.

Harper, C. and B. Le Beau (2003) *Food, Society, and Environment*. Prentice Hall: New Jersey.

Hart, G. (2003) *Disabling Globalization: Places of Power in Post-Apartheid South Africa*. Berkeley: University of California Press.

Held, D., A. G. McGrew, D. Goldblatt, and J. Perraton (1999) *Global Transformations: Politics, Economics and Culture*. Cambridge: Polity.

Held, D. and A. McGrew (2002) *Globalization/Anti-Globalization*. Malden, MA: Polity Press.

Latour, B. (1987) *Science in Action: How to Follow Scientists and Engineers Through Society*. Cambridge, MA: Harvard University Press.

LEAD (Livestock, Environment and Development Initiative) (1999) Livestock and Environment Toolbox. Food and Agriculture Organisation of the United Nations. Retrieved on July 16, 2003; http://lead.vurtualcentre.org/en/dec/toolbox/Indust/LossAgbi.com.

Lipton, M. (1993) Restructuring South African Agriculture. Pp. 359-408 in *State & Market in Post Apartheid South Africa*, edited by M. Lipton and C. Simkins. Boulder, Colorado: Westview Press.

May, J., I. Woolard, and S. Klasen (2000) The Nature and Measurement of Poverty and Inequality. Pp. 20-48 in *Poverty and Inequality in South Africa: Meeting the Challenge*, edited by J. May. New York: Zed Books.

Magdoff, F., J. B. Foster, and F. H. Buttel eds. (2000) Hungry for Profit: The Agribusiness Threat to Farmers, Food, and the Environment. New York: Monthly Review Press.

McMichael, P. (1991) Food, the State and the World Economy. *International Journal of Sociology of Agriculture and Food* 1: 71-85.

McMichael, P. (2000) Global Food Politics. Pp. 125-144 in *Hungry for Profit: The Agribusiness Threat to Farmers, Food, and the Environment*, edited by F. Magdoff, J. B. Foster, F. H. Buttel. New York: Monthly Review Press.

Morris, C. A. (1999) The Role of USDA's Beef Grading Program in the Marketing of Beef in 1999 Agricultural Marketing Outreach Workshop Training Manual; http://marketingoutreach.usda.gov/info/99Manual/grading.htm. (October 14, 2002).

National Agricultural Marketing Council (2001) Report on the Investigation into the Effect of Deregulation on the Red Meat Industry. Pretoria, South Africa: NAMC.

Posel, D. (2003) Have Migration Patterns in post-Apartheid South Africa Changed? Paper presented at Conference on African Migration in Comparative Perspective, Johannesburg, South Africa, 4-7 June, 2003. Retrieved August 10, 2003; http://pum.princeton.edu/pumconference/papers/1-Posel.pdf.

Ransom, E. (2003) Setting the Standard: Competing Values in the South African Red Meat Industry. Ph.D. dissertation, Michigan State University.

Reardon, T., J-M. Codron, L. Busch, J. Bingen, C. Harris (1999) Global Change in Agrifood Grades and Standards: Agribusiness Strategic Responses in Developing Countries. *International Food and Agribusiness Management Review*. 2 (3): 421-435.

Spriggs, J. and G. Isaac (2001) *Food Safety and International Competitiveness: The Case of Beef.* Oxford, CABI.

Stiffler, D. M., J. W. Savell, G. C. Smith, T. R. Dutson and Z. L. Carpenter (1984) Electrical Stimulation: Purpose, Application and Results. Report No: B-1375. College Station, Texas: Texas Agricultural Extension Service, The Texas A&M University System; http://savell-j.tamu.edu/pdf/es.pdf.

Tanaka, K. and L. Busch (2003) Standardization as a Means for Globalizing a Commodity: The Case of Rapeseed in China. *Rural Sociology* 68(1): 25-45.

Thompson, G. (2003) Water Tap Often Shut to South Africa Poor. *New York Times*, May 29, p. A1.

Tørres, L., H. Bhorat, M. Leibbrandt and F. Cassim (2000) Poverty and the Labour Market. Pp. 73-94 in *Poverty and Inequality in South Africa: Meeting the Challenge*, edited by J. May. London: Zed Books.

Troy, D. and R. Joseph (2001) Very Fast Chilling in Beef. The National Food Centre, Research Report No. 43. Castleknock, Dublin; http:www.teagasc.ie/research/reports/foodprocessing/4985/eopr-4985.htm.

Weatherspoon, D. D. and T. Reardon (2003) The Rise of Supermarkets in Africa: Implications for Agrifood Systems and Rural Poor. *Development Policy Review* 21(3): 333-355.

Winberg, M. (1996) *Back to the Land.* Johannesburg, South Africa: Porcubine Press.

World Bank (2001) *Poverty in the Age of Globalization.* Washington, DC: World Bank.

RICHARD JONES*, H. ADE FREEMAN†, GABRIELE LO
MONACO‡, S. WALLS§, AND S. I. LONDNER**

# 10. IMPROVING THE ACCESS OF SMALL FARMERS IN AFRICA TO GLOBAL MARKETS THROUGH THE DEVELOPMENT OF QUALITY STANDARDS FOR PIGEONPEAS

## 1. INTRODUCTION

Recent trends toward more liberalized domestic and export markets as important sources of economic growth provide new opportunities and challenges for African smallholder farmers. To take advantage of these opportunities, smallholders must find their competitive advantage. This implies access to well-organized marketing, distribution and post-harvest systems, effective market information, and technologies that allow them to be price and quality competitive.

Unfortunately, the long-term marginalization of agriculture in Africa since independence has left smallholders poorly equipped to develop their competitive advantage in international markets. Smallholders face high transaction costs and uncertainty arising from missing or incomplete input and product markets as well as information that restricts market access. Consequently, there is a need for policies that foster the most productive roles for public, private, and non-governmental organizations in support of African farmers, traders, and agribusinesses (Eicher, 1999). Working together, these actors can establish the institutional relationships that provide and facilitate access to technology, information, capital, and marketing arrangements – all necessary for developing a competitive advantage in international markets.

However, the emergence of a global agri-food system based on integrated international supply chains creates additional policy challenges (Busch, 2002). In East Africa, such challenges are seen clearly in the development of the horticultural sector where producers are linked to end markets dominated by supermarket chains in the United Kingdom and Europe. Similar trends are taking place in both domestic and regional markets for traditional commodities such as rice. In Kenya, one rice

* Richard Jones, Assistant Regional Director Eastern and Southern Africa, International Crops Research Institute for the Semi-Arid Tropics (ICRISAT).
† H. Ade Freeman, Director, Targeting Research and Development Opportunities, International Livestock Research Institute (ILRI).
‡ Gabriele Lo Monaco, Program Officer, MOVIMONDO.
§ Steve Walls, Chief of Party, Regional Agricultural Trade Expansion Support Program, Chemonics International.
** Steve Londner, Senior Advisor, Strategic Initiatives, TechnoServe, Inc.

*J. Bingen and L. Busch, (eds.), Agricultural Standards: The Shape of the Global Food and Fiber System, 177-191.* © 2006 *Springer. Printed in the Netherlands.*

miller sources locally, regionally from Tanzania, and internationally from Pakistan in order to process and package five different rice varieties to meet demand from local supermarkets and wholesalers. Furthermore, this miller further differentiates within varieties based on grades with hand-sorted grains at the premium end of the market and broken grains at the opposite extreme. For smallholders to remain active participants in these types of marketing arrangements, they must: meet exacting quality criteria, including size, color, texture, pesticide residues and taste; adjust production volumes rapidly to meet short-term market trends; track minor product innovations by changing planting material, planting methods and packaging; and, keep up with cost-reducing technical progress, in a context in which the partner retailer and its competitors have multiple sourcing (Kydd, 2002)

It has become increasingly evident that organizations like the International Crops Research Institute for the Semi-Arid Tropics (ICRISAT) – with a focus on technology to be transferred to farmers – are not responsive to these evolving demands of the global agri-food system (see Hall et al., 2001).

This chapter describes how ICRISAT, in partnership with private sector traders and processors, and TechnoServe, Inc. – an international non-profit business development organization – seeks to address these demands by establishing profit-oriented technology innovation systems in the pigeonpeas sub-sector. In response to the growing demand for pigeonpeas from India, ICRISAT and TechnoServe identified opportunities within already established marketing chains to capture increased benefits for smallholders based on adjusting the timing of production, improving product quality and making the seed commercially available.[1] A central argument in this chapter is that agricultural researchers and extension workers need to think beyond the farm gate and develop strategic partnerships with market players and policymakers to effect real change.

Following a review of the current structure and dynamics of domestic, regional and international pigeonpeas markets, this chapter examines the ways in which research focused on grades and standards can help improve the competitive position of smallholder African farmers.

## 2. TRADE AND MARKETING

### 2.1  Domestic and Regional Trade

Pigeonpeas are widely grown by smallholders in eastern and southern Africa (Table 1) for subsistence and as a cash crop.[2] Peas are consumed like a green vegetable, as cooked whole pigeonpeas, and as *dhal*.[3] It is the legume of choice and is particularly important in eastern Kenya, southern Malawi, northern Mozambique, southern Tanzania and northern Uganda where it is adapted to the agro-ecology of these areas. In Kenya there is a significant demand for *dhal* from the Asian as well as from the Kikuyu and Swahili communities who attach special significance to whole pigeonpeas as food for special occasions.

Table 1. Average production (Mt) and area (ha) of pigeonpeas in Kenya, Malawi, Tanzania and Uganda, 1980-82 and 1995-97; annual growth rate in production, 1980-97.

| Country | Production (Mt) 1980-82 | Production (Mt) 1995-97 | Area (ha) 1980-82 | Area (ha) 1995-97 | Annual production growth rate 1980-1997) |
|---------|---------|---------|---------|---------|---------|
| Kenya | 28,845 | 44,874 | 66,337 | 147,510 | 4.7 |
| Malawi | 85,000 | 98,000 | 127,333 | 143,000 | 0.8 |
| Tanzania | 22,667 | 37,333 | 36,667 | 56,667 | 2.2 |
| Uganda | 26,333 | 58,333 | 55,000 | 71,000 | 6.1 |

Source: Freeman et al., 1998

There is a significant domestic and regional trade in whole pigeonpeas, as well as for processing *dhal*. But since the crop passes through several intermediaries with little value being added before finally reaching end-users, the traditional marketing channels have high marketing and distribution costs. Typically rural assemblers bulk the crop and sell to middle men/traders in local market centers. The crop is then transported to larger produce markets where it is re-sold to transporters for delivery to processors and exporters. Table 2 shows marketing margins based on data for buying and selling prices for selected markets.

Table 2. Marketing margins (percent) for selected pigeon pea markets in Kenya[4]

| Marketing chain participant | Urban retail (supermarket) | Urban retail (open-air Market) | Urban retail of Dhal | Export of whole grain |
|---|---|---|---|---|
| Rural assembler | 6.0 | 8.4 | 8.1 | 3.3 |
| Rural wholesaler | 3.0 | 5.2 | 4.3 | 1.7 |
| Urban transporter | 5.3 | 24.4 | 7.0 | 2.9 |
| Urban processor/exporter | 31.4 | - | 41.9 | 60.3 |
| Urban retailer | 25.7 | 20.0 | - | 15.9 |
| Complete distribution chain | 71.4 | 58.0 | 61.2 | 84.1 |
| Producer share | 28.6 | 42.0 | 38.8 | 15.9 |

Source: Freeman et al., 1998

Total gross marketing margins in the distribution chain are highest for urban retail of *dhal* followed by retail of dry pigeonpeas in supermarkets. Correspondingly, farmers receive the lowest share of final consumer prices while urban processors receive the highest shares in both market channels. Without complete information of costs for transport, storage, processing, other transaction costs, and marketing risks, it is difficult to determine whether these margins reflect traders' profits or point to inefficiencies in the marketing system. Nonetheless, the much larger price spread between pigeonpeas producers and consumers in these market channels suggest that there might be opportunities for transferring a proportion of these margins to the advantage of producers (Freeman *et al.*, 1999).[5]

## 2.2   *International trade*

It is the export trade to India and other overseas markets that makes pigeonpeas different from other food crops, such as maize, that are also marketed domestically and regionally. While India is the world's leading producer of pigeonpeas, it regularly imports whole pigeonpeas to make up for domestic shortfalls in production. As Figure 1 indicates, the size of this demand fluctuates from year to year, depending largely on domestic production.

Figure 1. Indian imports of unprocessed pigeonpeas (MT)

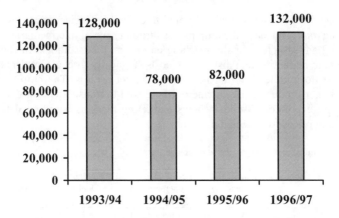

Source: Indian Foreign Trade Statistics

Trade in whole pigeonpeas from Kenya, Malawi, Mozambique and Tanzania has developed largely in response to the demand from India. Due to the unreliability of national statistics it is difficult to document accurately the development of pigeonpeas trade between eastern and southern Africa and India. Discussions with key informants involved in pigeonpeas trade suggest that the crop has been exported on a continuous basis at least from the early 1970's. Undoubtedly the presence of ethnic Indian communities in eastern and southern Africa, who were familiar with the pigeonpeas crop and had established contacts in India, was a major factor in the development of the pigeonpeas trade.

Table 1 shows the major expansion in pigeonpeas production between the early 1980s and the mid-1990s that is generally attributed to the producer incentives resulting from the move in the early 1990s towards market rates of exchange. However, an expansion of the area under cultivation and not increased productivity accounts for the increased production as smallholder farmers continued to plant low yielding local landraces with minimal use of purchased inputs. These varieties were suitable for the Indian market that accepted them as fair average quality (FAQ) grain containing up to 7% of foreign matter, weevil infested and damaged grain (Jaeger, 1998).

Several factors facilitated pigeonpeas as an attractive export crop for eastern and southern Africa. First, unlike maize, pigeonpeas have never been subject to government price controls or export bans because the crop was never considered strategically important for national food security. Second, since the African harvest takes place slightly before the main Indian harvest, traders can take advantage of higher prices at the end of the Indian season. Third, pigeonpeas productivity in India has not kept pace with population increase because farmers in high potential areas have switched from growing pigeonpeas to more input responsive crops, thereby marginalizing pigeonpeas production to less favored environments. Finally, during the era of over-valued currencies before structural adjustment policies were introduced in the early 1990's, the ready availability of pigeonpeas for export from eastern and southern Africa in exchange for hard currency provided a lucrative opportunity for traders to earn foreign exchange.

On the other hand, while the Indian import tariff of 35% made it unattractive for African *dhal* processors to export to India, it provided a marketing opportunity for the very same processors to export *dhal* to ethnic markets around the world. As a result, a thriving pigeonpeas processing industry developed in Kenya and Malawi.

## 2.3    Emerging Challenges in the Indian Market

India's pigeonpeas deficit is projected to continue to grow (Jaeger, 1998), but several challenges potentially threaten the long-term viability of pigeonpeas for smallholders in eastern and southern Africa who have few cash crop alternatives. First, Myanmar has become a major exporter of whole pigeonpeas to India and there is growing evidence that it can do so at lower cost than countries in eastern and southern Africa (Lo Monaco, 2002). Second, India itself has removed its export ban on *dhal* and provides tax incentives to exporters thereby making it harder for Kenyan and Malawian processors to compete in international markets. Third, several industrialized countries including the US, Canada, France, and Australia are entering the market to export non-traditional legumes, including chickpeas, yellow peas and pigeonpeas, to India.[6] Canada and France now export up to 300,000 tons of yellow peas annually to India. In late 2001 the French and Canadian yellow peas were available at US$200/MT compared with US$300/MT for pigeonpeas from Myanmar, and US$315/MT from Tanzania. Although there are definite taste preferences for the different types of legumes in India, Indian consumers are not price insensitive and will switch to alternative pulses if the price is right.

For countries in eastern and southern Africa to remain competitive, they must increase productivity, reduce transaction costs, and improve quality standards. High transport costs are of particular concern to landlocked Malawi where the cost of sending a fully loaded 20-foot container to Mumbai is US$1,800 compared to US$800-1,200 for Tanzania, and US$500-800 for Kenya. Transport costs from Myanmar to India are similar to those for Kenya, while improvements in transport infrastructure in Mozambique have reduced costs to below those of Kenya. However, transaction costs and productivity are by no means the complete story. Mechanical changes in milling indicate the need for changes in the type of pigeonpeas supplied by African producers.

The milling quality of pigeonpeas from Africa has generally allowed them to be traded in the Indian market at a premium over the international price. This premium is commonly perceived to be associated with bold grain size and white color,[7] which are traits of the Tanzanian variety "Babati White". Husk residues of white or cream varieties are less evident to visual inspection and millers historically preferred them to varieties with darker husks, such as those imported from Myanmar. But modern de-hullers are more efficient in removing the seed coat and this helps account for Myanmar imports forcing a 50% decline in the African premium price in late 2001 (Lo Monaco, 2002). Table 3 compares specific quality traits related to imported pigeonpeas for processing from Africa and Myanmar with yellow peas from Europe/North America that are targeted towards price sensitive consumers.

Table 3. Grain quality traits of pigeonpeas from Africa and Myanmar, and of yellow pea from Europe/North America.

|  | Africa | Myanmar | Yellow pea |
|---|---|---|---|
| Grain size | Medium – large | Medium – small | Large |
| Grain shape | Round | Round | Round |
| Easiness to dehull | Low | Fair | Very high |
| Cleanness | High | Low | High |
| Weeviled grains | Fair | High | Low |
| Homogeneity | High | Low | High |
| Average % milling yield | 65-70 | 65-75 | 90 |

Source: Lo Monaco, 2002

The results suggest that price premiums for African pigeonpeas are more a function of cleanness and fewer weeviled grains rather than grain size and color. Consequently, if African producers are to remain competitive they must establish standards for pigeonpeas that differentiate their product in terms of ease of de-hulling, cleanness, homogeneity and the ratio of weeviled grains.

The remainder of this chapter discusses ways in which collaborative work by regional organizations, national governments, the private sector, agricultural researchers and extension workers can help to develop such standards and thereby help to maintain the competitiveness of pigeonpeas for export from eastern and southern Africa.

## 3. ADDRESSING SEED SUPPLY ISSUES

Product quality is partly dependent on the crop variety. For farmers to meet established grades and standards and respond to changing product innovations they need to have access to seed varieties that are valued by end-users. This section discusses the importance of research and biological issues in a market-driven context as well as the institutional constraints on seed supply.

For non-hybrid crops such as pigeonpeas, farmers invariably use own-saved seed. Farmer seed systems are both resilient and flexible even under extreme conditions since traditional pigeonpeas landraces are indeterminate long-duration types that are well adapted to the farming systems where they are grown.[8] Consequently, farmers are reluctant to pay large premiums for improved and certified seed except for hybrids. However, test marketing of small seed packs shows that farmers are willing to purchase small quantities of more expensive, improved seed, but then save the germ-plasm instead of renewing it with new purchases (see Tripp, 2001). For self-pollinated crops like beans and groundnuts, seed saving in this way poses few problems. But for crops like pigeonpeas where there is some degree of out-crossing, this practice leads to a decline in the integrity of the variety and thereby weakens the value of the crop in markets where standards based on varietal integrity are important.

The International Crops Research Institute for the Semi-Arid Tropics (ICRISAT) has recently developed the first hybrid pigeonpeas and with yield increases of more than 30% (Saxena et al., 1996), the private sector has started to invest in pigeonpeas improvement because of the potential profits from hybrid seed sales. Pigeonpeas varieties that are resistant to *Fusarium* wilt[9] and that can be grown year-round in non-traditional pigeonpeas areas are now available. A next step involves updating and standardizing national policies to encourage new varietal testing and approval processes for new releases that could help assure the competitiveness of smallholders in the export market.

## 4. PARTNERSHIPS LINKING AGRICULTURAL RESEARCH AND MARKETS

In an emerging market economy, the real test of success of technological innovation is not in the test plot or the laboratory, but in the marketplace, which includes the broad range of actors dealing with input supply, production, harvest, storage, processing, and marketing. From this perspective, agricultural research plays a limited role in creating adequate incentives to spur the adoption of technological innovation. And yet, the adoption of technological innovation is essential for future growth and development. A major challenge involves the creation of the necessary institutional arrangements that will stimulate adoption of these new technologies by producers. As suggested above, farmers need a clear financial incentive to adopt varieties that meet the processors' quality standards. Why grow short-duration pigeonpeas that require the use of expensive pesticides when traditional long-duration varieties can be successfully grown without substantial additional costs?

Agricultural research institutions such as ICRISAT and its national agricultural research partners do not have a comparative advantage in market or business development to address this question, but they can catalyze the development of partnerships that will create the necessary incentives, thereby stimulating demand for new technologies. For an agricultural research institution to adopt this approach requires a fundamental change from the traditional supply side driven approach to technology dissemination that has had such limited impact in increasing agricultural productivity.

Studies by TechnoServe confirmed the preliminary observations of researchers with ICRISAT and its national agricultural research partners that pigeonpeas represented a significant market if farmers had access to the products of research that would satisfy the demands of high-value niche markets for pigeonpeas. Based on these findings, ICRISAT and TechnoServe agreed to collaborate on a detailed sub-sector analysis in each of the four major pigeonpeas producing countries in eastern and southern Africa in order to design interventions for overcoming identified constraints. TechnoServe's specialization in enterprise development, based on the philosophy that economically viable businesses will create income and economic growth for producers, was helpful in developing a more targeted understanding of the pigeonpeas sub-sector and in strengthening private-sector collaborators capable of stimulating demand for pigeonpeas technologies. The remainder of this chapter describes the evolution of the country strategies.

## 5. ADJUSTING PRODUCTION TIMING TO BENEFIT FROM SEASONAL PRICE RISES

In 1998 the TechnoServe office in Mozambique identified pigeonpeas as one of six commodities that held significant promise for business development in that country. Prior to the protracted civil war that ended in 1992, Mozambique had been a major exporter of whole pigeonpeas, mainly to India. Exports to India were disrupted throughout the war and were replaced by informal cross-border trade with neighboring Malawi (Ackello-Ogutu and Echessah, 1997).

TechnoServe's study of price trends in the Indian market suggested that if pigeonpeas from eastern and southern Africa could be shipped as early as May and maintained until October/November, (in contrast to the present situation where there is only an assured supply for two months starting in October), prices would be firmer. Such a strategy would not only improve prices, but also provide Indian processors a more reliable supply over time instead of a short term product glut. The message from the TechnoServe study was clear. Although India's pigeonpeas deficit is projected to continue to grow (Jaeger, 1998), the competitiveness of pigeonpeas in this market would depend less on quality and more on the amount, reliability and timing of supply.

ICRISAT, working with the *Instituto Nacional de Investigação Agronómica* (INIA), had already tested a range of improved short-, medium- and long-duration varieties and demonstrated the feasibility of extending the production season from May to October. That is, a possible technological solution in the form of short- and medium-duration varieties existed to respond to the marketing opportunity identified by TechnoServe. Nevertheless, a pest-control package had to accompany these varieties because of their greater susceptibility to insect pests.

Mozambique is a major producer of cotton that is grown largely by smallholders and marketed to companies that hold sole concessions for different geographical areas. The cotton companies provide inputs (seed and insecticides) to farmers on credit, which is then recovered from farmers when the crop is purchased. TechnoServe developed a business plan using data from ICRISAT and INIA that demonstrated the profitability of a cotton-pigeonpeas rotation, and presented this to the cotton companies. For agronomic reasons, cotton cannot be grown continuously on the same piece of land, and pigeonpeas were presented as an ideal rotation crop because of the market demand for pigeonpeas from India, and because of the fertility benefits from residual soil nitrogen that would boost the yield of subsequent cotton crops. By linking with the cotton companies, farmers would be able to access insecticides through the same institutional arrangements that are used to supply this input for cotton. The seasonal price differential that creates the incentive for this arrangement is significant. Over the past five years the average December to

February price, when the Indian crop hits the market, has been US$337/MT CIF Mumbai. In July – September, the corresponding five-year average high price has been US$465/MT, a 38% premium.

TechnoServe facilitated a visit for major Indian traders and processors to Mozambique. They visited with cotton companies, farmer associations and exporters, and were introduced to several improved pigeonpeas varieties developed by ICRISAT. They identified an improved short-duration variety (ICPL 87091) as having a good taste and appropriate milling characteristics. To further enhance the profitability, a specific brand, "Nacala Gold" was developed for ICPL 87091 exports from Mozambique. In time the idea is that this brand name will stand for a guarantee of a superior product that should be able to attract an additional US$10-25/MT (personal communication, 1999).

TechnoServe, cotton companies, ICRISAT and other collaborators are now working to supply the part of the demand for 100,000 metric tons *per annum* from May to September, a market that is projected to grow at 20% *per annum*. Seed is being multiplied and inputs supplied and financed by a range of agencies, including the cotton companies, farmer associations and exporters.

## 6. TARGETING HIGH-VALUE NICHE MARKETS BY MEETING EXACTING QUALITY CRITERIA

TechnoServe in Tanzania took a different approach and specifically targeted the demand from the communities of Indian and Caribbean origin in Great Britain. Research indicated a significant niche market for high quality grain (Jaeger, 1998) and buyer preference for bold cream-colored pigeonpeas from northern Tanzania. In addition, research indicates an annual demand for at least 1,500-3,000 MT. However, in contrast to the Indian market that is not quality driven,[10] European importers and brokers are very quality conscious. They demand strict compliance regarding seed cleanliness and breakage, and they pay a premium for pre-cleaned product of approximately US$100/MT over the world market price for unprocessed pigeonpeas. The final product is supplied to supermarkets as packaged dried whole pigeonpeas or to the canning industry. To meet this market's demands, traders buy grain from farmers, and then sort it by hand, capturing for themselves the price differential.

Clearly, smallholders receive obvious benefits if they can produce and supply this higher quality product. Accordingly, TechnoServe organizes small farmers in northern Tanzania into local groups in order to train farmers in village-level grain cleaning and handling. These groups are linked directly to exporters, who in turn are linked with identified European buyers. To facilitate and expand cash purchases from these groups, TechnoServe works with commercial banks to provide the exporters with working capital loan guarantees.

While TechnoServe was working on improving grain quality through hand sorting, ICRISAT was working with the national agricultural research and extension service to test a range of improved long-duration pigeonpeas varieties with farmers. These varieties were selected for their resistance to *Fusarium* wilt, and for their bold cream-colored seeds. Two consecutive seasons of on-farm testing confirmed that the preferred variety, ICEAP 00040 was resistant to wilt and approximately 30% higher yielding than existing landraces. European buyers who received samples of ICEAP 00040 from ICRISAT via TechnoServe, also expressed satisfaction with the grain quality of this variety. Fortuitously, the main exporter also runs a seed company, which is now multiplying ICEAP 00040 seed. Once this variety is more widely available, farmers should benefit from increased yields and, provided some degree of varietal purity is maintained, from the time saved that would otherwise be spent on hand sorting local landraces that tend to have more variable grain size and color.

Early data suggest that the incremental production costs for the farmers to adopt new, late-maturing varieties are small, and consist primarily of modest costs for seed, possible additional insecticides and harvesting. However, these are largely offset by savings from the elimination of pre-sorting prior to sale, especially since the sorting and grading is done on the farm and not by the buyers. Table 4 summarizes the potential financial benefits based on the substitution of traditional varieties with improved long-duration varieties.

Table 4. A comparison of traditional marketing in Tanzania versus selling to premium export markets[11]

| Production-marketing method | Yield | Selling Price $ per kg | Gross income | Net income | Additional income |
|---|---|---|---|---|---|
| Traditional mixed varieties, sold to agents & local market | 900 kg/ ha | $0.17 kg | $153/ ha | $92/ ha | N/A |
| Improved white varieties, sold directly to exporter | 1200 kg/ ha | $0.21 kg | $252/ ha | $191/ ha | $99/ ha |

Source: Pigeonpeas Sub-Sector Study, TechnoServe 1998

Pigeonpeas have now been exported to the UK market for two consecutive seasons, and in 2001 farmers received a price premium of 25%.

## 7.  ADDRESSING END-USER NEEDS THROUGH CHANGES IN PLANTING MATERIAL

There are 10 established pigeonpeas processors in Malawi, with a combined processing capacity of 20,000 metric tons, making Malawi the second largest pigeonpeas processing country in the world after India.[12] They have established a reputation as suppliers of superior grade *dhal*, and the country is the principal supplier of approximately 1,500 metric tons annually of dried pigeonpeas and processed *dhal* to the UK. Other markets for split pigeonpeas include the large Asian immigrant population in the US and Canada. However, the processors confront a significant challenge. In recent years, they have had difficulty maintaining quality standards both for whole dried pigeonpeas and processed *dhal* because of the limited supply of quality grain from producers. The cessation of hostilities in Mozambique and the re-establishment of direct exports from that country reduced the supply of pigeonpeas from Mozambique and consequently threatened the viability of their industry.

Until the mid-1990s these processors operated as competitors, but the reduced supply of pigeonpeas from Mozambique and the need for quality grain stimulated them to consider some degree of collaboration among themselves and with agricultural researchers.

In Malawi, the *Fusarium* wilt resistant variety ICP 9145 was hurriedly released after a severe wilt outbreak and widespread crop failure in 1987. Although this new variety was wilt resistant, Malawian traders and processors did not like its relatively small seeds and tight seed coat that reduced the percentage recovery of *dhal* from whole grain below the typical 70%.[13] Farmers also mentioned that ICP 9145 took a long time to cook, a function of the tight seed coat. In response to these shortcomings, another variety, ICEAP 00040, was selected after extensive testing both with farmers and industry players and has been released in Kenya, Malawi, and Tanzania. This variety combines *Fusarium* wilt resistance, bold cream-colored seeds, and fast cooking time and it is easily de-hulled.

In 1997 the Department of Agricultural Research and Technical Services (DARTS) and ICRISAT hosted a national planning workshop and invited one of the *dhal* millers to inform the industry players about efforts to increase pigeonpeas productivity. This led to the establishment of the Grain and Legumes Development Association Limited (GALDAL), a legally registered business for nurturing the development of grains and legumes in Malawi with a membership that includes eight pigeonpeas trading and processing companies.

GALDAL's first initiative was to promote the production of the improved long-duration variety ICEAP 00040. Extensive on-farm testing with smallholder farmers in two of the major pigeonpeas growing areas by DARTS confirmed the wilt resistance of ICEAP 00040 and, importantly for farmers, the faster cooking time and higher yield of this variety.[14] ICRISAT and DARTS supplied foundation seed of ICEAP 00040 to GALDAL, which then underwrote the cost of contracting farmers to multiply 100 tons of certified seed in the 1998/99 season, sufficient to plant 20,000 ha in the 1999-2000 season. Government inspectors carried out seed inspection and certification, but no clear strategy was devised to market the seed to farmers. The issue that the association and its partners now face is how to stimulate farmers' demand for the improved seed.

## 8. PRODUCT INNOVATION THROUGH CHANGING PLANTING MATERIAL

In Kenya, regular export of fresh green pigeonpeas to the UK has been maintained because determinate short-duration pigeonpeas are now available to farmers that can be harvested year round and there is a greater demand for convenience foods by immigrant communities in the UK. In fact, one UK importer indicated a willingness to enter into a contract for 40 metric tons of frozen pigeonpeas per month if only a supplier could be found. In addition, the large Indian and Afro-Caribbean communities in Europe and North America offer new potential markets that can be accessed through the application of improved processing technologies such as freezing. The recent introduction of refrigerated containers to the Kenyan market has relieved the major constraint to such an approach, and already exporters in other sectors are taking advantage of this facility.

Many Kenyan smallholder growers have contracts directly with commercial horticultural exporters who supply UK supermarkets with a variety of fresh vegetables. This trade, however, has been very seasonal because of the phenology of the traditional long-duration varieties grown by farmers. With the introduction of short- and medium-duration determinate varieties that are not so temperature and photoperiod sensitive, it is now possible to supply fresh pigeonpeas year round.

Based on its ongoing work in Kenya, in 1999, ICRISAT arranged for testing fresh pigeonpeas from 15 improved short-duration varieties to determine their storability and sugar content within the existing delivery chain used by a commercial horticultural exporter. Samples were also sent to the United Kingdom for market evaluation purposes. Helpfully, the results demonstrated that there were significant differences in the tested parameters, an important learning step. But equally important, it was learned that the UK market was more interested in green pigeonpeas rather than pigeonpeas with a purple seed coat – valuable information to feed back into the development process.

ICRISAT, with TechnoServe and other partners are now exploring how best to develop this nascent industry. An interesting feature of the horticultural sector is the close integration between the buyers on the one hand and the producers on the other. Quality is such an important consideration for horticultural exporters that these companies even employ graduate agronomists to work with contract growers to advise on all aspects of crop production.

## 9. CONCLUSIONS

The emergence of a global agri-food system based on global commerce and the world of supermarkets provides both new opportunities, and threats to farmers. There is an urgent need to change the way that we all do business. Otherwise, smallholder farmers in Africa, especially those in marginal environments, will become even further marginalized as others seize the opportunities and run with them. In the past, agricultural researchers largely focused their efforts on increasing crop productivity without paying much attention to profitability. It was assumed that farmers would readily adopt supply side interventions. But the reality has been somewhat different. Attitudes are beginning to change among researchers, and there is now widespread agreement that to ensure the relevance of agricultural research, farmers need to be involved in the selection, testing and evaluation of improved agricultural technologies. Unfortunately, this approach is yet to be extended much beyond the farm gate to the traders, processors and consumers of crops who together comprise the market in which farmers are increasingly anxious to participate. Unless farmers can find a ready market that is sufficiently attractive relative to other enterprises, they will still be reluctant to invest in new technologies.

Many actors involved in agricultural research and development are suspicious of the market and the role played by the private sector. Middlemen are still despised for the excessive profits they make from the labors of others rather than being recognized for the very considerable risks they often take. The types of arrangements described in this chapter indicate that there is a role for many different actors, but these actors need to work towards a common goal through the development of strategic partnerships for the benefit of smallholder farmers. Unfortunately there is insufficient understanding by policy makers and development investors of what needs to be done to foster such partnerships. This chapter does not pretend to provide all the answers, but it is hoped that the description of the market-based approach focused on a well-adapted crop grown by some of the poorest farmers in Africa will be of interest.

Agricultural researchers have developed pigeonpeas varieties that are both higher yielding and can meet the precise and varying quality requirements of end-users in terms of their grain size, color, processing characteristics, and delivery to market. Adoption of these new seed technologies is hampered by a lack of access to improved seeds as well as the lack of established quality standards within local market systems that can reward farmers for producing a differentiated product in terms of grain size and color, quality, or cleanliness.

Without the necessary market incentives, farmers are less likely to invest in improved seed and realize the productivity and quality gains that have been demonstrated from planting improved varieties. Even if farmers were sufficiently attracted by the superior agronomic performance (higher yield, early maturity, or disease resistance) the lack of improved seed would be a major constraint on the adoption of improved germplasm.

The introduction of simple and easily administered quality standards that are based on end-user needs, can help farmers, traders and exporters to benefit from niche markets that demand higher quality standards than the traditional export market for FAQ grain. The realization of price incentives will stimulate investment by interested parties in seed multiplication of improved pigeonpeas varieties. Success in pigeonpeas could be replicated in a wide range of other pulses and products.

Regional partnerships among international research institutions and business development agencies, working in close collaboration with the private sector and local institutions, hold great promise for identifying and implementing solutions to these complex constraints to agricultural and economic development.

## 10. NOTES

[1] There are many examples in smallholder agriculture where technological capability exists to increase productivity, timing of production, and product quality, but where institutional and organizational innovations are required to deliver benefits from research investments. Crop sales are one of the few avenues available to rural households to earn income, and yet the returns to household assets are low as a result of low productivity, inefficient markets, high transactions costs, and low producer prices. These factors combined result in low farm income. Evidence from livelihoods research in eastern and southern Africa indicate that poor farmers seek to increase their investments in agriculture as the preferred route out of poverty and therefore solutions to these problems are urgently required if poverty, which is endemic in rural areas of eastern and southern Africa is to be reduced.

[2] Pigeonpeas statistics are not routinely collected by most governments, and for some countries like Mozambique that was affected by war for nearly 18 years, no reliable statistics are available.

[3] *Dhal* is made by removing the seed coat and splitting the cotyledons. *Dhal* made from pigeonpeas is referred to as *Tur dhal*, although the terms *Toor*, *Tuver* or *Arhar dhal* are also used to describe the same product.

[4] The margins are gross marketing margins because the nature of some of the marketing systems - including both cash costs and implicit costs – makes it difficult to estimate marketing costs precisely.

[5] The removal of tariffs on agricultural produce traded between Kenya, Tanzania, and Uganda by the East African Community is likely to encourage increased cross-border trade. Similar cross-border trade in pigeonpeas takes place from northern Mozambique into Malawi that has the largest installed pigeonpeas processing capacity outside of India (Ackello-Ogutu and Echessah, 1997). This trade was undoubtedly stimulated by the protracted civil war in Mozambique that severely restricted internal movements within the country. Since the end of the war, Mozambican traders and entrepreneurs have become actively involved in the export of the crop direct from the deep-water port at Nacala. However in the case of Malawi, virtually all the crop is exported either as whole pigeonpeas or processed *dhal*.

[6] In addition, Australia made significant investments in pigeonpeas research, but the crop has never really taken off in that country.

[7] There is conflicting evidence on the milling yields of bold white grains with some authors reporting high recovery rates (Jambunathan and Singh, 1981) while Kurien (1981) found no strict correlation between the two characters.

[8] Smallholder farmers invariably intercrop pigeonpeas with cereals establishing both crops together at the beginning of the rainy season. The earlier maturing cereal is harvested at the end of the rainy season leaving the longer maturing pigeonpeas to mature on residual moisture several months later. The slow growing pigeonpeas crop does not compete with faster growing cereals, and because of its deep rooting system is able to continue growing well into the long dry season when the land would otherwise be unoccupied

[9] *Fusarium* wilt is a soil-borne disease which blocks the xylem vessels that transport water from the roots to the leaves causing the plant to wilt and die. In severely infected fields, 100% mortality can occur. Durable wilt resistance has been developed and incorporated into several pigeonpeas varieties. An impact assessment of *Fusarium* wilt resistance in India found that the total net present value of benefits from collaborative *Fusarium* wilt research is approximately $62 million, representing an internal rate of return of 65% (Bantilan and Joshi, 1996).

[10] Indian importers do not impose strict standards and rather high percentages of off-types and foreign matter are common.

[11] The implicit production cost of $33 per hectare is derived by distributing the total per hectare production costs of $152 between the intercropped maize and pigeonpeas, based on yields.

[12] For Malawi, export of the processed product is especially attractive, since it allows local agro-processors to capture additional value that helps offset higher freight costs from this landlocked country.

[13] As noted earlier, processors also prefer bold cream-colored pigeonpeas because the bold split cotyledons attract a premium price, and small pieces of seed coat that are not removed during the de-hulling operation do not reduce the price premium if their color blends in with the yellow cotyledons.

[14] For example, yields of ICP 9145 in on-farm trials averaged 100 kg/ha in 1997/98 and 165 kg/ha in 1998/99 compared with 108 kg/ha and 264 kg/ha for ICEAP 00040 over the same seasons (Ritchie et al., 2000).

## 11.   REFERENCES

Ackello-Ogutu, C. and P. Echessah (1998) Unrecorded Cross-Border Trade between Malawi and Neighboring Countries. Technical Paper No. 87, Nairobi: USAID/Africa Bureau, Regional Trade Agenda Series.

Bantilan, M .C. S. and P. K. Joshi (1996) Returns to Research and Diffusion Investments on Wilt Resistance in Pigeonpeas. Impact Series No. 1. Patancheru, Andhra Pradesh: International Crops Research Institute for the Semi-Arid Tropics.

Busch, L. (2002) Agribusiness and Market Linkages. Paper presented at a workshop on The Future of Agriculture in the Semi-Arid Tropics of Africa, Nairobi, Kenya

Carney, D. (1999) Approaches to Sustainable Livelihoods for the Rural Poor, *ODI Poverty Briefing Paper 2*, January, London: Overseas Development Institute.

Eicher, C. K. (1999) *Institutions and the African Farmer*. Third Distinguished Economist Lecture. Mexico D.F.: International Maize and Wheat Improvement Center.

FAO (1998) FAOSTAT.PC Database. Rome: Food and Agriculture Organization of the United Nations.

Freeman, H. A., R. B.Jones, S. N. Silim and M. A. Ochere (1999) The Pigeonpeas Sub-Sector in Kenya. Mimeo.

_____ (1998) Pigeonpeas Situation and Outlook in Southern and Eastern Africa. Mimeo.

Hall, A. J., V. R. Sulaiman, N.G. Clark, and B. Yoganand (2001) Shared Perspectives: A Synthesis of Obstacles and Opportunities. Pp. 35-40 in *Sharing Perspectives on Public-Private Sector Iinteraction* edited by A. J. Hall, B. Yoganand, V. R. Sulaiman and N. G. Clark. Delhi and Patancheru: National Center for Agricultural Economics and Policy Research and International Crops Research Institute for the Semi-Arid Tropics.

IFAD (2001) *Rural Poverty Report 2001: The Challenge of Ending Ruural Poverty*. Oxford: Oxford University Press.

Jaeger, P. M. L. (1998) The Indian Market for East African Pigeonpeas (*Cajanus cajan*). Mimeo.

Jambunathan, R. and U. Singh (1981) Grain Quality of Pigeonpeas in Proceedings of the International Workshop on Pigeonpeas, Vol 1, Patancheru: ICRISAT.

Kydd, J. (2002) Agriculture and Rural Livelihoods: Is Globalization Opening or Blocking Paths Out of Rural Poverty? AgREN Network Paper No 21. ODI.

Kurien, P. P. (1981) Advances in Milling Technology of Pigeonpeas in Proceedings of the International Workshop on Pigeonpeas, Vol 1, Patancheru: ICRISAT.

Lin, J. Y. (1998) Agricultural Development and Reform in China. Pp. 523-38 in *International Agricultural Development* edited by C. K. Eicher and J. M. Staatz Baltimore: John Hopkins University Press.

Lo Monaco, G. (2002) The Competitiveness of Eastern African Pigeonpeas Exports in International Markets. ICRISAT Working Paper.

Maxwell, S. (2001) Agricultural Issues in Food Security. Pp. 32-66 in *Food Security in sub-Saharan Africa* edited by S. Devereux and S Maxwell London: ITDG Publishing.

Ritchie, J. M., S. Abeyasekera, C. S. M. Chanika, S. J. Ross, C. B. K. Mkandawire, T. H. Maulana, E.R. Shaba, and T.T.K. Milanzi (2000) Assessment of Improved Pigeonpeas Varieties Under Smallholder Management. Pp. 180-189 in *Integrated Crop Management Research in Malawi: Developing Technologies with Farmers*, J.M. Ritchie (ed.). Chatham: Natural Resources Institute.

Saxena, K. B, Y. S. Chauhan, S. Laxman, R. V. Kumar, and C. Johansen (1996) Research and Development of Hybrid Pigeonpeas. Research Bulletin No. 19. Patancheru, Andhra Pradesh: International Crops Research Institute for the Semi-Arid Tropics.

Silim, S. N., P. A. Omanga, C. Johansen, S. Laxman, and P. M. Kimani (1994) Use of the Kenya Transect for Selecting and Targeting Adapted Cultivars to Appropriate Production Systems. Pp. 44-54 in *Improvement of Pigeonpeas in Eastern and Southern Africa – Annual Research Planning Meeting 1994* edited by S. N. Silim, S. B. King, and S. Tuwafe Patancheru, Andhra Pradesh: International Crops Research Institute for the Semi-Arid Tropics.

Tripp, R. (2001) *Seed Provision and Agricultural Development. The Institutions of Rural Change*. Oxford: James Currey.

World Bank (1999) *World Development Indicators*, Washington D.C.: World Bank.

PAUL THIERS*

# 11. CHINA AND GLOBAL ORGANIC FOOD STANDARDS:

*Sovereignty Bargains and Domestic Politics*

## 1. INTRODUCTION

This chapter considers the relationship between global standards of economic integration and local politics. The political study of international standards generally begins with assessments of relationships between nation states as negotiations are conducted, power and influence exerted, and national interests advanced. However, in addition to the analytical and theoretical tools of international relations, there is room for a comparative politics approach to global food and agricultural standards. This "politics matters" approach would focus on the internal political differences within nation-states.

International agreements have been depicted as *sovereignty bargains* in which nation-state governments give up some degree of national policy sovereignty in return for some specific state goal such as cooperation on environmental problems (Litfin 1998) or coordinated monetary stability (Jabko 1999). The sovereignty bargain concept opens the door for understanding nation-state political incentives. However, this view maintains an image of unitary states as the chief actors in global policy making and implementation. By failing to disaggregate politics within nation-states, it assumes that sovereignty and policy authority are solely controlled by central governments and are therefore theirs to offer at the international level. Even a two-level game approach, which emphasizes how domestic politics constrain and motivate the negotiating positions of nation-states, continues to depict central governments as the focal point for developing global regimes and standards.

This chapter uses the example of China's integration into the global organic food regime to support the following argument. Global standards do impact national sovereignty. But they also become embedded in domestic political struggles that are a function of unique domestic political economies. In other words, domestic actors appropriate international standards, and the global economic regimes of which they are a part, to gain economic and political advantage at various levels. In the process,

---

* Paul Thiers, Assistant Professor of Political Science, Washington State University, Vancouver.

*J. Bingen and L. Busch, (eds.), Agricultural Standards: The Shape of the Global Food and Fiber System*, 193-217. © 2006 *Springer. Printed in the Netherlands.*

the use and meaning of standards can be transformed, leading to unexpected and unintended outcomes.

In the case of Chinese integration into the global organic food regime, at least three levels of political interaction became significant. First, the sovereignty of the central government as the sole definer and enforcer of meaning was weakened as part of the bargain to obtain the economic benefits of global integration. Second, sectors of the Chinese bureaucracy used international standards and regimes as alternative sources of authority in an ongoing, domestic turf battle. Finally, international standards, and international buyers who insist upon them, were used by local elites to reinforce their authority over local people and resources.

This chapter begins with a brief theoretical discussion of the significance of local political economies for understanding the politics of global standards and a description of the specific political economy of China's bureaucracy and Chinese agricultural development. Following a discussion that juxtaposes the Chinese context with the globalization of standards for production, certification and marketing of organic food, the chapter offers examples of the interaction between global standards and Chinese politics at three levels; the national, the inter-ministerial, and the local. The chapter concludes by showing how the transformation of global organic food standards by domestic politics produced unintended consequences for the organization of organic agriculture in China and for the subsequent social and environmental impacts.[1]

## 2. CHINESE POLITICAL ECONOMY AND IT SIGNIFICANCE FOR GLOBAL ORGANIC STANDARDS

### 2.1 Some Conceptual Considerations

Haggard (1995) describes the new generation of trade and investment agreements as *deep integration* in which the universal requirements of the global market penetrate into policy areas previously considered solely the realm of domestic politics. Within this context, the domestic politics of global standards emerges. Specifically, as global standards, and the sovereignty bargain they represent, erode established patterns of *local* (sub-national) political authority and economic power, we see a local politics of co-optation or resistance. In addition, since local authorities become the primary actors called upon to implement and enforce global standards, these local elites commonly use global standards to maintain and increase their own power, even though this may subvert the original, internationally agreed intent of the standards.

This local politics of global standards will likely be most intense in relatively authoritarian political systems where the sovereignty bargain takes place with little domestic political discussion. Nearly a decade before global trade agreements became the subject of popular political protests in industrialized democracies, Grindle and Thomas (1991) noted that economic and trade policy formation often takes place in a politically closed environment where policy makers respond more to international forces than they do to domestic politics. More specifically, they predicted that the domestic politics of policy implementation would be most intense where policymaking structures are not democratic and where international forces play a direct role in policy formation.[2]

The adoption of global agricultural, and especially organic, standards in authoritarian systems such as China certainly meets these conditions. Such standards typically provide very limited opportunities for even central government policy makers to modify them to domestic conditions. Citizens and impacted groups such as workers, farmers or the business community typically have little knowledge that negotiations are taking place and fewer opportunities to influence the process. Even actors within the bureaucracy and at the local government level who will be called upon to implement, monitor and enforce the new standards have little or no role in negotiating the adoption of global standards. Consequently, they frequently attempt to block, modify or co-opt the standards *reactively* after the fact, depending upon their interests and capacities as shaped by the local political and economic context.

## 2.2    China's Political Economy – an Overview

By the close of the 20th century, China's political economy was a unique mix of entrenched authoritarian politics and gradually liberalizing markets. While the accelerating economic reforms of the past two decades have been transformative, China is still a long way from a free market, an open and accountable political system, and a liberal society. The continued expectation of strong state authority pervades all aspects of Chinese society including the recent development of organic agriculture.

China's planned political economy has long been described as a *fragmented authoritarian state* (Lampton 1987, Lieberthal and Oksenberg 1988, Lieberthal and Lampton 1992). From this perspective, the bureaucracy is seen as divided into a series of isolated policy systems. Vertical relationships within each system are formally established with a long chain of authority leading from the center to local cadres. However, at any given point on this vertical continuum horizontal relationships between entities belonging to different systems are informal and mutable. Since the cooperation of several of these entities may be required for policy implementation, agencies in different systems use negotiation and compromise, as well as the appeal to elites, to generate support for programs and policies. This process of negotiation and appeal commonly transforms policy objectives and instruments beyond their original intent. Therefore, explaining policy outcomes requires an understanding of "the resources, arguments, and specifics of the pertinent bargains that are made to permit policies to be adopted and implemented" (Lieberthal and Oksenberg 1988: 24). For new policy areas that fall across traditional bureaucratic lines, bureaucratic agencies may be less interested in compromise and more willing to struggle for bureaucratic control of new turf. This has certainly been the case in policies aiming to balance environmental protection and agricultural development. As described below, organic agricultural development has become embroiled in a turf battle between the Ministry of Agriculture and the State Environment Protection Agency over the power to define and control organic certification and marketing.

As economic reforms have inserted market incentives into a previously planned economy, fragmented authoritarianism has not gone away. Rather, the struggle between bureaucratic agencies has taken on new urgency as possibilities to use bureaucratic power for economic gain have greatly increased. The assumed role of state intervention in the country's planned economy has now been replaced by the operative assumption that state institutions will engage in "free" market activity to accumulate capital for maintaining operational budgets and for pursuing developmental goals.[3] As bureaucratic goals shift toward profit making, political authority takes on new significance as a way of enhancing economic competitiveness. In what I have described as the *fragmented entrepreneurial state* (Thiers 1999) State institutions (including local governments, sub-units of ministries, research institutions, army units and other entities) use political authority to gain market advantage as both regulators of, and competitors in the socialist market economy.

The economic reforms and market incentives were implemented earliest and most profoundly in the rural agricultural sector. During the 1980s a division of land use among individual families replaced collective production of the People's Communes. Household production and subsequent marketing reforms gave ever increasing amounts of autonomy and risk to peasant farmers in deciding what to grow, how to grow it, and how to market. China's farmers were clear winners in this first decade of the reform era as greater, though still limited, access to land and markets provided opportunities to enjoy the benefits of their own labor.

Ironically, and emblematic of the contradictions in the mixed economy, village, township and county government and party officials continue to exert influence over land (still officially held by the collective) and other resources within their jurisdiction. In the 1990s, many local governments reasserted their authority over local resources and people, and in some cases land-use contracts were renegotiated or lands were re-collectivized to further local government goals. In sum, the decentralization of economic decision making in the reform era has reduced central government control over local governments, but the lack of political reform has failed to replace central government authority with local, democratic accountability.

This is not to say that the dynamics of local authority in the reform era are simply a power struggle between newly free farmers and reactionary local elites. As the opportunities and risks of the market economy have expanded, both sides have seen the negative consequences of limited access to technology, capital and market information and the severe fragmentation of land holdings. The decision to re-collectivize, whether formally or informally, in order to foster local development can be seen as a function of the dependency of small farmers on local elites as the best or only source of information and resources. Whether farmer cooperation is voluntary or coerced, local government officials in many parts of rural China assume that they have both the capacity and the responsibility to direct agricultural development. As with other levels in the fragmented authoritarian state, there is also an assumption that local political authority will be used strategically to enhance the market success of local government led agricultural development. This context sets the stage for considering China's response to global organic food markets and standards.

## 3. GLOBAL ORGANIC STANDARDS IN THE CHINESE CONTEXT

The global organic food regime emerged incrementally in response to market needs and social movement ideologies. Virtually ignored by national governments for several decades, organic farmers and consumers developed their own production standards and non-governmental certification organizations as part of a social movement reaction against chemical intensive agriculture. In recent years, the organic industry has seen larger-scale production, an increase in international trade and corporate involvement, and greater levels of state regulation. The European Union and, more recently, the United States have developed national level standards that influence global standards through market pressure and trade regulation. But organic farmer associations and non-governmental certification organizations continue to play an important role in setting standards as part of a global organic community. This community achieves some institutional presence at the global level through the activities of the International Federation of Organic Agricultural Movements (IFOAM), an association of about 750 organic organizations and institutions worldwide. While IFOAM is not an international regulatory body, it performs an important norm setting function by convening meetings of member organizations and by organizing a global organic standards board. The IFOAM process produces an evolving set of core standards to which most certification organizations adhere in part or in whole. Those certifiers that comply with all IFOAM standards and procedures may obtain IFOAM accreditation, a designation of high status in the global organic community and a stepping stone to broad market access in the global industry.

Despite the absence of a formal regulatory body, the presence of national standards in the major importing countries (especially the EU), the norm setting role of IFOAM, and a degree of uniformity in the ideology of organic agriculture combine to establish a core set of recognized global standards. These standards focus on the production process, rather than the quality of the final product. They include no use of synthetic fertilizers and pesticides, the certification of land (rather than products) after a conversion period of about three years, and a complex set of certification procedures. These procedures include the review of long-term farm plans, on-site inspections, and a traceable audit trail for the production, processing and final sale of organically grown food. Of extreme importance is the expectation that inspection and certification will be conducted by an independent "third-party" with no financial connection to producers or buyers. The norms and standards of the global organic community reflect the assumption that organic farmers are autonomous, individual decision-makers with control over land and other resources. They also reflect the conviction that organic agriculture is a long-term movement toward ecological sustainability rather than a short-term strategy for marketing individual products.

The political economy of China's bureaucracy and of Chinese agricultural development stands in stark contrast to the assumptions on which global organic standards are based. State institutions at various levels act as regulators, organizers and competitors in organic production, certification and marketing. This is clearest at the local level where projects to develop organic agriculture are most often government led efforts to add value to agricultural production.[4]

It is not surprising that organic certification would be attractive to a system where political authority is used for market advantage, particularly where politics is monopolized by the party-state. Organic agriculture certification is always a political act, carried out by some authoritative body (whether governmental or non-governmental). It approves a production process as organic and thus enhances the product's market value. But in China, the dynamics of planned market authoritarianism and the fragmented entrepreneurial state become embodied in the certification process as competing state agencies struggle to assert their authority to define organic standards and to use those standards to control resources and privilege state entrepreneurs. In the Chinese context, this combination of politics and markets leads in a different direction than the non-governmental, social movement politics that characterized the origins of organic standards in the west. As will be seen in the following sections, Chinese expectations about organic agriculture, and the standards used to define it, reflect the characteristics of planned market authoritarianism and the fragmented entrepreneurial state. In China there is both a strong assumption that state authority will be the best and only definer of the meaning of organic and guarantor that standards are met, and a struggle between bureaucracies over which state fragment will exercise that authority.

## 4. NATIONAL SOVEREIGNTY AND THE BATTLE TO DEFINE ORGANIC AGRICULTURE IN CHINA: GREEN FOOD VS. THE INTERNATIONAL COMMUNITY

China's rocky integration into the global organic food regime illustrates the national level sovereignty bargain involved in the acquiescence to global standards in return for market access. Chinese actors began the process with the assumption that the national government was the sole definer of meaning and regulation within national boundaries. Over more than a decade, this position was gradually eroded as standards and procedures were adjusted to come closer to global norms. Where such adjustments were insufficient, international actors were allowed onto Chinese territory to act as trainers, regulators and definers of meaning. Yet Chinese actors continue to maintain whatever elements of state sovereignty and authority they can, both because of domestic political imperatives and because such authority is profitable within the fragmented entrepreneurial state.

The first effort to certify and market what might be called quasi-organic food in China depended on central government authority without reference to the international organic industry or movement. China's "Green Food program," was the brainchild of the Ministry of Agriculture's State Farm System (SFS), the sector of Chinese agricultural production most deeply rooted in the planned economy and its centralized, top-down authoritarian administration.[5] The SFS initiative can be seen as an effort to seek a comparative advantage in competing with the more productive and flexible family farm sector that had emerged through a decade of land and market reform. In the late 1980s, as state planners negotiated the details of the Eighth Five Year Plan, the SFS Planning Office proposed that state farms be allowed to specialize in the production of "pollution-free food." They argued that increasing concern over consumer poisonings due to pesticide residues was creating a domestic and international market niche for foods grown under strictly controlled chemical use. The assumption behind this argument was that the dismantling of the communes and the devolution of control over production to smaller units and to peasant farmers was responsible for the irrational over use of farm chemicals. The SFS claimed that they, more than other production units, still maintained the high degree of control over production practices, as well as post harvest processing and distribution, necessary to ensure food safety. The Chinese state Council (China's cabinet) and the Ministry of Agriculture (MOA) approved the plan with the caveat that a more innocuous title be used (to avoid the implication that all other food was, in fact, polluted) and "Green Food" was born.

Over the next four years, an elaborate organizational infrastructure was created that reflected the centralized planning and bureaucratic origins of the Green Food program. In 1990, the first year of official operation, 127 enterprises (all apparently SFS units) applied for the right to use the Green Food label. The State Farm System expanded an existing network of food testing laboratories in an effort to quickly assess the validity of applicant claims (Han 1990). The China Green Food Development Center (GFDC) was created as a division of the SFS charged with the development of standards, certification, and administration of the new label. By the end of 1993, Green Food development offices had been set up at the provincial level in every province except Tibet and Taiwan. Although formal standards were still under development, officials claimed to have authorized the Green Food label on more than 200 products. In the absence of a set of production or product standards or on-site inspection procedures, residue testing of final products was the primary tool for defining Green Food.

The rapid expansion of the program was possible because of the existing SFS network and because of the organizational and political support from MOA and the State Council. Through a series of proclamations, the central government made it clear during these years that the MOA had sole authority to use the Green Food label and that individual units must be certified by the GFDC before labeling their products. Several central policy documents, including China's Agenda 21, prominently mentioned Green Food. Green Food was officially linked to the "Three Highs" program, an MOA initiative to designate and subsidize specific farms and counties as demonstration sites for high-yield, high-quality, and high-efficiency agriculture. The SFS network and MOA's agricultural bureaus located in every county provided the program with an organizational infrastructure as well as access to "production bases" across China. Thus, legitimacy, access and subsidies provided by association with the central government made it unnecessary for Green Food officials to consider market access and the possibility that external standards might contest Green Food authority. It was not until Green Food attempted to enter the global organic market that the significance of existing global standards became apparent.

### 4.1    Green Food – State Entrepreneurship and the Global Organic Market

Before examining Green Food's experience with global standards it is important to examine how Green Food operates as an entrepreneurial state unit. The central government granted Green Food the authority to certify products and to levy certification fees. But Green Food also uses this authority to enhance its earnings by persuading clients to accept the agency's more profitable entrepreneurial input supply and export services. For example, in order to obtain Green Food certification, a producer must agree to export products only through Green Food's export company and to buy production inputs through Green Food. Green Food has some trouble enforcing these requirements, and some Green Food certified producers have complained about the high price of Green Food inputs and its monopoly on product exports.[6] If Green Food did not make certification contingent upon purchasing its input products and accepting its export services, it would have to find other ways to reap the benefits from its certification authority such as offering farmers a price premium or better terms of trade based on its certification.

An original goal of Green Food was to ensure food safety in order to keep open international markets for *conventional* Chinese products.[7] It was not until 1993 that Green Food actively began pursuing the international organic market. That year, Green Food joined the International Federation of Organic Agriculture Movements and began referring to its products as organic in translated promotional literature. Green Food appears to have been quite naive (or perhaps duplicitous) in its assumption that their IFOAM membership and their own certification label would be enough to gain acceptance with international organic buyers. The assumption among Green Food officials was that, as the authorized representative of the Chinese government, they had the right to define what constituted organic in Chinese agricultural production. Since Green Food standards allowed for the restricted and controlled use of some chemical fertilizers and pesticides, it was only the lack of transparency about these standards that allowed Green Food to attract some interest from the international community.

International skepticism came to a head at the 1995 IFOAM conference in Seoul, Korea when a representative of a rival Chinese certifier (described below) publicly accused Green Food of defrauding the international community. This accusation burst the legitimacy of Green Food's organic claims in the international arena and made it clear that foreign buyers would not defer to Chinese state sovereignty in the definition of organic. Green Food never officially backed down from its position that, as the certification organization designated by the Chinese Government to define "green food" (and therefore organic food) within China, non-Chinese institutions should recognize its sovereignty. However, it did begin to take steps to harmonize with the standards of the global market.

Green Food made two major procedural concessions as soon as foreign buyers expressed their unwillingness to accept Chinese state authorized certification. First, it reclassified its products as part of a long-term effort to build a Chinese certification label acceptable to the global community. Second, it reluctantly and temporarily yielded a measure of state sovereignty directly in return for market access.

In 1995 Green Food reclassified its original certification label as "A-Grade Green Food" and introduced an "AA-Grade" label which it hoped would quickly satisfy international buyers.[8] The initial AA-Grade standards amounted to little more than a ban on "harmful" chemicals and did little to appease the global community. Since that time, Green Food has incrementally developed a set of AA-Grade standards that are approaching international expectations of organic. Beginning in late 1995, Green Food sought training on certification procedures and international definitions of organic from foreign experts representing IFOAM, the European Union and other organizations (Geier 1996). It has also collected and studied standards published by a number of foreign governmental and nongovernmental certifiers. In taking these steps, and through interactions with foreign inspectors brought in by buyers, Green Food has gradually gained an understanding of international expectations from a certification organization. While the language of sovereignty and governmental authority is still present in Green Food's domestic rhetoric, it has made significant concessions to the international community in its formally written standards. Green Food continues to offer AA-Grade standards as "organic" and claims that some Asian buyers have begun to accept this claim. However, the bulk of the global organic community still does not recognize AA-Grade Green Food as organic, thereby indicating that further concessions may have to be made.

While the ongoing process of standards harmonization has dragged on, Green Food has had to resort to a more direct and, it hopes, temporary measure to gain foreign market access. Green Food now facilitates the *re-certification* of its Chinese producers by international, nongovernmental certification and inspection organizations, even though some staff members are indignant that foreign buyers don't "trust" Chinese certification in China. From a western perspective, it may not seem surprising that an international, non-governmental organization should be considered more credible than an official arm of the Chinese state, but for many in China this is hard to accept. In any event, Green Food has little choice. Without a certification label that is accredited in the importing country, no sale will take place. One German buyer explained that they see Green Food as only a "pre-certification" label, not essential but useful as an indication of meeting international standards.

Green Food's resentment of the need for foreign re-certification is not simply a matter of national pride. The downgrading of Green Food's authoritative role from certifier to facilitator threatens the agency's ability to use its political authority to enhance profitability. As rural producers begin to deal with foreign certifiers and buyers directly, they may conclude that they do not need Green Food certification. Some Chinese trading companies are now moving into the organic food business using foreign (or alternative Chinese) certification and their own export authority, thereby cutting Green Food out of the loop and eroding its authoritative position. As a result, not only does Green Food lose certification fees, it loses the leverage to its certification authority to promote input sales and trade services enterprises. Not surprisingly, while Green Food has learned to present itself as a quasi-nongovernmental body in its dealings with the foreign community, it continues to stress its authoritative state identity within its own network of producers.

Green Food is clearly in a bind. It needs to relinquish state sovereignty and accept global standards to gain foreign recognition. Yet it needs to maintain state authority to exert control in the domestic arena. This paradox directly affects the ways in which Green Food attempts to harmonize with global standards. It explains why Green Food is willing to make certain concessions and not others. A few examples will illustrate the ways in which Green Food moves to meet the letter of global standards while continuing to pursue methods that allow it to meet its domestic political and economic goals.[9]

It was relatively easy for Green Food to rewrite its standards to prohibit synthetic fertilizers and pesticides. But the question of how to verify this prohibition remained. Instead of stressing on-site inspection and a rigorous audit trail, Green Food developed a two-tier approach. First, it would continue to rely on product residue testing in centralized laboratories. Second, it began requiring AA Grade producers to sign input supply contracts stating that they would buy all of their production inputs directly from Green Food. The official justification for this unusual method was that by channeling all inputs through Green Food offices, they could ensure that no prohibited materials were used. But the underlying assumption that producers who had to buy only Green Food approved inputs would never pay for additional, unapproved inputs on the open market, is debatable and largely a matter of individual economic calculation. What is clear, however, is that this method enhanced Green Food's potential profits from the sale of agricultural inputs. At a 1997 national meeting of Green Food producers and administrators where the input supply contract system was announced, the director of the Green Food affiliated company that would sell the products stressed that these contracts were needed to comply with strict global standards for quality control.

A second major modification of Green Foods standards required the certification of land instead of the certification of products.[10] Under the A-Grade Green Food system of certifying individual products, farm enterprises can rotate "organic" and conventional crops. The size of the production area might change from year to year as individual peasant farmers are brought into or moved out of Green Food production of a specific crop. Green Food officials have proposed a unique solution to this problem, the designation of "AA-Grade Production Bases" that would be subject to tight administrative control. Minimum size requirements (more than 1333 hectares for grain production bases, more than 133 hectares for fruits or vegetables) would ensure the scale of production needed to support a permanent, on-site Green Food management office guaranteeing constant oversight. Green Food officials seem convinced that this will satisfy the literal expectation of land certification while adhering to "Chinese circumstances." It would certainly help Green Food maintain its authority at the local level and detect contacts with foreign buyers, alternative certification organizations, production input suppliers and export service companies.

Green Food has had great difficulty meeting a third requirement from the global organic food regime that the certification organization be independent from organic producers and buyers. This "third-party" standard runs contrary to Green Food's very structure. At the national level, Green Food is associated with certification and export trade. At the local level, Green Food uses the state farm network and the MOA's county and township agricultural bureaus to organize both production and certification. These local government units hold political authority over land and other resources needed for agricultural production. Many Green Food processing enterprises are owned by the very state units that certify them.

The primary strategy for attempting to meet the third-party certification requirement seems to be symbolic compliance at the national level. The central Green Food office appears to have become fully aware of this problem in late 1997 or early 1998. Up to that point, the ties between Green Food certification and its export service and production input businesses were very open. These units shared offices and some officials had two titles on their business cards. As late as 1997 one certification official said that business profits could be used to support the certification office. By 1998 the same official stressed the financial and physical separation of the entities at the national level. However, in that same year, managers promoting the input supply business still stressed the link between certification authority and the input supply contracts described above.

While national level businesses have now officially been spun-off, at the local level the structural connectedness between certification and production continues unabated. As late as 2001, a county manager of a Green Food certification office and processing center boasted that they were "one unit with two names" (*yige danwei, liangge paizi*). The same official emphasized that administrative authority was essential in organizing production. This integration is systemic throughout Green Food at the local level and may prove impossible to sort out. The dynamics of the fragmented entrepreneurial state provide strong incentives for local officials to maintain state authority even as they move further into entrepreneurial activity. These entrepreneurial officials are likely to be unimpressed by sovereignty bargains negotiated at the national level. After a decade of concessions to global standards, the third-party certification requirement may turn out to be a deal breaker for Green Food; there may be some structural concessions that national leaders are simply unwilling or unable to make in their efforts to satisfy global standards.

## 5. THE USE OF GLOBAL STANDARDS IN BUREAUCRATIC TURF WARS: THE MINISTRY OF AGRICULTURE VS. THE STATE ENVIRONMENTAL PROTECTION ADMINISTRATION

As Green Food was establishing its extensive domestic network for production, certification and marketing of quasi-organic food, another state agency, the Organic Food Development Center (OFDC) based in Nanjing, China, pursued a very different course by directly embracing global organic standards. Global standards, and the global community they represent, constitute an alternative source of authority that not only allowed OFDC to best its more powerful rival in the international market, but also became an important new weapon in a domestic political turf battle between two agencies.

OFDC illustrates the new power of global institutions within domestic politics. The unique history of this institutional rival to Green Food is the story of a Chinese state institution growing increasingly more connected to global sources of legitimacy and to global standards even as it continues to be embedded in the domestic politics of Chinese bureaucracy. The Organic Food Development Center grew out of an institutional effort by the Chinese State Environmental Protection Agency (SEPA) to extend its administrative jurisdiction to rural and agricultural issues. In 1978, SEPA established the Nanjing Institute of Environmental Sciences (NIES) which, through its Rural Ecosystems Division, conducted and published field research on ecological agriculture that represented its first challenge to the hegemony of the Ministry of Agriculture in agricultural development.

Even located far from the hub of ministerial activity in Beijing, its focus on environmental problems in agriculture afforded NIES some national recognition through a governmental contract to carry out some of the MOA's Eco-Counties program in the 1980s. In addition, its position as the most radical Chinese voice for sustainable agriculture gained it considerable attention in the international community concerned with agro-ecology. In the mid-1980s, Rural Ecosystems Division staff attended several international meetings which exposed them to the increasingly social and political (as opposed to purely biological) orientation of agro-ecology research in the developing world. It also brought them to the attention of international organizations interested in fostering this more social conception of sustainable agriculture in China.[11]

In 1986, the Rockefeller Brothers Fund (RBF) began a 10-year series of grants to the Rural Ecosystems Division to promote an integrated approach to sustainable agricultural development in China. RBF money kept the division afloat in a time of central government budget reductions and provided division staff with important exposure to the global community. RBF arranged and sponsored numerous foreign tours and internships to important centers for agro-ecology and organic agriculture, as well bringing leaders of those movements to Nanjing to conduct seminars and training workshops. The division's interest in organic agriculture, including organic certification is directly traceable to these contacts. In 1989, NIES joined the International Federation of Organic Agriculture Movements. In 1993, RBF sponsored an important trip to Germany and the Netherlands where division staff met with IFOAM officials and visited organic farms, processors, retail stores and non-governmental certification organizations. In the following years, the division pursued rapid integration into the international organic community.[12] Within a span of only seven years, this Chinese state institution became closely associated with an organic movement and industry that had been developing in North America and Europe for several decades.

In 1994, the entire Rural Ecosystem Division was renamed as the Organic Food Development Center for the express purpose of becoming an organic certification body for China.[13] Consistent with the features of the political economy of the fragmented entrepreneurial state, changing the purpose of the division represented a specific effort to emulate global certification organizations and to develop an independent revenue stream in the face of declining Central Government contributions to the Rural Ecosystems Division and the RBF stipulation that its last grant was contingent upon the division proposing a long-term strategy for self-sufficiency. The first step toward developing this strategy came as early as 1990 when a Dutch tea trading company asked the division to assist a European organic certifier in inspecting and certifying organic tea production areas in Anhui and Zhejiang Province. By facilitating this and other inspections in 1991 and 1992, the division realized that foreign trading companies would pay for the services of a certification organization recognized by the global community. By late 1993, the Rural Ecosystems Division had made a clear decision to pursue fee-for-service organic inspection and certification as a long term funding strategy. After this decision was made in consultation with RBF and other international institutions, the division sought SEPA's permission so that OFDC would also have central government authority for its operations.[14]

The creation of OFDC clearly differs from that of most comparable public and private organic certification organizations in North America and Europe. OFDC emerged into organics very quickly, but without significant input from Chinese organic farmers or from a domestic organic movement. Instead of developing standards and procedures that responded to the expressed needs and interests of farmers or local consumers, OFDC simply accepted standards recognized by the international community. This facilitated its rapid access to the international market, but reduced the opportunity to tailor standards toward local ecosystems and local priorities.

The OFDC relationship with the US-based Organic Crop Improvement Association (OCIA) illustrates the way in which it consciously modeled itself after existing international organizations.[15] OFDC staff met OCIA president Tom Harding in 1993 when they toured Germany and the Netherlands where Harding was also serving as an official with IFOAM. In 1994, Harding visited OFDC and trained two individuals to be OCIA inspectors. In 1995, OFDC, while still a governmental division within SEPA formally became the Chinese national chapter of OCIA. This created an unusual status from both the Chinese and the international perspectives: OFDC was now both a sub-unit of a Chinese state ministry and a chapter of an international non-governmental organization, accountable to the bylaws and policy decisions of that NGO. This gave OFDC both national and global authority, a clear advantage over Green Food in efforts to enter the international organic market.

Its status as an OCIA chapter brought important benefits to OFDC. OCIA provided training for OFDC inspectors and served as a model for OFDC organization and procedures. In addition, OFDC adopted OCIA standards almost in their entirety, thereby putting it on the road to acceptance in the global community.[16] By using the OCIA label, OFDC was pursuing a deliberate strategy to gain legitimacy in the international organic market (Li 1997). OCIA was accredited by IFOAM, a status that would have taken OFDC years to accomplish on its own, and its label was accepted in Japanese, North American and, in a few cases, European markets. Thus, in one step, OFDC gained the authority to inspect and certify Chinese agricultural products for the lucrative international market.

However, in the short term OFDC's selection of OCIA as an international source of legitimacy turned out to be a double-edged sword. In December of 1997, OCIA officially lost its accreditation with IFOAM, presumably in part due to problems with certification in China. Accreditation was restored and OFDC maintained its relationship with the re-accredited OCIA. But it also used this crisis to diversify its associations with international certification and accreditation bodies, particularly those associated more closely with the European Union. OFDC learned the hard way that choosing the right patron is as important in the global arena as it is in domestic Chinese politics.

As a step toward greater autonomy, OFDC applied directly for IFOAM accreditation. After a lengthy process involving on-site assessment by IFOAM delegations and other documentation, OFDC's application was approved in December 2002. IFOAM accreditation marks a major milestone in OFDC's path toward full acceptance as part of the global organic community.

## 5.1    Green Food and OFDC competition in the international arena

The global organic community is quite comfortable interacting with two Chinese-based certification organizations. As part of a global movement and industry with social movement origins, non-governmental certifiers have moved easily across nation state borders and operated in overlapping regions depending on the attractiveness of their certification label to producers, brokers, and consumers.[17] But in China, the assumption that the state will monopolize all political authority, and the fragmentation of that authority in practice, produces a very different scenario. OFDC's institutional heritage lies in an effort by the State Environmental Protection Agency to encroach on policy issues traditionally dominated by the Ministry of Agriculture. With the rising importance of market incentive in the fragmented entrepreneurial state, it is not surprising that Green Food and OFDC have each struggled to be recognized as China's sole designated state certifier.[18] The turf battle has been, at times, acrimonious. As one MOA official complained, OFDC exists because SEPA is "trying to eat from our rice bowel" (*Huanbaoju yao chi women de fan*). While the Chinese supra-ministerial State Council tends to support Green Food, it has refrained from proactive moves to close down OFDC, thereby leaving the two rivals to battle it out or eventually seek compromise.

What is significant for the study of global standards is the extent to which these two adversaries within the domestic political economy of China have carried their battle into the global arena. While Green Food takes advantage of the infrastructure, economic resources and political clout afforded by its relationship with its parent ministry[19] on the domestic front, OFDC has relied on global connections, including the global standards and the cultural norms of an NGO.

As a result, OFDC has repeatedly outmaneuvered or outpaced Green Food in the global arena. For example, Green Food joined IFOAM four years later than OFDC and it seems to have assumed that this was simply a symbolic step that would provide automatic recognition of Chinese sovereignty over the definition of Chinese organics. In contrast, OFDC recognized the significance of IFOAM as the dominant institution in international standards setting and monitoring and, as noted earlier, used its relationship with IFOAM at the 1995 IFOAM conference in Seoul, South Korea to improve its competitive position by exposing Green Food's violation of global organic standards and setting Green Food's international market ambitions back by perhaps a decade. Furthermore, while Green Food was hurriedly seeking foreign guidance on what standards it needed to change, OFDC gained representation on IFOAM's standards board and began participating in its standard setting discussions. OFDC has now received IFOAM accreditation, a step that Green Food is still a long way from undertaking.[20]

OFDC has been proactive in establishing positive links with foreign certification organizations. While the OCIA affiliation has not been without costs, it has clearly been advantageous in bringing OFDC rapid exposure and experience in the international community. As OFDC has diversified its links, particularly to bodies certifying for the European market, it has positioned itself for a further expansion of the market value of its label. Green Food has viewed foreign certifiers as a necessary evil (to re-certify its own products for the global market) and a potential threat to its control of Chinese producers.

Finally, OFDC has tapped international development organizations for money and connections. The 10-year relationship with the Rockefeller Brothers' Fund was essential for OFDC's financial survival and global connectedness in its formative years. After RBF support concluded, OFDC established a multi-year project with the German development organization GTZ[21] specifically to improve its organizational capacity and move towards EU and IFOAM accreditation. The financial, institutional and networking support afforded by these projects has been instrumental in allowing OFDC to survive and expand at a time when central government resources were being withdrawn.

## 5.2    Observation

Traditional assumptions about Chinese state sovereignty and the authoritarian nature of Chinese society, in combination with the tremendous advantages of size and infrastructure enjoyed by Green Food, suggest that Green Food would dominate production, certification and market share in the battle to lead Chinese organic agricultural development. This appears to hold true for production, since the area of OFDC-certified land has not surpassed one percent of the land claimed to be certified by Green Food. Green Food domestic and foreign conventional market sales have expanded rapidly,[22] but there are no significant examples of AA Grade Green Food being sold in the international organic market without re-certification by a foreign certifier. OFDC certified exports to international organic buyers have risen rapidly from US $600,000 in 1996 and US $3-6 million in 1997 to $15 million in 1999 and $30 million in 2000 (Thiers 1999, Du 2001, Smith 2002). Green Food's domestic expansion of its quasi-organic, A-Grade label has been impressive and its use of foreign re-certification has allowed it to sell some of its AA-Grade products abroad. But in terms of independently certified sales in the global organic market, OFDC is the only functioning Chinese agency. Significantly, since 2000 a few prominent Green Food certified producers (including at least one state farm) have quietly switched to OFDC certification despite their administrative ties to the Ministry of Agriculture. At least one Green Food technical advisor and an important

Green Food administrator have also switched to working in the OFDC system. For those with an economic or ideological interest in global organics, OFDC's success and Green Food's failure in meeting global organic standards is beginning to trump political loyalty toward state institutions.

For a production unit or administrator to move from one ministerial system to another is a new and significant development in Chinese political culture where access to power and resources have traditionally been bound up with ministerial identity. Such moves illustrate the rising importance of global sources of authority, including global market standards, in domestic political considerations. No other factor can explain the counterintuitive "David beats Goliath" direction in the battle between OFDC and Green Food. OFDC's very survival in the face of MOA animosity and State Council neglect would probably not have been possible without the money, status and connections gained through its identification with the global organic community. The fact that OFDC appears to be flourishing illustrates the role of global standards as an alternative source of authority in the domestic politics of even relatively closed political systems such as China.

Global standards will continue to influence Chinese domestic politics. OFDC's pursuit of IFOAM accreditation increased the pressure for it to become a formally independent NGO in order to meet IFOAM expectations of legal personhood. This in turn has challenged Chinese expectations that domestic NGOs should not carry out economic, political or organizational activities, all of which are common in western organic certification NGOs. A more significant challenge may come through further development of global organic standards. Within IFOAM there is an ongoing discussion, soon to be codified into core standards, requiring certification organizations to include a "social justice" component in their certification criteria. If a social justice standard is to have any meaning in the Chinese context, it will come into direct conflict with current expressions of local Communist Party and government power in rural China.[23]

## 6. GLOBAL STANDARDS AND THE REINFORCEMENT OF LOCAL POWER THROUGH QUALITY CONTROL

Among other things, global standards represent an alternative source of authority in a previously closed political system. As such, this new authority can be used to challenge or to reinforce existing expressions of power. In China's fragmented entrepreneurial state, where governmental sub-units use central state authority for market advantage, these sub-units will use the authority implied by the mandate to enforce global standards to obtain market advantage as well. In other words, state authority and global authority can be combined to reinforce established power relationships. But in doing so, farmer empowerment and autonomy are precluded, thereby compromising important assumptions of the global organic movement.

In the case of Chinese organics, state officials have framed global standards as the need to enforce *quality control*. Since control of the behavior of others is assumed to be a state function, regulation by alternative institutions, such as farmers' or consumers' associations, is not an option. There is also little room for an assumption of the organic movement that individual farmers, secure in land ownership and market access, will pursue organic agriculture primarily because it is in their own interests as long-term stewards of land. Instead, the assumption of state control merges with the new priority of quality control to enhance state power at several levels.

We have already seen this phenomenon as Green Food officials used the strict requirements for quality control in the global organic community to justify an enhancement of their own authority. The proposal requiring AA-Grade Green Food production only on large, centrally controlled production bases was advanced principally in order to justify the on-site presence of permanent, Green Food administrators. Further, the input supply contract system requiring Green Food certified producers to buy all inputs from the central Green Food company ostensibly was justified as the best way to ensure that prohibited materials would not be used. Even the claimed monopoly on Green Food certified exports was rationalized as a check against "fake" products reaching the international market.

At the local level, global organic standards also become embedded in local struggles to challenge or maintain traditional and local lines of control in the era of economic reform. When the Peoples' Communes dissolved in favor of de-collectivized household level production and marketing in the 1980s, commune cadres, now county and township officials, saw their control over resources and developmental decisions erode. The disposition of land, in particular, became complicated as short-term use rights were given to peasant farmers in the form of land contracts, while formal ownership of land remained in the hands of the local, state dominated collective. Through peasant struggles and central government reforms, the length of land contracts was gradually extended to increase farmer incentives to invest in long-term production. At the same time, local industries, including input production and agricultural processing facilities, were held by the local state or collective as "off budget enterprises" frequently managed by local institutions, such as county agricultural bureaus.[24]

The rise of value-added agricultural production as a local developmental strategy (among many other factors) provided a rationale for the formal or informal re-collectivization of land in order to coordinate the scale of production needed to satisfy the demands of outside markets. Very often, local government or Communist Party officials and institutions coordinate these developmental plans. But there is still a politics of control over production decisions and profits. It is within this local politics that global standards become an important political tool. Local governments may be best suited to implement, monitor and enforce the strict, external demands of the organic market. But enforcing standards through local state power requires a reassertion of control over land, labor and other resources.

The mix of local political authority and global standards is illustrated most clearly in the organization of large numbers of peasant farmers into large organic "production bases."[25] Foreign buyers need to buy products in much larger quantities than can be produced on the small holdings of most households. On production bases, foreign buyers (and foreign and Chinese certifiers) deal with a single entity responsible for all production within the base. In most cases (though not all) this is done either directly through a local government institution or state farm, or indirectly through a government affiliated company.

This mode of operation, however, requires some means to ensure that all peasant farmers within a production base comply with organic production practices. Some managers report that, so far, all farmers within a production base have been willing to comply. But organic farming often carries additional costs in terms of labor, ecological risk, and the short-term deferral of profits. Given that families will have varying calculations regarding these costs, it is unrealistic to expect that all farmers will be equally willing to go organic

The secret to eliciting farmer compliance lies in the local government's ability to move farmers in and out of these bases. State managers of both Green Food and OFDC certified sites refer openly to this as the use of "administrative measures" (*xingzhen zuofa*) and "land rotation" (*zhuanliu*) to replace farmers unwilling to comply with organic standards with more compliant farmers. Again, local officials cite the strict quality control standards of the global organic market as their justification for taking these steps. While the balance between coercion and voluntary compliance appears to vary considerably from site to site, farmer knowledge that local officials could move them to other land almost certainly plays a role in farmer behavior. The general picture is probably best seen, not as a pattern of constant coercion, but rather as one of farmer dependency on local elites and an absence of democratic tools for local accountability.[26]

The availability of administrative authority to elicit farmer compliance can increase profitability for local elites and those who buy their products. In the absence of such authority, the only way to recruit additional farmers to organic production would be to pass on greater economic incentive either directly in the form of higher prices or through government subsidy. The use of local state authority in China means that economic incentives to farmers can be reduced and profits directed elsewhere. Local governments may direct these profits toward local development or local corruption. They may also attract foreign buyers by offering organic products at marginally lower prices.[27]

### 6.1    The Absence of Farmer Participation

What is missing, of course, is the autonomy and participation of the small, independent, organic farmer. Organic standards emerged to meet the self-regulating needs of such farmers in the context of American and European political economy.[28] Within the political economy of rural China, institutionalizing farmer participation is problematic due to both logistic and political barriers. OFDC, because of its connections to the international community, has attempted to include farmer input in the development and implementation of standards. OCIA International requires that a chapter be formed by at least five certified farmer/members and that certification be controlled by a certification committee elected by its members. As the China Chapter of OCIA, OFDC has a formal board and certification committee, officially made up of participating farmer/members. However, some of these "farmer/members" are actually major processors, collective farm managers, or trading company owners who are not themselves engaged in agricultural work.[29] The top positions on OFDC's Board of Directors, Certification Committee, and Standards Committee are staffed by OFDC officials (Anon 1998). Thus, despite the formal presence of participatory institutions reflecting the traditional grassroots origins of organic certification, there is no evidence of meaningful participation by agriculturists in the day-to-day management or strategic development of OFDC. With even less connection to the international community, Green Food makes no effort (symbolic or otherwise) to include feedback from peasant/farmers in the development and administration of its standards.

In recent years, farmers' associations have formed at the village, township and even county level, primarily as collaborative efforts to expand marketing options or access technical information. Given the role of farmers' associations in the organic agriculture movement elsewhere, it is reasonable to ask if such associations might develop around organic production and marketing and become a force for greater farmer autonomy and input. While several organic farming sites officially have associations, most appear to be local government-led, with the association providing a format for government companies to extend inputs and technical advice and procure final products for processing and marketing. Three recently formed organic farming associations, two in Anhui and one in Guangdong are reported to be autonomous from their local governments. In one of the Anhui associations, while there is a high degree of overlap between the association and the Party leadership at the village level, the association appears to make production and marketing decisions independently from the interests of the township or county government.

However, it is significant to note that this relatively independent organic farming association was established with the aid of an international poverty relief project, and not in response to foreign buyers or foreign market standards. There is no evidence that global markets or standards support the emergence of autonomous farmers' associations in opposition to local government control. To the contrary, local governments have sometimes used the economic power of global corporations to undercut and disrupt independent farmers' organizations (Ren 1996). Given the advantages that local authoritarian politics offers global capital in quality control, in ease of procurement and in profitability, it seems unlikely that global market integration will become a force for a redistribution of power at the local level.

This is where the specific content and local applicability of global standards becomes most important. A comparative politics perspective should always ask if the specific global standards at issue reinforce or disrupt existing power relationships in the local political economy. In this context, the current IFOAM proposal to expand organic standards to include social justice requirements is potentially very significant. Just as OFDC used global organic standards as a tool to establish itself as an alternative to the dominant Green Food program, social justice standards could theoretically become a tool used by peasant farmers to attack local government domination. However, this will depend on the appropriateness of the new social justice standards for the specific political economy in rural China and the capacity for certification of compliance within that political economy. This would require a high degree of specificity which, given the universal nature of global standards, seems highly unlikely.

## 7. OUTCOMES AND UNINTENDED CONSEQUENCES

The combination of the standards of the global organic industry and the national and local political economy of China led to unintended outcomes in the organization of certification and production, and in their social and environmental effects (also see Thiers 1999, 2002). First, state institutions clearly dominate the organization of organic certification. While these institutions to some degree have learned to present a nongovernmental identity to the international organic community, they stress their state identity as an additional source of status and authority in their dealings with domestic actors. This reflects both Chinese political culture and the self-interest of the certification organizations. It also coincides with the rise of state involvement in setting and administering organic standards in other parts of the world. Unlike the west, Chinese state certifiers seem unlikely to be balanced by domestic non-governmental counterparts in the near future.

The role of the state is also more pronounced in the organization of production. Partially as a consequence of this, and in response to the needs of the global industry, the incentives in Chinese organic agriculture are toward large-scale production. For similar reasons, many of these units stress the production of specific, marketable crops with less emphasis on integrated crop rotations. The term *plantation organics* might be applied to some of these production bases.

The social impacts of organic agriculture in China are still under study. On site observations and secondary data support the expectation that farmers will receive fewer benefits in a system where political authority can be substituted for economic incentive. Local government claims that preferential contracts, higher prices, and free inputs are given to organic farmers were sometimes disputed in farmer interviews. There do seem to be benefits in terms of market access and market risk, but there is little evidence that integration into the global organic market does much to reduce preexisting levels of coercion and dependency. As discussed above, global industry and local authority often work together to mutual benefit.

The environmental impacts of integration into global organic markets are impossible to assess in any comprehensive way. On most sites observed, there was evidence of clandestine use of chemical pesticides. This may be because peasant farmers who receive little economic benefit and who are unsure of the long-term stability of land tenure see little incentive to comply fully with organic standards. Some farmers also seem to lack basic understanding of standards or the environmental significance of organic agriculture.

Even where political control is sufficient to overcome cheating and obtain certification, there still seems to be a lack of long-term stewardship. In one such location, intercropping had given way to a single crop in demand in the Japanese market, and serious soil erosion problems were being ignored. This may be due to a lack of incentive on the part of peasant farmers and a lack of knowledge or direct observation on the part of production base managers. The globally certified organic production bases of China have fostered relationships between foreign buyers, international certifiers and enterprise managers at the expense of long-term relationships between steward-farmers and the land.

## 8. CONCLUSION

In this chapter the example of Chinese integration into the global organic food market illustrates the domestic politics of global standards. The adoption of global standards does impact on national sovereignty as national level institutions negotiate for global acceptance. But the benefits of state sovereignty will be maintained where possible and, in some cases, sovereignty bargains may not be entirely at the discretion of central government actors. Where established, decentralized interests are threatened by global standards, local elites may resist meaningful change. The notion of "sovereignty" hides the fact that, in many political systems, state authority is not bundled up in a single block at the national level. The global community may find that national leaders are bargaining with chips off that block that are not theirs to offer. Green Food's domestic advantage in connections to production units may prove to be its undoing as local governments refuse to separate their production and certification authority.

Global standards also become tools in domestic political battles. The ministerial war between MOA and SEPA for jurisdiction over sustainable agriculture is an ongoing domestic affair. However, OFDC's advantages in the international arena played a decisive role in its continued existence and apparent victory in this one battle.

Finally, global standards become embedded in local struggles to challenge or maintain existing power relationships. By interpreting global organic standards as a requirement for strict control, local elites justify the continued use of coercion and dependency. Farmers who are unable to become fully empowered participants in organic agriculture, may choose the weapons of the weak in the form of clandestine chemical use or simply the neglect of long-term stewardship.

This case illustrates the catch-22 of global standards – universal design and local application. Global market standards reflect the economic goals of universal production and marketing processes. However, these standards, like the global economy they represent, must still articulate within specific locations with diverse political economies. Even in an era of market globalization, the diversity of local politics still matters. When local politics are ignored, a diversity of unanticipated outcomes will result.

In the case of Chinese organics, we see that organic agriculture may meet the universal demands of the organic industry. But the promise of the organic movement will be unfulfilled until domestic political changes bring permanent ownership of land and local democratic accountability to the Chinese countryside. Global standards could conceivably play some role in stimulating that process of domestic political change, though only if they specifically and directly confront issues of power inequality. Even so, the struggle is still that of local people who may or may not find these standards to be a useful tool.

The specifics of this case aside, these findings argue for a comparative politics approach to the study of global standards. The ubiquitous expansion of the global market and the one-size-fits-all design of global standards do not reduce the need for a detailed understanding of the economic, political, social and even ecological conditions in which standards are implemented and certified. Specific consideration of institutional arrangements and self-interested sectors will facilitate empirical observation and theoretical analysis of implementation capacity, resistance and co-optation. Such an approach would anticipate, rather than being surprised by, unintended consequences. This might in turn lead to a better design of global standards and certification regimes.

## 9. NOTES

[1] This study is based on 23 field visits to organic or quasi-organic production sites in six Chinese provinces in 1997, 1998 and 2001. 173 officials, entrepreneurs, researchers and practitioners were interviewed and extensive secondary sources were reviewed.

[2] A decade later this claim found an interesting parallel in the justification given by anti-globalization critics for street protests in western democracies: that agreements such as the World Trade Organization were being negotiated without full debate by established democratic institutions.

[3] Of course state bureaucrats may also engage in market activity for personal gain. Opportunities for bureaucratic corruption have increased significantly in the reform era.

[4] At virtually all locations visited in this study, local government officials described their organization of organic production, certification and marketing as an effort to add value to local agriculture by differentiating their products and gaining access to a lucrative, international market.

[5] China's State Farm System (SFS) has historical associations with the Chinese military dating back to the pre-revolutionary tradition of stationing troops in border regions as agricultural laborers. The post 1949 SFS performed these same functions with gradually less direct association with the military and a continued emphasis on the reclamation of "wasteland" for conversion to agriculture. The SFS currently includes more than 2000 farms on 39 million hectares of land, organized with varying degrees of hierarchical administration. State farms are best understood as the state owned enterprises of Chinese agricultural production, processing and distribution. Like other state owned enterprises, state farms have been challenged by the economic reforms as market incentives have increased the productivity and competitiveness of the locally controlled collective sector and the newly emerging private sector. The SFS has instituted a number of attempts at structural reform to try and improve competitiveness by capitalizing on the system's high degree of vertical integration and hierarchical control of production (IBRD 1998, Hill 1994, Han 1994, Liu 1993). The original conception of the Green Food program was consistent with these initiatives.

[6] Some enterprises refuse to sign input supply contracts and go to other trading companies for export services specifically for this reason. Green Food has trouble enforcing these requirements precisely because of the breakdown in central state sovereignty represented by the operation of alternative foreign and Chinese certification organizations as described below.

[7] During the 1980s, a series of highly publicized chemical residue scares had caused the closure of some export markets in East and Southeast Asia to specific Chinese food products.

[8] The fact that Green Food began working on the AA-Grade standards before the IFOAM meeting in Seoul indicates that they were aware that their original standards were unacceptable. This realization probably came about gradually through private discussions with international buyers. However, Green Food certainly did not advertise the discrepancy and has consistently translated the term Green Food (luse shipin) as "organic" in English language publicity.

[9] For a more lengthy discussion of Green Food efforts to meet specific global standards from the perspective of implementation and enforcement problems see Thiers (2002).

[10] The inspection and certification of farm land is an essential component of organic certification as it ensures that the entire farm operation, including the production of non-marketable crops, complies with standards and supports the integrated quality of organic farming. Before a farm gains certification, it must go through a multi-year "conversion period" during which time no chemical pesticides or fertilizers can be used. This system also provides a strong incentive against cheating as the potential gains in yield for one crop are unlikely to warrant the risk of loosing a multi-year investment in the organic status of the land.

[11] As one example of this recognition, in the early 1990s, the Rural Ecosystem Division was contracted by the United Nations Environmental Program to provide training sessions on sustainable agriculture for participants from across China and other parts of Asia.

[12] OFDC staff attend all major IFOAM events and, since 1997, OFDC Director Xiao Xingji serves on the influential IFOAM Standards Board.

[13] The Rural Ecosystem Division continued to exist on paper but all of its staff, offices, laboratories and research sites, even its business cards, were converted to OFDC.

[14] OFDC's official Chinese name is the "Organic Food Development Center of the State Environmental Protection Agency of China" (*Guojia Huanjing Baohu Zongju Youji Shipin Fazhan Zhongxin*). It uses this full title on all Chinese documents and in dealings with Chinese state actors at all levels, indicating the continued importance of OFDC's state identity.

[15] OCIA is one of the dominant, organic certification organizations in North America and is also active in Central and South America and in Asia. OCIA certifies through both a central office in the United States (OCIA International) and through member chapter organizations, a flexible and relatively decentralized structure that allowed it to grow from four chapters certifying just over 100 farms in 1986 to 79 chapters in 28 countries certifying more than 35,000 "grower members" on 1 million hectares ten years later.

[16] While this wholesale adoption of global standards did not leave much room to accommodate Chinese political, economic or ecological peculiarities, OFDC standards require only a two year conversion period to be eligible for organic certification while OCIA requires three, and clients who want to use the OCIA label pay two to three times as much in fees.

[17] The recent rise in nation state regulation of certification has checked this fluidity somewhat. The European Union, for example, requires that foreign certifiers meet criteria for equivalency with EU standards.

[18] OFDC's claim rests primarily on its accusation that Green Food may have state authority but it is not organic. Green Food's claim rests on its dismissal of the much smaller OFDC as insignificant or as a chapter of an international (and therefore non-Chinese) organization.

[19] SEPA and MOA are mismatched competitors. MOA operates from a position of strength and traditional ownership in agriculture. In addition to the strengths of a production ministry, MOA has an extensive infrastructure throughout rural China with an institutional presence at the county and township level, extensive systems for development and extension of science and technology, and a nationwide infrastructure for the purchasing, processing and even retailing of agricultural products. As a regulatory agency, SEPA has less resources and lower governmental status. SEPA's institutional network is largely arranged for the regulation of industrial pollution in urban areas, lacking staff and infrastructure in the countryside. Both SEPA officials and academic observers in China agree that in the formulation and implementation of environmental regulations pertaining to agriculture, SEPA must rely on MOA largesse and cooperation.

[20] One Green Food official expressed hope in 1997 that uniform standards coming out of the United States Department of Agriculture would be easier to match and would eventually become the global norm. Since then, USDA has had to rewrite its draft standards in the face of domestic movement pressure while IFOAM has grown and developed links to the European Union. Assumptions that superpower sovereignty will trump global norms may prove accurate in the long run but they are not serving Green Food well in its immediate task of entering the global market.

[21] GTZ is the commonly used acronym for *Deutsche Gesellschaft für Technische Zusammenarbeit*.

[22] Green Food publications claim that by 2000 domestic and international sales had reached US$4.8 billion and US$200 million respectively (Liang 2002). The great majority of this is A-Grade Green Food. While Green Food sometimes refers to all of this as "organic" it clearly does not meets global standards. Even the small AA-Grade portion does not reap global organic prices without re-certification by other organizations.

[23] Of course, OFDC representation on the IFOAM organic standards board may mean that Chinese perspectives will begin to impact global standards. The extension of "global" (western) standards to ever more diverse parts of the world creates the possibility of blowback as those new participants justifiably claim the right to participate in the renegotiation and development of standards.

[24] For more details and perspectives on this extremely complicated set of transformations in the local political economy see Blecher and Shue (1996), Zhou (1996), and Oi (1995).

[25] The term "production bases" (*shenchang jidi*) is used throughout both the Green Food and OFDC systems.

[26] At issue here is the vulnerability of land use contracts. The central government repeatedly calls on local government elites to respect the validity of these contracts but has been unable to achieve uniform compliance. A 1999 survey of actual land tenure practices in 17 provinces found that 82% of surveyed

villages had experienced some form of land reallocations since the original de-collectivization. More than half of farmers surveyed had low confidence that their land tenure was secure (Prosterman et al 2000). Such a survey may under-report cases of ad hoc or individual reallocation undertaken to punish or control individual peasant farmers who may fear additional reprisals.

[27] During this study, a meeting between a county government official and a prospective foreign organic buyer was observed. As the official spread out a map and began speculating as to which of "my villages" and "my farmers" would be mobilized to fulfill buyer demands, it became clear that, even in organic agriculture, the combined authority of local politics and global markets can work in synergy.

[28] Many would argue that the political economy of organic agriculture in the west has also shifted toward a lack of farmer (or farmworker) autonomy with the rise of a large scale, corporate dominated, organic food industry (Guthman 1998, Buck et al. 1997). I would point out that the presence of an ideological organic movement and established democratic and legal institutions (i.e., labor law and an independent media) however imperfect, create at least some check on farmworker exploitation in the west. At present, these factors are completely lacking in China.

[29] One member of the OFDC board is the closest thing to an autonomous organic farmer located during this study. This individual rents suburban land from a municipal government which he farms himself with minimal governmental interference. Ironically, his family operated organic farm is so small, and his individual market opportunities so limited, that he does not bother to obtain organic certification.

## 10. REFERENCES

Anon., D. Quanguo, Y. Shipin, K. Jishu, J. Zai, and N. Juxing (1998) The Fifth All-China Organic Food Development Technical Workshop Held in Nanjing. *Youji Shipin Shidai (Organic Food Times)* (4):22.

Blecher, M., and V. Shue (1996) *Tethered Deer*. Stanford, CA: Stanford University Press.

Buck, D., C. Getz, and J. Guthman (1997) From Farm to Table: The Organic Vegetable Commodity Chain of Northern California. *Sociologia Ruralis* 37 (1):3-20.

Du, X. (2001) *Youji Nongye Gailun (Introduction to Organic Agriculture)*, Beijing: China Agricultural University Press.

Geier, B. (1996) *Development of the Organic and Green Food Product Sector in China*. Beijing: China-EU Centre for Agricultural Technology.

Grindle, M. S. and J. W. Thomas (1991) *Public Choices and Policy Change: The Political Economy of Reform in Developing Countries*. Baltimore: Johns Hopkins University Press.

Guthman, J. (1998) Regulating Meaning, Appropriating Nature: The Codification of California Organic Agriculture. *Antipode* 30 (2):135-154.

Haggard, S. (1995) *Developing Nations and the Politics of Global Integration*. Washington, DC: The Brookings Institution.

Han, B. (1990) The Beifang Foodstuff Checking and Testing Center. *Beijing Review*, August 13-19: 28.
_____ (1994) State Farms Eye the Market. *Beijing Review*, December 5-11: 14-17.

Hill, K. (1994) China's State Farms Go Corporate. *China Business Review*, November-December: 28-31.

IBRD (1998) *Staff Appraisal Report China: State Farms Commercialization Project*. Beijing: World Bank, Rural Development and Natural Resources Sector Unit, East Asia and Pacific Region.

Jabko, N. (1999) In the Name of the Market: How the European Commission Paved the way for Monetary Union. *Journal of European Public Policy* 6: 475-495

Lampton, D. M. (1987) *Policy Implementation in Post-Mao China*. Berkeley: University of California Press.

Li, Z. (1997) Tantan Woguo Youji Shipin de kaifa. Discussion of the Development of Organic Food in China. *Youji Shipin Shidai (Organic Food Times)* (1):6-13.

Liang, Z. (2002) *Green Food Development and Sustainable Agriculture Development in China*. Beijing: China Green Food Development Center.

Lieberthal, K. G., and M. Oksenberg. (1988) *Policy Making in China: Leaders, Structures and Processes*. Princeton: Princeton University Press.

Lieberthal, K., and D. M. Lampton (1992) *Bureaucracy, Politics, and Decision Making in Post-Mao China*. Berkeley: University of California Press.

Litfin, K., ed. (1998) *The Greening of Sovereignty in World Politics*. Cambridge, MA: MIT Press.

Prosterman, R. L., B. Schwarzwalder and Y. Jianping (2000) *RDI Reports on Foreign Aid and Development #105: Implementation of 30-Year Land Use Rights for Farmers Under China's 1998 Land Management Law*. Seattle, WA: Rural Development Institute.

Liu, C. (1993) Greater Global Access for State Farms. *Beijing Review*, April 5-11: 18-20.

Oi, J. (1995) The Role of the Local State in China's Transitional Economy. *The China Quarterly* 144 (December):1132-1149.

Ren, J. (1996) Synthetic Report. In *Zhongguo Nongcun Minjian Zuzhi: Nongcun Zhuanye Jishu Xiehui de Yanjiu (Rural Non-governmental Organizations in China: Research on Rural Specialized Technological Associations)*, edited by J. Yao. Beijing: Beijing Agricultural Science and Technology Press.

Smith, G. (2002) *A Matter of Trust: The Organic Food Market in China*. Honors thesis, Sydney: University of New South Wales.

Thiers, P. (1999) *Green Food: The Political Economy of Organic Agriculture in China*. Ph.D. thesis, Eugene, OR: University of Oregon.

_____ (2002) From Grassroots Movement to State Coordinated Market Strategy: The Transformation of Organic Agriculture in China. *Government and Policy*. 20(3): 357-373.

Zhou, K. (1996) *How the Farmers Changed China*. Boulder, CO: Westview Press.

JIM BINGEN[*]

# 12. COTTON IN WEST AFRICA:

## *A Question of Quality*[1]

### 1. COTTON, QUALITY AND DEVELOPMENT

In September 2003 Africa's cotton farmers made world headlines in helping to bring down the Fifth Ministerial Conference of the World Trade Organization at Cancún. Led by cotton farmers from Bénin, a delegation from Chad, Burkina Faso and Mali asked the WTO to scrap US and European cotton subsidy programs and accept their Cotton Poverty Reduction Initiative. Based on a report by Oxfam showing that African farmers lose $300 million per year from northern cotton subsidies, the delegation clearly stated its desire for free trade and an equitable chance to compete in the world market (Watkins 2002). Cotton accounts for 30-40% of the export earnings for several West African countries and the average annual $4 billion spent on cotton subsidies easily surpasses the annual allocation of foreign assistance to these countries (Baffes 2003). However, despite the compelling evidence favoring the demands from Africa's cotton farmers, others warn of the equally pernicious consequences of ending subsidies. Some argue that if eliminating cotton subsidies in North America and Europe made African cotton production more attractive to corporate investment, machines would replace rather than enrich African family farmers (Lind 2003).

This chapter argues that US and European cotton subsidies must be ended, but that doing so will contribute little to African development unless the question of quality receives equal attention. Just as the narrowly-conceived World Bank-led push to privatize the cotton sector throughout West Africa fell short of transforming the lives of cotton farmers, so too will the "getting the prices right" approach to ending subsidies.

No one approach will turn cotton into the powerful engine of development. Indeed there are numerous economic efficiencies to be achieved: reduced export taxes, a better trade-related infrastructure, reducing production costs, etc (Baffes 2003). But a focus on cotton quality standards offers new insights into the development dilemmas of West African cotton. More specifically, the question of quality allows us to identify the opportunities and implications of continuing trade negotiations for the empowerment and quality of life of family cotton farmers in West Africa.

Concerns with quality have been an integral part of the colonial history of cotton in West Africa from the time when colonial administrators were interested primarily in a substitute for American cotton to the late colonial period with its focus on

[*] Jim Bingen, Professor, Department of Community, Agriculture, Recreation and Resource Studies, Michigan State University.

*J. Bingen and L. Busch, (eds.), Agricultural Standards: The Shape of the Global Food and Fiber System, 219-242. © 2006 Springer. Printed in the Netherlands.*

producing a quality fiber for export markets (Bassett 2001; Roberts 1996). More recently, it has become generally accepted that this new "era of quality" offers the opportunity to help assure the profitability and ecological sustainability of small farmer cotton production (Bourge 1995). Estur (2002: 13) notes, "one of the best ways of improving the profitability of the African cotton industries is to improve the quality at every stage".

In response, national cotton companies in West Africa reject the narrow, liberal economic focus of the World Bank's critique of "managed monopolies." They argue instead that the real development issue is not one of firm structure, but one of maintaining a competitive world market position by assuring quality control. Confronted with the pressure to privatize, the companies maintain that quality standards are the way to assure competitiveness in the world market.

This chapter examines several ethics and value issues raised as the Malian national cotton company, the Malian Company for the Development of Textiles (CMDT, *Compagnie Malienne pour le Développement des Textiles*), demonstrates its new entrepreneurial, quality standards strategy to define and enhance a distinguishable world market reputation for "Malian cotton" in collaboration with its French-based partner, (DAGRIS, formerly the French Company for the Development of Textile Fibers (CFDT, *Compagnie Française pour le Développement des Fibres Textiles*). Different ethical issues are explored as the cotton company implements at least three different sets of quality standards from production through processing and marketing. First, the international agronomic research arrangements required to control the quality of cotton seed and to develop improved varieties – both of which are instrumental in assuring the company's competitive international market position – involve significant political questions concerning the emergence and nature of a national agricultural research capability in a new global era. Second, the adherence to a quality standard based on cotton that is cultivated and hand-picked raises two important concerns: the implications of this standard for the viability and the personal well-being of peasant cotton farmer livelihood strategies; and, the implications for environmental stewardship. Third, the industrial processing (ginning) standards required for the international textile market – and the grading process used to meet these standards - poses complex questions concerning peasant farmer control, power and democratic processes in agricultural and rural development.

## 2. AN APPROACH TO QUALITY STANDARDS

In order to get beyond headline stories about subsidies or biases in World Bank policies, this chapter identifies and examines how quality standards are used to govern several "systems of negotiation" or "collective action" related to cotton production, processing and marketing. Drawing from convention theory, the analysis focuses on the rules, norms and conventions that are used to negotiate and assure quality standards among networks of actors (Eymard-Duvernay 1995; Wilkinson 1997). Instead of assuming that a commodity like cotton has a well-defined and general standard of quality that is established "once and for all," this approach suggests that quality standards are continually defined and re-defined through series of transactions or negotiations. In other words, quality standards are seen as properties or rules that emerge as "mechanisms of clarification" through which various actors maintain agreement about the relationships between themselves and with things.

In each of these situations, different sets of principles or "worlds" may be drawn upon to justify different forms of collective action. For example, in the "market world," quality can be defined principally in terms of price or the use of specified commercial criteria. On the other hand, in an "industrial world," standards of reliability would be more commonly used to evaluate the quality of a commodity like cotton. In any given situation, multiple worlds may be evoked to justify the relationship between an action or process and quality standards. Consequently, a key analytic issue involves identifying the compromises that are reached between these different worlds and the ethical and value implications of the mediation between the different forms of evaluation (Murdoch, Marsden, and Banks 2000).

From this perspective, several interrelated themes are used to discuss how attention to quality standards offers new insights on the relationship between cotton and democratic development in West Africa. The first theme addresses the networks of actors engaged in setting and implementing quality standards. Particular attention is given to the implications of the use of different sets of principles to assure this engagement (e.g., relying on established rules for quality as opposed to permitting more localized discussions of quality standards) by different sets of actors. As Eymard-Duvernay suggests, quality is tied to maintaining agreement among networks of actors and the engagement of all actors is important in assuring quality standards (Eymard-Duvernay 1995).One of the critical questions to explore involves whether managed monopolies like the national cotton companies in West Africa can reconcile centralized control with more localized, open and democratic processes in order to meet quality standards in the world cotton market.

A second theme builds from the notion that a commodity like cotton is defined by its performance (Latour 1987), and that it contains within it all the information necessary for its exchange (Wilkinson 1997). As noted above, different "worlds" with their particular sets of principles and criteria are used or evoked to define and apply quality standards for exchanging a commodity. Under these conditions, networks of actors develop and rely upon sets of instruments or methods that embody the norms of these worlds. The instruments (e.g., grading and testing equipment and procedures) mediate between these worlds by reducing the margins of negotiation among actors thereby facilitating the exchange of the commodity. In this way, the commodity is "known" to all actors.

However, cotton from West Africa represents a case in which instrumentation is commonly not available to define fully the commodity before its exchange. Different actors may also find local testing and grading procedures an unacceptable means for "defining" the quality of the cotton to be traded. In this situation, an organization usually becomes the guarantor of the exchange. In doing so, the characteristics and reputation of this partner become an important part of the negotiations and exchange. Key questions of concern relate to the conditions upon which an organization's reputation is established, the interests served in securing and maintaining this reputation, and the implications of this process for African development. Addressing these questions should provide insights on the effects of "transnationalization on the organization of local production," or the links between different local spaces and commodity-based networks of production and exchange (Marsden and Arce 1995).

A third theme draws from the concern with the ecological norms or conventions related to the quality standards of commodities (Murdoch, Marsden, and Banks 2000). Most agricultural commodities, including cotton, carry some type of identification and reputation related to "place." This may involve a focus on the personal knowledge and trust relationships that help to define the quality of a product. At the same time, this involves the relationship to, or "embeddedness" of the production and marketing activities to the natural resource base and the ways in which these relationships are used to define quality standards. In addition to drawing our attention to important environmental issues related to cotton production, this theme offers us another means to examine how negotiations over quality standards provide insights on the distribution of power in a global commodity chain.

## 3. COTTON QUALITY AT THE GRASSROOTS – THE ORGANIZATIONAL IMPERATIVE

### 3.1    Cotton Production in West Africa

Two features of West African cotton production and marketing set the stage for discussing cotton quality. First, cotton is grown under rainfed conditions on small farms that have limited access to animal drawn equipment and that rely largely on family labor for cultivation and harvesting.[2] Second, practically all of the cotton produced under these conditions is sold to the world export market. Thus, in the absence of policy protection against the vagaries of weather or the world market, smallholder farmers bear most of the risks associated with production. But at the same time, these defining features of West African cotton – a hand harvested crop produced under rain fed conditions by unpaid family labor – create a quality standard used to assure its competitiveness on the world market (Béroud 2001).

Despite these risks, West African farmers have increased the land in cotton about 6% per year since the mid-1990s and their production accounts for almost 13% of world exports. These farmers generate between 30 to 50% of the national GDP across the region and produce almost all of the region's staple food crops and oilseeds. With access to agricultural equipment and supplies, cotton farmers are also responsible for increasing food grain production throughout most of the region. As one observer notes, "there is some evidence that there is an agricultural revolution in cotton production zones, with cotton driving a process of "extensification" on the one hand and intensive production of cereals as cash crops for urban markets on the other" ( also see Goreux 2003; Hussein 2004).

For various demographic and ecological reasons, this "extensification process" means that farmers are cultivating more marginal lands in order to maintain and/or increase production. While this practice generates short-term earnings, in the longer-term it may easily weaken the West African cotton quality standard and its competitive position in the world market. The soils on more marginal lands respond less favorably to inorganic fertilizer thereby contributing to the downward trend in yields and plant strength that renders cotton more susceptible to disease and pest damage. Since the mid-1990s yields have remained steady or declined (e.g., 2% per year in Mali) at the same time as farmers have confronted new pest control problems from bollworms and whiteflies.

### 3.2    Organizational Issues in West African Cotton Production

It has been widely acknowledged for years that the accomplishments and quality reputation of West African cotton derive largely from the integrated research, production and marketing operations of the region's national cotton companies that are affiliated with the French-based conglomerate, DAGRIS (*Développement des Agro-Industries du Sud*; ex-CFDT, *Compagnie Française pour le Développement des Fibres Textiles*) (See Bingen, Carney, and Dembelé 1995; Lele, Walle, and Gbetibouo 1989). The establishment of such integrated operations, including ginning facilities, was central to assuring cotton quality during the colonial era (Isaacman and Roberts 1995). For the over 40 years since political independence, applied research has been closely linked with the improvement and distribution of cotton varieties to farmers who have received close supervision and advice (*encadrement* and *vulgarisation*), production credit, guaranteed purchase prices and collection for their harvested crop. In fact, it might be argued that the production of high quality cotton under rainfed and smallholder conditions requires the integration of all these activities (Groupe de Travail Coopération Française 1991).

In addition to alleviating some smallholder risk by assuring input supply and guaranteeing purchase at a fixed price, some suggest that such an integrated structure reduces many pesticide-related environmental and health issues that commonly arise under more "open" or more "liberalized" arrangements (Béroud 1999). More specifically, many argue that the expertise and commercial interests represented through integrated operations help to assure the timely delivery and quality of agricultural equipment and supplies, including seed selection and multiplication with attention to adaptability and purity, fertilizers, pesticides, plows and seeders. However, a recent study of a new farmers' cooperative alliance, suggests that experienced farmers in collaboration with a national non-governmental organization can meet the logistic requirements and meet the quality control conditions necessary to assure the delivery of quality equipment and supplies to smallholders (Bingen 2003).

For almost 10 years the World Bank (2000) has argued that this type of "managed monopoly model" suffers from two serious weaknesses. First, it presumably limits incentives to minimize costs and stifles entrepreneurial decision making, thereby rendering it vulnerable in a highly competitive global market.

Second, the viability of the model "...is based primarily on its ability to tax producers and accumulate profits in times of high export prices, and to rely on budgetary support from national governments in times of low international prices" (The World Bank 2000: 1). Both the 1998-1999 management scandal in the CMDT, the Malian national cotton company (*Compagnie Malienne pour le Développement des Textiles*), and the producer cotton boycott of 2000 would appear to confirm the World Bank position.

In response, the national cotton companies in Benin, Togo and Côte d'Ivoire have partially privatized ginning and marketing operations, while the Malian company has established an Office for Quality Assurance focused on setting up quality circles as a way to move away from top-down management practices. None of the reforms have targeted the production purchase guarantee, exclusive collection rights or the standardized prices for inputs and seed cotton. Nor have the reforms addressed one of the farmers' long-standing, principal concerns: the accountability of the national companies to their farmers. From the April 2001 *Etats Généraux du Monde Rural* in Mali to the most recent *Etats Généraux du Secteur Coton*, farmers continue to condemn the self-serving activities of the CMDT and the lack of structural change that would protect farmers' interests. Finally, the proposed reforms do not address the importance of maintaining ginning efficiency. In principle, the "managed monopoly" model helps to reduce ginning costs, and thereby creates a basis for offering a higher price to growers, since it has the capacity for estimating the timing and amount of the harvest and for collecting the harvested cotton according to a schedule that assures a steady supply of seed cotton to keep the mills running continuously.

West African cotton farmers welcome and support all efforts to remove the subsidies used by several industrialized countries to protect their world cotton market share. Nevertheless, they are equally concerned with resolving important structural constraints on their full participation in cotton marketing, including an annual evaluation of the principal marketing agent, COPACO, and the direct involvement of farmer representatives in assuring how quality standards can be met through all production and marketing activities. The challenge is whether the farmers' demands for quality control gain traction over calls by major international corporate actors to use quality as a restriction that assures farmer access to diverse and expanded sources of cotton.

## 4. CREATING QUALITY

### 4.1    Cotton Varieties and Quality

Some believe that the ancestor of all lint-bearing cotton species, *Gossypium herbaceum subsp. africanum* is African since it grows wild and is the only wild species of *Gossypium* that bears lint (see Bassett 2001). There is evidence that "new world" varieties of cotton entered Africa between the 16th and early 18th centuries as part of the slave trade, and when colonial agronomists and botanists started to study local cotton varieties in the late 1800s, they were surprised at the degree of hybridization in these varieties. African growers had been experimenting for years to develop plants with higher yields and with the qualities of importance to local cloth spinners - color, fiber length, ease of hand-ginning. In particular, these spinners appreciated the labor-saving qualities of medium and long-staple cotton (see Roberts 1996). However, in response to the demands from the European textile industry for cotton of even length and uniform color that was comparable to the market standard set by the US medium staple upland varieties at that time, colonial agronomists introduced American cotton varieties into West Africa (Isaacman and Roberts 1995).

The focus on spinning quality by the textile industry continues to "set the standard" for all cotton breeding, production and marketing. Spinning quality is measured by four sets of fiber characteristics: fiber length and length uniformity; strength; fineness and maturity; and a low percentage of broken fibers. The challenge in meeting this standard in West Africa, or producing and marketing cotton that meets these quality features, involves accommodating the divergent interests of the textile industry, the growers and the national cotton companies.

For the textile industry, changes in textile technology, particularly the replacement of ring spinning by new high speed rollers, requires greater uniformity in length, less short fiber, higher strength and more mature cotton. By meeting these criteria, and producing cotton with 'high spinnability,' "higher prices can be expected and producers will have no difficulty in marketing their product" (May 2003: 39). In other words, the production technology and the final product drives the value placed by the textile industry on those fiber properties that directly affect the quality of the yarns and the efficiency at which they are produced (Estur 2004).

On the other hand, producing cotton under the smallholder conditions common in West Africa often requires a trade off between quality and yield (May 2003). Fiber length, and fineness and maturity are primary components of quality for the textile industry. But they are only secondary components of yield – of principal interest to both growers and the national cotton companies. In other words, breeding for these quality characteristics may hamper the selection of varieties more responsive to grower and company interests (Gillham, Bell et al. 1995). In addition, fiber length, as well as fineness and maturity, may be compromised by a combination of environmental factors and cultivation practices (see Malloum 2002). These include erratic weather conditions (extreme temperatures or erratic rainfall distribution) that are common throughout West Africa. These also include common smallholder cultivation practices such as late sowing (as planting cereal crops takes priority), insufficient or inappropriate fertilizer application (when some of the fertilizer required for cotton is used for food crops) and expanding cultivation onto poorer soils (as one strategy for increasing production by increasing the area cultivated). For Gillham (1995: 66), "good agronomic practices are ... especially true for cotton. ... Cotton is a crop that has to be really 'tamed' from A to Z to achieve its optimum production potential."[3] Meeting these standards makes it important for plant breeding to be closely supported by adequate fiber and spinning testing that facilitates selection based on these multiple criteria and that can develop varieties adapted to the range of diverse environmental conditions found in most West African cotton producing countries (see Gillham, Bell et al. 1995).

The sophistication of the ginning facilities also contributes to meeting these multiple quality standards and to creating cotton that meets the 'high spinnability' quality standard. In addition to minimizing damage to the fibers during processing, the ginning equipment must have the capacity for removing foreign matter (seed coat fragments, leaves, stems) and damaged ("sticky") bolls that can create numerous problems during spinning. Ginners must also guard against creating neps, or tiny knots of immature fibers, that causes white specks in fabrics after dyeing (Hamai 2003).

While the raw material is the most important factor influencing yarn quality (Estur 2004), creating quality is a continuing process of seeking consistency and minimizing variability to respond to multiple priorities in breeding, cultivation, processing and spinning.

### 4.2    Meeting Quality Standards in Mali

Given the difficulties in improving the historically cultivated varieties (*Gossypium hirsutum*, *Gossypium punctatum*), colonial agronomists introduced   Allen (a US variety) from Sudan in the early 1920s (see Bassett 2001). As Table 1 shows, Allen varieties dominated breeding and production in Mali until the network of French-supported research stations in West and Central Africa made other improved varieties available. In fact, as Anthony (1986) notes, the results from this Africa-based, applied research network are largely responsible for the impressive growth of cotton production throughout West Africa and for the development of quality African cottons that tend to be longer and finer than the 'bread and butter' cottons of the American Cotton Belt.

Table 1. Cotton Varieties in Mali

| Variety | Years Grown | Origin |
|---|---|---|
| Allen 49T | 1955 - 61 | USA |
| Allen 151 | 1956 - 67 | USA |
| Allen 333-57 | 1961 - 71 | USA |
| BJA 592 | 1967 - 82 | Central African Republic |
| BJA SM 67 | 1972 - 73 | Central African Republic |
| B 163 | 1978 - 89 | Central African Republic |
| ISA 205-B | 1988 – 93 (?) | Côte d'Ivoire |
| GL 7 | 1991 - 95 | Côte d'Ivoire |
| Stam F | 1991 - 95 | Togo |
| NTA 88-6 (N'Tarla) | 1992 -> | Mali |
| STAM 42 | 1994 -> | Togo |
| G 269-2 | 1992 - 93 | Côte d'Ivoire |

After several years of distributing the same variety throughout its production region, the Malian cotton company now distributes up to nine different varietal types (e.g., NTA 88-6, 90-5, 93-2, 93-13, 93-15) in order to achieve optimum yields and quality under different agro-ecological conditions. However, varietal improvement requires continuing trade-offs between grower and company priorities. For example, in the mid-1990s, the company introduced a variety (GL 7) that was resistant to weeds, more fertility tolerant and had longer fiber. But farmers did not accept it because the low number of seeds per boll reduced the weight of the harvest and the quantity of processed seed meal available for animal feed. On the other hand, farmers prefer the Stam and NTA 88 varieties. But these varieties are also susceptible to weeds and to insects, thereby making it difficult to meet both production and quality standards. The time for weeding cotton often overlaps with the time for weeding cereal crops. And in response to high costs, most farmers spread out pesticide use with partial applications, thereby compromising the effectiveness of the pesticides. As the Malian cotton company expands into new cotton growing areas, the adaptation of varieties to new agro-ecological conditions becomes a major challenge, and one which could encourage more of an effort to integrate farmers into varietal development programs (Dembelé and Yattara 2000).

In the mid-1980s, the Malian cotton company turned its attention to breeding for a higher ginning ratio, or focusing varietal improvement to increase the weight of lint (fiber) as a percentage of the seed cotton purchased from farmers for processing. This focus on higher ginning ratios by national cotton companies is one of the distinguishing features of West African cotton in comparison to other regions of Africa. The ratio of all current varieties is 42%, and all new varieties must achieve a 43% to 46% ginning ratio. Even the smallest increases in ginning ratios translate into significant earnings. For example, if the national company markets 500,000 tons annually, a 1% higher ginning ratio (or an increase of 50,000 tons at 100,000 CFA/ton) provides an additional five billion CFA.[4] Despite the significance of this type of research, Malian researchers do not have immediate access to fiber and spinning testing facilities. All new varieties must be sent to France for fiber and spinning tests, thereby preventing the joint consideration of both the agronomic and technological research results in the same year.

In addition to the ginning ratio, the cotton program in Mali has increased field productivity and fiber length, thereby responding to the concerns of growers and developing a quality standard that attracts buyers to "Malian cotton." At issue is the continuing viability of this research as the once vibrant and essential regional research programs that were the source of new varieties and other improvements are moribund. Furthermore, reduced revenues force national companies away from long-term research and toward more immediate and problem-solving research. Consequently, instead of financing research that might improve the color of Malian cotton, the cotton company focuses on responding to immediate pest control problems.

In summary, if the elimination of cotton subsidies in North America and Europe did generate higher world market prices for growers in West Africa, measures would also need to be in place in order to assure the institutional investment required to meet continuous changes in quality standards. Smallholder grower relationships with the world market or the international textile industry are currently mediated by national cotton companies. Thus, without a commitment to assuring the long-term agronomic research supported by an investment in acquiring a national technological testing capacity, higher producer prices may prove to be only a short-term solution to improving the livelihoods of West African cotton farmers.

## 5. MEASURING QUALITY

### 5.1    The Sciences of Measuring Cotton Quality

"Cotton is a natural product. There are considerable variations of quality that arise under the influence of the differences in the seed varieties, soils, climate, fertilizers, insect damage, irrigation practices, method of harvesting and ginning. To classify and grade these various cottons accurately is extremely important in … cotton trading. It determines the market value and provides the quality data for spinners to make the yarn production plan" (Hamai 2003: 3).

The signatories to the Universal Cotton Standards Agreement[5] meet every three years in the US to review and consider revisions to two sets of cotton standards: those used for grading or classifying cotton; and those used for calibrating the fiber testing instruments to select cotton for specified fiber standards. Based on this agreement, the Standardization and Engineering Branch of the US Department of Agriculture accepts the responsibility to prepare and distribute physical samples of the grade and calibration standards for use by cotton classers, private companies and governments around the world.

With American Upland Cotton as the reference, there are two sets of grade standards that rely on a visual grading process. The first set of standards describes the color of the lint and it includes 25 color grades and five categories that fall below the grade. From these, each year the USDA prepares sample boxes of fifteen of these grades, and descriptions of the remaining grades based on the physical color grade standards, for worldwide distribution. Since the color of cotton deepens over time, and especially when stored under conditions of high temperature or relative humidity, new sample boxes are prepared annually. The second set of standards describes cleanliness in terms of seven grades of leaf or trash content in the cotton. The USDA also prepares physical samples of these for grading. Based on these sets of standards, cotton is graded into categories called Good Middling, Strict Middling, Middling, Strict Low Middling, Low Middling, Strict Good Ordinary, and Good Ordinary.

In conformity with the International Calibration Cotton Standards (ICCS) Program, the USDA also distributes four sets of calibration standards used in instrument testing. The first set includes standards for fiber length, the length uniformity index, and fiber strength that are based on the Universal High Volume Instrument (HVI) Calibration Standards for American Upland cotton.[6] The second set involves the measurement of micronaire or fiber fineness and maturity by air flow instrument tests. A third set measures the percentage area and particle count of trash with an HVI video trashmeter. Finally, reflectance (Rd or the degree of grayness) and the degree of yellowness (+b) are measured by an HVI colormeter. In addition, the ICCS Program sets standards for the atmospheric conditions in the cotton grading rooms and conditioning practices and procedures to be followed in the grading process.

The challenge for West African cotton companies involves developing the capacity to use both sets of standards – the visual and the machine. All of West Africa's cotton is currently graded or classed by hand, and even though most of this cotton has a quality suitable for the international textile industry, manual grading glosses over its true value (Estur 2002; Macdonald 2002). But in addition to undervaluing the region's cotton, the continuing reliance on manual grading threatens to marginalize West African cotton on the world market. Continuing improvements in the sophistication of spinning technology that generate more exacting specifications of cotton fiber, combined with the competition from better synthetic fibers and declining profit margins in the textile industry, all indicate that machine grading, or HVI classification, will play a major role in the continued success of the cotton industry (Dunavant 2002).

Thus, in order to remain competitive on the world market, the issue for West African cotton involves identifying how and under what conditions both sets of standards can be used. Manual or visual grading relies on valuable artisanal or craft type expertise, while the use of machine grading relies on a combination of operator skills plus the assurance of a reliable infrastructure (electricity, temperature and humidity controls, etc.) to support the sophisticated HVI technology. In the absence of being able to assure this minimum infrastructure, often because of the unreliable supply of electricity or inadequate maintenance facilities, West African cotton companies must consider organizational alternatives to acquire a machine grading capacity and thereby seek to remain competitive on the world cotton market.

In addition to the color and cleanliness of cotton lint, the manual grading process involves a feeling and "hand-pulling" process to determine softness and measure fiber length according the internationally accepted standard lengths that range from $1^{1/16}$, $1^{3/32}$, $1^{1/8}$, to $1^{5/32}$ inches. For some, and especially the Cotton Company (*La Compagnie Cotonnière*), an affiliate of DAGRIS that manages the international marketing for most of West Africa's cotton, this process "is an art that neither machines nor technology have yet replaced" (DAGRIS 2002). In fact, some argue that given the variations in machine calibrations as well as wide variability of conditions under which these machines operate around the world, the consistency and reliability of grading by an experienced classer surpasses that of HVI classification (see Macdonald 2002).[7]

DAGRIS (2002) compares the expertise required and process followed in manual cotton grading with that in evaluating wine. With cotton however, the "touch" and "pull" of the cotton is all-important. To evaluate the "touch" or feel of the cotton, the classer observes how quickly a small sample of cotton resumes its form after being pressed in the palm of the hand. In this way, the suppleness of the cotton helps to determine its quality. With this test completed, the classer moves to assessing the "break" of the cotton as the means to identify fiber length. This step involves holding a small sample between the thumb and forefinger of each hand and pulling it multiple times to determine the uniformity of fiber length in the sample. This process also allows the classer to determine three other important features of cotton. First, hand manipulation quickly exposes any seeds or fragments of seed coats that remain in the cotton fiber. Second, this process allows the classer to identify the prevalence of immature fibers (neps) that were not extracted during ginning. Third, pulling helps determine the cotton's "stickiness" that results from inadequate pest management and that creates serious problems during spinning. Finally, the most experienced classers are known to rely as much on taste and sound, as they do on touch and feel. Some run fibers across the tongue to assess "stickiness." Others do part of the pulling process next to their ears in order to assess the brittleness of the sound when the fibers separate and break.

In contrast to the "sensory science" relied upon by classers, machine testing with the HVI system must meet several precisely calculated conditions (Malloum 2002). For HVI analyses to be of reliable quality, the system must be in perfect operating condition and properly calibrated. The room temperature must be maintained at 20°C within a range of plus or minus 1°, with the relative humidity at 65% within a range of plus or minus 2%. In addition, the cotton samples must be conditioned to reach a humidity level between 6.75% and 8.25%. These hygrometric variations influence the measurements of the key characteristics of tenacity and elongation. It is generally agreed that cotton fiber reaches hygroscopic equilibrium in four hours, which means that a sample may be analyzed if it has been subjected to standard conditions (65% relative humidity and a temperature of 20°C) for at least four hours. When these conditions are met, HVI systems provide the textile industry with more detailed fiber information that allows spinners to improve fiber blends and quality (Schroder 2003).

Proper air conditioning is indispensable for the HVI systems to operate correctly. In addition, a reliance on HVI systems requires the capacity to: assure the instruments are regulated to conform to international standards; verify the procedures that guarantee the precision of the HVI results; test the instruments periodically; and, assure the quality of the classification process. Currently, none of these conditions can be met in West Africa (Gourlot 2000). The inadequate electric supply throughout the region creates a major constraint on operating an HVI system and thereby meeting the international textile industry expectation for HVI standards. In addition, HVI systems require regular and sophisticated maintenance, and replacement parts that are commonly available only from Europe (Malloum 2002). Consequently, unless some fundamental infrastructure issues are resolved, and in the absence of at least a regionally-based parts and maintenance capacity, the quality reputation for West African cotton may evaporate in the face of demands for "machine science" grading.

## 5.2    Measuring Cotton Quality in Mali

The Malian Cotton Company operates seventeen ginning facilities in the country's cotton growing region. These gins are located strategically in order to optimize the operation of the gins and the collection of cotton from widely dispersed villages. The geographical distribution of the gins is designed to assure a steady supply of seed cotton in order run the gins on a regular schedule. By assuring a regular supply of seed cotton, the company can improve ginning efficiency and thereby the production of higher quality fiber.

Toward the end of each processing season (or early in the calendar year), the CMDT cotton graders, who work out of the four classification rooms in the company's ginning facilities, convene in Le Havre, France at the headquarters of the Le Havre Cotton Exchange and the French Cotton Association (AFCOT, *Association Française Cotonnière*) with other cotton graders from West and Central African cotton companies that are affiliated with DAGRIS and with DAGRIS/Cotton Company graders, to set the grading standards for the coming year. In order to assure the acceptability of African cotton on the world market, these discussions may include representatives from the textile industry. These discussions use the USDA-supplied sample boxes and samples of cotton fiber identified by variety to specify the classification grades that each country will use to grade and label its cotton fiber.

In Mali, it is agreed that for the purposes of grading, cotton fiber should be first separated by variety and between the two major types of gins that operate in the country. One category of gins has fiber cleaning and humidity control for both seed cotton and fiber. Another category includes all those without these features. Seventy percent of Malian cotton is ginned in the first type of facility and it is classed and labeled by five levels of $1^{st}$ quality cotton (Sarama, Juli/S, Juli, Roky, Roky/C) or two levels of $2^{nd}$ quality cotton (Yoro, Taro). The remaining 30% of the cotton from gins without a fiber cleaning or humidity control capacity is classed and labeled into three quality classes: $1^{st}$ quality (Kati/S, Kati, Liba, Liba C); $2^{nd}$ quality (Kola, Luko); and, $3^{rd}$ quality (Bati, Bajo, Fako). Sample boxes representing these classes are prepared and used in each of the CMDT classification rooms.

The CMDT maintains classification rooms in four of its ginning facilities. Each of these windowless rooms is specially outfitted with air conditioners to keep the temperature at 20-21°C, humidifiers to keep the humidity at 50-55% and special lights that mimic outside lighting. Working with an assistant/apprentice who is responsible for cutting and preparing the 250 gram sample from each bale produced in the gin, an experienced classer can grade up to 3,500 samples per day. Each sample is identified by bale and variety, classed as $1^{st}$, $2^{nd}$ or $3^{rd}$ category and then labeled based on the composite grading of color, cleanliness, length and "feel." In order to provide a quality guarantee for the purposes of marketing, one of every twenty-five samples is sent to the COPACO grading room in Paris for HVI verification. Clearly, if the CMDT could maintain HVI instruments in each of its grading facilities, this step would be unnecessary. Furthermore, the company would be able to use the full range of criteria for grading its cotton fiber.

The absence of a capacity to operate HVI equipment to international standards does create a dependency relationship between CMDT and COPACO. But it is a relationship that still strengthens CMDT's role in the world cotton market. On the other hand, the current approach to grading continues to give second place to the interests of growers. In doing so, the process weakens the fidelity of farmers to the company and could eventually jeopardize the quality of cotton available from Mali. The issue between the farmers and the company arises because the farmers sell one product, seed cotton, while the CMDT uses another product, cotton fiber, to pay the farmers. As discussed between the company and the farmers since the early 1990s, the question is one of relying upon the company's "industrial classification" that grades cotton fiber, or one based on "village classification" that grades seed cotton. Rather than grading seed cotton and paying farmers directly, the CMDT pays farmers for a product (cotton fiber) different from what the company collected from them at the village collection point. In addition, there are several steps in the collection and ginning process that both undermine farmer confidence and the individual incentive to produce high quality cotton.

Farmers deliver all of their cotton to a common, village-level collection point that is managed by their "village association." Another member of the association weighs and "grades" the cotton as either $1^{st}$ or $2^{nd}$ quality based largely on color and cleanliness. Some associations use simple sample boxes distributed by the CMDT graders to help assure some conformity and alleviate unnecessary arbitrariness among members of the same association at this point in this process. Each farmer receives a receipt indicating the quantity and quality delivered. However, each individual's cotton is mixed with that from other farmers, and the cotton becomes identified with the association, not with the farmer. Consequently, while farmers still have an incentive to deliver $1^{st}$ quality cotton, the loss of a personnally identifiable quantity dilutes this incentive and encourages farmers to try to hide lower quality cotton within higher quality loads. Some empirical verification of this may be found in reports from some CMDT graders that the quality of $1^{st}$ grade cotton has declined about 10% decline over the last five years.

Other procedures further weaken the individual incentive to deliver uniformly high quality cotton. Most associations keep $1^{st}$ and $2^{nd}$ quality separate at the village storage point, and the collection truck driver receives a copy of the weight and grade receipts from each village association in order to assure that each association is paid accurately for the quantity and quality of its cotton. But both of these distinctions are blurred as different qualities of seed cotton are mixed during loading at the collection points and when seed cotton from other villages is added to make a full truck. Thus, when the truck arrives at the gin, only the receipts carried by the driver link the cotton back to the village and eventually serve to calculate the payment to each association.

When COPACO confirms the cotton fiber quality, the CMDT pays the associations according the quantity of $1^{st}$ and $2^{nd}$ quality seed cotton collected at the village. Each association is responsible for distributing the payment according the initial collection receipts. Given the need for COPACO confirmation, the delay between harvest and payment to the farmer may be as long as six months, often creating serious cash flow problems for many farmers. Moreover, the associations and the farmers do not benefit from any market price differences based on the quality labels assigned to each bale.

Clearly, these procedures require a level of farmer confidence in the ginning and grading process that neither the farmers nor the CMDT have been able to assure. For a short time during the 1990s, the farmers tried to resolve this issue and gain a measure of confidence by assigning representatives to oversee the ginning and grading process at each of the gins. However, the farmers quickly realized their inability to assure oversight at each gin and they have reluctantly accepted the

CMDT industrial classification system. Nevertheless, the controversies continue as many associations complain that their cotton was downgraded as a result of mistakes made during the ginning process. For example, villagers commonly complain that the cleaning machines and gins are run faster than recommended in order to meet or exceed ginning quotas. In doing so, seed cotton is improperly cleaned. Stems and leaves remain, as well as broken seeds that gum up the machines, and result in a "dirtier" cotton with high levels of foreign matter in each bale.

Given this dependence upon the ginning process, the loss of any identity with their cotton, and their removal from marketing, it is difficult to encourage farmers to make an extra effort to deliver high quality cotton. The marketing and grading procedures between the CMDT and the farmers create a dependency relationship without any of the benefits of participation that could arise from ways to build farmer confidence, fidelity and quality assurance. Furthermore, this has significant long-term implications related to the legitimate demands to remove cotton subsidies and raise the world market price for African farmers. Higher world market prices would offer an initial earnings boost for farmers. But unless national companies like the CMDT improve their quality assurance procedures, they risk jeopardizing their world market position and the long-term incomes of small-scale farmers.

## 6. MARKETING QUALITY

As suggested earlier, the case of Malian and West African cotton illustrates the importance of an intermediary organization or agency between supplier and buyer that defines and guarantees the quality of the cotton to be traded. The CMDT and most of the national cotton companies in West Africa lack the HVI instrumentation that can define adequately or provide the complete specifications of cotton fiber for the purposes of the world market. To compensate, the CMDT relies upon its agent, COPACO (the *Compagnie Cotonnière*), the marketing affiliate of DAGRIS, to handle its marketing.[8]

For Mali, this relationship with COPACO is only the most recent manifestation of an historical Franco-African relationship built around developing cotton production to supply the French textile industry. Since the creation of the *Association Cotonnier Colonial* (AAC) around the end of the 19th Century, the French government and textile industry have collaborated closely to fund research, production and marketing initiatives around the world (Bloud 1925). After almost 40 years of mixed experiences with largely public initiatives, in 1949, the French government and textile industry created a mixed, public-private company, the French Company for the Development of Textiles, (CFDT, *Compagnie Française pour le Développement des Textiles*[9]) to lead a major cotton development program that would be supported by the government's overseas development program (FIDES) and a special tax on the French textile companies (*Fonds d'Encouragement à la Production Textile*). This new company was given full responsibility for all development aspects of cotton production, and it worked closely with the newly established Institute for Cotton Research (IRCT) to establish and fund a network of cotton research sites across West and Central Africa (Groupe de Travail Coopération

Française 1991) that has long been known for its contribution to the development of African cotton (Lele, Walle, and Gbetibouo 1989).

In June 2001 the CFDT was reorganized into DAGRIS (The Southern Agro-Industrial Development Company, *Développement des Agro-Industries du Sud*), an industrial holding company with 64% government capital and 36% from employees, textile associations and private banks. The purpose of establishing DAGRIS was to move away from the development service orientation of the CFDT and foster a more entrepreneurial approach to cotton development focusing on quality control as much as production and marketing. Of critical importance for West and Central Africa, DAGRIS is expected to diversify its cotton supply, with African sources dropping from 88% to 80% of what is marketed. As this occurs, national companies like the CMDT will need to consider the "quality implications" of a continuing marketing relationship through an agent instead of selling through international brokers as practiced by the cotton companies in Cameroon, Bénin and the Côte d'Ivoire.

Most cotton is marketed through brokers, or companies that purchase cotton without attention to national identification or labeling in grading.[10] For these companies, successful marketing depends more upon access to diverse supplies than upon representing cotton specifically labeled from a particular country. Consequently, the grading or quality assurance process, including the annual standard setting meetings in Le Havre, as discussed above, is central to the relationship. By marketing through an agent, quality becomes the becomes the basis for developing customer loyalty, and for DAGRIS, one way in which African farmers can minimize the risks associated with the liberalization of the cotton sector in their countries. Further, DAGRIS is working with Max Havelaar to develop a fair trade certification process for some African cottons, and with the French Association for Quality Assurance, (AFAQ, *Association Française d'Assurance Qualité*) for a Malian-labeled cotton. Without question, there are advantages and disadvantages to marketing through brokers or through agents. But for most West African countries, working through an agent seems to be an effective means to maintain a positive world market reputation based on both quality and reliability of supply (Estur 1992). This relationship, however, does little to help West African countries deal with the looming challenge of another quality issue: worker protection through environmental standards related to pesticide use.

## 7. THE ENVIRONMENTAL CHALLENGE TO QUALITY

In Africa, as elsewhere, cotton depends heavily upon two sets of practices that could jeopardize the quality label of African cotton if environmental and/or human safety concerns begin to play a greater role in setting the standard for quality. For several years, cotton productivity has stagnated throughout West Africa, giving rise to concerns that the continuing use of inorganic fertilizers weakens already fragile soils. In addition, recent cases of pesticide poisoning in Bénin, as well as reports of water pollution and the disappearance of beneficial insects such as bees, raise serious questions about recommended pest management practices based on synthetic pesticides. The cotton companies and researchers usually respond to these issues by blaming the farmers for not following recommended practices. At the same time there is very little international pressure at the current time from the industry, consumers, or fair trade organizations that encourages companies to build environmental or human safety criteria into the quality standards and labeling of cotton grown by African farmers.[11] However, on the one hand, as the demand for organic cotton increases, and, on the other hand, as corporate efforts to promote the use of cotton varieties genetically modified for insect resistance in Africa become more significant, both environmental and human safety criteria will find an important place in the quality debate.

### 7.1    Soil Fertility and Soil Erosion[12]

The use of inorganic fertilizers is a production requirement for farmers in West and Central Africa to market cotton through companies like the CMDT. While in part responsible for enhancing and maintaining the productivity of cotton, the continuing use of fertilizer has contributed to two worrisome soil problems.

First, the continuing use of fertilizer on the same fields – an increasingly common practice in the absence of fallowing land – increases soil acidity and depletes the soil of organic matter. This is the principal reason why yields continue to stagnate and in some cases decline in the older cotton regions throughout West and Central Africa. Second, the availability of fertilizer engenders further environmental degradation that is infrequently acknowledged. For years it has been widely known that farmers "borrow" from their supplied cotton fertilizer – or short the required application – and use these captured quantities – however small – to enhance in some small way their food crop production. Consequently, in order to compensate for any shortfall in their expected cotton production these same farmers bring additional and commonly more marginal land under cotton cultivation. Such practices not only enhance the susceptibility of the already marginal lands to erosion, but also reduce the effectiveness of the fertilizer used on cotton.

The challenge under these conditions lies not in rejecting fertilizer use, but in finding ways to improve soil quality with organic fertilizers and to reduce soil erosion. The national company cotton programs have become increasingly sensitive to the natural resource management issues raised by the widespread and long-term use of fertilizer. The response by these companies, however, has been limited. Soil protection measures are commonly promoted in a project-like manner as an activity separate from and additional to regular production and harvesting practices. Furthermore, natural resource management (soil protection and health) concerns take a back seat to breeding and pest management in the cotton research programs supported by the companies. But even the passing nod to dealing with these issues risks being sacrificed as the companies respond to World Bank pressures to "liberalize" their activities by transferring responsibility for non-production activities, such as natural resource management, to other firms or government agencies.

7.2     *Pest Management*

Insects – not diseases or fungi – are the main cause of crop damage and losses in cotton throughout sub-Saharan Africa. These insects include aphids, sucking and pricking insects as well as worms (bollworms) that attack the leaves and bolls and feed on the cotton plant at various stages in its life cycle. Insect damage varies widely by country, but in areas where damage is considered to be "relatively moderate," yield losses are about 30 per cent per year. For years, cotton pests have been controlled through the use of treated seeds to improve germination, and program spraying, i.e., a specified number and type of applications at pre-determined periods during the growing season. The common practice throughout West and Central Africa involves a 14-day program with the total number of applications ranging from four to six. Some undocumented evidence indicates that such program treatments reduce pest loses by about ten percent. But the costs of these practices account for 25 to 30 per cent of the total input costs for cotton.

The expected and continuing resistance to these pesticides indicates that the cotton companies, farmers and the international community face an environmental and human health issue of some concern. In 1995 cotton bollworm (*Helicoverpa armigera*) resistance to the relatively non-toxic pyrethroids became problematic and was compounded by additional damage from whiteflies (*Bemisia tabaci*). In response, the cotton companies in West and Central Africa decided to re-introduce endosulfan, a highly toxic chlorinated hydrocarbon for control, and to fund research on the use of a more powerful pyrethroid insecticide. This is the classic "pesticide treadmill" response in which increasingly more powerful formulations are regularly required to respond to the resistance developed by insects. As researchers address this problem, they have been able to reduce the volume of pesticides used by increasing the toxicity by weight. A study by the Sahel Institute in Mali confirms this phenomenon. Researchers found that while the volume of pesticides used declined by 44 per cent, the proportion of active ingredient per volume has increased 40 per cent (Camara, Haïdara, and Traoré 2001).

The insecticides used are pyrethroid-organophosphate mixtures that are moderately toxic to mammals and usually quite toxic to birds, fish and beneficial insects, including bees.[13] However, few, if any, environmental studies have been completed. Farmers report the disappearance of bees in the older cotton growing zones, and there have been discussions of the possibility of cotton pesticide residues in honey. Governments and cotton companies have permitted only very limited environmental impact studies of pesticides. A few groundwater pollution studies have been carried out, but only long after the growing season and the last pesticide application. The few studies that have been undertaken found pesticides in over 25 per cent of the wells studied and at levels that exceeded the EU residue standards for drinking water.

With respect to the human safety risk, the most widely publicized incident involved endosulfan poisoning in Bénin during 2000. Thirty seven people were killed and at least another 36 become seriously ill. This type of disastrous incident usually does not involve direct contamination from spraying, but from eating food – in this case maize – that becomes contaminated from sprays used on cotton, and drinking from re-used pesticide containers. In addition, as many observers have pointed out for several years, farmers do not wear protective clothing and practically nothing is known about the chronic poisoning that occurs from inhalation and dermal exposure, especially since low protein diets engender a higher susceptibility to pesticide poisoning (see Adjovi 1998; OBEPAB 2000). There is anecdotal evidence as well of cattle deaths from eating treated stalks of cotton that have been left in the fields after harvest. Moreover, it is widely alleged, but not well-documented, that pesticides are frequently used for fishing and for "hunting."

The CMDT in Mali has started to move away slowly from a program approach to pest management. First, cotton seed is no longer automatically treated before distribution. The treatments were not improving germination rates and farmers were feeding the extra treated seed to their animals. Second, the company has started to introduce an integrated pest management program (IPM) that relies on scouting or field observations of pest presence instead of pre-determined dates for spraying. However, almost ten years after introducing integrated pest management, it is not widely implemented. It is estimated that the program covers less than ten per cent of the total cotton zone. Farmer resistance or hesitation to adapt the practices does not appear to account for the low level of program application. On the contrary, the IPM procedures are designed for non-literate farmers, and during informal field surveys farmers express considerable interest in exploring ways to cut pesticide use and costs. Instead, the procedures are designed to be closely supervised and it appears that the low adoption rate reflects considerable hesitancy on the part of the cotton company and of researchers to allow farmers more freedom in their pest management decisions.

In West Africa there are two diametrically opposed alternatives to addressing many of the environmental and human safety concerns raised by current production practices. Small efforts are underway in both Mali and Senegal to promote organic cotton production but it confronts serious dilemmas with pest management and the problem of low soil fertility. At the other end of the spectrum, Monsanto has explored the introduction of Bt cotton into West Africa. Most of the national companies, however, do not feel that Bt cotton responds to their preoccupations. Furthermore, there is as a general feeling that requiring the seed to be sold each year - in contrast to the free distribution of seed by the companies each year – would be impossible to implement. Consequently, unlike developments in Southern Africa, it is highly unlikely that either organic cotton or Bt cotton can help to resolve many current environmental and human safety issues.

## 8. QUALITY AND EMPOWERMENT

The voice of Malian cotton farmers during the 2001 Estates General for Cotton was clear: Undertake the policy and organization reforms required to improve the farmers' price for cotton and access to equipment and supplies without privatizing the cotton sector. For these farmers, these demands had gone unanswered, especially by the World Bank, for 10 years. As one farmer was reported to have said, "if the World Bank has been really interested in helping us since the early 1990s, is it possible that it is deaf?"[14] But the farmers' requests went far beyond these important, but not surprisingly, instrumentalist demands. They challenged expected norms of bureaucratic discourse (Brulle 2000), and recommended several measures that directly addressed many of the dimensions of quality standards discussed in this chapter.

With respect to the theme of creating quality, the farmers called for the introduction of an improved variety of cotton, and for training that would help them improve their cotton harvesting and storage practices. Related to the theme of measuring quality, they asked to become full members of the CMDT's new Quality Assurance Unit. Finally, in terms of the theme of marketing quality, the farmers proposed an annual performance evaluation of COPACO that would be used to assign it an annual marketing quota, instead of operating as the sole buying agent.

Despite the pertinence of the farmers' recommendations regarding quality standards and marketing, studies of global commodity chains suggest that gaining acceptance for them confronts significant hurdles. As Gibbon (2001) argues, power in a commodity chain like that of cotton is associated primarily with coordinating the procurement of cotton from numerous supply sources on a continuing basis and for numerous clients. No individual or association of producers from Africa has the capacity to provide the volume of cotton that would make a difference on the world market. Further, the success of an agency like COPACO, or any other international cotton trader derives principally from its accumulated market knowledge, its world market reputation as a reliable source for specific quantities of quality cotton and its capacity to respond to the demands from the textile industry. Under these conditions, producers would need access to very specialized "insider trader" knowledge in order to evaluate the performance of COPACO or to evaluate alternative international trading arrangements.

Clearly, the success of the West African delegation at the September 2003 WTO meetings in Cancún indicates that African producers can be heard and start to make a difference on the world market.[15] Nevertheless, success on subsidies will do little to change the structure of the world market and the small role that West African cotton plays in this market. With this in mind, the West African cotton producing countries are beginning to explore possibilities for re-establishing a West African textile industry geared both to the local market and to adding value to the region's cotton by producing thread, cloth and garments for export.

The challenges to such an initiative are even more daunting than those confronting African farmers in the world cotton market. Just after political independence in the 1960s, there were about 40 textile factories operating in West Africa. There are now about 20 factories, and 95% of the region's cotton is exported as cotton fiber. Previous efforts to establish a regional industry geared to a West African market were undercut by dumping of cheap cotton fiber from other parts of the world and massive imports of second hand clothing. If such dumping can be prevented, a West African Development Bank study indicates that it should be possible to capture at least 25% of the region's cotton crop for a regional industry by 2010.[16]

Such a move could keep quality standards front and center in the trade debate and offer African farmers the opportunity to play a more direct role in the commodity chain. For example, it is conceivable that African farmers could participate in some type of mixed industry-trade group that would be responsible for regional procurement and replace the international traders upon whom farmers currently depend. In principle, such participation would create the conditions for farmers to see the direct and strategic role that quality standards have throughout the commodity chain from cultivation to harvesting and village-level storage through ginning. These are some of the "critical standards points" where both cotton farmers and the national cotton companies need to focus in order to catch up to the world quality standards for cotton (Fok 2002).

A region-wide structure oriented toward the development of a West African regional textile market and around which farmers could organize is already in the making. In 2000, the West African Network of Farmer Organizations and Producers (ROPPA, *Le Réseau des Organisations Paysannes et de Producteurs de l'Afrique de l'Ouest*) was established to create a regional capacity to represent the interests of West African farmers in rural development and agricultural policy discussions held under the auspices of the West African Economic and Monetary Union (UEMOA) and the Economic Community of West African States (ECOWAS). Following the Cancún meetings, ROPPA's most recent initiative involves a Plan of Action for the Sustainable Development of the West African Cotton Sector that includes the creation of a regional cotton market.[17] In order to establish this market, the Plan of Action calls for an examination of the fiscal and tariff measures required to encourage the development of a regional textile industry, the economic incentives for promoting local and artisanal enterprises, and the removal of barriers to intra-regional trade. While the Plan falls short of addressing how quality standards could be used strategically to realize its objectives, it takes a step in this direction by calling for more farmer involvement in managing the means for creating quality – the availability of improved seeds and supplies such as fertilizer and pesticides. This strategy confirms that recommended by the International Cotton Advisory Committee (ICAC) to "… develop cooperation and the regional integration of inputs and farm products and textiles, while eliminating tariff and non-tariff barriers" (Estur 2002: 13).

But this strategy requires an initial and long-term investment in empowering farmers to become directly responsible for providing supplies and equipment and in strengthening various types of farmer-centered inter-professional associations, such as ROPPA. The recent creation of a farmers' collective, the Upper Niger River Valley Union and Associated Economic Enterprises (UGOA, *Union des GIE de l'Office de la Haute Vallée du Niger et Associés*) offers one model for promoting this type of farmer involvement. With support from a national non-governmental organization, this collective economic group is now in its third year of consolidated supply and equipment orders for farmers in about 80 villages that allows them to negotiate lower input prices and reduced distribution costs. Clearly, the continuing success of such a group depends heavily upon its capacity to supply quality inputs reliably and over time.[18]

Over the long-run this is the type of collective action required if the international concern over subsidies is to be translated into concrete and constructive results for cotton farmers in West Africa. This type of collective group offers a basis upon which cotton farmers can negotiate among the different "worlds" of quality standards. In particular, groups like UGOA represent one way for cotton farmers to become more fully engaged in the network of actors concerned with assuring quality standards. In doing so, this type of collective action represents an important step toward reconciling control and commodity chain coordination with more localized, open and democratic processes.

## 9. NOTES

[1] Research for this chapter was supported in part by National Science Foundation Grant No. SBR 9810149. Any opinions, findings, and conclusions or recommendations expressed in this material are those of the authors and do not necessarily reflect the views of the National Science Foundation. K. Edmond Dembèlé provided important data and invaluable insights that helped to frame some of the arguments in this chapter. However, he is fully exonerated from any responsibility for the positions taken, or the errors in this chapter.

[2] In other parts of the world, cotton is also cultivated under irrigated and flood recession conditions. Under these conditions, yields can double those under rain-fed conditions.

[3] Fiber length can also be jeopardized by the excessive or inappropriate use of cleaners during the ginning process.

[4] It is important to note that the ginning ratio is not just a function of the variety. Newer gins can achieve a 43-44% ginning ratio from varieties bred for a 42% ratio.

[5] This agreement originally took effect in 1924 and has now been signed by 24 cotton merchant and spinners associations in 21 countries, including the US Department of Agriculture. The conference is attended by the signatories as well as by representatives of producers, ginners, shippers, exchanges, and other actors in the cotton industry. This discussion of international cotton standards is taken from http://www.ams.usda.gov/cotton/ctnsta.htm.

[6] The standard for fiber or staple length includes graduations of one thirty-seconds of an inch ranging from 13/16 inches upwards. The length uniformity index is the ratio between the mean length and the upper half mean length expressed as a percentage. Fiber strength represents the force in grams to break a specific sized bundle of fibers.

[7] Earlham (2003) discusses the variability among HVI machines in grading rooms around the world and the lack of confidence in the repeatability of HVI results. There is no international agreement on HVI instrument testing, and the calibration standards issued by the USDA, as noted above, act as guidelines.

[8] COPACO, formerly the Maison Ernest Siegfied, was founded in 1862. It specializes in marketing African cotton, and handles more than one-half of the annual harvest from West and Central Africa, but is represented in 45 countries and represents 6% of the world market.

[9] The CFDT was first known as the Textile Company for the French Union, *La Compagnie des Textiles de l'Union Française*.

[10] In comparison with other internationally-traded commodities, the world cotton industry is not highly concentrated. Nineteen companies market almost 40% of the world's cotton (Guitchounts 2004)

[11] See Ingram, 2002.

[12] See Bingen, 2003a.

[13] These mixtures commonly include dimethoate (an organophosphate and a general use pesticide) as well as either cypermethrin or deltamethrin (synthetic pyrethroids, that are restricted use pesticides because of their toxicity to fish).

[14] Cited by Dembèlé, 2001.

[15] And the recent WTO ruling in favor of Brazil's contention that cotton subsidies paid to US cotton farmers violate international trade rules certainly reinforces efforts by West African producers to continue their international lobbying campaign.

[16] Reported in United Nations, Office for the Coordination of Humanitarian Affairs, Integrated Regional Information Network (IRIN) "Compromise Deal on Cotton Subsidies in Preparation." http://www.irinnews.org, 2/24/2004.

[17] ROPPA. 2004. Plan d'Actions du ROPPA et des OPPA pour le Développement Durable des Filières Africaines de Coton. Cotonou, Bénin. 14 mai 2004.
[18] See Bingen, 2003.

## 10.  REFERENCES

Adjoin, E. V. (1998) Quand l'Or Blanc Intoxique ses Producteurs. in *SYFIA International*; http://www.syfia.com/presse.

Anthony, K. (1986) Sub-Saharan Africa Agricultural Research Review: Cotton Research. The World Bank, Washington, DC.

Baffes, J. (2003) Cotton and Developing Countries: A Case Study in Policy Incoherence. The World Bank, Washington, DC.

Bassett, T. J. (2001) *The Peasant Cotton Revolution in West Africa. Côte d'Ivoire, 1880-1995.* Cambridge and New York: Cambridge University Press.

Béroud, F. (1999) Développement Rural en Afrique: l'Exemple des Filières Cotonnières. Intégration ou Dérégulation? *Revue Coton et Développement – Le Monde Diplomatique*, 3 Mai 1999: 2-6.

_____ (2001) Cotton Production in Francophone Africa. *Cotton: Review of the World Situation* 54 (March-April):11-14.

Bingen, J. (2003) The Upper Niger River Valley Union and Associated Farmers' Enterprises (UGOA ): A Case Study of a Farmer Cooperative Alliance for Agricultural Input Supply in Mali. Unpublished paper. East Lansing, Michigan.

Bingen, J. (2003a) Pesticides, Politics and Pest Management: Toward a Political Economy of Cotton in Sub-Saharan Africa. Pp 111-126 in *African Environment and Development: Rhetoric, Programs, Realities* edited by B.I. Logan and William G. Mosely Burlington, VT: Ashgate Publishing.

Bingen, R. J., D. Carney, and E. Dembelé (1995) The Malian Union of Cotton and Food Crop Producers: The Current and Potential Role in Technology Development and Transfer. ODI Research and Extension Network, London.

Bloud, H. (1925) *Le Problème Cotonnier et l'Afrique Occidentale Française. Une Solution Nationale.* Paris: Librairie Emile Larose.

Bourge, J. Y. Le (1995) Vous avez dit Qualité? *Coton et Développement* 13:27.

Brulle, R. J. (2000) *Agency, Democracy, and Nature. The US Environmental Movement from a Critical Theory Perspective.* Cambridge and London: The MIT Press.

Camara, M., F. Haïdara, and A. Traoré (2001) Etude Socio-économique de l'Utilisation des Pesticides au Mali. Institut du Sahel, AGROSOC / Sécurité Alimentaire – Gestion des Ressources Naturelles. Université de Hanovre, Institut des Sciences Economique – Projet Politique des Pesticides. FAO, Projet Gestion des Pesticides au Sahel, Bamako, Mali.

DAGRIS (2002) Le Classement: Un Savoir Faire et Une Technologie. DAGRIS, Paris.

Dembelé, S. and A. Yattara (2000) La Recherche et le Développement de la Filière Cotonnière au Mali. Pp. 45-52 in *Role et Place de la Recherche pour le Développement des Filières Cotonnières en Evolution en Afrique.* Actes du Seminaire, 1-2 Septembre 1999, edited by M. Fok, J.P. Deguine, C. Gaborel (Editeurs Scientifiques). Montpellier, France: CIRAD.

Dembèlé K. E. (2001) "Synthese du Processus des Etats Généraux du Secteur Coton du Mali." Unpublished manuscript.

Dunavant, B. III (2002) Advantages of the High Volume Instrument System.The 21st Century Cotton Industry: Growth Through Private Investment. 61st Plenary Meeting.Cairo, Egypt, September 7-12, 2003. ICAC.

Earlam, N. (2003) Problems Caused by Insufficient Knowledge About Cotton Quality: A Merchant's Perspective. The World of Cotton – Developments and Remedies. 62nd Plenary Meeting.Gdańsk, Poland, September 7-12, 2003. ICAC.

Estur, G. (1992) La Commercialisation du Coton: le Système CFDT-COPACO. *Coton et Développement* 1:16-18.

_____ (2002) Cotton: Engine of Economic Growth in Africa. *Cotton: Review of the World Situation* (Nov.-Dec.):10-13.

_____ (2004) US Exports: Is Quality at Issue? Cotton: *Review of the World Situation* (Jan.-Feb.):13-16.

Eymard-Duvernay, F. (1995) La Négociation de la Qualité. Pp. 39-43 in *Agro-alimentaire: Une Economie de la Qualité,* edited by F. Nicolas and E. Valceschini. Paris: INRA and Economica.

Fok, M. (2002) Cotton Future in Western and Central Africa: The Challenge of Combining Technical and Institutional Innovations. OCL 9:115-223.

Gibbon, P. (2001) Upgrading Primary Production: A Global Commodity Chain Approach. *World Development* 29,2:345-363.

Gillham, F. E. M., T. M. Bell, T. Arin, G. A. Matthews, C. Le Rumeur, and A. B. Hearn (1995) Cotton Production Prospects for the Next Decade. The World Bank, Washington, D.C.

Goreux, L. (2003) Reforming the Cotton Sector in Sub-Saharan Africa (Second Edition). The World Bank, Washington, DC.

Gourlot, J-P. (2000) Les Tendances dans la Standardisation du Coton sur le Marché Mondial. Pp. 113-116 in *Rôle et Place de la Recherche pour le Développement des Filières Cotonnières en Evolution en Afrique*. Actes du Seminaire, 1-2 Septembre, 1999, edited by M. F. J-P. Deguine, C. Gaborel (Editeurs Scientifiques). Montpellier, France: CIRAD.

Groupe de Travail Coopération Française (1991) *Le Coton en Afrique de l'Ouest et du Centre. Situation et Perspectives*. Paris: Ministère de la Coopération et du Développement.

Guitchounts, A. (2004) The Structure of World Trade. *Cotton: Review of the World Situation* (Jan.-Feb.):16-20.

Hamai, A. (2003)The Problems in International Trade Caused by Insufficient Knowledge about Cotton Quality. The World of Cotton – Developments and Remedies. 62nd Plenary Meeting.Gdańsk, Poland, September 7-12, 2003.ICAC.

Hussein, K. (2004) Importance of Cotton Production and Trade in West Africa. Cotonou, Benin.

Ingram, M. (2002) "Producing the Fiber Naturally: Technological Change and the US Organic Cotton Industry." *Agriculture and Human Values*. 19, 4: 325-336.

Isaacman, A. and R. Roberts (1995) Cotton, Colonialism, and Social History in Sub-Saharan Africa: Introduction. Pp. 1-39 in *Cotton, Colonialism, and Social History in Sub-Saharan Africa*, edited by A. Isaacman and J. Hay. Portsmouth, NH: Heinemann.

Latour, B. (1987) *Science in Action: How to Follow Scientists and Engineers Through Society*. Milton Keynes, England: Open University Press.

Lele, U., N. van de Walle, and M. Gbetibouo (1989) Cotton in Africa: An Analysis of Differences in Performance. The World Bank, Washington, DC.

Lind, M. (2003) The Cancún Delusion, *The New York Times* Opinion. www.nytimes.com, accessed 9/14/2003. New York.

Macdonald, A. (2002) Market-based Incentives for Improving Cotton Quality, The 21st Century Cotton Industry: Growth Through Private Investment. 61st Plenary Meeting.Cairo, Egypt, September 7-12, 2003.ICAC.

Malloum, I. (2002) Utilization and Constraints of the High Volume Instrument (HVI) Classification System in Chad. The 21st Century Cotton Industry: Growth Through Private Investment. 61st Plenary Meeting, Cairo, Egypt, September 7-12, 2003.ICAC.

Marsden, T. K. and A. Arce (1995) Constructing Quality: Emerging Food Networks in the Rural Transition. *Environment and Planning* A 27:1261-1279.

May, O. L. (2003) Breeding Cotton With Enhanced Fiber Qualities Amidst Technologically Evolving Yarn and Textile Manufacturing Industries.The World of Cotton – Developments and Remedies. 62nd Plenary Meeting, Gdańsk, Poland, September 7-12, 2003.ICAC.

Murdoch, J., T. Marsden, and J. Banks (2000) Quality, Nature, and Embeddedness: Some Theoretical Considerations in the Context of the Food Sector. *Economic Geography* 76:107-125.

OBEPAB (2000) Les Accidents Causés par les Pesticides Chimiques de Synthèse Utilisés dans la Production Cotonnière au Bénin. Organisation Béninoise pour la Promotion de l'Agriculture Biologique, Cotonou, Bénin.

Roberts, R. L. (1996) *Two Worlds of Cotton. Colonialism and the Regional Economy in the French Soudan, 1800-1946*. Stanford: Stanford University Press.

Schroder, H. F. (2003) Impact of Cotton Classing on the Optimal Use of Fiber Quality. The World of Cotton — Developments and Remedies. 62nd Plenary Meeting, Gdańsk, Poland, September 7-12, 2003.ICAC.

*The World Bank* (2000) Cotton Policy Brief: The Administered Monopoly Model in the Era of Competition and Globalization. The World Bank, Washington DC.

Watkins, K. (2002) Cultivating Poverty. The Impact of US Cotton Subsidies on Africa. *Oxfam International*, Washington, DC.

Wilkinson, J. (1997) A New Paradigm for Economic Analysis? *Economy and Society* 26, 3: 305-339.

V

# CONCLUSIONS AND FUTURE AGENDA

JIM BINGEN* AND LAWRENCE BUSCH†

# 13. SHAPING A POLICY AND RESEARCH AGENDA

This chapter draws upon the case studies in this volume to suggest a continuing research and policy agenda on food and agricultural standards. We discuss this research agenda in terms of five themes that emerge from issues raised by the case studies in this volume, as well as continuing work at the Institute for Food and Agricultural Standards. These themes are: private and public standards, the multiplicity of standards, third party certification, new technologies and standards, and standards and power. Each of these themes cuts across traditional disciplinary boundaries and offers opportunities to apply and expand upon an analytical framework based on the concepts of negotiation, access and outcomes. By way of introduction to a presentation of our agenda, a brief review of these concepts is useful.

The concept of *negotiation* orients our inquiry toward an identification of the groups or interests represented during the creation, modification or maintenance of food and agricultural standards. It draws our attention to three characteristics of negotiations. First, standards are negotiated on a continuing basis; they are always being discussed, reformulated, redesigned in light of legal, institutional, and technological changes as well as other (possibly conflicting) standards. Second, standards are applied locally and thus subject to site-specific and local interpretation and negotiations. This is true even for standards that claim universality. Third, all standards negotiations raise issues of fairness and self-governance. This is the case because there are always winners and losers in the adoption of (changes in) standards.

Food and agricultural standards are rules and as such allow or deny *access* to marketing opportunities. Meeting certain standards may require a level of capital investment that precludes certain groups from producing and selling in a particular market. Similarly, meeting standards may require certain organizational or technical skills or technologies; such skills and technologies are always distributed unevenly leading to uneven access. Finally, governments and private groups may also use standards strategically and deliberately to protect an industry or activity.

The *outcomes* of food and agricultural standards include both distributive and environmental effects. Efforts to meet specified standards can and do redistribute income, wealth, power, status and prestige among different groups within a supply chain or even among third parties. For example, consider the concerns raised by farmers adhering to organic standards over decisions by their neighbors to plant crops that meet standards defining them as genetically modified. Similarly, the need

* Jim Bingen, Professor, Department of Community, Agriculture, Recreation and Resource Studies, Michigan State University.
† Lawrence Busch, University Distinguished Professor, Department of Sociology, Michigan State University.

*J. Bingen and L. Busch, (eds.), Agricultural Standards: The Shape of the Global Food and Fiber System, 245-250. © 2006 Springer. Printed in the Netherlands.*

to "make the grade" in producing or processing a particular product may raise important environmental and/or human rights concerns.

## 1. PRIVATE AND PUBLIC STANDARDS

The case study discussions in this volume provide convincing evidence of the interrelationships between, and the necessity for both public and private agencies in developing, modifying and implementing food and agricultural standards. Nations can and do use food and agricultural standards strategically for economic development, as illustrated by the case of soybeans in Brazil. More commonly, governmental agencies are responsible for creating and enforcing standards to regulate food safety, environmental protection, plant and animal health, and worker health and safety among others. In contrast, private firms or commercial groups, such as the OIV, use standards to capture and protect market share, manage competition, or even create markets through specialized labeling as with COPACO in the case of cotton.

With "free market" principles now dominating global economic activities, important shifts among standards setting and enforcement bodies are occurring. In particular, international bodies are becoming more important players, just as non-profit and corporate groups seek greater influence within changing sets of national and international public regulations and standards. Consequently, instead of neatly delineated public and private responsibilities for food and agricultural standards, we now confront a constantly evolving and changing global network of relationships among public and private, mandatory, voluntary, and national and international standards bodies.

The case of the OIV illustrates the complexities and the ambiguities that arise within this global network. As Hanin et al. explain, one question before the OIV concerns finding ways in the context of the WTO of accepting the coexistence of several systems based on different underlying principles and goals. But the ambiguous international standing of OIV further complicates this process. The WTO has not accepted the OIV request for recognition. This weakens the OIV position, and as Hanin et al. point out, "raises the possibility that trade decisions concerning the wine sector might be contrary to the principles upon which the OIV consensus has been built and sustained, thereby disrupting the coherence of OIV as well as generating significant sectoral change." Parallel to this position, Ransom concludes that "national and international bodies regulating global trade would do well in following the lead of local South African officials." Ways need to be found for "acknowledging who benefits and who loses economically and socially from the adoption of specific standards."

Clearly, today's food and agricultural standards are being negotiated in a new institutional context in which some, as Ilcan and Phillips warn, will continue to be marginalized. But at the same time, as Kennedy argues, and as the recent WTO decision on cotton subsidies suggests, many will be economically better off. However, as Jones et al. and Bingen suggest, it may take various types of expensive, long term collaborative efforts among businesses, research institutions, NGOs, and public bodies to help farmers, traders and exporters in non-industrialized countries meet the quality standards required in the global marketplace.

As we think of a research agenda focusing on the evolving relationships between public and private food and agricultural standards, some of the key questions might include the following. Does the current mix of public and private standards bodies best serve the public good? Should this mix differ by product or commodity? What rights should various groups (e.g., producers and consumers) have with respect to public and private standards setting and enforcement? How can we avoid a decline in trust and democratic governance in standards development and enforcement? Better still, how can trust and democratic governance be enhanced through standards?

## 2. THE MULITIPLICITY OF STANDARDS AND THIRD PARTY CERTIFICATION

As the overview in the introductory chapter and some of the case studies remind us, until quite recently food and agricultural standards were standardized. Governmental agencies or authorized private organizations certified conformity and corporations competed principally on price and commercial quality of the goods. In this "economy of quantities" negotiation among actors and ethical concerns were defined largely in commercial terms. Without question, standards for standardization continue to be an important part of our food and farming systems. However, as several of the contributors to this volume have discussed, standards are beginning to be used to differentiate markets.

With the opening of global markets, and especially the emergence of global food oligopolies in the processing and retail sectors, firms prefer to minimize price competition, and to differentiate their products (Nicolas and Valeschini 1995) as much as possible on other qualities such as trust, societal and environmental benefits, attachments to place, etc. In this "economy of qualities," other worlds of standards including the family, the environment, human rights, taste, safety, and animal welfare become relevant. In other words, in an economy of qualities there are different standards of goodness depending on the world to which one wishes to appeal. Thus, various groups appeal to the environment, to worker health and safety, to paying fair wages, etc. These worlds may be consonant with each other or they may conflict (e.g., phyosanitation v. worker safety).

To achieve a measure of coherence among these worlds, several international efforts are underway to develop a unified certification standard aiming at a "certified once, accepted everywhere" standard. In collaboration with the International Federation of Organic Agriculture Movements (IFOAM), the ETC Group (Action Group on Erosion, Technology and Concentration, formerly the Rural Advancement Fund International, RAFI) has led one such effort to develop social stewardship standards for sustainable and organic agriculture. The "goal is to build a model of an alternative food system by creating an economic incentive for social equity and just working conditions through the establishment of a "social justice" food label" (Henderson, Mandelbaum et al. 2003).

These efforts raise a concern about the role of Third Party Certification (TPC) in setting and enforcing food and agricultural standards. Third Party Certification (TPC) has become commonplace so rapidly that few studies of it exist.[1] Nevertheless, TPC is now the norm rather than the exception at many junctures in the agrifood system. Third party certifiers are private or public organizations that use scientific theories, tests, and data as well as technical artifacts to independently verify process and product quality and safety claims. They are usually distinguished by their claimed independence from both buyer and seller. Third party certifiers play an increasing role in negotiating issues of risk in society; yet, little is known about the emerging forms, tools, and functions of third party certifiers or the scientific, legal, and ethical issues that the process of third party certification engenders. Some work helps us understand how third party certifiers negotiate issues of risk in society (Deaton 2004). However, we have a much less clear understanding of the societal and policy implications that arise as third party certifiers seek to reconcile differing scientific and value claims in the certification process.

With the global restructuring of our food systems, increasing numbers of producers, distributors, processors, retailers, consumers, policy makers, regulators, and social movements around the world are involved in the production, processing, distribution and regulation of food and agricultural products. These diverse sources of supply, processing and distribution become increasingly remote from historically close and local control. Consequently, transnational firms rely upon independent agencies or groups to certify that their inputs, products, processing and production processes meet a range of quality, safety, labor, human rights and environmental standards demanded by governments and society.

These conditions lead to four critical questions for inquiry. First, to what extent is third party certification being used to exclude certain groups from markets? As several case studies in this volume illustrate standards can be used to restrict access. There is no particular reason to expect that third party certification would not have the same effect.

Second, third party certification shifts enforcement from visual or direct inspection to the development and archiving of documentation. This coincides with a shift from product standards to process standards. Thus, a firm or farm might be documented as meeting specified standards and still follow questionable labor or damaging environmental practices. As noted above, and with a focus on organic agriculture, this is precisely one of the issues that the IFOAM-RAFI effort on social stewardship standards tries to address. Can such efforts be effectively implemented and enforced?

An answer to this question will depend in part on a third issue: trust. The use of third party certification suggests that buyers do not fully trust those from whom they buy goods or services. In fact, third party certification simply transfers trust in the seller to trust in the certifying firm. How do we certify the certifiers and assure that their behavior is ethical?

Finally, process standards, such as those often enforced through third party certification, tend to block innovation. They impose a standard for the process – a right way to do things – and thereby reduce innovation that might lead to cheaper, more efficient, or more effective processes. In contrast, product standards encourage the development of cheaper, more efficient, and more effective ways of producing the same product for the final consumer. What are the ethical principles upon which third party certification should be based?

## 3. NEW TECHNOLOGIES AND STANDARDS

Biotechnologically altered food products represent one arena in which there is already considerable debate over safety and environmental standards. Miller et al. discuss at least one aspect of these issues in their review of the mix of technical, scientific and the social issues raised during the Starlink™ corn case. As the authors conclude, "as the challenges of biotechnology become increasingly complex, understanding the indivisibility of technoscientific and ethical/political problems in the Starlink™ case helps us to appreciate the larger context surrounding standards setting and food safety."

The introduction of nanotechnologies raises comparable challenges and poses several questions of particular relevance to food and agricultural standards. These new biological, transport and communication technologies raise a number of questions of socially and ethically acceptable use (Busch, 2000). For example, how much personal data should be made available to the retail sector about the buying patterns of individual consumers as registered by RFID chips? How much monitoring of employee movements is acceptable? In short, there is a need for standards for nanotechnologies as they may be employed in various elements of the agrifood system. Of concern here is who should set the standards, how should they be administered, how much flexibility the standards should have, and how they should be adapted to differing cultural expectations. Without such standards for use, nanotechnologies almost certainly will be at the center of protracted public controversy comparable to that surrounding the use of biotechnologies.

At the same time, nanotechnologies can be used to test whether standards are met. For example, various nanotechnologies may be used to detect spoiled products, tampering, or degrees of freshness. In some instances nanotechnologies may replace older technologies used for these purposes (e.g., labels with expiration dates), but in other instances they may permit a wide range of new standards (e.g., for consumer detection of pesticide residues, traceability from the hindquarter of a particular cow to the steak on the table for dinner).

Some of the key questions driving a research agenda include: Who should be responsible for designing and implementing standards for nanotechnologies? What should be the roles of the public and private sectors in standards formation and implementation? What should the scope of these standards be, given the novelty of these technologies? How can we avoid the polarization that took place with the introduction of the new agricultural biotechnologies?

## 4. STANDARDS AND POWER

As discussed in most of the case studies in this volume, and as embodied in the focus of our conceptual framework, we are concerned with "who benefits" and "who loses" in the creation, modification and enforcement of standards. To paraphrase Harold Lasswell, standards are about who gets what, when, where and how. For example, as Bingen argues, part of the future of cotton in West Africa involves finding a way to shift income away from processors (ginners and traders) back to small farmers. Jones et al. offer a more challenging scenario for smallholders linked to markets dominated by European supermarket chains. To remain active participants in these types of marketing arrangements, small farmers must dramatically improve their management capacity to meet exacting quality criteria, adjust their production volumes to short-term demands, and adapt new agronomic and post-harvest practices to changing market requirements. But not all African farmers require the kind of collaborative assistance recommended by Jones et al. Ransom reminds us that in South Africa the large feedlot producers, large retailers, and wealthy consumers actively support concentration and centralization in the red tender meat industry. Many others, especially smaller producers, do not.

The GMO controversy between the US and the EU illustrates another type of power issue that adapts principles to serve specific political interests. The continuing debate between the US and the EU over the standards for defining risk from GMOs, the appropriate scientific tools for detecting it, and the ethical principles for managing it (e.g., precautionary v. familiarity principles) directly affect the interests of farmers, processors and retailers on each side of the Atlantic. More generally, this debate illustrates a common feature of international agreements in the area of food and agricultural standards. Each country interprets these standards within the framework of its own national laws and regulatory principles. Consequently, when fundamentally different assumptions guide national frameworks and regulatory principles, and when the provisions of the agreement do not explicitly acknowledge these assumptions, deep disagreements arise.

For example, the EU and the US are both concerned about microbial contamination of food products. Both parties have signed the Sanitary and Phytosanitary (SPS) Agreement and the Agreement on Technical Barriers to Trade (TBT). Nevertheless, despite adverse decisions at the WTO's appellate body, the EU continues to apply the precautionary principle to microbial evidence, while the US uses risk assessment, relative risk, and risk-based standards. However, at the same time, the EU applies the principles of risk analysis to its acceptance of raw milk cheeses, just as the US adopts policy guidelines consistent with the precautionary principle for some non-GMO related products. A good example is the US argument for destroying a flock of sheep imported from Belgium for cheese production on the grounds that there is a remote possibility that they might have the disease known as scrapie (Busch 2002). While it should be clear that food and agricultural standards set the "rules of the game" in several types of market or exchange relationships, Thiers reminds us that such standards can also impact national sovereignty. The Chinese response to the global organic food market illustrates "the domestic politics of global standards." Particularly instructive in this case are the ways in which various bureaucratic actors used international standards as alternative sources of authority in domestic turf battles, and how local elites also used these standards to reinforce their authority over local people and resources. As Thiers warns, both instances easily lead to behavior that threatens the integrity of the standards.

Sylvander and Biencourt draw our attention as well to the influence of local agreements in global standards setting. "In the global raw milk negotiations, it is clear that local agreements will carry considerable weight as those representing local agreements will seek to protect their investments in these agreements." Ilcan and Phillips express a similar concern when they ask about the possibility of developing global standards that recognize "culturally diverse knowledges." At issue is a better understanding of the forces and conditions required for standards without standardization, or harmonization without uniformization in the global economy. What kind of universally recognized quality standards can be developed without radically altering local cultural norms?

Addressing these and the other questions posed in this chapter offers a challenging opportunity to integrate technical matters, behavioral and social research, and ethical and policy analysis. There is clearly a need for scholars and scientists, and practitioners to develop conceptual and methodological tools that transcend disciplinary boundaries and explicitly incorporate ethical concerns. We hope the issues raised and cases discussed in this volume can be used to begin to train a new generation of scientists and ethicists who understand and can work effectively on these ethical and policy issues with industry, government policy-makers, labor, consumers, and citizens in both national and international arenas.

## 5. NOTES

[1] In general, Third Party Certification refers to auditing by some organization external to the company being audited (i.e., the First Party). The term Second Party is usually used to refer to the seller, while the Fourth Party is usually reserved to the various organs of state regulation. (See Tanner 2000).

## 6. REFERENCES

Busch, L. (2002) The Homeletics of Risk. *Journal of Agricultural and Environmental Ethics* 15:17-29.

Deaton, B. J. (2004) A Theoretical Framework for Examining the Role of Third-Party Certifiers. *Food Control* 15:615-619..

Henderson, E., R. Mandelbaum, O. Mendieta, and M. Sligh (2003) Toward Social Justice and Economic Equity in the Food System. A Call for Social Stewardship Standards in Sustainable and Organic Agriculture. Rural Advancement Fund International, Pittsboro, NC.

Nicolas, F. and E. Valeschini (1995) *Agro-Alimentaire: Une Economie de la Qualité.* Paris: INRA and Economica.

Tanner, B. (2000) Independent Assessment by Third-Party Certification Bodies. *Food Control* 11:415-417.

# INDEX

# The International Library of Environmental, Agricultural and Food Ethics